Praise for *Humanism in Business*

Values make a difference. For the most part, having a 'purpose beyond profit' has proven one of the best ways for a company to be profitable and socially valuable. Some of the earliest socially responsible businesses achieved this purpose beyond profit from the religious convictions of their founders. In this more secular age, there are many who will be interested in how such values translate into the pragmatic, success-oriented business environment of today. Those seeking a rigorously academic study from an avowedly humanistic perspective will find a wealth of food for thought in *Humanism in Business*.

Mallen Baker, *CEO Business Respect and Development Director for Business in the Community in the UK*

This book is a most crucial and insightful collection showing persuasively how humanism can be practiced creatively at the core centre of economic development policy agenda, not being a rhetorical flourish but the fundamental basis of economic prosperity and sustainability. Many contributors to this collection illuminate the role of business within society and its potential as a life-serving organ for positive social change. It offers an intriguing blueprint for how the world would be better with a more life-conducive economic system. A must-read for world policy leaders of the future.

Kriengsak Chareonwongsak, *Member of Parliament, Thailand*

This book stresses the theme of humanism in business in terms of seeking the goal of sustainability, not only in terms of the earth's resources, but also in terms of relationships to all the contributors to the creation of wealth. Call it sustainability plus.

Paul Lawrence, *Professor Emeritus, Harvard Business Sch̄ꭉ*

The notion that "humanism in business" is an oxymoron is r sensical, discredited by both history and logic. Ultimately, busine the centralization and utilization of physical, financial resou human energy and intellect within organizations great and small – the societal function of providing the goods and services essential

human survival and well-being. How this function is fulfilled has varied greatly over time and place. An important factor in determining the "how" are the values which underlie the society and are manifested in the operations of its business institutions and those who lead them. The editors and authors of this creative volume demonstrate convincingly that business activity in the twenty-first century is not, and cannot, be governed by mechanistic markets operating autonomously of broader societal values and expectation. It is our humanistic traditions developed over millennia from philosophical, religious and cultural sources that in the final analysis define the appropriate role of business in society. Congratulations to the editors of this volume for underscoring this point so convincingly.

Edwin M. Epstein, *Professor Emeritus, International and Area Studies and Haas School of Business, University of California, Berkeley*

In the last few decades business has become increasingly aware that shareholder value cannot be the only indicator for success. Sustainable development and corporate social responsibility (CSR) concepts attempt to address negative trade-offs. But at the heart of the matter stands a humanistic attitude, an ethical stance towards all we do, be that in business or as private individuals.

Claude Martin, *former Director General, WWF International*

Humanism in Business

What is the purpose of our economic system? What would a more life-serving economy look like?

There are many books about business and society, yet very few of them question the primacy of GDP growth, profit maximization, and individual utility maximization. Even developments with a humanistic touch like stakeholder participation, corporate social responsibility, or corporate philanthropy serve the same goal: to foster long-term growth and profitability. *Humanism in Business* questions these assumptions and investigates the possibility of creating a human-centered, value-oriented society based on humanistic principles. An international team of academics and practitioners present philosophical, spiritual, economic, psychological, and organizational arguments that show how humanism can be used to understand, and possibly transform, business at three different levels: the systems level, the organizational level, and the individual level. This groundbreaking book will be of interest to academics, practitioners, and policymakers concerned with business ethics and the relationship between business and society.

HEIKO SPITZECK is a lecturer at the Doughty Centre for Corporate Responsibility, School of Management, Cranfield University.

MICHAEL PIRSON is a lecturer at Harvard Extension School and a research fellow at the Hauser Center for Nonprofit Organizations, Harvard University.

WOLFGANG AMANN is Executive Director of the MBA program at the University of St. Gallen, Switzerland.

SHIBAN KHAN is Senior Researcher at IMD, Lausanne, Switzerland.

ERNST VON KIMAKOWITZ is studying for a PhD at the Institute for Business Ethics of the University of St. Gallen, Switzerland.

Humanism in Business

Edited by
HEIKO SPITZECK
MICHAEL PIRSON
WOLFGANG AMANN
SHIBAN KHAN
ERNST VON KIMAKOWITZ

CAMBRIDGE
UNIVERSITY PRESS

HF
5387
. H859
2009

CAMBRIDGE UNIVERSITY PRESS
Cambridge, New York, Melbourne, Madrid, Cape Town, Singapore, São Paulo, Delhi

Cambridge University Press
The Edinburgh Building, Cambridge CB2 8RU, UK

Published in the United States of America by Cambridge University Press, New York

www.cambridge.org
Information on this title: www.cambridge.org/9780521727624

First published 2009

Printed in the United Kingdom at the University Press, Cambridge

A catalogue record for this publication is available from the British Library

Library of Congress Cataloguing in Publication data
Humanism in business / Heiko Spitzeck . . . [et al.].
    p.   cm.
Includes bibliographical references and index.
ISBN 978-0-521-89893-5 (hardback) – ISBN 978-0-521-72762-4 (pbk.)
    1. Business ethics.   2. Economics–Moral and ethical aspects.   3.   Economics–
    Social aspects.   4. Humanism–Social aspects.   I. Spitzeck, Heiko.
HF5387.H859 2008
174'.4–dc22
2008037142

ISBN 978-0-521-89893-5 hardback
ISBN 978-0-521-72762-4 paperback

Contents

Figures

Tables

Editors and contributors

Editors

Wolfgang Amann

Wolfgang Amann is a member of the faculty of the University of St. Gallen and Executive Director of the MBA-HSG. He co-founded Humanistic Management Network in 2005. He previously taught at Henley Management College in Henley-on-Thames, UK and IMD (International Institute for Management development) in Lausanne, Switzerland. He has also held visiting academic positions at the Wharton School of the University of Pennsylvania, the Indian Institute of Management (IIM) in Bangalore, and Hosei University in Tokyo. He has directed, delivered, and contributed to open and in-company programs, as well as courses on strategy, internationalization, governance, and sustainability in the US, Europe, China, India, and Japan. He has (co-) authored more than seventy case studies for these programs, with his case series on Hindustan Lever in India winning the 2006 oikos Sustainability Case competition. He received two teaching awards (in 2006 and 2007), when his course "Corporate Strategy and Governance" was chosen as the CEMS course of the year of all CEMS business schools in seventeen European countries. Wolfgang Amann's primary expertise relates to successful internationalization and sustainability strategies. His special emphasis within humanistic research lies in broadening strategic and organizational goal systems, as well as creating innovative but feasible win-win-win situations for employees, organizations, and society.

Shiban Khan

Shiban Khan leads the research initiative on Access to Medicines in India at IMD, Switzerland, and is a co-founder of Humanistic Management

Network. She is also a visiting tutor at Henley Management College, UK. She has served as the executive director of oikos International, a student-driven organization that focuses on integrating sustainability into management education. Shiban has worked on sustainability and development issues in Europe, North America, and South Asia. Her research interests lie in a contextual focus on sustainability, social trusteeship theory, purpose-driven environmental communication, and comparisons between the Eastern and Western ethos in humanistic business principles. With a Master's in Environmental Studies from the University of Pennsylvania, she is currently completing her PhD at the University of St. Gallen on the connotation of corporate sustainability in the Indian context.

Michael Pirson

Michael Pirson is a co-founder of Humanistic Management Network. He received his PhD in Organizational Behavior from the University of St. Gallen, Switzerland. He is currently a lecturer at Harvard Extension School and a research fellow at Harvard University, researching organizational trust and well-being. In his teaching, he focuses on management dilemmas in the twenty-first century and social entrepreneurship as a model for humanistic management. Before receiving his doctorate, Michael worked in international management consulting. He also gained experience in the political arena while working on Hillary Clinton's Senate campaign, and has started several social enterprises in the area of economic development. He currently serves on the board of three NGOs based in the USA.

Heiko Spitzeck

Heiko Spitzeck is a lecturer at the Doughty Centre for Corporate Responsibility at Cranfield University School of Management. He has been a visiting scholar at the University of California at Berkeley and a researcher at the Institute for Business Ethics at the University of St. Gallen, Switzerland. He co-founded Humanistic Management Network in 2005 and leads current research projects related to humanism and business. Between 2004 and 2006, he served as a director of oikos International. His research looks at organizational behavior, especially learning and innovation from business and society interactions. Before starting his academic career, Heiko worked for the international consulting firm Accenture in Munich. He studied European business studies at the Universities of Bamberg, Germany and Seville, Spain.

Ernst von Kimakowitz

Ernst von Kimakowitz is currently pursuing his PhD at the Institute for Business Ethics of the University of St. Gallen in Switzerland. The title of his thesis is "The Interaction between Transnational Corporations and Small and Medium-sized Enterprises in Developing Economies." He also works as an independent consultant on projects related to corporate social responsibility and economic development. His mandates include consulting engagements for the United Nations Conference on Trade and Development (UNCTAD), as well as for various private sector clients. For five years he was with an international management consulting firm in London, England, working in various industries. He holds an MSc (Econ.) from the London School of Economics and Political Science (LSE). His undergraduate studies were in political science and business administration at the Johannes Gutenberg University of Mainz, Germany and the Universidad de los Andes in Mérida, Venezuela. He is a German citizen with a lively interest in international issues.

Contributors

Omar Aktouf

Omar Aktouf is Professor of Management at L'École des hautes études commerciales de Montréal (HEC Montréal) and a founding member of Humanism and Management at HEC. Before joining HEC, Dr. Aktouf was a senior manager in several firms, including a major petroleum company. His academic background includes psychology, management, and development economics. He has researched a number of complementary areas including organizational culture, project management, symbolism and speech within organizations, as well as epistemology, methodology, and pedagogy of administration "sciences." He is the author of numerous books and articles on these subjects, which have been translated into several languages, including

French, Spanish, Portuguese, German and English. He is an active international lecturer, speaker, and consultant, having provided consulting services to numerous large and small companies. He is the recipient of several awards and prizes, including "Best French Canada Business Book Award" for 2003 (*La Stratégie de l'Autruche*).

Joseph L. Badaracco

Joseph L. Badaracco, Jr., is the John Shad Professor of Business Ethics at Harvard Business School. He is also Senior Associate Dean and Chair of the MBA Program. Badaracco has taught courses on business ethics, strategy, and management in the School's MBA and executive programs. Badaracco is a graduate of St. Louis University, Oxford University, where he was a Rhodes Scholar, and Harvard Business School, where he earned an MBA and a DBA. Badaracco serves on the Faculty Committee of the Harvard Center for Ethics and the Professions, and he is also the faculty chair of the Nomura School of Advanced Management in Tokyo. In recent years, Professor Badaracco was chairman of the Harvard University Advisory Committee on Shareholder Responsibility and served on the boards of two public companies. He has taught in executive programs in the United States, Japan, and many other countries, and has spoken to a wide variety of organizations on issues of leadership, values, and ethics.

Matt Cherry

Matt Cherry is Executive Director of the Institute for Humanist Studies and has spent more than fifteen years as a professional leader in the humanist movement in three countries. In May 2004, and again in 2006, Cherry was elected president of the United Nations NGO Committee on Freedom of Religion or Belief. He also is an NGO delegate to the UN, representing the International Humanist and Ethical Union (IHEU). Before joining the Institute for Humanist Studies in 2000, Cherry served as Executive Director of the Council for Secular Humanism, publisher of *Free Inquiry*, the most widely circulated humanist magazine in the US. During his five years at the Council, Cherry was Acting Executive Director of the International Humanist and Ethical Union, Executive Editor of *Free Inquiry* magazine, and editor of *Secular Humanist Bulletin*. Cherry has also worked in the Netherlands as Secretary for Development and Public Relations for the International Humanist and Ethical Union (IHEU) and in the UK for the British Humanist Association (BHA).

Claus Dierksmeier

Claus Dierksmeier is Associate Professor of Philosophy at Stonehill College, Easton, Massachusetts. He was previously Assistant Professor in Practical Philosophy at the University of Jena in Germany (1998–2002) and a visiting professor and research fellow in Spain, Uruguay, and Argentina (2001–2). He received his PhD in 1997 with a dissertation on Immanuel Kant's religious philosophy. He earned his professoral degree (*Habilitation*) in 2002 for a study of the German philosopher Karl Christian Friedrich Krause and his influence in Latin American political thought. Claus Dierksmeier has published widely in German, English, and Spanish. His current research is into the various philosophical notions of freedom and their relevance for a just society. He also works on economic philosophy and business ethics.

Bill Drayton

Bill Drayton is the CEO and founder of Ashoka, Innovators for the Public. He has been a social entrepreneur since he was a New York City elementary school student and was a McKinsey and Company consultant for almost ten years, gaining wide experience serving both public and private clients. For four years he was Assistant Administrator at the US Environmental Protection Agency. He also served briefly in the White House, and taught both law and management at Stanford Law School and Harvard's Kennedy School of Government. Bill has received many awards for his achievements. He was elected one of the early MacArthur Fellows for his work, including the founding of Ashoka. Yale School of Management gave him its annual Award for Entrepreneurial Excellence. In 2005 he was selected one of America's Best Leaders by *US News & World Report* and Harvard's Center for Public Leadership. In the same month he was the recipient of the Yale Law School's highest alumni honor, the Yale Law School Award of Merit, for his substantial contribution to public service.

Greg Epstein

Greg M. Epstein serves as the Humanist Chaplain of Harvard University. He also sits on the executive committee of the thirty-eight-member corps of Harvard Chaplains. In 2005 Greg received ordination as a Humanist Rabbi from the International Institute for Secular Humanistic Judaism, following five years' study in Jerusalem and Michigan. He holds a BA (Religion and Chinese) and an MA (Judaic Studies) from the University of Michigan, Ann Arbor, and a Master's of Theological Studies from the Harvard Divinity School. He is an advisor to two student groups at Harvard College, the Secular Society and the Interfaith Council, and to the Harvard Humanist Graduate Community.

Dieter Frey

Dieter Frey is Dean of the Faculty of Psychology and Educational Science as well as Professor of Social Psychology at Ludwig Maximilian University in Munich (Germany). In addition, he is Academic Director of the Bavarian Academy for Elite Training and a member of the Bavarian Academy of Sciences. Before coming to Munich he was Professor of Social and Economic Psychology in Kiel and from 1988 to 1989 he was Theodor Heuss Professor at the Graduate Faculty of the New School for Social Research, New York. In 1998, Dieter Frey was elected German Psychologist of the Year. His extensive research interests include basic social psychology (e.g. decision processes, information seeking, group processes) as well as organizational psychology (e.g. leadership and innovation) and behavioral finance.

Adrian Henriques

Adrian is an advisor on corporate responsibility, social accountability, and sustainability. He has produced research on social sustainability and taught accountability and social auditing at Warwick University Business School. Adrian has been a Council Member of the Institute of Social and Ethical Accountability and was for five years a member of the Global Reporting Initiative Steering Committee. He is also a member of the Association of Chartered Certified Accountants' Social and Environmental Committee. Adrian is currently Visiting Professor of Accountability and CSR at Middlesex University Business School.

Formerly Head of Accountability at the New Economics Foundation, he has also worked for the International Society for Ecology and Culture, an NGO campaigning on economic globalization. For a number of years Adrian was a management consultant for Price-waterhouseCoopers in financial services. His publications include *Corporate Truth: The limits to transparency*, and *The Triple Bottom Line – Does it all add up?*

W. David Holford

W. David Holford is a professional engineer, as well as a PhD student in management at L'École des hautes études commerciales de Montréal (HEC Montréal) under the supervision of Dr. Omar Aktouf. He is also Assistant Professor of Management at the University of Quebec at Montreal (UQAM). His field of interest is the humanistic dimension of management and its ramifications for both risk/crisis creation and knowledge management. He has co-authored several articles with Dr. Omar Aktouf, and recently won major scholarships and prizes for academic excellence (2004–7). Prior to embarking in his studies, Mr. Holford worked for nineteen years in the aerospace industry (Pratt and Whitney, Canada), the last nine in senior engineering management.

Aileen M. Ionescu-Somers

Aileen Ionescu-Somers is the program manager of IMD's research project on Corporate Sustainability Management (CSM). Previously she was head of the International Projects Unit at the World Wide Fund for Nature (WWF International), and held program management roles within the Africa and Latin America regional programs. She holds a BA, MA, HDipEd, and MSc in Environmental Management and a PhD in the area of corporate social responsibility in the food and beverage sector from the National University of Ireland (UCC). She is currently completing her book *Business Logic for Sustainability: An Analysis of the Food and Beverage Industry*.

Stephan Kaiser

Stephan Kaiser is an assistant professor at the Ingolstadt School of Management, Catholic University of Eichstätt-Ingolstadt. In 2001, he earned his PhD at the same university. Earlier, he studied business administration at the Universities of Regensburg and Wales (EMBS Swansea). His current research focuses on positive organizational studies, human resources, professional services firms, as well as knowledge, technology, and organizations.

Jean-Pierre Lehmann

Jean-Pierre Lehmann is a professor at IMD. His areas of special interest include globalization, global governance, trade and development, the role of business in the reduction of poverty and inequality, and the socio-economic, cultural, and business dynamics of Asia. He acts in various leading capacities in a number of public policy institutes and organizations, as an advisor to governments and corporations, and as a frequent commentator in the international media. He is the author of several books and numerous articles and papers primarily dealing with globalization, modern East Asian history, and East Asia and the international political economy. In 1995 he launched the Evian Group, an international coalition of corporate, government, and opinion leaders, united by a common vision of enhancing global prosperity for the benefit of all by fostering an open, inclusive, and equitable global market economy in a rules-based multilateral framework. A leading voice on global trade and investment issues that acts as a forum for dialogue and a birthplace of ideas, the Evian Group also engages actively in advocacy to counter the forces of protectionism and chauvinism.

Klaus Leisinger

Klaus M. Leisinger is President and CEO of the Novartis Foundation for Sustainable Development and Professor for Development Sociology at the University of Basel. He pursues academic and practical field work on a wide range of development-related topics, among them foreign aid and international development, good governance, health policy in the least developed countries, business ethics, and corporate responsibility. Klaus Leisinger serves as invited lecturer or visiting professor at several universities worldwide and was awarded an honorary doctorate in theology by the University of Fribourg. He has held advisory positions in a number of national and international organizations, such as the United Nations Global Compact, the United Nations Development Programme (UNDP), the World Bank (CGIAR), the Asian Development Bank, and the Economic Commission for Latin America (ECLA). From September 2005 to December 2006, Klaus Leisinger served as special advisor to the United Nations Secretary-General for the UN Global Compact.

Thomas Maak

Thomas Maak is Senior Researcher at the Institute for Business Ethics and Reader in Corporate Responsibility at the University of St. Gallen in Switzerland. As visiting faculty he also co-directs a research stream within the PwC-INSEAD initiative on high-performing organizations at INSEAD, France. He has held visiting positions at the School for International and Public Affairs at Columbia University, New York and at Georgetown University's McDonough School of Business in Washington, DC. His research and teaching focus on business ethics, corporate citizenship, integrity management, and responsible leadership. Thomas is a member of the Executive Committee of the European Business Ethics Network (EBEN). As consultant and advisor he has worked with leading corporations such as Shell, PricewaterhouseCoopers, Volkswagen, and DONG Energy. Among his many publications is *Responsible Leadership* (with Nicola Pless, 2006). He has also served as guest editor for the *Journal of Business Ethics*.

Domènec Melé

Domènec Melé is Professor of Business Ethics and holds the Chair of Economic and Ethics at IESE Business School, University of Navarra, Spain. He earned his doctorate in industrial engineering from the Polytechnic University of Catalonia and his PhD in theology from the University of Navarra. Before joining IESE in 1986 he was Professor of Chemical Technology at the Polytechnic University of Valencia. Over the last twenty years, he has written extensively and carried out research in the areas of business ethics and Christian social thought. His areas of specialization include economic and business ethics, international management ethics, corporate social responsibility, Christian ethics and spirituality in management, ethics in organizational cultures, and philosophy of management. Domènec Melé also chairs the bi-annual International Symposium on Ethics, Business and

Society led by IESE since 1991 and is the co-founder of IESE's Center for Business in Society. Currently, he serves as section editor of the *Journal of Business Ethics*.

Oliver Rapf

Oliver Rapf is head of Business & Industry Engagement, Climate Change Programme, WWF International. Based in Brussels, Oliver is the leader of the Business & Industry (B&I) strand of WWF's global climate change program. He collaborates with a multitude of companies and sectors on corporate carbon management, and works with a global team to develop new cutting-edge partnerships to mitigate climate change. Oliver Rapf is a registered advisor on sustainable business practices to the European Commission, focussing on B&I performance in sustainable energy and climate change. Since 1997 he has overseen WWF projects on sustainable energy and efficient housing, as well as climate change mitigation strategies and impacts. He has headed the German NGO delegation to several UN climate conferences. Before joining WWF he worked for an environmental think tank and a spatial planning institute. Oliver studied at universities in Heidelberg, Bonn, and Vancouver and has a Master's in Geography, Political Science, and Economics.

Gordon Müller-Seitz

Gordon Müller-Seitz works at the Technical University of Berlin, Department of Sociology of Organization for the Research Project "Path Creating Networks: Inventing Next Generation Lithography in Germany and the US." He received his PhD at the Department of Organisational Studies and Human Resources, Catholic University of Eichstaett-Ingolstadt, Germany. His research interests lie in positive emotions, networks, innovative technologies, knowledge management, and professional services firms. He has published his ideas among others in *Organization* and *Industry & Innovation*.

Julian Nida-Rümelin

Julian Nida-Rümelin is Professor of Political Theory and Philosophy at the Ludwig Maximilian University in Munich, Germany. He currently also holds the position of visiting professor at the University of St. Gallen, Switzerland. Between 2001 and 2002 he was state minister for culture and media and member of the German federal government. Prior to that he was Professor of Philosophy at the University of Göttingen. He studied philosophy, physics, mathematics, and political science in Munich and Tübingen. Julian Nida-Rümelin has received various honors, among them an honorary professorship at Humboldt University in Berlin and the award "To the Patron of the German Book" of the Börsenverein des Deutschen Buchhandels.

Lynn Sharp Paine

Lynn Sharp Paine is John G. McLean Professor of Business Administration at Harvard Business School, where she is a member and former chair of the general management unit. Ms. Paine's research focuses on the leadership and governance of companies that meld high ethical standards with outstanding financial results. A member of Phi Beta Kappa and a *summa cum laude* graduate of Smith College, Ms. Paine holds a doctorate in moral philosophy from Oxford University and a law degree from the Harvard Law School. A faculty associate of the Harvard University Edmond J. Safra Foundation Center for Ethics, Ms. Paine also serves on the Advisory Board of Leadership Forum International (LFI) and the academic council of the Hills Program on Governance at the Center for Strategic and International Studies. She was a member of the Conference Board's Blue-Ribbon Commission on Public Trust and Private Enterprise formed after the corporate scandals of 2002. Before joining the Harvard faculty, Ms. Paine served on the faculties of Georgetown University's Business School, the University of Virginia's Darden School of Business, and at the National Cheng Chi University in Taiwan, where she was a Luce Scholar in 1976–7.

Miguel Pereira Lopes

Miguel Pereira Lopes is an invited assistant professor at Faculdade de Economia, Universidade Nova de Lisboa, in Lisbon, Portugal. He received his PhD in Organizational Psychology from Universidade Nova de Lisboa. In the past, he has worked as a senior manager at major national and multinational companies. His current research focuses on the emergence of positive behavior in organizational settings, social networks, and positive leadership.

Claudia Peus

Claudia Peus is Assistant Professor of Social and Organizational Psychology at Ludwig Maximilian University in Munich, Germany. From 2005–7 she was a visiting scholar at the Sloan School of Management, Massachusetts Institute of Technology and a post-doctoral fellow in the department of psychology at Harvard University (2006–7). Her research interests focus on the impact of leadership on employees' attitudes and behaviors, leadership development, women in management, and cross-cultural psychology. In addition to her academic work, Claudia Peus has been involved in executive education and organizational development programs for numerous multinational companies including Allianz Global Investors, E.ON, and Goodyear.

Miguel Pina e Cunha

Miguel Pina e Cunha is an associate professor at the Faculdade de Economia, Universidade Nova de Lisboa, in Lisbon, Portugal. He received his PhD from Tilburg University (the Netherlands). His current research focuses on organizational improvisation, emergent change, organizational bricolage, and positive organizing.

Nicola M. Pless

Nicola Pless is Research Director and Reader in Responsible Leadership at the University of St. Gallen in Switzerland. She is also a visiting senior research fellow in INSEAD (France), where she co-directs the PwC-INSEAD research stream on "Developing Responsible Leadership." She holds a Master's degree in business administration from the University of Bayreuth, a PhD in organizational theory from the University of St. Gallen, and a diploma in clinical organizational psychology from INSEAD. Prior to joining above-mentioned faculties she worked as a vice president in the financial services industry and served at the World Bank Group in Washington,

DC. Her research, writing, and teaching focus on corporate social responsibility, responsible leadership, and leadership development. She has delivered training and consulting services for the International Finance Corporation, Deutsche Telekom, Volkswagen, Pricewater-houseCoopers, and DONG Energy. She has published three books and several articles in practitioners' and academic journals. Her latest book, *Responsible Leadership* (with Thomas Maak), was published in 2006.

Oliver Salzmann

Oliver Salzmann is a research associate at IMD, Lausanne. He works for the research project on Corporate Sustainability Management (CSM) in IMD. He holds a Master's in industrial management from Dresden University of Technology and a PhD in corporate sustainability management in the energy sector from Berlin University of Technology. Since joining IMD in 2001, he has conducted empirical research in several areas, including private households and sustainable consumption, the business case for corporate sustainability, and stakeholders' perceptions and activities with respect to corporate social and environmental responsibility.

Amartya Sen

Amartya Sen is Lamont University Professor and Professor of Economics and Philosophy at Harvard University and was until recently the Master of Trinity College, Cambridge. He has served as President of the Econometric Society, the Indian Economic Association, the American Economic Association, and the International Economic Association. He was also Lamont University Professor at Harvard earlier, from 1988–98, and before that was Drummond Professor of Political Economy at Oxford University and a fellow of All Souls College (where he is now Distinguished Fellow). Prior to that he was Professor of Economics at Delhi University and at the London School of Economics. His research has ranged over a number of fields in economics, philosophy, and decision theory, including social choice theory, welfare economics, theory of measurement, development economics, public health, gender studies, moral and political philosophy, and the economics of peace and war. Among the many awards he has received is the Nobel Prize in Economics 1998.

Ulrich Steger

Ulrich Steger holds the Alcan Chair of Environmental Management at IMD and is Director of IMD's Forum on Corporate Sustainability Management. He is Director of the DaimlerChrysler Partnership Programs and Allianz Excellence Program and Co-Director of Building High Performance Boards. He also holds an Honorary Professorship in International Management at Berlin Technical University. He was minister of economics and technology in the state of Hesse and a member of the managing board of Volkswagen, in charge of environment and traffic matters and the implementation of an environmental strategy within the VW group worldwide. He has published extensively, most recently *Inside the Mind of the Stakeholder: The Hype behind Stakeholder Pressure* (2006).

Peter Ulrich

Peter Ulrich, born 1948 in Berne, Switzerland, is Full Professor of Economic and Business Ethics and Director of the Institute for Business Ethics at the University of St. Gallen, Switzerland. After his studies in business administration, economics and social sciences at the University of Fribourg (1967–71) and his doctorate at the University of Basle (1972–6), he spent four years as a management consultant in Zurich. A scholarship from the Swiss National Science Foundation enabled him to complete his habilitation thesis ("Economic Sciences and Their Philosophical Foundations," 1986) at the University of Witten-Herdecke, Germany for a *venia legend*. In 1984, he was appointed as Full Professor in Business Administration at the University of Wuppertal, Germany. In 1987, he was appointed to the first chair for Business Ethics at a German-speaking faculty in St. Gallen. In the twenty years since then, his approach of integrative economic ethics has become widely accepted in the German and European debate.

Allen L. White

Allen L. White is Vice President and Senior Fellow, Tellus Institute, Boston, and directs the institute's corporate design program. Dr. White co-founded the Global Reporting Initiative in 1997 and served as Chief Executive through 2002. In 2004, he co-founded Corporation 2020, an initiative focused on designing future corporations to sustain social purpose. He advises multilaterals, foundations, corporations, and NGOs on corporate responsibility and sustainability strategy, policy, and practice. He has held faculty and research positions at the University of Connecticut, Clark University, Tufts University, and Battelle Laboratories, and is a former Fulbright Scholar in Peru and Peace Corps worker in Nicaragua. Dr. White has served on advisory boards and committees of a multitude of non-profit organizations in the US and abroad. He is Chair of GAN-Net, a non-profit organization dedicated to building capacity and building the movement of global, multistakeholder civil society organizations. He is a member of the Steering Committee of the Institute for Responsible Investment, Boston College Center for Corporate Citizenship, and, since 2004, has served as Senior Advisor to Business for Social Responsibility.

Stephen B. Young

Stephen B. Young, Global Executive Director of the Caux Round Table, is a lawyer and writer. He has served as Dean of the Hamline University School of Law and as an assistant dean at the Harvard Law School. He has taught law and Vietnamese history and served on the boards of numerous non-profit organizations. While Dean of the Hamline University School of Law he initiated the *Journal of Law and Religion*. Young studied anthropology and government at Harvard College and took his law degree at Harvard Law School. In 2004 Berrett-Koehler of San Francisco published Young's book *Moral Capitalism*. It has been translated into Japanese, Spanish, Polish, and Croatian. Young has contributed chapters to a number of recent books on ethics and corporate social responsibility and blogs regularly for the *Twin Cities Daily Planet*. As an attorney, Young has both served corporate clients and litigated in state and federal courts. In 1966 Young discovered the Bronze Age site of Ban Chiang in northeast Thailand, now a UNESCO world heritage site. In 1975 Young initiated efforts to open the United States to refugees from South Vietnam and later served on the Citizens' Commission for Indochinese Refugees. He later suggested the framework of a United Nations trusteeship interim administration for Cambodia as a means to end the civil war in that country.

Muhammad Yunus

Muhammad Yunus earned the nickname "banker to the poor" by giving small cash loans to the poorest people in Bangladesh. Yunus completed his PhD in economics at Vanderbilt University in 1969. He taught at Middle Tennessee State University before returning to Bangladesh in 1972 to teach at Chittagong University. His first loan was given to a group of very poor village women in 1974, an amount equivalent of $27. Yunus founded the Grameen Bank two years later to institutionalize this small-scale loan giving, usually to people who had no collateral and would have been turned away by the traditional banks. This notion of "microcredit" has now become a worldwide phenomenon, giving millions the opportunity to pull themselves out of abject poverty. Yunus and Grameen were jointly given the Nobel Prize for Peace in 2006. By that time the bank had helped more than six million borrowers, the vast majority of them women. In awarding the prize, the Nobel Committee stated: "Lasting peace cannot be achieved unless large population groups find ways in which to break out of poverty. Microcredit is one such means."

Acknowledgements

Every attempt has been made to secure permission to reproduce copyright material in this title and grateful acknowledgement is made to the authors and publishers of all reproduced material. In particular, the publishers would like to acknowledge the following for granting permission to reproduce material from the sources set out below:

Chapter 9 excerpted from *Development as Freedom* by Amartya Sen, New York: Alfred A. Knopf, 1999. Reproduced with kind permission of Alfred A. Knopf, a division of Random House, Inc.

Chapter 11 excerpted from *Value Shift: Why Companies Must Merge Social and Financial Imperatives to Achieve Superior Performance* by Lynn Sharp Paine, New York: McGraw-Hill, 2003. Reproduced with kind permission of The McGraw-Hill Companies.

Chapter 19 excerpted from *Corporate Truth: The Limits to Transparency* by Adrian Henriques, London: Earthscan, 2007. Reproduced with kind permission of Earthscan Ltd.

Chapter 22 excerpted from *Leading Quietly: An Orthodox Guide to Doing the Right Thing* by Joseph L. Badaracco, Boston: Harvard Business School Press, 2002. Reproduced with kind permission of Harvard Business School Publishing.

Chapter 24 originally published as Chapter 1 of *Social Entrepreneurship: New Models of Sustainable Social Change*, edited by Alex Nicholls, Oxford: Oxford University Press, 2006. Reproduced with kind permission of Oxford University Press.

Humanistic Management Network: paving the way towards a life-serving economy

In the Aristotelian concept of the economic system, the economy served political goals. As far as these political goals were democratically legitimized, the economy directly served the people. The humanist credo of "man as the measure of all things" (*Protagoras*) led us to a free, liberal, and democratic world. However, the current global economic system more often than not treats humans as instruments for profits or GDP growth, ignoring the democratic rights and liberties they enjoy within their nation-states. The effects are injustice, environmental degradation, and unhappiness – even for those who currently profit from the existing system. To counter these inhumane effects, Humanistic Management Network creates and disseminates *actionable knowledge* that puts humans first and supports the creation of a life-serving economic system.

Humanistic Management Network's *vision* is to encourage businesses to embrace a more 'life-serving' approach by integrating humanistic values into their core strategy. Our *mission* is to influence business academia, management, and the general public in defining the purpose and role of business in a global society. We foster the creation and dissemination of actionable knowledge to change business practices towards humanistic ideals.

In a first step, Humanistic Management Network is focusing on the creation of a research platform based on humanistic principles. We are establishing a common research agenda for researchers of various disciplines and fields to address the need for a life-serving economy and to build our network of likeminded think-tanks and research groups around the world. In a second step, we will create products and services based on humanistic principles and offer them to organizations in consultations. In a third step, we will use the insights gained from research and practice to influence public discourse and policy decisions towards a human-centered economy. These three steps will be the basis of a continuous feedback loop, which will

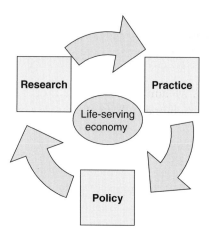

Figure A.1 Humanistic Management Network's integrated approach for a more life-serving economy

slowly but systematically support the creation of a life-serving economic system in which authentic human needs will be served.

Humanistic Management Network currently consists of the editorial team of this book.
They are:

Wolfgang Amann
Shiban Khan
Michael Pirson
Heiko Spitzeck
Ernst von Kimakowitz

Our pledge

If we do not take responsibility for reshaping our economic system and business organizations, who will? And even if – in the end – our collective efforts fail to reach the goal of a humane future, we can say that we tried our best in order to achieve it. Or as Martin Luther put it: "Even if I knew that tomorrow the world would go to pieces, I would still plant my apple tree."

This is easy to demand but hard to live up to. However, if we do not strive for the highest goals right at the beginning, we will not get very far at all. This is why we as editors pledge the following and encourage any reader, student, colleague, and critic to hold us accountable to this and to indicate if we lose our way to a humane future.

Our pledge:

- As *researchers*, we aim to generate *actionable knowledge* to help others to grow as humans. We will focus on publishing books and articles of which we can be proud, but we will also act on this knowledge as teachers and consultants.
- As *teachers*, we will make sure that our students understand the duality of success and humanism and, in case of doubt, to strive to make man the measure of all things. Our duty as education professionals is to help our students grow professionally and as humans.
- As *consultants*, we make sure that we combine our ideals with our capabilities to generate pragmatic solutions that make a difference to humans as well as to business.
- As *citizens*, we will foster discourse on humanism in business to enable people to understand the challenges of our shareholder economy and to start thinking of creative solutions.
- Finally, we hold ourselves accountable, open to discourse, and undertake to be transparent, to develop measures for academic accountability.

This pledge mirrors what this book is about: reflection, principles, and action. However, as editors, we would not be the servants we strive to be, if we were merely satisfied with the publication of a book that includes a pledge. We are striving for a real-life impact towards a more humane business environment.

Where do we go from here?

We encourage fellow researchers from diverse disciplines to cooperate and evaluate the interactions between business and society, and, we hope, to exemplify that humane and successful organizations and institutions are feasible. This would encourage practitioners to experiment with similar life-conducive endeavors. In the same spirit, we encourage practitioners to share their stories of what worked and what did not. Research, case studies, etc. would help to initiate a constructive public discussion about humanistic values in our current business environment – a topic that we believe affects each of us.

We believe in the power of change through dialogue and insight. Just talking about humanism and business will generate change: change in individuals, in organizations, and in systems. Let us start the dialogue and try to keep it alive. We therefore encourage every reader with ideas on how we can approach the idea of a humane form of business to contact us at info@humanetwork.org. In order to make this idea come true, we all need to stand together and show courage when this is required.

When your grandchildren ask you what you did to give them a life-conducive world in which to grow up, what will your answer be?

Please visit us at www.humanetwork.org.

Introduction: humanism in business

MICHAEL PIRSON, ERNST VON KIMAKOWITZ,
HEIKO SPITZECK, WOLFGANG AMANN,
AND SHIBAN KHAN

The king is dead, long live the king?

Before and during the Middle Ages many societies were organized around a dominant power such as a king or priest. Serving the central ruler was the raison d'être of the state, its economy, and its inhabitants, which often resulted in human costs. In the era of enlightenment,[1] proponents of Liberalism broke with this tradition and boldly proclaimed individual freedoms as the central tenet of organized society.[2] Consequently, societies transformed, economies experienced an upsurge, wealth was created at unprecedented rates, and a growing number of citizens were able to pursue their life goals more freely. The industrial revolution that followed is often regarded as a direct result of these societal changes, supporting the argument that Liberalism's empowering effects on the individual were at the epicenter of long-lasting and profound progress in human development.

When analyzing the current state of our societies, one could almost conclude that these advances are being partially reversed in a world in which a new king is worshipped: profit.

This new king's main constituents are shareholder-value-maximizing businesses, and one of his strongest allies is GDP growth, which has generally become a central societal goal – an end rather than a means. In other words, we treat the achievement of GDP growth as an objective in its own right and not as a tool that we can use to achieve an objective. This is difficult to grasp: why are even the wealthiest societies looking for, let's say, an extra half percentage point of

---

[1] For the relationship between enlightenment and religion, see Epstein (chapter 3 of this volume).
[2] For a historical review of humanistic thought, see Nida-Rümelin and Cherry (chapters 1 and 2 of this volume).

growth without contemplating what that extra income could best be used for? Why is no one asking whether a specific problem requiring attention truly lacks financial resources or whether other factors are responsible for it? Is it possible that the measures taken to achieve that little extra growth might exacerbate the problems that the additional growth earnings are supposed to tackle? Given that between 1995 and 2005 cumulative GDP growth in the OECD countries was close to 30 percent,[3] there seems to be little evidence that growth alone solves societal problems. Would it not seem more sensible to first agree on an objective and then determine the appropriate tool? This may or may not be to nourish GDP growth.

We have accepted our new king and his entourage all too readily, often at the expense of other important aspects of human existence, such as a clean environment, strong social relationships, and self-determination. Just as the Age of Enlightenment "civilized" the state in order to serve its people, we would like to see a renewed liberalization – one that is based on similar notions, but that will allow us to "civilize" the *economic* system.

Don't get us wrong here: we are not advocating some socialist Utopia, nor are we anti-market or anti-globalization sentimentalists. We gratefully acknowledge the tremendous progress that has been brought about by free-market economies in terms of human development. We believe in the power that markets have to unleash individual creativity and to allocate goods and services more efficiently than any centrally planned process could. We also believe that tremendous opportunities arise for humankind from an economy that is inter-connected and inter-dependent on a global scale. However, like early humanists, we are not ready to accept the given order without inquiring into potential variations on this given order.

It sometimes seems astounding that the fall of the Berlin Wall was largely viewed as a victory of capitalism over communism, rather than a liberating event that enabled us to engage in a discourse – unclouded by ideological confrontation – on our economic future. The Western world's victory pose may have been an understandable reaction at the time, but today, nearly twenty years later, it is time to stop patting our

---

[3] See www.oecd.org/LongAbstract/0,3425,en_2649_201185_36396771_1_1_1_
1,00.html for statistical information on the economies of the OECD countries.

own backs and return to work. We should not be exploiting yesterday's conflicts to silence challenges to the status quo.

The debate that we believe needs to be held is not about free markets vs. centrally planned markets, but about the need to decide when and where free market forces should govern an issue and when and where we have other, more appropriate tools to find a life-serving solution. A free market is amoral,[4] indifferently creating great wealth, as well as great hardship. Consequently, moral beings should use it wisely and responsibly, rather than blindly trusting a "one-size-fits-all" approach.

As a starting point, we draw on the Aristotelian concept according to which the character of the economy is a life-conducive, life-serving one. This is a view inspired by Protagoras, according to which the purpose of the economy is to cater to authentic human needs, to enable humans to develop their full capabilities.[5] We believe that the currently dominant form of capitalism, shareholder capitalism, suffers from several shortcomings in this regard.

In the following section, we will briefly elaborate on some of the challenges that we believe lie within our current, shareholder-oriented capitalism. We will also introduce the rationale and the questions that have led to this book being compiled, as well as the outline and the flow of the various contributions.

Challenges to shareholder capitalism

The current economic set-up often fails to meet expectations in respect of its life-conduciveness and respect for humanity. Closely following the structure of this book, our analysis of these shortcomings is based on three levels: a systemic level, an organizational level, and an individual level.

The systemic level

Environmental destruction is one of the most obvious problems of our current system. Industrialized nations use more resources than the

---

[4] To avoid misunderstandings: amoral means without a moral capacity, it therefore means neutral towards or "unaware" of moral concerns but it does not mean immoral. Immoral would mean markets have a negative moral capacity, which they don't.

[5] For human capabilities, see Sen (chapter 9 of this volume).

planet can provide. As an illustration: if everybody on this planet were to consume natural resources at the rate of an average American, five planets' worth of resources would be required; at the rate of an average European, three planets (Boyle, Cordon, and Potts 2006). All in all, humanity is currently using the productive capacity of nearly 1.3 planets to satisfy its needs (WWF 2006). The situation is set to exacerbate with continued global growth. In economic terms, this is irresponsible, as we are living off our planetary capital and not the interest generated by it. This lack of sustainability is, however, supported by the logic of our current system. Shareholder capitalism is short-term-oriented and, when applied rigorously, rewards plundering over preserving. Consequences such as external effects are often ignored and, according to neoliberal reasoning, the state should not be involved, as it hampers entrepreneurial freedom.

Increasing inequality is another problem that is likely to have significant repercussions on the stability of our political and economic systems. Current trends in globalization have led to a world in which the rich get richer, and the poor get disproportionately poorer (Sachs 2005). One sixth of the world's population lives in extreme poverty. An additional one and a half billion people live at a subsistence level, leading lives characterized by problems such as a lack of drinking water. The level of poverty and inequality pricks the conscience of many people, but is also a threat to the stability of the overall system. Political unrest, collectivization, and even terrorism are fed by the increased level of inequality, which often leads to a loss of individual and collective dignity. Shareholder capitalism is mostly blind to these consequences and has not yet provided satisfactory ways to deal with these issues.

The organizational level

At the organizational level, businesses face the challenge of decreasing levels of stakeholder trust. A long list of corporate governance scandals since the beginning of the millennium, along with the arguments sometimes presented to justify "downsizing," "rightsizing," or outsourcing activities, has shaken the foundation of trust that citizens once had in "their" companies. Trust is, however, commonly viewed as the key enabler for cooperation, motivation, and innovation, all of which are required to achieve an organization's peak performance and its eventual success. Surveys indicate that stakeholder trust in businesses is decreasing dramatically, specifically in shareholder-value-maximizing, large, and global companies (World Economic Forum 2006).[6] Research finds that the decline in trust is heavily contingent upon a lack of value congruency between stakeholders and the organization (Pirson and Malhotra 2006). Profit maximization goals are perceived as inherently opportunistic; hence, one of the business community's challenges is to re-establish trust.

We observe that many corporations are facing a decreasing level of employee commitment, indicative of the growing lack of mutual commitment. The Hay Group (2002), for example, finds that 43 percent of American employees are either neutral or negative towards their workplace.[7] According to a Gallup study,[8] 71 percent of US employees are either not engaged or actively disengaged, showing an alarming inner withdrawal rate. Jensen (2001: 278) argues that the goal of profit maximization is partially responsible for this. He posits as self-evident that: "Creating value takes more than acceptance of value maximization as the organizational objective. As a statement of corporate purpose or vision, value maximization is not likely to tap into the energy and enthusiasm of employees and managers to create value." Hence, shareholder-value-maximizing organizations are under-utilizing their employees' potential.[9]

The individual level

On the individual level, we observe an interesting anomaly. While the current system is credited with creating more wealth for many, the

---

[6] These findings are based on a global public opinion poll involving a total of 20,791 interviews with citizens across 20 countries (n = 1,000 in most countries), conducted between June and August 2005 by respected research institutes in each participating country, under the leadership of GlobeScan. (A full list of participating institutes, with contact details, is available at: www.weforum.org.) Each country's findings are considered accurate to within three percentage points, nineteen times out of twenty.

[7] Peus and Frey address this challenge, presenting a humanistic organizational culture and humanistic leadership principles (chapter 15 of this volume).

[8] Gallup Study, "Engaged Employees Inspire Company Innovation". The study revealed that 56 percent of US employees are not engaged and 15 percent are actively disengaged at work. http://gmj.gallup.com/content/24880/Gallup-Study-Engaged-Employees-Inspire-Company.aspx

[9] The alternative is labeled social entrepreneurship, which is outlined by Maak and Pless, Drayton, and Yunus (chapters 21, 23, and 24 of this volume).

average level of life satisfaction has not necessarily increased (Easterlin 2001). GDP growth and growth in well-being have decoupled. Factors that contribute to well-being have a relatively low correlation with material wealth once a certain wealth level has been achieved (Diener and Seligman 2004). From a systemic perspective, the quality of a government in terms of democratic and human rights, the level of corruption, the stability of the system, high social capital, a strong economy with low rates of unemployment and inflation all contribute to subjective well-being. On an individual level, the quality of social relationships, good physical and mental health, and a generally positive attitude towards life are central drivers of well-being. Materialism as an attitude, for example, is considered toxic for well-being (Diener and Seligman 2004; Elias 2002). The current system, however, largely sustains itself by serving material needs that lie beyond those that increase well-being and by an endless attempt to generate new needs, which can in turn only be satisfied by the unsustainable use of available resources.

Why this book?

By highlighting the issues described above, we hope to demonstrate that the current shareholder model of capitalism faces severe functional as well as moral challenges.[10] Current economic endeavors are often short term oriented; we create unsustainable wealth, not sustainable well-being. Furthermore, the pursuit of profit maximization and GDP growth has largely become an end in itself. In short, humans are currently not the measure of all things, nor can this problem be solved by using the same economic logic that created it in the first place.[11] Therefore, we argue that we need to take a step back and ask some very basic questions: what is the purpose of our economic system? What would a more life-serving economy look like and what is the role of business therein?

To start this discussion, we wish to present humanism as a lens through which to view potential alternatives.[12] Humanism is a

---

[10] Which is why Aktouf and Holford call for a "radical humanism" (chapter 6 of this volume).

[11] As Albert Einstein once observed: "The problems that exist in the world today cannot be solved by the level of thinking that created them."

[12] For the concept of socio-economic rationality, see Dierksmeier and Ulrich (chapters 4 and 8 of this volume).

philosophy, an approach to life, and a movement that focuses on creating a human-centered, value-oriented society.[13] Thus, we believe that humanism has much to offer in the search for answers to the questions raised above.

We wish to make it clear that humanism comes in many different flavors. We do not endorse any one specific strand, be it religious or secular. Rather, we wish to demonstrate humanism's unifying potential and inclusive character, while acknowledging the impossibility of covering it exhaustively within this book. We do, however, believe that a globally inter-linked economy needs a globally accepted framework if we want to fully reap the benefits that can arise from it. To achieve global acceptance, this framework cannot be based on only one people's culture, religion, or regional character. The framework must have an ethical basis rooted in humanity itself to appeal to everyone, everywhere. As we will see later in this book, humanism offers just that because it is based on reason and the universal desire to lead an ethical life. It can therefore accommodate any number of cultures, religions, and regional characters under its roof.

Our objectives in compiling this book are twofold: first, we wish to contribute to the creation of a common research agenda for humanism in business. Second, by looking beyond the research agenda, we wish to help to define and strengthen the common ground to enable practitioners and policymakers to engage in a discourse on a human-centered economy. It will be up to the reader to decide if and to what degree we have succeeded.

In this book, we present humanism and its relevance for business. We have brought together contributions from various research disciplines, such as philosophy, economics, management, and psychology, which all too often operate independently. We will start by examining humanism's philosophical and historical roots in order to create an understanding of what humanism means in today's economic world. Then, we will examine the role of business within society and its potential as an agent for positive change. Finally, we will suggest ways in which current business frameworks and management practices can be enhanced to embrace a more life-serving business conduct in which "humans are the measure of all things." In conclusion, we will illustrate the role of the individual in the economic

---

[13] For a philosophical grounding, see Nida-Rümelin (chapter 1 of this volume).

system and consider how each of us can contribute to changing the current system to a more life-conducive one.

Part 1. Philosophic-historical grounding of humanism

This book commences with insights from humanist philosophers from throughout history, clarifying the current understanding of the term. Philosophy is, after all, the mother of all sciences. Julian Nida-Rümelin outlines the principles of humanistic thought and demonstrates the need to reconcile and re-integrate business with humanism. These views are complemented in a historical review by Matt Cherry that describes the effects that humanism or humanists have had on politics, business, and social movements over time. Greg Epstein traces humanist traditions in the world's religions and outlines the comparative advantage of humanism, which is its open anthropology and cultural inclusiveness. Turning to business, Claus Dierksmeier reflects critically on how current business ethics are constrained by economic thought and calls for an economic philosophy based on human freedom. Steven B. Young subsequently looks at the global economy from a moral point of view and points out that the stewardship principle is "humanism at its best" within the economic sphere. Omar Aktouf and W. David Holford argue that the instrumentalization of humans is one of the greatest challenges for humanism in business, and Domènec Melé concludes this section, demonstrating that humanistic elements have always been present in economic thought. These antecedents allow us to envision a more humanistic economy in the future.

Part 2. Towards an integration of humanism and business on a systems level

Following the philosophical grounding, we now direct our attention towards the current state of humanistic values in the global economy, and develop a vision of the role and responsibilities that business has in society. The starting point is Peter Ulrich's depiction of a humane society and the role of businesses within such a society. Amartya Sen's contribution links Dierksmeier's call for human freedom with Ulrich's desire to civilize economic forces, presenting the well-known capability approach as the way that development should be engendered. Klaus M. Leisinger focuses on core humanistic values and universal human rights, and outlines the role business could and should have in their promotion, presenting a business case for corporate human rights engagement. Lynn Sharp Paine demonstrates in the following contribution that the relationship between social and business objectives is not antagonistic by nature but that managing this duality symbiotically is the crux of business success in the twenty-first century. Part 2 concludes with an assessment of the current state of affairs and a call for action by Ulrich Steger.

Part 3. Humanistic management

Focusing on the organizational level, we ask how organizations can be managed humanistically. Allen White examines the deficiencies of current governance mechanisms and explains what humanistic governance systems could look like. Michael Pirson describes the newly emerging field of social entrepreneurship as a blueprint for humanistic management and draws lessons for corporations. Claudia Peus and Dieter Frey stress the importance of humanistic cultures and present examples of humanistic leadership principles. Miguel Pereira Lopes, Miguel Cunha, Stephan Kaiser, and Gordon Müller-Seitz explain that positive organizational scholarship is the academic backbone of humanistic management. Oliver Salzmann, Ulrich Steger, and Aileen Ionescu-Somers temper our optimism with a current assessment of corporate behavior and managerial incentives. They call for effective stakeholder pressure to spur corporations towards the humanistic mode. Oliver Rapf describes the case of WWF, demonstrating that partnerships between businesses and NGOs can accelerate that process.

Part 4. The individual as a change agent for a humane business society

This part concentrates on the individual's role within business and as a force for change. Adrian Henriques elaborates on how human dignity can be preserved within a business context. He focuses on ethical codes as regulative moments and honesty as a personal lever for humanistic cultures. Jean-Pierre Lehmann manifests his belief in the power of individuals and holds that through their engagement, a more humane free-market society is possible. Thomas Maak and Nicola Pless argue that there is a new type of leader emerging: one that is less driven to obtain power, but motivated to serve others. Servant leaders focus on the growth of their followers' capabilities. Once they are motivated and have the capacity to take action towards a humane world – in business and beyond – the followers will ideally become leaders and change agents themselves. Joseph L. Badaracco argues that the most effective changemakers are often people you do not notice. He calls these principled, everyday people "quiet leaders," as they contribute to positive change effectively but without fanfare. Bill Drayton focuses on social entrepreneurs as role models for a humanistic business society because they create social value by employing entrepreneurial means. He also elaborates on the societal mechanisms required to support the social entrepreneurial revolution. Finally, Muhammad Yunus presents his experiences as a social entrepreneur and spreads hope that social entrepreneurs are the solution to our current problems. He presents specific steps that businesses can follow to become more life-conducive.

These four parts present a good overview of current academic thought and research on a more humane economy and the role of business therein. We wish to thank John Silva and Ilse Evertse for their tremendous interest and support in the review process. We also gratefully acknowledge the guidance of Paula Parish at Cambridge University Press.

With your interest piqued, we know that you will enjoy reading about the challenges that the authors of this book pose to our current king and his allies.

Isn't it time to crown a new king? One that we can expect to serve us all better: humanity!

Heiko Spitzeck
Michael Pirson
Wolfgang Amann
Shiban Khan
Ernst von Kimakowitz

St. Gallen, July 2007

References

Boyle, D., Cordon, C., and Potts, R. 2006. *Are You Happy? New Economics Past, Present and Future*. London: NEF.

Diener, E. and Seligman, M. 2004. "Beyond Money," *Psychological Science in the Public Interest* 5(1): 1–31.

Easterlin, R. 2001. "Income and Happiness: Towards a Unified Theory," *Economic Journal* 111: 465–84.

Elias, M. 2002. "Psychologists Now Know What Makes People Happy," *USA Today*, December 10.

Hay Group 2002. "Engage Employees and Boost Performance." CIPD/Bath study. Toronto: The Hay Group.

Jensen, M. C. 2001. "Value Maximisation, Stakeholder Theory, and the Corporate Objective Function," *European Financial Management* 7(3): 297–317.

Pirson, M. and Malhotra, D. 2006. "Stakeholder Trust – What Matters to Whom?" Paper presented at Academy of Management Conference, PDW, Atlanta, August.

Sachs, J. 2005. *The End of Poverty: Economic Possibilities for Our Time*. New York: Penguin Books.

World Economic Forum, 2006. "Decline in Trust." www.globescan.com/news_archives/WEF_trust2005.html (accessed June 26, 2007).

PART I

Philosophic-historical grounding of humanism

1 | Philosophical grounds of humanism in economics

JULIAN NIDA-RÜMELIN

Elements and variants

There is a vast variety of usages of the term "humanism." Humanism is commonly associated with what was called the *studia humaniora* in late medieval and early modern times. Reading classical authors such as Cicero or Seneca, and later Plato and Aristotle, expressed a humanistic attitude in education and learning. Italian Renaissance humanists like Petrarch recommended reading the Latin and Greek texts of ancient times. They thought that this would help to develop one's personality, to become *mitis* and *amabilis*, mild and friendly. The early humanists of the Italian Renaissance did not see scholarship as an end in itself. Scholarship was merely a side-effect of a general program of human refinement.

Let us take this as the first key element of humanism: the idea that human nature is not given, that it can be refined and that education and learning is an adequate means to refine human nature. The idea of educating the human personality is a key element of humanism at all times. It rests on a tradition of philosophical thought that has its origins in Socrates and Plato. For them, instead of authorities, instead of political institutions, instead of holy texts it is reason alone that justifies belief and action. All Platonic dialogues are constructed around this philosophical stance. "Truth" is "adequately justified true belief," as Socrates argues in the *Theaetetus* dialogue. Rhetoric is a cheating art if it is used to win the battle of arguments instead of finding out the truth. In order to find out what is true and what is false, scrupulous investigations are necessary and patient exchange of arguments can lead – dialectically – to the detection of truth.

This leads to the second key element of humanism: reasoning and reason, what is called *logos* in Greek. Plato was quite optimistic about human nature. He was convinced that if a person had understood

15

what is just he would act justly without further motive. Put in modern terms: if a person has good reasons to act and if the person has the necessary insight into these reasons the person will act accordingly. This point of view might be called "intellectualism." But whereas a certain trait of intellectualism can be found in all variants of humanism from ancient times to the present, the strength and centrality of intellectualism in humanism varies. For Aristotle, 40 years younger than Plato, the basis of morality is primarily habituation, not insight. But Aristotle, too, acknowledges the role of principles and their philosophical groundings.

Reasoning is inclusive. It includes all those human beings that have the capacity for reasoning. Historically, however, it takes effort for this inclusiveness of reasoning to be philosophically acknowledged. It is the Hellenistic movement called *Stoa* that probably for the first time in history adopts a universalistic stance. Reasoning addresses all humans, not merely Greeks or citizens of the Hellenistic empire. Reason, the *logos*, governs the world and the life of reasonable persons. The Stoicist sees himself as part of a reasonable, ordered *kosmos*, and this fosters an attitude of indifference towards events that cannot be controlled by the person (the so-called *adiaphora*) and a calmness of the soul (*apatheia*). Universalism is the third key element of humanism. Humanism addresses all persons; there are no essential differences of ethnicity, nation, race, social status, or culture.

This opposition to collective identities binds humanism to individualism as the fourth key element. Humanistic values address the individual, not the collective. For humanism there are no differences between individuals belonging to different communities that cannot be bridged, howsoever these communities might be constituted. Humanism relies on the possibility of communication, on common values and their accessibility to everybody, independently of collective belongings. This individualism is not necessarily atomistic. It does not presuppose that human individuals are "unencumbered selves."[1] Neohumanistic thought, which was especially strong in Germany

---

[1] A term used by Michael Sandel to criticize philosophical and political liberalism. See Sandel, Michael. 1984. "The Procedural Republic and the Unencumbered Self," *Political Theory* 12(1): 81–96. See also Taylor, Charles M. 1985. "Atomism," in C. M. Taylor, *Philosophy and the Human Sciences. Philosophical Papers 2*. Cambridge: Cambridge University Press, pp. 187–211.

during the nineteenth century, emphasized the role of language, tradition, and culture for the constitution of the human individual without giving up the humanistic essentials, including individualism.[2]

These four mutually dependent key elements of humanism are at least present in all modern variants. Some of these emphasize one or two of the key elements and stress the others less. The humanism of classical Greece places emphasis on individualism, reason, and education but does not yet grasp the universal inclusiveness of reasoning. Early modern variants of humanism underscore scientific forms of reasoning, education, and refinement but neglect individualism, which fosters Utopian models of a perfect, harmonious social system.[3] Even Plato has been accused of collectivism by Karl Popper,[4] although the value of "autarkeia" (self-government) plays a central role in Platonic thought.

Some proponents understand humanism as a kind of atheism. This can be seen as an overemphasis of (scientific) reason. Indeed the intellectual movement of modern humanism had to fight against Church authorities for many centuries. Some humanists, like Erasmus of Rotterdam, joined or helped the Protestant separation from the Catholic Church. Other humanists were obviously religious and remained bound to Christianity without giving up the autonomy of reason.

Early socialist thought was partly bound to humanism, like the Fabian Society in England or Charles Fourier in France. Even the ethical socialists in Germany like Fries and Nelson can be labelled as humanists in the tradition of Kantian thought. Western Marxists discussed the topic of humanism, and it is not misleading to divide twentieth-century Marxism into a humanistic and a scientistic branch. Scientistic Marxism relied on the "eternal laws" of historical materialism, and the core of this theory was political economy. The theory of class struggle fostered a collectivist understanding and alienated Marxism from its humanistic sources. Humanists among

---

[2] An especially interesting example is Wilhelm von Humboldt, who could be labeled as communitarian in terms of his theory of culture and language on the one hand, but on the other argued in favor of liberal individualism, self-reliance, and self-responsibility, and a state which grants individuals the capacity to decide for themselves which life they want to live.

[3] More, Thomas. 1518. *Utopia*. Basel; Campanella, Tommaso. 1623. *Civitatis solis*. Frankfurt; Bacon, Francis. 1627. *Nova Atlantis*. London.

[4] Popper, Karl. 1945. *The Open Society and Its Enemies*. London: Routledge.

Marxists were more interested in Marx's early writings, the relation between Marx and Hegel and German idealism in general. Jean-Paul Sartre obviously thought that an existentialist transformation of Marxism would save its humanistic content.[5]

A similar split can be observed in liberalism between those who emphasize human rights and human autonomy and understand liberty as anthropologically founded in man's reasonable nature, and those who reduce liberty to the freedom to buy and sell goods and services in the marketplace. The term "liberalism" as it is used in the political arena in the USA is mostly bound to the first, humanistic tradition, whereas "liberalism" and "neoliberalism" as it is used in most European nations emphasizes the second, economistic form of liberalism. This has led to the introduction of the term "libertarianism" to distinguish economistic from humanistic forms of liberalism. It goes without saying that this demarcation is too general to cover all the philosophical and political variants of today's liberalism.

Given the multitude of humanist paradigms, it seems necessary to reconstruct the key elements of humanism on philosophical grounds. I will try to do this in the second part of this chapter.

Philosophical grounds of humanism

In this section I will try to give a systematic outline of what I take to be the philosophical grounds of humanism. These precepts are related to the historical variants of humanism already mentioned, but it is not the aim of this philosophical reconstruction to include all, or even most, characteristics of the intellectual and cultural movements that have been labelled "humanism." Instead it is the aim of this section to develop a coherent account of humanism. Hence, if some forms of what historically has been called humanism are not covered it does not make this account inadequate.

In order to develop a coherent account of humanism it is helpful to discriminate between theoretical (or metaphysical) humanism on the one hand and practical (or ethical) humanism on the other. Theoretical humanism is a view of man as an anthropological theory. Theoretical humanism assumes that reason is essential for what we believe and how we act. The exchange of reason is a central mode of human

[5] Sartre, Jean-Paul. 1946. *L'existentialisme est un humanisme*. Paris: Nagel.

interaction. Even human interaction that is based on interdependent emotions is constrained and at least partly constituted by the exchange of reasons. If A hates B this is not only a simple emotional fact that has to be taken into account, it is also in need of justification. Hate is certainly an emotion, neither a belief nor an action, but this emotion would not be justified if B were not guilty of some wrong-doing. To be guilty of some wrongdoing is a prerequisite for rendering hate rational. One may add that even if this prerequisite is met, hate would seldom be justified. Some take it as an essential of Christian ethics that one has to love even one's enemies. Buddhist authorities and Stoicist ones reject certain emotions as irrational altogether. But if we keep to our lifeworld-reactive attitudes, hate can and must be justified.

The exchange of reason is a mode of communication ridden with conflict. But these conflicts are of a different nature than conflicts of mere interests. In a conflict of interests one person aims at X and another person aims at not-X and both try to reach their aims taking the other person as part of the given conditions of action. In conflicts *modulo* reasons there is a neutral authority involved: Both appeal to rationality and hopefully to the same or at least sufficiently similar criteria of rationality.

Rationality includes fallibilism. We can be wrong about reasoning, and this implies epistemic tolerance. It implies that even if our opinion differs from somebody else's and we think we have good reasons for our opinion and that the other person has no good reasons for hers, we do not exclude the possibility that she is right and we are wrong. Dogmatism is a form of epistemic irrationality. Reasoning as a form of interaction aims at convincing, i.e. at a change of belief justified by good reasons. It does not aim at belief change as such. The result of successful reasoning is a consensus that is quite different from a consensus reached by force or intimidation. Both parties can agree without regret.

Discourse ethics bridges the gap between theoretical and practical (or ethical) humanism. Discourse ethics relies on those norms that constitute the interaction of giving and taking reasons.[6] The

---

[6] Habermas, Jürgen. 1983. "Diskursethik – Notizen zu einem Begründungsprogramm," in J. Habermas (ed.), *Moralbewußtsein und kommunikatives Handeln*. Frankfurt a. M.: Suhrkamp; and Brandom, Robert B. 1994. *Making It Explicit*. Cambridge, MA: Harvard University Press.

proponents of discourse ethics, however, tend to overestimate these
norms. This has led to the assumption that all relevant normative
claims can be reduced to the constitutive rules of rational discourse.
Rational discourse and the community of language rely on three basic
principles[7]: (1) truthfulness, (2) trust, and (3) reliability. These three
principles are closely interrelated and can be explicated only in relation to each other. If I am truthful I can expect a confident person to
adopt those beliefs that I hold given that they accept my reasoning. To
adopt the beliefs of a truthful person is a rational act only if this
person is reliable, i.e. forms her beliefs on the basis of good reasons.
The process of language learning can be understood only if in most
cases our beliefs and our utterances based on those beliefs are reliable.
Our utterances are based on our beliefs if we are truthful. Confidence
is rational only if other persons can be expected to be truthful and
reliable. Truthfulness and reliability are not sufficient for language
learning if the interacting persons lack confidence. We disappoint a
confident person if we are either not truthful, or not reliable, or both.
A truthful and reliable person is disappointed if the listener is not
confident. We could never learn what an utterance means if in general
we would not and could not expect truthfulness and reliability.

Theoretical humanism is a metaphysical point of view that is deeply
embedded in our everyday practice of communication. But this does
not mean that the whole of theoretical humanism is based on communication or can be reduced to the constitutive rules of communication. Truthfulness, confidence, and reliability are important and
central but not exhausting norms of ethical humanism. Theoretical
humanism is an anthropological assumption that might be called
"metaphysical" because a good deal of what we know about human
beings rests on these assumptions. These assumptions seem to have an
a priori necessary status regarding this knowledge; ethical humanism
embraces a certain type of ethical norms. These norms rest on the
assumption of human nature being reasonable and the idea of
refinement and self-refinement (*Bildung*). Reason is not just given; it is
the result of education, learning, and the development of one's personal character. Ethical humanism takes human nature to be framed
by ethical norms. These ethical norms become relevant for the

---

[7] Nida-Rümelin, Julian. 2001. *Strukturelle Rationalität. Ein philosophischer
Essay über praktische Vernunft*. Stuttgart: Reclam, chapter 6, pp. 104ff.

refinement of human nature not only by (intellectual) insight but also by the everyday practice that conforms to these ethical norms.

In its most elaborated form ethical humanism becomes the theory and practice of autonomy. Kantian ethics understood in this sense marks the most elaborate form of ethical humanism. Kantian philosophy can be understood as an explication of humanism in both dimensions – theoretical and practical. In both dimensions autonomy is the central concept: autonomy of belief and autonomy of practice. The autonomous person weighs (theoretical) reasons in order to form (rational) belief. The autonomous person weighs (practical) reasons in order to bring about a (rational) decision. The person is autonomous insofar as reasons alone affect her beliefs and her actions. She is autonomous insofar as these reasons are her reasons, reasons she accepts.[8] This does not contradict an objectivist interpretation of reasons.[8] Humanism understood as the theory and practice of autonomy is more than an approach based exclusively on communication and its constitutive rules. Negative and positive liberties, the liberty that restricts interventions and the liberty that guarantees the means necessary to live an autonomous life consist in more than the conformity to the rules of (rational) discourse. The dignity of man is more than the prerequisite of communication. The dignity of human beings presupposes the capacity to act and judge on the basis of reasons (rationality), it takes human beings as free and responsible; they are not just forced by causal laws but free to act and judge and at the same time responsible for giving reasons for their actions and judgments. Rationality, freedom, and responsibility are three aspects of the same phenomenon: to believe and decide (partly also to feel) according to reason.

---

[8] This is certainly a difficult matter. I deal with it in *Strukturelle Rationalität* (2001). Since I am not yet perfectly happy with the answers I gave in this booklet regarding the objectivity of reasons I will deal with it again in the sequel about responsibility (Nida-Rümelin, Julian. Forthcoming. *Begriff Verantwortung*. Stuttgart: Reclam). For present purposes I think it is not necessary to discuss this point further, but it should be said that most present-day Kantians reject objectivism regarding reasons and prefer constructivism regarding reasons. See Rawls, John. 1999. "Kantian Constructivism," in Samuel Freeman (ed.), *John Rawls: Collected Papers*. Cambridge, MA: Harvard University Press, pp. 303ff; and Korsgaard, Christine. 1996. *Creating the Kingdom of Ends*. Cambridge: Cambridge University Press, and her 2002 Locke Lectures at Oxford under the title "Self-Constitution: Agency, Identity, and Integrity."

Is humanism reconcilable with economics?

First it should be emphasized that there is an essential common element in humanism and economic theory: both accounts take the human individual as their starting point. Moreover, both accounts rely on the human capacity for reasoning. Both accounts are hostile to collectivist and naturalistic anthropologies.

Economics as a discipline originated from Scottish moral philosophy during the European Enlightenment. One of the founding fathers of utilitarianism, Jeremy Bentham[9] tried to establish rational normative criteria for good legislation. Every single person counted as equal, independent of social status and origin. Utilitarianism follows humanistic impulses not only in its origin but also in its present-day variants.[10] Classical liberalism was closely bound to utilitarianism. John Stuart Mill, one of the leading theoreticians of liberalism, was a utilitarian ethicist at the same time. But in fact there is a central problem. Whereas the original impulses of the utilitarian movement were liberal, universalist, and rationalist it became more and more clear that utilitarian principles can justify collectivist practices: To maximize the total sum of happiness efficiently can include the instrumentalization of one person for the sake of one or several others. Under certain conditions even slavery can be justified by utilitarian principles.

There are three main flaws in utilitarianism:

First, utilitarianism has no adequate understanding of human rights and liberties. According to utilitarian principles rights and liberties can only be justified as efficient means of maximizing the total sum of happiness, but it seems obvious that an adequate understanding of rights and liberties justifies the corresponding norms humanistically, i.e. understanding rights and liberties as expressing respect for the individual human person, her dignity, and autonomy.

Second, the integrity, even the personal identity of the utilitarian agent is threatened if she follows utilitarian principles in her everyday practice. No project that might be essential for leading an upright and coherent life will

---

[9] Bentham, Jeremy. 1789. *Introduction to the Principles of Morals and Legislation*. London.

[10] See Hare, Richard Mervyn. 1963. *Freedom and Reason*. Oxford: Clarendon Press; and Hare, Richard Mervyn. 1981. *Moral Thinking. Its Level, Method and Point*. Oxford: Clarendon Press; or Brandt, Richard Booker. 1979. *A Theory of the Good and the Right*. Oxford: Clarendon Press.

survive if the duty to maximize the total sum of happiness has priority in each moment of the agent's life.

Third, utilitarianism lacks the conceptual means to give an adequate account of cooperation. Utilitarian agents maximize the same value function. They can coordinate their actions interpersonally, but they cannot cooperate. Cooperation is the answer to diverging subjective values that would lead to suboptimal results if everybody optimized his or her values individualistically. If cooperation were excluded as an option of choice in the prisoner's dilemma, only utilitarianism could help to establish collective rationality or – in other words – could avoid Pareto-inefficient results.[11]

Present-day economics is based on rational decision and game theory. The utility theorem of von Neumann and Morgenstern[12] can be taken as the theoretical core of modern economics. This theorem transforms preference relations that are coherent into two interrelated functions, the utility function and the probability function. These two functions represent two different yet interrelated propositional attitudes: desires and expectations, conative and epistemic attitudes, or, put in different terms, normative and empirical judgments.[13] The theorem itself is neutral regarding the content of epistemic and conative attitudes. It postulates coherence in the form of different criteria like transitivity, connectivity, or monotonicity. The criteria are formulated such that desires and beliefs, conative and epistemic attitudes, normative and empirical judgments are interdependent, i.e. the first type of attitude cannot be ascribed to the person independently from the second and vice versa. The utility theorem states that if and only if these two interdependent attitudes are coherent can they be represented by ascribing simultaneously a utility and a probability function. Both of these functions represent subjective states or dispositions of the respective person. Therefore "utility" is a misleading term. It is subjective value and subjective probability; it is subjective desire and subjective expectation or subjective normative and subjective empirical judgment. The basic theorem of rational choice,

---

[11] Nida-Rümelin, Julian. 1993. *Kritik des Konsequentialismus.* Munich: Oldenbourg, chapters 7 and 10, and Nida-Rümelin, Julian. 1997. "Why Consequentialism Fails," in G. Holmström-Hintikka and R. Tuomela (eds.), *Contemporary Action Theory.* Dordrecht: Springer, vol. II, pp. 295–308.
[12] Von Neumann, John and Morgenstern, Oskar. 1955. *Theory of Games and Economic Behavior.* Princeton: Princeton University Press.
[13] Nida-Rümelin, *Strukturelle Rationalität.*

utility theory and decision and game theory, is to be understood coherentistically and not consequentialistically. *Decision-theoretic and economic rationality is based on coherent preferences and coherent expectations.* It is conceptually independent from any specific kind of motivation. Insofar as a human practice is coherent it can be described using the conceptual means of decision theory. If any coherent practice can be so described and if a practice governed by humanistic principles is a specific form of coherent practice then humanistically motivated and governed behavior is rational in the decision-theoretic sense and meets the criteria of present-day economic rationality.

This result will probably seem strange to many readers. They are accustomed to the opposition between humanistic and economic values, between deontological traits of morality and consequentialist rationality in the economic sphere. But if my argument is correct this opposition does not hold logically or conceptually. This opposition is the result of a specific reading of economic rationality that fills the decision-theoretic conceptual frame with a consequentialist account of rationality and a narrowly economistic interpretation of subjective values. But neither of these accounts is required if one takes the coherentist basis of present-day economics seriously. Present-day economics does not impose any restrictions on the subjective values that a human individual adopts; nor does it presuppose that human individuals are exclusively motivated by the desire to optimize the consequences of their actions. Ethical humanism does not allow the misuse of human beings as mere means. Ethical humanism is committed to certain deontological norms based on dignity and self-respect that have to be interpreted in absolute terms, i.e. that cannot be included in weighing processes regarding consequences of human action. It is for example not permissable to enslave a human being for the sake of the overall benefits which this enslavement may produce for other human beings. Deontology can, as we argued above, be integrated[14] into the conceptual frame of present-day economics. *There is no incompatibility between humanism and economy. There are philosophical grounds of humanism that can and should be extended to economic practice.*

---

[14] Nida-Rümelin, Julian. 2005. "Why Rational Deontological Action Optimizes Subjective Value," *Protosociology* 21: 182–93.

References

Bacon, Francis. 1627. *Nova Atlantis*. London.

Bentham, Jeremy. 1789. *Introduction to the Principles of Morals and Legislation*. London.

Brandom, Robert B. 1994. *Making It Explicit*. Cambridge, MA: Harvard University Press.

Brandt, Richard Booker. 1979. *A Theory of the Good and the Right*. Oxford: Clarendon Press.

Campanella, Tommaso. 1623. *Civitatis solis*. Frankfurt.

Habermas, Jürgen. 1983. "Diskursethik – Notizen zu einem Begründungsprogramm," in J. Habermas (ed.), *Moralbewußtsein und kommunikatives Handeln*. Frankfurt a. M.: Suhrkamp.

Hare, Richard Mervyn. 1963. *Freedom and Reason*. Oxford: Clarendon Press.

1981. *Moral Thinking. Its Level, Method and Point*. Oxford: Clarendon Press.

Korsgaard, Christine. 1996. *Creating the Kingdom of Ends*. Cambridge: Cambridge University Press.

More, Thomas. 1518. *Utopia*. Basel.

Nida-Rümelin, Julian. 1993. *Kritik des Konsequentialismus*. Munich: Oldenbourg.

1997. "Why Consequentialism Fails," in G. Holmström Hintikka and R. Tuomela (eds.), *Contemporary Action Theory*. Dordrecht: Springer, vol. II, pp. 295–308.

2001. *Strukturelle Rationalität. Ein philosophischer Essay über praktische Vernunft*. Stuttgart: Reclam, chapter 6, pp. 104ff.

2005. "Why Rational Deontological Action Optimizes Subjective Value," *Protosociology* 21: 182–93.

Forthcoming. *Der Begriff Verantwortung*. Stuttgart: Reclam.

Popper, Karl. 1945. *The Open Society and Its Enemies*. London: Routledge.

Rawls, John. 1999. "Kantian Constructivism," in S. Freeman (ed.), *John Rawls: Collected Papers*. Cambridge, MA: Harvard University Press, pp. 303ff.

Sandel, Michael. 1984. "The Procedural Republic and the Unencumbered Self," *Political Theory* 12(1): 81–96.

Taylor, Charles M. 1985. "Atomism," in C. M. Taylor, *Philosophy and the Human Sciences. Philosophical Papers 2*. Cambridge: Cambridge University Press, pp. 187–211.

Von Neumann, John and Morgenstern, Oskar. 1955. *Theory of Games and Economic Behavior*. Princeton: Princeton University Press.

2 | *The humanist tradition*

MATT CHERRY

It has been said that humanism is "as old as human civilization and as modern as the twentieth century" (Elias and Merriam: 109). To avoid becoming dated, I would suggest that humanism is as ancient as humanity and as new as the latest scientific discovery. Or, to put it more prosaically, humanism is a recent name for a philosophy with ancient roots that seeks constantly to update itself in the light of new knowledge.

The terms "humanism" and "humanist" have been used in many different contexts. They have referred to the educational program of Renaissance scholars, as well as to movements in art, literature, psychology, architecture, and other cultural fields. While these senses differ, they all share a central focus on humanity, often representing a move away from concerns with divinity. Thus the *Encyclopedia of the Social Sciences* defines humanism as, "That which is characteristically human, not supernatural, that which belongs to man and not to external nature, that which raises man to his greatest height or gives him, as man, his greatest satisfaction."

Today, the term "humanism" is most often used in reference to a comprehensive worldview, or life stance, that the *Merriam Webster Dictionary* defines as "a doctrine, attitude, or way of life centered on human interests or values; *especially*: a philosophy that usually rejects supernaturalism and stresses an individual's dignity and worth and capacity for self-realization through reason." Even more specifically, the *Chambers Pocket Dictionary* defines humanism as, "seeking, without religion, the best in, and for, human beings."

The humanist philosophy of pursuing the good life based on reason and humanity has been embraced by a wide variety of thinkers in different cultures for thousands of years. But not until the twentieth century did the word "humanism" become the common term for this worldview, as self-described humanist groups first appeared to defend and advance this historic philosophy.

Tracing the history of the humanist philosophy can be difficult. Unlike revealed faiths, which can usually trace their origins to a clear act of creation, such as the revelations of Mohammad for the religion of Islam or Joseph Smith for the Church of Jesus Christ of the Latter Day Saints, humanist thinking has developed gradually and in many different places. Humanism has evolved rather than being created.

Strands of humanist thought can be seen throughout human history. Just as most human societies have held a wide range of beliefs in gods and supernatural forces, it seems too that most societies have included skeptics who have doubted these gods and sought to explain the world solely in natural terms. Many of these skeptics emphasized that happiness here on earth was more important than speculative notions about life after death. Similarly, human communities have always developed moral codes, and some have justified these codes by appeals to reason, humanity, or community, rather than to gods and the supernatural.

When humanists today identify historic thinkers, or schools of philosophy, with their own worldview, they are of course isolating and highlighting just some threads from a larger, more complex fabric. With the benefit of hindsight, we pick out key moments in the evolution of humanist thought, applying modern labels and highlighting developments that may have gone unnoticed by contemporaries. Before we go on to look at some individual strands from the history of humanist thinking, it is important to emphasize that threads of humanist thought have been part of the fabric of all societies. While there are examples of stand-alone humanist communities – the Epicurean gardens of classical Greece and Rome, or the nineteenth-century freethinker communities founded by German émigrés to the American Midwest – humanist ideas have generally been developed and practiced as part of the wider culture of the day. So, unlike some faith communities, humanism cannot be viewed as a belief system set apart from the rest of society like a patch in a quilt. Humanism is a thread that can be found throughout the quilt, sometimes prominent, sometimes blending in, often almost invisible.

In addition to humanist thought that stood outside of, or in opposition to, religion, we also see more or less humanist thinkers within many religious traditions. For example, such revolutionary thinkers as Siddhārtha Gautama (the Buddha) in the Hindu world, Zhuangzi in ancient China, Averroes (Ibn Rushd) in the Islamic world, Maimonides in medieval Judaism, and Erasmus in Christendom, were responsible for bold steps in a humanist direction, but they placed their teachings within a religious context. This chapter's focus on picking out the distinctively humanist strands in many different schools of thought may relegate the more religious elements of these philosophies to the background. To some extent the history of humanism is the story of the increasing secularization of philosophy and society. Yet it is also important to remember that no history of humanism can be entirely separated from a history of progressive ideas in religion.

Unfortunately, humanist thought has been persecuted throughout history. Attempts to develop morality in humanist terms have frequently been attacked as threats to religious orthodoxy. In truth, criticism of supernatural claims usually does undermine religious authority. Thus, public expressions of humanist ideas have often been suppressed and destroyed, and, at other times, such ideas have probably been voiced only in private. Nevertheless, there do exist accounts of humanist thought in many different cultures over many thousands of years. Sometimes the strongest remaining indications of humanist thinking in a society are seen in reports of the destruction of heretical works or in the arguments of apologists who are defending religious orthodoxy against the skeptics of the day.

Humanism has often been portrayed as a Western invention, but in fact humanist ideas have arisen independently in cultures all over the world. The humanist heritage of ancient Greece shaped Western civilization and therefore is central to the development and spread of humanism in the modern world. However, India and China have older humanist histories. These rich humanist traditions reveal that common principles can arise in the most diverse environments, and suggest that the humanist goal of living an ethical and fulfilling life guided by reason is an aspiration with universal appeal.

The atheist materialism of ancient India

In India, which is still home to a thriving humanist movement, humanist thought can be traced back at least 2,700 years, and perhaps further. Indeed, Amartya Sen points out that, "Sanskrit and Pali have a larger literature in defense of atheism and agnosticism than can be found in any other classical language: Greek or Roman or Hebrew or Arabic" (Sen 2001).

The most popular humanist movement in ancient India was the Carvaka school. It promoted a materialist philosophy, Lokayata, that denied a separate spiritual realm in favor of a belief that mind and everything else in the world can be explained in terms of matter. As so often in the history of freethought, most of the references to this important school of thought come from the religious contemporaries who sought to rebut and ridicule it. Jawaharlal Nehru, the humanist and founding prime minister of India, lamented that "much of the literature of materialism in India was destroyed by the priests and other believers in the orthodox religion during subsequent periods" (Nehru 1989: 100).

Materialism in India may be almost as old as Indian philosophy itself, dating back over 3,000 years. But the most commonly referenced text of the Carvaka philosophy is the *Brhaspati Sutra* of around 600 BCE. The teacher Brhaspati is quoted as saying, "There is no heaven, no final liberation, nor any soul in another world, nor do the actions of the four castes, orders, etc., produce any real effect" (King 1999: 16). This quotation is cited by the theologian Sayana Madhava in *Sarvadarsanasamgraha*, in the fourteenth century CE. Neither the *Brhaspati Sutra* nor any other original text of the Carvaka or Lokayata philosophy has been preserved. From the Hindu rebuttals of their materialist opponents, it is clear that the Lokayatikas criticized the Hindu priesthood, denied the immortality of the soul, and developed a naturalistic philosophy of the cosmos. Krishna Mishra, a contemporary of the Buddha, summarized Lokoyata teaching in these words: "only perceptual evidence is authority. The elements are earth, water, fire and air. Matter can think. There is no other world. Death is the end of all."

The ancient opponents of the Carvakas portrayed them as selfish hedonists, but it appears that they actually promoted a moral philosophy centered on human well-being. In the Hindu epic poem the *Mahabharata*, composed in the middle of the first millennium BCE, a Carvaka is put to death for criticizing the king's warmongering. The historian of Indian thought Dale Riepe observes, "It may be said from the available material that Carvakas hold truth, integrity, consistency and freedom of thought in the highest esteem" (Riepe 1961: 75).

The humanist agnosticism of ancient China

Starting in the sixth century BCE, a series of Chinese philosophers developed humanistic ethical systems that remain influential to this day. In contrast to the thoroughgoing atheism of the ancient Indian materialists, the Chinese adopted a more agnostic approach to supernatural claims. Arguing that reliable knowledge of the supernatural was impossible, they sought other foundations for morality, such as an understanding of the natural world, human nature, and society.

The most famous of these teachers is Confucius (*c.* 551–479 BCE). Confucius dismissed questions about the spiritual realm, instead promoting a practical outlook that rendered the gods irrelevant. When Confucius was asked how to serve ghosts, he replied, "You are not able even to serve man. How can you serve the spirits?" (Confucius 2000: 99). The Confucians tried to replace traditional religious beliefs with an ethical system focused on responsibility to family and society. Confucianism emphasizes benevolence, respect for others, and reciprocity as the foundations of social order. An early expression of the golden rule of ethics is found in the Analects of Confucius: "Tzu-kung asked 'Is there a single word which can be a guide to conduct throughout one's life?' The Master said, 'It is perhaps the word *shu*. Do not impose on others what you yourself do not desire.'" (Confucius 2000: 99).

Confucius' follower Mencius (*c.* 372–289 BCE) emphasized the inherent goodness and reasonableness of human nature, and strove to define a morality that all human beings could follow. This humanist ethics stressed the four virtues of benevolence, justice, courtesy, and wisdom. A later Confucian, Hsün-Tzu (or Xun-Zi, *c.* 300–215 BCE) took a less charitable view of human nature than Mencius, believing ethical norms were needed to rectify man's corrupt nature. Hsün-Tzu was a declared skeptic, saying that heaven (*tian*) is simply the natural world and that all events have natural causes. From this belief he argued that people should focus on the human, social realm, rather than dealing with claims about heaven.

Classical Greece and Rome

In the sixth and fifth centuries BCE, the Greek world experienced a cultural flowering that was to transform human civilization. Many of history's most influential philosophers, historians, dramatists, and statesmen lived in Athens and other Greek city-states within a period of just three or four generations. This explosion in human understanding played an essential role in creating the world we live in today.

Classical Greece was extraordinary in many ways. Its drama and art are almost as influential in shaping the modern world as its philosophy and politics. In all of these areas, Greek culture is notable for its focus on humanity. Whether in statues celebrating the human body, in plays exploring the human condition, in politics that created the first democracies, or in philosophy that recognized that "man is the measure of all things," Greek culture explored and celebrated humanity.

The focus on the human rather than the divine is well illustrated by the philosopher Protagoras (*c.* 481–411 BCE). In his work, now lost, *Of the Gods*, Protagoras said, "About the gods I have no means of knowing either that they exist or that they do not exist or what they are like to look at; many things prevent my knowing – among others, the fact that they are never seen and the shortness of human life." Protagoras made a statement often associated with humanism: "Man is the measure of all things, of the reality of those which are, and of the unreality of those which are not." Passed down without context, the precise meaning of this is unclear. Humanists have taken it to mean that humankind is the ultimate source of values. Plato, on the other hand, accused Protagoras of a thoroughgoing relativism. The Athenians prosecuted Protagoras for impiety, banishing him from the city and burning his works in the marketplace.[1]

Protagoras may have developed the questioning dialogue as a means of seeking truth. But this method of inquiry is most associated with Socrates (*c.* 469–399 BCE). The Socratic method can be seen as profoundly humanistic in the way it encourages untrammeled inquiry that is open to all parties. Whereas the great religious prophets of human history claimed to bring "God's truth" and absolute commandments, Socrates is famous for saying he knew nothing and brought not answers but a method of questioning.

Starting in the fifth century BCE Leucippus and Democritus developed the atomist theory which said everything in the cosmos was ultimately composed of material atoms and that all of our knowledge of the world comes from our senses. Epicurus (*c.* 341–271 BCE) took

---

[1] The source of this claim, and all the extant sayings of Protagoras, is Diogenes Laertius, *Lives of Eminent Philosophers*, ed. and trans. R. D. Hicks. Cambridge, MA: Harvard University Press, vol. II, pp. 462–7.

this materialist philosophy of nature and used it as the foundation for a profoundly humanist philosophy of the good life. He suggested that two things prevent people from trying to live a full and happy life: fear of the gods and fear of an afterlife. But the materialist philosophy of the atomists removed both the fear of the supernatural and the fear of death. Death meant annihilation for the person, because the mind (or self) is composed of atoms that disperse upon death. Epicurus spoke of his "Four Herbs" to relieve the maladies of life:

> There is nothing to fear from gods,
> There is nothing to feel in death,
> Good can be attained,
> Evil can be endured.

Epicurus described the purpose of philosophy as "the art of making life happy." He argued that nature and reason both show that pleasure is the sole good and pain the sole evil. But, contrary to some caricatures, the Epicureans did not encourage wanton indulgence in sensual pleasures. Epicurus argued that intellectual pleasures were better than physical ones – although both were necessary to live a full and happy life – and that "tranquility of the soul" was a key component of pleasure. Hedonistic indulgences might lead to short-term gratification, but one avoids them if they will cause disturbance and suffering in the longer term. The Epicureans therefore argued for moderation and balance in all aspects of life. In one of Epicurus' few surviving writings, his *Letter to Menoeceus*, he wrote, "It is impossible to live pleasantly, without living wisely, virtuously and justly, just as we cannot live wisely, virtuously and justly without living pleasantly." Epicurus also believed in the equal worth of all human beings. In fact, one reason that the Epicureans were accused of licentiousness was that they allowed women and slaves to join their communities as equal participants. Tragically, this promise of equality was denied for more than 2,000 years until the birth of the modern women's liberation movement and the still unfolding feminist revolution.

Nearly all of Epicurus' writings have been lost, but his teachings inspired the Roman poet Lucretius (*c.99–c.55* BCE) to write his monumental *On the Nature of Things*. Lucretius' poem, which even outlines an early version of the theory of evolution by natural selection, helped transmit Epicurus' materialist philosophy to later generations.

Perhaps the most important classical Greek contribution to world culture was the idea that human excellence can be taught. The Greeks created the concept of "liberal education," which they saw as a way to bring out the best in each and every human being. The heart of the Greek concept of liberal education was a program of subjects that included philosophy, logic, rhetoric, grammar, mathematics, astronomy, literature, and drama. When the Romans adopted this education system they named it *studia humanitas* – the study of humanity. The Renaissance scholars who revived the *studia humanitas*, almost a thousand years after the fall of Rome, became known as "humanists." Our modern term "humanism" also ultimately derives from the Latin *humanitas*.[2]

The Islamic world

After the fall of Roman civilization in the West, the wisdom of the ancient Greek philosophers was preserved in the Muslim empire built by Mohammad and his successors. It was not until the fifteenth century that the great classical philosophies were reintroduced to Europe in the rebirth of learning known as the Renaissance.

In centers of learning from Baghdad to Cordoba, between the eighth and twelfth centuries, major advances were achieved in mathematics, astronomy, optics and chemistry. Philosophy was pursued in the tradition of Aristotle, dominated by the central Asian Avicenna (Ibn Sina, 980–1037 CE) and Averroes (Ibn Rushd, 1126–98 CE) of Cordoba in Spain. Despite Islam's severe prohibitions against heresy and apostasy, a number of figures from the Muslim world gave open expression to skeptical and humanistic views. As so often in the history of free thought, we know about these heretics mostly from the religious polemics directed against them. The ninth-century Persian theologian Ibn al-Rawandi is accused of advancing skeptical arguments against central tenets of Islam that amounted to a case for atheism. He was a contemporary of Abu Isa al-Warraq, a scholar in Baghdad who not only wrote refutations of Christianity but also questioned Islam itself. The blind eleventh-century Syrian poet Abu Ala Al-Ma'arri denied divine providence and wrote, "Religions have

---

[2] See Walter, N. 1997. *Humanism: What's in a Word*. London: Rationalist Press Association, for a thorough history of the term "humanism."

only resulted in bigotry and bloodshed, with sect fighting sect, and fanatics forcing their beliefs onto people at the point of a sword. All religions are contrary to reason and sanity." For good measure, he declared that "the world holds two classes of men – intelligent men without religion, and religious men without intelligence" (Nicholson 1921).

Less outspoken, but more famous, was the great mathematician and poet Omar Khayyam (1048–31). His scientific work demonstrated his belief that the world could be explained by natural laws, while his poetry revealed a compassionate humanity. Khayyam's skepticism of divine providence is often taken as evidence of his humanist sympathies. It may also have been a response to the violent upheavals wracking the Muslim world during his lifetime.

After the time of Averroes, political turbulence and religious orthodoxy stifled free inquiry in the Muslim world and its science and philosophy went into decline. But Averroes' commentaries on the works of Greek thinkers, particularly Aristotle, helped to reconnect Europe with its classical past and sparked the Renaissance.

The Renaissance and the birth of science

The Renaissance began as a movement to regain the intellectual glories of the classical world, but ended by giving birth to the modern world. The Renaissance (from the French term meaning "rebirth") describes the period in European history starting in the late fourteenth century and continuing through to the early seventeenth century. The characteristic intellectual outlook of the period is known as "Renaissance humanism."

Renaissance humanism marks the transition between medieval supernaturalism and the scientific and secular outlook of modernity. While modern humanism owes much to Renaissance humanism, there are some important distinctions between the two forms of humanism. Contemporary humanists do not believe in God or the supernatural, whereas most Renaissance humanists believed in a god, often the traditional Christian God. What both kinds of humanists have in common is a focus on the concerns of this world, a belief in the "dignity of man," and a commitment to developing human potential. The French essayist Michel Montaigne (1533–92) captured this humanist spirit when he took a motto from the Roman poet Terrence and carved it above his desk: "I am human; nothing human is foreign to me."[3]

As the Renaissance progressed, leading thinkers became increasingly skeptical of medieval Christian doctrine. Frustrated humanist reformers fanned the flames of the Protestant Reformation sparked by Martin Luther (1483–1546). Meanwhile, Christopher Columbus' discovery of the New World opened up new horizons for European thinkers, even as the Americas were ruthlessly conquered by "Sword and Cross." The Reformation and the spread of the printing press gave more opportunities for exploring humanist ideas. The Church's response to these new ideas was often brutal. The Italian scientist Giordano Bruno (1548–1600) defended Copernicus' view that the Earth orbited the Sun, criticized Christian ethics, and called for tolerance of differing religious belief. In 1600, the Inquisition burned Bruno at the stake for refusing to recant these views.

Galileo Galilei (1564–1642) also suffered at the hands of the Inquisition for promoting the Copernican view that the Earth orbited the Sun. He avoided execution by renouncing this view. Galileo can be seen as the most important figure in the birth of modern science. His many discoveries revolutionized humanity's understanding of the cosmos. And he successfully argued that observation, experiment, and mathematically quantified measurement were the essential bases for scientific study of the world.

The French philosopher Pierre Gassendi (1592–1655) revived the atomism of Epicurus, arguing for an empirical approach to physics based on a mechanistic theory of causation. In England, Francis Bacon (1561–1626) argued in favor of science based on reason and factual evidence. Bacon was not a great scientist like Galileo, but he played a crucial role in articulating and promoting the new empirical science. Bacon saw that in addition to increasing human understanding, science could be used to benefit humankind. In *Novum Organum* (1620), his most important work, he argued that humanity should, "Pursue science in order that the human estate may be advanced." It was this commitment to the scientific study of the world – combined with the increasing secularism and individualism of European culture – that gave birth to the Age of Reason.

---

[3] In Latin: "Homo sum, humani nil a me alienum puto."

The Age of Reason

The Age of Reason, also known as the Enlightenment, starts in the seventeenth century and reaches its high point in the middle of the eighteenth century. It marks humankind's emergence from the "Ages of Faith" into a new age enlightened by reason, science, and respect for humanity. The thinkers of the Enlightenment believed that human reason could discover the natural laws of the universe, determine the natural rights of humankind, and thereby achieve continuous progress in human knowledge, technology, and society.

A major stimulus for the Enlightenment was the scientific discovery of universal natural laws. By the late seventeenth century, thanks to the work of scientists such as Copernicus, Galileo, and Newton, universal laws were established for mechanics, optics, and gravity. The thinkers of the Enlightenment focused on developing this knowledge of the natural world, and on trying to apply the scientific method to the study of humanity and society.

While some of the leading Enlightenment figures were atheists, and others were Christians, the most distinctive religious attitude of the Enlightenment was deism. Deists believed in a "god of nature" that created the universe but then left it to run by itself. The deist "Creator" could not contravene the laws of nature. Deism rejects the theistic belief in a personal god who answers prayers, talks to prophets, and intervenes in human affairs. Just as the philosophers of ancient China and Greece believed that gods and the supernatural were too unknowable to serve as a basis for human ethics and knowledge, the deists generally believed that ethics and knowledge must be grounded in human reason and nature, not in claims of supernatural revelation. In most areas there is little practical difference between deists and godless humanists. However, in some cases, such as Rousseau and Robespierre, deists criticized atheism as a threat to society and argued for a deistic "civic religion."

Though still dangerous, skepticism of religious claims became increasingly common as the seventeenth and eighteenth centuries progressed. The English political theorist Thomas Hobbes (1588–1679) and the great ethical philosopher Baruch de Spinoza (1632–77), from Amsterdam's Jewish community, have each been cited as the first modern atheist philosopher. However, both rejected charges of atheism. Spinoza developed a form of pantheism, arguing that the universe was composed of one single substance and that "God" and "Nature" were just two different names for that underlying substance. And while Hobbes argued that all substance is material, he claimed that his materialism did not deny the existence of God, but merely demonstrated that God must be material. Although Hobbes and Spinoza both knew their lives could be threatened by charges of atheism, they also benefited from the intellectual freedom that was, intermittently, made possible by the turmoil of the seventeenth-century wars of religion.

Hobbes is considered the founder of modern political philosophy. His great work *Leviathan* was written near the end of the English Civil War. In the natural condition of humankind, argued Hobbes, life is "solitary, poor, nasty, brutish, and short" (Hobbes 1994: 76). But the constant "war of all against all" is in nobody's best interest. Rather, it is in everyone's interest to live under a strong central authority that ensures peace and the security to pursue a living: "the passions that incline men to peace are fear of death, desire of such things as are necessary to commodious living, and a hope by their industry to obtain them" (Hobbes 1994: 78). According to Hobbes, government is based on a social contract, where the governed give up some of their freedoms in return for the state guaranteeing their security and the rest of their rights. Hobbes also argued for a negative version of the golden rule: "Do not that to another, which thou wouldst not have done to thyself" (Hobbes 1994: 99). This negative version, also espoused by Confucius, has been dubbed "the silver rule." Hobbes contrasts it with the Christian golden rule, which encourages actively doing *for* others: to Hobbes, that is a recipe for social chaos.

Writing in more tranquil times, the Scottish philosopher, David Hume (1711–76), wrote skeptically about miracles[4] and about religion.[5] A thoroughgoing skeptic, Hume was critical of the ration-alistic deists who believed that natural rights and justice were inherent in human nature in the form of natural laws that would one day be discerned as clearly as the laws of physics. In ethics, according to one

---

[4] Section X of *An Enquiry Concerning Human Understanding* (1748).
[5] *Dialogues Concerning Natural Religion*, whose publication Hume prudently delayed until after his death.

noted biographer, Hume "produced one of the first completely and consciously secular systems in the modern era" (Flew 1961: 272).

Another great figure of the Scottish Enlightenment was Adam Smith (1723–90). Like Hobbes, Smith was the son of a clergyman yet rejected Christianity early in life. Smith's first work, *The Theory of Moral Sentiments* (1759), was an empirical study of human moral judgment and behavior. Smith's secular moral theory posited an innate human desire to sympathize with others and arrive at impartial moral judgments. According to Smith, individual conscience arises from our relationships with others. Smith's second book, *An Inquiry into the Nature and Causes of the Wealth of Nations* (1776), provided an intellectual rationale for free trade and capitalism that is influential to this day. Although Smith's work marks the birth of political economy as a field separate from moral philosophy, the interpenetration of morality and economics is still prominent in his theories. A unifying theme in his books is the exploration of how individual self-interest – distinct from selfishness, which lacks sympathy for others – could contribute to the well-being of the whole of society.

Enlightenment thought was championed by a group of influential French philosophers called the *philosophes*. The high-point of the French Enlightenment was the creation of the *Encyclopédie* – the first comprehensive account of human knowledge – compiled between 1751 and 1765 by Denis Diderot with the help of fellow *philosophes* such as D'Alembert, La Mettrie, Helvetius, and D'Holbach. The *Encyclopédie* clearly expressed their naturalistic thinking and their skeptical attitude toward religion.

One contributor to the *Encyclopédie* broke away from its emphasis on reason and science. Jean-Jacques Rousseau (1712–78) inspired the Romantic ideal of recovering human goodness by returning to nature. In contrast to Hobbes, Rousseau's political philosophy was based on his belief that humanity is essentially good but is corrupted by society. An opponent of representative democracy, Rousseau argued that individuals should submit to the authority of the "General Will" of the people as a whole. Rejecting atheism and Christianity, Rousseau believed in a "natural religion" of simple morality based on belief in a benevolent creator and argued that the state should adopt this as a "civil religion."

Another influential political thinker of the Enlightenment was Charles de Secondat, Baron de Montesquieu. Montesquieu's *Spirit of*

Laws (1748) had a more empirical basis than the speculative theories of Rousseau, and developed the concept of a democratic republic with a "separation of powers" to help guarantee individual freedoms. Perhaps the most famous of the *philosophes* was François-Marie Arouet, better known as Voltaire, who is still revered for his crusades against injustice and his stinging critiques of Christianity.

Revolutions

Across the Atlantic, the intellectual leaders of the American colonies were drawn to the new thinking of the Enlightenment. Many of the most distinguished leaders of the American Revolution (1775–83) – Jefferson, Washington, Franklin, Madison, and Paine – were powerfully influenced by Enlightenment thought. In fact, Thomas Jefferson, author of the Declaration of Independence, even described himself as a follower of Epicurus.[6] Skeptical of religious authority, the leaders of the American Revolution – deist and Christian alike – believed separation of church and state was necessary to guarantee freedom of conscience. Montesquieu's idea of the separation of powers between the executive, legislative, and judicial branches of government inspired the development of the "checks and balances" of the new republic's political structure. The Enlightenment concept of inalienable freedoms – the right to "life, liberty and the pursuit of happiness" – underpinned the American Revolution, the United States Constitution, and the Bill of Rights, and has become woven into America's fundamental image of itself.

The American Revolution can be viewed as the culmination of the Age of Reason, when ideas that were once heretical came to form the basis of a new nation: a nation based not on ethnicity or religion, but on the promise of individual rights and freedom. The American model has proven remarkably resilient and open to progress. Initially restricting its rights to the elite of white, male landowners, the United States of America has gradually, sometimes wrenchingly, extended equal rights to women and minority ethnic groups.

The French Revolution that followed soon after the birth of the United States of America proved far more problematic. Enlightenment

---

[6] "I too am an Epicurian." In Jefferson's letter to William Short, October 31, 1819.

ideals influenced the French Revolution, especially its secularism and republicanism, and were articulated for the ages in the Declaration of the Rights of Man (1789). Tragically, the intolerance and mass murder of the "Reign of Terror" (September 1793 to July 1794) went against the most basic principles of the Enlightenment. The betrayal of the Revolution's initial ideals and its transformation into a murderous tyranny pitted humanist reformers against authoritarian radicals. The leaders of the Terror, principally Maximilien Robespierre (1758–94), envisioned a French Republic based on virtue, where the highest and noblest goal of any citizen would be service to the state, which embodied the "General Will." A deist follower of Rousseau, Robespierre believed faith in the divine was necessary for the moral and political health of the nation. He even started the cult of Supreme Being, intending to make this the civil religion of post-revolutionary France. Robespierre declared that "the basis of popular government in time of revolution is both virtue and terror: virtue without which terror is murderous, terror without which virtue is powerless. Terror is nothing else than swift, severe, indomitable justice; it flows, then, from virtue" (Stearns, 1947).

Tragically, these revolutionary themes were to be repeated many times over the next two centuries. Even without belief in divine commandments or a heavenly afterlife, secular true believers have repeatedly demonstrated the dangers of subjugating individual rights in the here-and-now to the goal of ushering in a future heaven on earth. Robespierre became the first of many modern revolutionary leaders to justify inhuman acts in the name of transcendent ideals.

The American and French revolutions thus mark the violent eruption of Enlightenment ideas onto the political stage. The echoes of these eruptions are still felt today. And the contrast in the methods and outcomes of these revolutions has continued to haunt the modern world in general and secularist ideology in particular.

These revolutions also marked a popularization of humanist ideas. Writers such as Thomas Paine (1737–1809) gained a huge audience for Enlightenment philosophy with bestselling books such as *The Age of Reason* and *The Rights of Man*, as well as through mass-produced pamphlets. At the same time, the Industrial Revolution was expanding the middle class, creating a new urban class, and destabilizing long-established social structures. As more people sought to create a humane and rational society, they increasingly questioned the religious and political status quo. At the same time, Christianity's moral and political support for the existing power structures – "the Alliance of Altar and Throne" – pushed anti-clericalism to the fore-front of the radical and progressive agenda.

Anti-clericalism in the Latin world

The identification between Church and State was particularly strong in the Latin world – the Italian and Iberian peninsulas and Central and South America. The struggle between progressive freethinkers and Catholic conservatives was a dominant political theme in these regions throughout the nineteenth and twentieth centuries. (Another humanist influence in Latin America was Positivism, the secular Church of Humanity formed by the French sociologist August Comte in the mid-nineteenth century. Positivism was most significant in the republic of Brazil, and its motto of "Order and Progress" still appears on the Brazilian flag.)

A quick look at the most celebrated leaders of Latin liberation movements reveals the pivotal importance of humanist freethinkers. In the early nineteenth century Simon Bolívar (1783–1830), the great liberator of South America, embraced the humanist ideals of the American Revolution. A freethinker who personally rejected religion, Bolívar's anti-clericalism was probably also a political necessity in view of the Roman Catholic Church's support for continued Spanish control of Latin America. Bolívar led the fight for independence in what are now the countries of Venezuela, Colombia, Ecuador, Peru, Panama, and Bolivia (the latter named after him). In contrast to Bolívar, who had been born into an elite family descended from Spanish conquistadors, the most revered leader in Mexico's history, Benito Juárez (1806–72), was an indigenous "Indian" who grew up in extreme poverty, speaking only the native tongue of the Zapotecans. Yet like Bolívar, Juárez became a freethinker and, despite armed resistance, curtailed the power of the Catholic Church and the mili-tary, while trying to create a modern civil society and free-market economy. Similarly, the great hero of Italy's *Risorgimento*, Giuseppe Garibaldi (1807–82), was a freethinker who had to literally fight the Catholic Church, and liberate the lands still under the temporal control of the Vatican, in order to unify the lands of Italy into an independent state.

Unfortunately, many of these battles between freethinking liberals and Church-backed autocrats had to be fought again and again in the twentieth century, often with even more bloodshed. The Catholic Church backed fascist regimes in Italy, Portugal, and Spain, while helping military juntas dictate political life in much of twentieth-century Latin America. To this day liberal and socialist movements in the Latin world have a strong anti-clerical flavor.

Liberalism, socialism, and secularism

The nineteenth century saw rapid industrialization and urbanization in Europe and the growth of popular movements that were critical of religion and existing power structures. These included moderate reformers who wanted to improve existing institutions so that all people in society could access the benefits of modern democracy, education, and industry. Others were more radical, seeking the complete replacement of existing political, economic and social institutions. Many of these movements embraced humanist ideas, seeking to improve the human condition without religion.

In Britain, important moderate reformers included the utilitarians under the leadership of Jeremy Bentham (1748–1832). Utilitarians rejected religion and belief in the supernatural, and arguing that "the greatest happiness of the greatest number is the foundation of morals and legislation" (Bentham 1843: 142) they advanced a wide-ranging program of ethical, political and legal reform. Their influence can be seen by the number of utilitarian policies that were considered shocking during Bentham's lifetime but are now standards of free societies: the abolition of slavery, equal rights for women, separation of church and state, legalization of homosexuality, abolition of corporal punishment for children and adults, the right to divorce, free trade, and animal rights. Bentham's "secular godson", John Stuart Mill (1806–73), was his most important philosophical heir. Mill developed Bentham's utilitarianism to place greater emphasis on individual rights. He wrote important works on philosophy, logic, and economics, but today Mill is most celebrated for his book *On Liberty*. Considered a foundational text of liberalism, *On Liberty*, explores the nature and limits of the power that can be legitimately exercised by society over the individual. It argues that each individual has the right to act as he wants, so long as these actions do not harm others.

Another important follower of Bentham was Robert Owen (1771–1858). However, over time Owen moved away from the liberalism of Bentham and became one of the progenitors of socialism. Whereas Bentham thought that free markets and the right for workers to choose their employers would free the workers from the excess power of the capitalists, Owen came to believe that there could only be economic justice if the community controlled the means of production. Owen is considered the founder of the cooperative movement, which is based on the principle that the workers in an enterprise are its owners and decision-makers. Unlike other forms of socialism, "co-ops" do not require changing the structure of a state's entire economic system and therefore can be freely pursued by a minority within a capitalist economy. Co-ops remain popular on a small scale with ventures such as community farms and stores, as well as mutual funds and some banks.

Like the utilitarians, Owen was a freethinker who criticized the power of the Church. One of his followers was George Jacob Holyoake (1817–1906), who coined the term "secularism" for a worldview that rejects considerations of theology in favor of improving life in this world. Holyoake set up "secular societies" across Britain to advance this philosophy. The first president of the National Secular Society (founded in 1866) was Charles Bradlaugh (1833–91), who in 1880 was elected as the first openly atheist member of the British Parliament. He was a member of the Liberal Party and was critical of the socialism espoused by many of his fellow secularists.

While all socialists believe that property and the distribution of wealth should be subject to control by the community, there have been many differences about how to do this. Some, like Owen, wanted this control to be exercised directly by the workers through popular collectives such as worker cooperatives. Others wanted state control of the means of production on behalf of the people. There were also differences about how to bring about this new socio-economic structure. Some socialists sought gradual and peaceful change; others thought only violent revolution would work.

Similar divisions between liberals and socialists, and between reformers and revolutionaries, could be found throughout the Western world during the early industrial period. Humanist thinkers were prominent, even dominant, in all these movements. Reform movements in Europe were largely stifled by conservative rulers until the pressure for change led to an explosion in 1848. The 1848 "Spring of Revolutions" saw uprisings and revolutions in almost every country between Britain and Russia. The revolts were suppressed and achieved little in terms of political change.

Many freethinkers in Germany responded to the failures of 1848 by emigrating to the United States, in some cases setting up freethought communities in the newly colonized Western states. Swiss and French followers of the French socialist Charles Fourier set up about 40 Utopian communities in the US during the same period. In this, they were following the lead of Robert Owen, who had established a socialist community at New Harmony, Pennsylvania, in 1825. None of these secular Utopian communities lasted more than a generation or two.

The "Spring of Revolutions" further radicalized sections of the progressive movement, many of whom rallied around the *Communist Manifesto* issued by Karl Marx and Friedrich Engels early in 1848.

Marx and dialectical materialism

Any serious history of humanist thought must address Marxism and its legacy. Karl Marx (1818–83) wrote his doctoral thesis on the materialist theories of Democritus and Epicurus, but he went on to develop an entirely new worldview called dialectical materialism. In the twentieth century the impact of Marxism was to prove deep and extraordinarily harmful.

Marx saw himself as overturning the Romantic Idealism of Hegel, who had argued that the abstract "Ideal" determined the historical development of the world. But Marx accepted Hegel's dialectic: the process of historical determinism leading to a more perfect world. Thus, as Pat Duffy Hutcheon summarizes it, Marx's "unique brand of materialism was founded, not just on an assumption of order in nature, but on an unshakeable commitment to a particular pattern in which that order was to be expressed: to an immutable dialectic of history acting upon a world of matter. The specific material relations fuelling the process he identified as the technologies of production – which determine the nature of economic relations. These in turn, he said, shape all other socio-cultural institutions, including science and religion" (Hutcheon 1996: 103–4). Like Hegel, Marx subordinated the rights of the individual to the state, but, more like Rousseau, it was not the existing state that trumped individual rights but the vision of a future state, a state that would perfectly express the general will of the people.

Marx believed that the future communist state would be created by the proletariat's violent overthrow of bourgeois capitalist society. He dismissed as "Utopian" the idea that the future communist state could be created by peaceful social reform. In fact, Marx argued that dialectical materialism was the only true expression of the forces of history and passionately attacked all other forms of socialism. Marx's political followers adapted some of his teachings – notably Lenin argued that the dictatorship of the proletariat could usher in a communist state even in economically backward feudal states like Russia – but they seem to have adopted wholesale his authoritarian intolerance.

In the twentieth century Marxists gained power first in Russia and then China and scores of other countries. Marxist rejection of representative democracy justified small minorities seizing power through military force. The belief that the dictatorship of the proletariat would usher in the perfect society bred contempt for individual rights and led to violent suppression of alternative views of the world, both humanist and religious. Looking back from the twenty-first century, the moral bankruptcy of Marxism is as apparent as its economic failure.

Marxism was clearly materialist and atheist, but it has long been a matter of debate as to whether it should be classified as "humanist." A school of avowedly "Marxist humanists," active between the 1950s and 80s, focused on Marx's early writings on "alienation"[7] to propose a form of "socialism with a human face." The most famous of these were Alexander Dubcek and other leaders of the 1968 "Prague Spring." Other Marxists[8] argue that by the time of his definitive work, *Das Kapital* (1867), Marx had abandoned his humanist focus on dignity and alienation. Certainly, the actual Marxist regimes of the twentieth century denied personal autonomy and trampled on human

---

[7] In *Economic and Philosophic Manuscripts* (1844), Marx argues that people who must work for subsistence wages to meet their most basic needs are no longer autonomous agents but have become "objectified" and have therefore lost their human dignity.

[8] Notably the French Marxist Louis Althusser.

dignity, and therefore do not deserve the name "humanist." Ironically, the prominence of Marxism and its inhumanities in the twentieth century have resulted in a twenty-first-century humanist movement that is devoted to the ideals of human rights and individual freedom, at the same time as it has led many conservatives to view all humanists as tainted by the totalitarian politics and failed economics of Marx.

Evolution

In looking at the humanist tradition – and the forerunners of modern humanist thought – we have been picking out a few strands of thought against a background of superstition and unquestioned authority. But by the nineteenth century, the humanist strands have become a prominent part of the intellectual fabric of the day. Yet for those positing a naturalistic explanation of the world and humanity's place in it, the development of life, and its myriad species, remained a central challenge. The challenge was met by the theory of evolution, first explained by Charles Darwin in *The Origin of Species: By Means of Natural Selection* in 1859. Darwin galvanized the scientific community and shook intellectual Christianity to its foundations. Evolution explained how intelligent beings could arise from a process lacking intelligence. It not only overturned the biblical claim that humans and all the other species had been created by God as separate and unchanging forms, but also removed the need to propose an intelligent "Creator" to explain the amazing complexity of life on earth.

The explanatory power of Darwin's theory meant that it was rapidly accepted by the scientific community. At the same time, humanist thinkers were quick to highlight the broader implications arising from evolutionary theory's challenge to religion. Thomas Henry Huxley (1825–95) became known as "Darwin's Bulldog" not only for his work popularizing evolution but also for his unflinching challenge of the biblical account of creation. Huxley coined the term "agnosticism" for his belief that it was impossible to demonstrably prove whether or not God existed. The theory of evolution provoked a crisis of faith in the Victorian intelligentsia. The Christian-turned-agnostic Matthew Arnold famously evokes this philosophical sea change in his 1867 poem "Dover Beach," where he speaks of the "Sea of Faith" once "at the full . . . But now I only hear / Its melancholy, long, withdrawing roar."

After Darwin, naturalistic philosophy and humanist thinking dominate the mainstream of intellectual debate, and that intellectual debate is broader and more diverse than ever before. Instead of picking out mere threads of humanist thought, a study of post-nineteenth-century humanism must deal with a rich and complex tapestry. Such a study would breach the confines of this brief introduction to humanist thought. But before bringing this chapter to a conclusion, we should look at the development of the modern humanist movement.

Organized humanism

Some of the ancient schools of humanist thought, such as Epicureanism, were associated with organized movements. These schools of thought disappeared with the decline and fall of the Roman empire and the rise to power of the early Christian Church. The humanist organizations that exist in the world today have all been created in the last two centuries.

In Western societies dominated by Christianity, usually enforced by the power of the state, it has been difficult and dangerous to criticize religious views or advance an alternative way of understanding the world. Historically, this has usually meant that humanist views have been hidden, or only expressed in coded language by small groups of people. While there are reports of secret societies of atheists and freethinkers in the sixteenth, seventeenth, and eighteenth centuries – for example, among Freemasons – public groups of freethinkers did not become widespread until the nineteenth century. The growth of humanist groups also corresponds with the general growth of civil society and the spread of issue-based voluntary organizations.

The nineteenth-century humanist groups adopted a bewildering variety of names to describe their worldview. In English alone titles included: Rationalist, Freethinker, Atheist, Secularist, Naturalist, Positivist, Agnostic, and Ethical Culture. Some of these groups were primarily anti-clerical, focused on critiquing religion and the power of the clergy, while others saw themselves as new, progressive, non-theistic forms of religion. "Humanist" was not widely used in its modern sense until the publication of the *Humanist Manifesto* in the US in 1933. The term "humanist" quickly spread as the preferred description for non-theistic people and groups who believed in

promoting human welfare without reference to gods or the supernatural. Increasingly, these groups saw themselves neither as religious
nor anti-religious but as a positive, ethical replacement for religion.[9]

After the Second World War, leaders from Britain, the Netherlands,
India, and the USA led the way in creating the International Humanist
and Ethical Union (IHEU), a new global umbrella organization for
national humanist groups. The president at its founding congress was
the biologist Sir Julian Huxley, founding secretary-general of
UNESCO and grandson of T. H. Huxley. By 2007, the IHEU included
more than 100 member organizations, from over 40 countries, whose
mission is to promote humanism as a "life stance": a contemporary
worldview offering a framework for everyday life. One important
focus of humanist groups in the second half of the twentieth century
was individual "self-determination": the right to give meaning and
shape to one's own life. This led humanist groups to push for greater
personal autonomy in matters of sex and reproduction, and for
greater control over medical decisions, including the right to end
one's life.

Beyond the twentieth century

The growth of humanist organizations has been relatively slow
compared to the growth of humanism in the general population.
According to the *World Encyclopedia of Christianity*, "the number of
nonreligionists . . . throughout the 20th century has skyrocketed from
3.2 million in 1900, to 697 million in 1970, and on to 918 million in
AD 2000" (Barrett *et al.* 2001). Many of these non-religious people
are not humanists, and most of those who are do not identify themselves as such. However, it has been argued that these figures actually
underestimate the number of functional humanists because of the
many people who are only nominally religious.[10] Clearly, the role of
avowedly humanist organizations is only one small component of the
humanist influence on society.

---

[9] For a summary of the views of the modern humanist movement see either the
   IHEU Amsterdam Declaration or the Humanist Manifesto III at www.
   humaniststudies.org.
[10] For a good overview of the growth of irreligion see: "Why the Gods are Not
   Winning" at www.edge.org/documents/archive/edge209.html#gp.

The twentieth century was also notable for the rise and fall of secular totalitarianism. In part, the past century's totalitarian ideologies sprang from certain strands of Enlightenment thinking, such as the belief in the inevitable progress of humankind towards a perfect society. Other strands of Enlightenment thought were always skeptical about the inevitability of progress or the possibility of human perfection. In reacting to the horrors of the twentieth century, such liberal humanists as Karl Popper, F. A. Hayek, Hannah Arendt, Isaiah Berlin, and Jacob Bronowski emphasized human fallibility and rejected the very possibility of a perfect society. In doing so, they explicitly rejected the absolutism of Marx and Rousseau and reached back to some of the ideas of liberal Enlightenment philosophers such as Hume, Smith, and Montesquieu. Popper coined the term the "Open Society" to describe a society which guarantees individual freedom, allows a multiplicity of belief systems to compete in the marketplace of ideas, and provides the means for peaceful change. Political philosopher John Rawls developed an imaginative new version of social contract theory to justify the open society, while John Dewey and Jürgen Habermas also provided non-foundational rational justifications for such adaptive social structures. In this view, tolerance, pluralism, and critical inquiry are not simply necessary evils, they are actually a positive benefit to society. If our ideas and social structures are fallible and open to improvement, then free inquiry and debate are essential to the process of learning and developing.

This model of the open society, and the experiences fighting the tyrannies of the twentieth century, should give humanists new strength to fight some old foes: the resurgence of Christian fundamentalism in the US and Islamic fundamentalism across the world. Yet humanism in the twenty-first century will have to do more than refight the old freethought battles against religious power and obscurantism. The technological possibilities and challenges unleashed by the rapid progress in science require a new ethical framework that embraces a scientific understanding of humanity and our place in nature. The challenges of bio-technology will loom large in the coming century. And economics, as well as personal ethics, must adopt an ecological dimension. In the prevailing liberal free-market system, businesses are principal drivers of social change, so an immediate challenge for humanists is to make humanist values relevant to different business sectors and individual enterprises.

While working for rational ethics and the humane use of technology, the humanist movement also needs to work at the personal level. The humanist thinking that gave birth to modern science, unleashing wave after wave of technological and social revolutions on a world used to gradual change and rigid rules of behavior, must also help individuals cope with continual change. The high levels of social and psychological disturbance in even the most prosperous societies, and the continuing appeal of the facile comforts of religious certainty and New Age mysticism, suggest that far more needs to be done to help people cope with a fast-changing world. For individuals to flourish in the fluid global society of the twenty-first century, humanists need to find ways to make the goal of "self-realization through reason" accessible to all. Perhaps the re-emergence of China and India as global leaders will see a new focus on ethical philosophies that are rooted in those cultures' distinctive humanist traditions and yet share the universal values that have emerged since the European Enlightenment.

This chapter began by saying that humanism seeks constantly to update itself in the light of new knowledge. The twentieth century saw the growth of the social sciences and the birth of the scientific study of the mind. Some of the most influential schools in this field, such as Freudian theory, proved to be humanistic but not really scientific. Nonetheless, Freudianism, like Marxism, was for a period influential as a grand narrative informing intellectual debate across the sciences, humanities, and in general culture.

Today, a neoDarwinian evolutionary model seems to be the closest to such a dominant overarching view, or paradigm. Humanist thinkers such as the biologist E. O. Wilson, the cognitive philosopher Daniel Dennett, and the sociologist Pat Duffy Hutcheon closed the twentieth century with calls for a new "consilience" uniting the social and natural sciences, and even the humanities, within a common framework grounded in evolutionary naturalism. They suggest that if the social sciences, including economics, can be unified with the natural sciences, then these sciences can help guide the evolution of our culture in a more rational and humanistic direction. That sounds like a twenty-first-century challenge worthy of the humanist tradition.

References

Barrett, David B., Kurian, George T., and Johnson, Todd M. (eds.) 2001. *World Christian Encyclopedia: A Comparative Survey of Churches and Religions in the Modern World*. Oxford: Oxford University Press.

Bentham, J. 1843. *The Works of Jeremy Bentham*, vol. X. Edinburgh.

Confucius. 2000. *Analects of Confucius*, trans. D. C.Lau. Hong Kong: The Chinese University Press, 2000.

Elias, J. L. and Merriam, S. 1980. *Philosophical Foundations of Adult Education*. Malabar, FL: Robert E. Krieger.

Flew, A. 1961. *Hume's Philosophy of Belief*. London: Routledge & Kegan Paul.

Hobbes, T. 1994. *Leviathan*, ed. E. Curley. Indianapolis: Hacket Publishing.

Hutcheon, P. D. 1996. *Leaving the Cave: Evolutionary Naturalism in Social-Scientific Thought*. Waterloo, ON: Wilfrid Laurier University Press.

King, R. 1999. *Indian Philosophy: An Introduction to Buddhist and Hindu Thought*. Edinburgh: Edinburgh University Press.

Nehru, J. 1989. *The Discovery of India*. Oxford: Oxford University Press.

Nicholson, R. A. 1921. *Studies in Islamic Poetry*. Cambridge: Cambridge University Press.

Riepe, D. 1961. *The Naturalistic Tradition of Indian Thought*. Seattle: University of Washington Press.

Sen, A. 2001. "Other People," *Proceedings of the British Academy* 111: 319–35.

Stearns, R. P. 1947. (ed.) "Maximilien Robespierre, Speech to the Convention of February 5, 1794," in *Pageant of Europe: Sources and Selections from the Renaissance to the Present Day*. New York: Harcourt, Brace & Co.

Humanism and culture: balancing particularity and universalism among the world's religions

GREG EPSTEIN

I grew up as the product of global capitalism and the amazing diversity it has recently spawned in certain parts of the world. I spent my young boyhood in Flushing Queens, New York City, an area that has been radically transformed by the 1960s US immigration reforms. My friends were primarily recent refugees or the children of immigrants from a myriad of nationalities, religions, and ethnicities. My street boasted a Pakistani pizzeria, a Korean barbershop, a Dominican market; it was rare to see English-language signs or billboards in certain areas. I loved my neighborhood's different food and music, its many temples and traditions, languages, histories, and myths. Even more, I loved the fact that we, the children growing up in such a unique setting, formed boundary-transcending friendships so easily and harmoniously – most of the time.

Of course there were flare-ups; we were young boys. One of the worst involved a number of us from various backgrounds "overcoming" our differences for the unfortunate purpose of verbally harassing a Sikh classmate, Puneet, because of his *dastaar*, or turban. It was an obvious physical marker differentiating him from the rest of us, and I am ashamed to admit today that we had difficulty seeing beyond it, and used to give him a cruelly hard time about it. Fortunately Puneet's parents had the wisdom to encourage him to fight back, but not with fists. Over time, he learned to deliver retorts about how obnoxiously convenient it was that we were all able to see the foreignness of his turban, but we couldn't imagine any strangeness in, say, the skullcap and fringed *tallit* I wore to the synagogue on Jewish holidays, or in the very symbolism of eating the body and blood of one's God every Sunday. And over more time, we couldn't help but begin to realize he had a point.

The lesson I began to learn from our little skirmishes with Puneet is quite possibly at the root of many of the sectarian so-called *clashes of civilizations* today, whether involving Catholics vs. Muslims, Jews vs. Arabs, Protestants vs. Catholics, Indians vs. Pakistanis, or other pairing. *Clashes occur when we take pride in our own culture but fail to see how others could take pride in theirs; or when we apply the laws of rationality – and cynicism – to discussing another's inherited religious beliefs or customs, but fail to understand that we too have beloved traditions that seem bizarre in the eyes of others.*

Today, as the Humanist Chaplain of Harvard University, I am a member of another diverse community. But in my new neighborhood, I no longer have the option of being a kind of continual tourist among all the religions and cultures on campus, unsure what to believe in or where to situate myself when conflict arises. With an opportunity to help educate future leaders from every corner of an uncertain world, the stakes are too high to ignore the twenty-first century's demand for resolutions to cultural and religious differences, not merely economic or political ones.

Perhaps especially because of my childhood misadventures in misunderstanding the different creeds and rituals of my diverse collection of peers, I am proud to have chosen a career as an advocate for Humanism, wherein it is my professional responsibility to promote the idea of *deeds before creeds*. I have come to affirm that we humans live in the one and only world – the natural world. There is no evidence for a life after this one where we can atone for crimes against our fellow humans, or be rewarded for putting our people above others. The meaning of life is derived from working together with others to uphold the social contracts we create and shape, wherein all must be considered equally deserving of the freedom to build lives of dignity, regardless of ethnicity, gender, sexuality, or religious background.[1]

---

[1] And yes, Harvard does have a Humanist Chaplain. My position is a permanent part of Harvard; partially endowed, it has existed for over 30 years. This may represent a bit of a paradox, even an oxymoron, but then again seeming oxymorons can be among the world's most worthwhile ideas: as in the case of "Humanism in Business." For more on the Humanist Chaplaincy at Harvard on the internet, visit http://harvardhumanist.org.

The universal and the particular

As our world grows smaller and more interconnected, we are in ever greater need of a universal ethic for all humanity. But should our new global neighborhoods, from Flushing to Harvard to Jerusalem to Brussels or Buenos Aires, have to lose their culture's distinctiveness in order to achieve unity? Should I tell my students who come from many places that each must give up his or her heritage in order to take part in my Humanistic community? No. In this chapter, I will argue that for diverse twenty-first-century communities such as universities, cities, villages, nations, or even corporations, Humanism promotes a single set of ethical ideals valid for all people but should not seek to impose a single monolithic culture on all of us. A truly transnational Humanism for the modern world is one that allows us to actively celebrate our distinct cultural and other kinds of identity, while still affirming universal Humanist principles.

On a practical level, where should we find the balance between universal Humanism and particular identity? How can we allow for individuals and groups to honor that which is unique to their heritage while expecting them not to indulge in the temptation to see themselves as above others? First, we must acknowledge that within each cultural group, there are distinctly humanistic voices – that when we look to resources for grounding democracy and this-worldly, humanitarian outlook in longstanding tradition, we can each find sources of inspiration among the *minority voices* within our own cultural traditions. Second, we must begin to imagine newly reworked cultural identities for the modern world, which draw on ancient minority voices as well as more recent traditions to create *cultural humanisms*; and finally, we must work with individuals within our various traditions that may not agree fully with Humanism's inherent questioning of many of their beliefs and practices, but who could nonetheless fully endorse such goals as universal human rights, representative and constitutional *democracy*, and a more progressive and just global capitalism. Still, before we can come to any conclusion about how Humanism and culture should best be combined, we will need to achieve a more precise understanding of what we mean by the two terms.

Humanism

"Humanism" is a term that has been used to refer to a number of distinct and different phenomena. Some use the term in reference to the classical Greco-Roman philosophical tradition, known in Latin as *studia humanitas*, which challenged priestly and cultic authority in favor of reason and critical thinking. Others use the term to mean, as it did in the Renaissance, the nervy assertion that there is more of value to human life and knowledge than obedience to God and theology. Still others speak of Humanism as referring to the more radical approach of the French Positivist philosopher August Comte, who was convinced Notre Dame cathedral would one day become the Temple of the Worship of Man.

This plurality can be frustrating if we are attempting to find a simple definition, but to therefore pronounce (or denounce) Humanism so nebulous as to defy definition altogether would be going too far. An equally complex pluralism would frustrate any intellectually serious attempt to define religions such as Christianity, Judaism, Islam, Buddhism and others, or even philosophical schools such as existentialism; and yet surely these phenomena can nonetheless be understood in some cohesive way, even if loosely so.

By Humanism, then, I refer to the contemporary world view described by the American Humanist Association as "a progressive philosophy of life that, without supernaturalism, affirms our ability and responsibility to lead ethical lives of personal fulfillment, aspiring to the greater good of Humanity." This philosophy, which I prefer to call "Humanism *with a capital H*," can be and most likely is affirmed on some conscious or unconscious level by many if not most of the world's hundreds of millions of agnostics and atheists (see Zuckerman 2007 for statistical analysis). We "capital H" Humanists pride ourselves on using empiricism, a limited tool but nonetheless the best one available to humans, to determine truth about the nature of the world; and we base our views as to what is ethical upon whether or not it is good for human beings, not what any god or deity has commanded.

"Capital H Humanism," or contemporary life-stance Humanism, must then be distinguished from "lowercase h humanism," or Renaissance humanism. The latter is not a comprehensive view of life but rather the notion, which evolved in Europe during the Renaissance (though its roots go back farther); that humans should strive for knowledge beyond the "mind of God," and that we should use critical thinking to attain knowledge of the world around us, rather than relying exclusively on the world around us. Thus Copernicus and Galileo, while still believers in Christianity, are symbols of Renaissance humanism. Renaissance humanism forms part of the foundation of modern life-stance Humanism, but also of much of contemporary liberal Christianity and Judaism, and thus progressive Christians, Jews, Humanists, and others should see themselves not as enemies but natural allies, tracing their intellectual approach to life back to the common precedent of Renaissance thinking. And of course Muslims and others can be included in this unifying view, because Muslim philosophers in Cordova and elsewhere were among the medieval figures who most inspired that which eventually became the Renaissance.

Cultural identity

Turning our attention back to the modern world, we must understand that even a universal worldview such as modern Humanism cannot exist in a vacuum. Humanist philosophy can only be combined with the other elements that go into making a person. One of the most salient of these elements is culture. Culture can be many things – the attitudes, practices, values, customs, diet, music, and aesthetic sensibility associated with a particular group of people, whether that group is ethnic, national, or organizational. For our purposes, perhaps the concept of cultural identity can be quickly summarized best as in tension with another concept – that of being a "citizen of the world." Humanists have largely leapt to embrace the concept that people ought to consider themselves to be equally loyal to all people, and consider themselves at least potentially "at home" in all countries or cultures. However, as Kwame Anthony Appiah poignantly notes in his recent *The Ethics of Identity*, world citizenship becomes problematic when it almost inevitably conflicts with each person's unavoidable situatedness in a particular identity (see Appiah 2005). Appiah argues that while a universal identity may be a worthy ideal, we must acknowledge that each time we enter a new culture or country, we cannot help but bring with us the baggage that is our roots; his thesis is that rather than trying to avoid this inevitability we should try to mold it into an identity of "rooted cosmopolitanism."

This is not to say that each person can have only one culture. Obviously we all have more than one influence upon our cultural identities, and, as Amartya Sen argues in his 2006 work *Identity and Violence*, conflicting cultural identities can serve a helpful purpose in preventing one of our allegiances becoming so absolute as to promote belligerence. I agree with Dr. Sen's point; however, I stress that we need not treat the idea of a *primary* cultural or ethnic identity as an evil unto itself. Sen argues that we must place "reason before identity"; I would accept this premise but argue that in many cases Humanism could benefit by celebrating identity, *within reason*.

Minority voices: roots of humanism in the world's great religious traditions

One of the biggest misunderstandings in and about the contemporary Humanist movement is the assumption that Humanism is an exclusively "Western" tradition. Humanism, we are taught, began with the rational philosophers of ancient Greece and Rome whose work was picked up after a fallow millennium by the Renaissance and came to a head in the Enlightenment that swept Europe from the eighteenth century. Darwin, Nietzsche, Marx, Freud: the fact that these European men of the late colonial era are some of the cardinal saints of Humanism is one of the few facts upon which most Humanists, and their enemies, can agree. But an understanding of Humanism that makes no effort to look for inspiration beyond these great men and for what they stood, is a Humanism that fails at one of its primary goals. It fails to *embrace all people*, because it fails to recognize that all people have contributed to what it means to be a human being in today's world, as well as to what it means to be a Humanist.

The earliest intellectual and spiritual movement that began to approach the naturalism (or belief that only the natural world exists – as opposed to supernaturalism) of contemporary Humanism as defined above was probably not the Greeks as is generally assumed but rather the Lokayata movement in India, a philosophical school dating back nearly three thousand years. The Lokayata were skeptical of the Gods, believed the world was made up only of natural materials and forces, and presaged the even more Humanist Carvaka movement in the middle of the first millennium CE, a proudly atheistic school of thinkers who valued happiness in this world and dismissed the possibility of rewards in any future world or life.

Seeds of Humanism around the world

The middle centuries of the first millennia were labelled the "axial age" because so many of the world's great religious and philosophical traditions were then in key stages of development. Around the time Protagoras was deeming man "the measure of all things," not only had the Lokayata and Carvaka already forcefully articulated comparable ideas in India, important developments had already occurred elsewhere in the world to emphasize a naturalistically ethical message. Gautama Buddha was yet another Indian who sought insight and understanding, not God's will. Sen has strongly praised the Buddha for having utilized "a special strategy of combining his theoretical skepticism about God with a practical subversion of the significance of the question by making the choice of good behavior completely independent of any God – real or imagined" (Sen 1998: 23).

In China, the Confucian and Taoist philosophical schools that emerged in the sixth century BCE are notable for having focused on human needs, behavior, and ethics, as opposed to the supernatural (despite the fact that later followers of the school's founders – Confucius and Lao Tzu – often devolved into a worship of spirits and ancestors their predecessors had hardly intended). Confucius is well known to have developed, in his *Analects*, an early version of the "golden rule" that one should not do to others what one would not want done to oneself. But perhaps the greatest significance of his thought is that it is entirely centered upon human social relationships and on attaining an ethical harmony among people in this life, as opposed to any future existence. This is a rare occurrence in any culture, regardless of the era. And while these are by no means the only examples of early Humanisms in ancient times, we should also note some key steps taken around the world in the direction of Humanism in late antiquity and medieval times. The Muslim philosopher Averroes or Ibn Rushd differed markedly from other Islamic authorities in his notion that the human soul is *not* eternal, and encouraged a reason-based vision for Islamic jurisprudence. Yet, from his own time to the present, he has been acknowledged by Muslims, Christians, and Jews as one of the most important philosophers.

Averroes was born in Cordova in 1126, during the too often forgotten classical period in which the "Abrahamic" faiths enjoyed dynamic co-existence in and around Arab-conquered Spain.

Elsewhere, there were other great medieval Muslim thinkers such as Avicenna, the Persian physician-theologian born in 980, who cultivated a rational, neoPlatonic view of God as the first cause of all things. Avicenna saw all human beings as connected by a kind of collective consciousness, and underplayed the idea of immortality though he did not deny it explicitly. One could go on this way about the seeds of Humanism to be found in ancient Jewish wisdom literature, or in the thought of Moses Maimonedes, also from the classical Spanish period; one might choose to elaborate on the Humanistic qualities in early African religions, such as the religious system of Nigeria's Yoruba people, which, in the words of Nobel Prize winning author Wole Soyinka, "drastically reduces the absolute authority of deities over the lives of human beings and therefore reduces the dependency of human beings on the interpreters of the extraterrestrial authority" (Allen 1997).

I have no desire to enter into an argument as to which ancient culture was the most Humanistic – such a question would not only be pointless but also impossible to answer. My point is rather that if we create a discourse about Humanism which fails to recognize these significant milestones in Humanist history from around the world, in effect we are creating a contemporary Humanism that privileges Western heritage. In other words, we are subtly but powerfully implying that Judeo-Christian (with heavy emphasis on the *Christian*) culture is the normative culture for a Humanist and that while Humanists will deign to receive individuals from other backgrounds, those received will be expected to identify with a supposedly more Humanistic Western heritage than with their own. If this were all Humanism stood for, its opponents would be right to accuse it of being little more than a form of European imperialism, a kind of intellectual colonialism. Fortunately, an authentic Humanism embraces its influences and manifestations outside of a Christian cultural context (just as it acknowledges that even Christianity itself has been influenced by a wide variety of prior influences, ranging from Judaism, Greek philosophy and earlier Near Eastern civilizations).

Of course one might argue that the thinkers listed above were merely minority voices within their traditions, and moreover not very influential today. But even in the contemporary Western world Humanism has not become the dominant political or philosophical voice. In the US and in even in Europe, there are many other influential voices such as militant nationalism, the Vatican, Evangelical Churches, New Age spirituality, or a kind of nihilism and a crass, unreligious but hardly Humanistic commercialism.

Humanism has been a powerful force in the West, and in other parts of the world, as *a minority voice* in each of the human cultures it has touched. This may be hard to see, for example, in the contemporary Arab world, which is now in the throes of an Islamic backlash against Humanism. But we must remember that this is a backlash against more than simply outside influences: half a century ago, the great leadership in the Arab and Muslim world was secularist, from Ataturk's Turkey to Jinnah in Pakistan, to Nasser in Egypt, to the PLO. Thus, Arabs or Muslims looking for a new and Humanistic way of understanding their own identity would need to give up traditional theology but they would not need to give up a sense of being "insiders" in their own cultural milieu. They would need to embrace science and democracy but they could honestly say that they were influenced in that direction by their own ancestors such as Ibn Rushd and Ibn Sinna, or Jinnah and Ataturk just as much as by Marx or Freud. This would be a powerful realization because it would take the emphasis off the idea of a "clash of civilizations" and refocus on the fact that within each culture there are a variety of voices, and we each can choose which of those voices to identify with.

The emergence of cultural Humanisms

The fact that Arab and Muslim cultures, and essentially all cultures, contain strong Humanistic minority voices is of the utmost relevance to prospects for a global Humanistic business in the twenty-first century. This is because such voices must assume greater prominence in order for a Humanistic business to make the world smaller without enflaming the divisions between cultural groups; divisions which are often intensified by economic gaps between nations, regions, and so-called *civilizations*.

Any vision for a more Humanist global business will obviously involve a critique of the present state of international economic activity. This is appropriate so long as we understand that on the one hand, our critique of the present must not lead us back to failed experiments with communism or socialism, or into an ultimately defeatist negation of the concept of globalization itself; and on the other hand, Humanist business must succeed better than it does today in benefiting all human beings, rather than primarily members of wealthy societies who are presently capable of investing their wealth. What we want is a healthy and progressive globalization where economic growth is negotiated mutually and multilaterally among a diverse collection of people and peoples. This is not the cultural "haves" dispensing their wisdom on Darwin and Adam Smith to the cultural "have-nots." Fortunately, an emerging phenomenon exists that can provide a better theoretical and practical paradigm in which to envision mutually successful interaction among peoples today. This phenomenon is yet unnamed, but we might refer to it as "cultural Humanism."

Multiple identities, rational priorities

Cultural Humanism is a way that individuals and communities can affirm an ongoing identification with their cultural, ethnic, religious and/or national *heritage*, while at the same time affirming their commitment to universal Humanistic principles. It means taking pride in and appreciating one's identity as European or a Buddhist or a Jew or a Rwandan, while renouncing any elements of those identities that conflict with being a citizen of the world. Pride in one's ancestry and many of its traditional festivals and rituals or a desire for one's people, country, or region to do well, can in many cases be consistent with this type of Humanism. But for Humanists, theological views that one's people was specially "chosen" by God or is superior to another people must be criticized, revised, and replaced by an acknowledgement that all people have evolved naturally from common origins and must now afford one another universal dignity and rights in order to thrive.

For a cultural Humanist a singular vision of identity (where one's allegiance to America, or Allah, or "Asian values" or Europeanness, etc., is seen as overridingly important in nearly every situation) is also replaced, but not by a renunciation of all culture or nationality. Rather, cultural Humanism's vision is of *multiple identities*, where one can be, as Amartya Sen glibly points out, at the same time, an Asian, an Indian citizen, a Bengali with Bangladeshi ancestry, an American or British resident, an economist, a dabbler in philosophy, an author, a Sanskritist, a strong believer in secularism and democracy, a man, a feminist, a heterosexual, a defender of gay and lesbian rights, with a non-religious lifestyle, from a Hindu background, a non-Brahmin, and a non-believer in an afterlife (and also, in case the question is asked, a non-believer in a "before-life" as well). (Sen 2006: 19)

Sen's description, essentially a self-portrait and test-case for his principle that we must prioritize reason before identity as we choose how to understand ourselves, is indeed compelling. But it does not address what we should do, as individuals, when we encounter situations in which a particular component of our identity, especially the national, religious, or cultural component, matters a great deal. In fact even Sen himself, while a great Humanist and a man who has contributed to the well-being of all people, has with his actions and choices placed more importance on his Indian heritage than on many other competing parts of his identity. Much of his early work as an economist was devoted to thinking about the well-being of India's economy; and recently much of his energy as a philosopher and lover of literature has been spent commenting on the history of Indian thought. This does not make Sen a traitor to the rest of humanity, however; it merely makes him a cultural Humanist, or more specifically, an Indian Humanist.

There are three chief ways in which cultural Humanism is currently emerging as a viable form of identity around the world today. First, Humanists are combining Humanism with a progressive interpretation of their *national cultures* to create distinctly American, Dutch, British, Norwegian, and other versions of Humanism. In other words, Humanists in these and many other nations have banded together to form strong national organizations, with local chapters, for the dual purpose of representing Humanistic values in their countries while also celebrating the rhythms of life as national citizens, from a Humanistic point of view. Members of the American Humanist Association, for example, proudly participate in the American "civil religion" of holidays and traditions such as Independence Day, Martin Luther King, Jr. Day, or Labor Day, but they may choose their own way of participating in certain parts of the American "liturgy," for example by omitting the words "under God," added during the McCarthyite attacks on "Godless communism" in the 1950s, from the

"Pledge of Allegiance" to the US flag. They also tend to invent or emphasize ceremonies of their own in place of more traditional rituals which may make them uncomfortable: a December 24 holiday celebrating "Human Light" instead of Christmas, or treating the anniversary of the UN Universal Declaration of Human Rights as a major occasion.

Formalized cultural Humanism

Another form of cultural Humanism that goes even farther than the national variety is one in which Humanists choose to formally celebrate their Jewish or Christian religious and/or ethnic heritage by joining explicitly Humanist churches or synagogues, led by openly atheistic rabbis, ministers, or lay clergy. This occurs primarily, but not exclusively, within two American-based movements: Unitarian Universalism and Humanistic Judaism. Unitarian Universalism (UU) is a 250,000-member religious body that in fact no longer formally calls itself "Christian," though it was formed in the early 1960s in a merger of two liberal Christian denominations: the Unitarians and the Universalists. Upon this movement's founding, the majority of its leaders were self-identifying Humanists and many of its large and prestigious churches (the Unitarians traced their heritage back to the Calvinist founders of the Massachusetts Bay Colony and were largely responsible for turning Harvard into the US's leading university) across the United States were converted to Humanist centers. However, the UUs decided early in their history as a united movement not to officially endorse any creed, including Humanism, and thus today one is likely to experience any number of liberal religious perspectives in their company. Humanistic Judaism, meanwhile, is a movement founded around the same time as UUism with an understanding of Judaism as a culture, ethnicity, and heritage as well as a religion. Led by a dynamic rabbi named Sherwin T. Wine, Humanistic Jews declare that they identify with the history, culture, and fate of the Jewish people while affirming Humanism as their philosophy of life. They often attend synagogues, hire rabbis to lead them in celebrating Jewish holidays as well as weddings, funerals, and other ceremonies, and study Jewish literature and history. However, they are the most open of all Jewish denominations in terms of welcoming non-Jews into their communities; and they do not pray to any deity, subscribe to a doctrine of the Jews as a "chosen people," or revere the Torah as more than a great classical text. They tend to use their strength as congregations to support progressive interpretations of Zionism, including Jewish–Palestinian dialogues, human rights campaigns, and certainly negotiations in good faith towards a two-state solution to the Palestinian–Israeli conflict.

Still a relatively small movement, Humanistic Judaism is nonetheless growing in the US and around the world despite having been misunderstood both by Humanists who suspect it of being too "Jewish," and by Jews who see its deep commitment to Humanism as offensive or problematic. Moreover, I would argue that its *potential* relevance eclipses its current size, because it provides an outstanding example of cultural Humanism as a way one can gain the benefits of associating with a close-knit, particular community, while respecting and working with all people. Still, I should disclose: I am both a member of the Society for Humanistic Judaism, the movement's core organization, and an ordained Humanist rabbi.

If it were limited to the few communities mentioned above, the idea of cultural Humanism, however, would be much less significant than it is in the world today. Here we must remember that, as I stated above, "cultural Humanism" is merely a working title, and should be replaced if it ultimately distracts from the powerful concept I hope it represents. What *is* clear is that there is a previously unconscious and now increasingly conscious movement in many different cultural milieus around the world to combine Humanistic philosophy with the culture of a particular group. Every cultural, religious, and ethnic group, after all, has its share of "non-believers" and others that would probably best be categorized as Humanists, in the sense that regardless of what they believe and do not believe about God or theology, they all tend to believe that human beings and their needs are most important when determining right and wrong.

The hopes and values of these groups of Humanists have been eloquently documented in recent years by some of the world's finest intellectuals. Amartya Sen, in *The Argumentative Indian* (2005) and *Identity and Violence* (2006) has sketched the outlines of an Indian identity thoroughly informed and inspired by Humanism. Tu Weiming, Harvard's renowned Harvard-Yenching Professor of Chinese History and Philosophy and of Confucian Studies, has devoted his scholarly career to making the case for Confucian

Humanism, an affirmative, spiritual vision of Chinese and East Asian identity that makes an explicit commitment to universal human rights, ecological conservation, ecumenical dialogue, and progressive capitalism (or at least progressive anti-communism) (see Weiming 2004). The Muslim apostate Ibn Warraq (a pen-name taken by Islamic heretics over the years) has been prolific and increasingly known in recent years in his production of books and materials describing the process of turning to Humanism from an Islamic perspective, and of attempting to bring about an "Enlightenment" in contemporary Islam by means of critical scholarship on the Qur'an, the history of intellectual and theological liberalism in Muslim circles, and on those who have "left Islam" as a dogmatic system of supernatural beliefs and accompanying rituals (see Ibn Warraq 2002, 2003). Noted French Buddhist scholar Stephen Batchelor makes a passionate plea for agnosticism and naturalism as a historical element of Buddhist philosophy and an important aspect of contemporary Buddhism in his recent bestselling work *Buddhism without Beliefs* (Batchelor 1997). And Anthony Pinn, a leading young Harvard-educated scholar of African American religion, has become an articulate spokesperson for "African American Humanism" with several excellent recent books and essays that envision a cultural sort of Humanism as a real and exciting solution for some of the problems of a black community in the US and beyond that clearly has a distinct cultural identity but could stand to benefit from expressing its uniqueness in ways that will open it up to a richer experience of connection to humanity as a whole (see Pinn 2004, 2001).

Common cause with like-minded others

Any transnational "cultural Humanism" would achieve its greatest strength and potential for success if it could mobilize Humanists to work together with like-minded others, or together with "lower case h humanists." After all, many of the core values of contemporary Humanism have been internalized by non-Humanists around the world. Though it was once not necessarily so, today Humanists and liberal theists the world over can agree that life's highest priority is not to bring on the rapture while piously living in wait for heaven, but rather building the best world humans are capable of building, here on earth. We can agree that family planning is more important than

ancient laws of sexual purity; that broad-ranging education and free
inquiry are better than narrow sectarian schooling; that universal
human rights must be promoted whether they are divinely ordained or
not; that, as Amartya Sen argues, economic development *is* freedom,
and that the freedom to live a life of dignity is of the utmost
importance to all people. These are some of the many values
"Humanists" and "humanists" hold in common, and one of the most
basic ways all can work towards such goals together is via the promotion of "interfaith dialogue" (with Humanists, atheists, and
agnostics represented, of course) within and beyond the walls of
institutions such as universities, corporations, and NGOs.

Progressive capitalism as a goal for global Humanism

If we can create a Humanism that successfully integrates insights from
all the world's religious and cultural traditions, we will be capable of
influencing the manner in which people interact with one another,
including the ways they do business with one another. This is in fact
what Marxism originally intended; it was designed as a replacement for
Judeo-Christian and then ultimately all cultural identities. In retrospect,
Marxism went too far in denying multiple identities and the pull of
culture. Marxism also tried to impose one culture along with one set of
values on all people. But a more humble and flexible Humanism for the
twenty-first century can promote progressive capitalism by allowing us
to be distinct, to be ourselves, while inspiring us to see all peoples as
equal and to work for justice in the only world we have.

References

Allen, N. 1997. "Why I Am a Secular Humanist: An Interview with Nobel
    Laureate Wole Soyinka," *Free Inquiry* 17(4), www.secularhumanism.
    org/library/fi/soyinka_17_4.html.
Appiah, K. A. 2005. *The Ethics of Identity*. Princeton: Princeton University
    Press.
Batchelor, S. 1997. *Buddhism without Beliefs: A Contemporary Guide to
    Awakening*. New York: Riverhead Books.
Ibn Warraq. 2002. *What the Koran Really Says: Language, Text, and
    Commentary*. Amherst, NY: Prometheus Books.
    2003. *Leaving Islam: Apostates Speak Out*. Amherst, NY: Prometheus
    Books.

Pinn, A. 2001. *By These Hands: A Documentary History of African American Humanism.* New York: New York University Press.

2004. *African American Humanist Principles: Living and Thinking like the Children of Nimrod.* New York: Palgrave Macmillan.

Sen, A. 2005. *The Argumentative Indian: Writing on Indian History, Culture, and Identity.* New York: Farrar, Straus, and Giroux.

2006. *Identity and Violence: The Illusion of Destiny.* New York: W. W. Norton.

Weiming, Tu. 2004. "The Ecological Turn in New Confucian Humanism: Implications for China and the World," in T. Weiming and M. E. Tucker, *Confucian Spirituality*, vol. II. New York: The Crossroad Publishing Company.

Zuckerman, P. 2007. "Atheism: Contemporary Numbers and Patterns," in M. Martin (ed.), *The Cambridge Companion to Atheism.* Cambridge: Cambridge University Press, pp. 47–65.

4 | A requisite journey: from business ethics to economic philosophy

CLAUS DIERKSMEIER

Introduction

To put humans first in business and to implement humanistic values in management are noble endeavors. In order to make room for more humane business practices, however, a new kind of business ethics is requisite: one that does not subordinate its principles to the narrow confines of short-term profit maximization. Since discussion in business ethics is often influenced and framed by the theoretical foundations of academic economics, the demand for a new business ethics translates into the need for a critique of the economic paradigms underlying traditional business ethics. In that vein, a departure from certain reductionistic economic theories, namely from basic assumptions of neoclassical economics, becomes crucial. Instead of construing human agency within a matrix of self-centered utility calculations, the real human being needs to be reintroduced into economic theory, and we must recognize the eminent role of human freedom. In pursuit of a humanistic business ethics, an economic philosophy based upon the notion of human freedom must be advanced.

The ethical challenges of globalization

With astounding speed, the global exchange of products and services is transforming the natural and cultural face of the earth. Biological systems vanish, customary rules of behavior fade, legal frameworks dissolve, languages die out, and many traditional religions are on the wane. In their stead, driven by an exponential increase in information exchange, novel forms of interaction are taking hold; various new ways of life are quickly spreading, from their origins in the remotest localities on earth and even from cyberspace, all around the globe.

Are we heading toward a paradise of freedom and autonomy in which all human needs are met, or, are we facing endless war, civil strife, environmental destruction, and cultural poverty? Are we nearing one global culture or "multiple modernities?" And what will be the future role of the corporations? Will they become an integral part of a global civic society, and close ranks with the various non-governmental organizations that work toward the betterment of human life? Or will business impede our advancement toward a more humane society? In brief, will corporations foster or hinder human progress?

On a very basic level, both the main problem and its likely solution seem to be clear: humankind can halt the current "race to the bottom" only through implementing global ecological and social standards of business. Hence, we need agreement on a normative framework for the worldwide use of economic liberty (Cornia 2004). Before we attempt, however, to convince the business world of such a framework, the feasibility of our goals must be tried by economic theory. Business ethics, after all, does not exist in isolation from economics; without the latter, the former lacks important theoretical foundations. *Ultra posse nemo obligatur*: no one is obliged to do what she cannot achieve. If economics were to inform us that business, by its very nature, is incapable of incorporating moral perspectives, then all talk about value management and humanistic business ethics would be pointless. Thus, in order to advocate a normative position, we must examine whether economics allows for such ethical considerations.

Bygone business ethics

Although business decisions have always been made under conditions of uncertainty, in recent years (in conjunction with economic globalization) the level of general uncertainty has risen steeply. Corporate social responsibility can no longer be entrusted to the law alone; the limited scope of national jurisdiction faces a transnational traffic of goods, services, and persons. The more complex modern business relations grow, the less they fit neat legal categories. Corporate activity beyond the law, i.e. moral leadership, is required, but a consistent conceptualization of such leadership proves a challenging task. Divergent cultural, religious, and political values demand the attention of modern executives; thus, bringing ever more undefined variables into the management calculus (Vitell, Nwachukwu, and Barnes 1993). Add some postmodern moral vagueness to the mix, and acts of both individual corruption and corporate malfeasance are to be expected. When, however, managers look to academia for moral orientation, the traditional business ethics fails them for several reasons:

One, conventional business ethics is reactive, not proactive. Classical business ethics textbooks examine the errors of the past. Rarely do they encourage speculation about future problems. *Two*, classical business ethics is case-based rather than principle-oriented. Case-to-case comparisons work well in stable socio-cultural and legal contexts, but not so well in today's ever-changing global economy. *Three*, customary business ethics individualizes moral responsibility by focusing on character (e.g. in "whistle blower" scenarios). Today's moral challenges, however, demand intelligent structures rather than acts of personal heroism; systemic problems need systematic solutions. *Four*, traditional business ethics favors conditional premises ("If you want to avoid bad press, don't cook the books!"). Proactive management, however, needs unconditional adherence to values regardless of vicissitudes and transient disadvantages (Ulrich 2008). *Five*, the economic sector is a major force for societal change, since it educates people and societies through practice. Eclectic in nature and cut off from philosophical discourses about the good, "business ethics as usual" cannot anticipate the optimal direction of societal change; its advice remains largely arbitrary and unsystematic.

Business ethics redux

Current literature on successful efforts in corporate social responsibility agrees mostly on the "hard facts" of corporate ethics; for example, if business ethics is to succeed, corporations need to do more than simply propagate a code of ethics. Companies should also educate employees on the application of such codes, audit their performance (optimally, through independent agencies), and report honestly about shortcomings and accomplishments. Furthermore, the integral implementation of ethics management systems is important. Corporate ethics must, for instance, be coordinated with internal promotion structures, lest the latter undermine the efforts of the former. Promotions which are oriented solely at *quantitative* parameters, such as sales, production, and cost reduction, should yield then to promotions based also upon *qualitative* standards, such as stakeholder involvement, employee satisfaction, etc. As upright business practices do not always allow for the short-term maximization of profits, promotion management must take care not to punish employees who adhere to the corporate code of ethics and thus "make lesser numbers." It is only then that employees will be convinced of the integrity of their firm's moral initiatives. Under this condition alone will they bring their personal initiative, their creative thinking, their productive energies, and their enthusiasm to bear on policies that otherwise lack zest, and – most importantly – success. And the outside reflects the inside: a corporation typically persuades the public of its ethics only insofar as it convinces its own personnel.

The "soft facts" of the underlying corporate culture are, however, just as important for the achievement of ethical goals as the "hard facts" that can be captured by ethical audits. When a corporation strives for higher ethical standards, a transformation of its entire corporate culture must take place. In the same way that individuals are driven ahead by the tensions between their own ideals and how they are being perceived by others, a corporation relates to itself through idealistic symbols and a careful consideration of its image in society. Symbolic communication is of the utmost importance. It is imperative that there exist a normative ideal, conveyed in clear language and unambiguous imagery, in order to allow for the intended ethical orientation.

The ideals of a modern, humane business ethics must be both inspiring and demanding. As for individuals, some pragmatism is in order for corporations as well, yet too much of it crowds out any idealism and all the enthusiasm, energy, initiative, and innovation that come with noble ideals. Corporations, much like individuals, perform better when reaching out beyond the scope of their present possibilities than when they rest complacently within their limits. The presence of a lofty, yet attainable, corporate ideal coherently expressed through all sectors of corporate culture often is in itself a considerable force towards the achievement of its aims.

The mechanistic self-portrayals of old – the corporation as a "machine" for mere profit-maximization – fail utterly in this respect. Human beings do not appreciate being viewed and treated like cogs in a machine; it offends their sense of dignity. Moreover, this model does not provide the leeway necessary for ethical action. An agent who is not free cannot be held responsible, and a mechanism set up solely for profit-maximization is not free.

Corporations must also avoid symbolic inconsistency. If a corporation describes itself in metaphors of "family life" or by the imagery of an "organism," it is markedly contradictory to try to get rid of the respective "family members," or "limbs," as soon as they appear to be temporarily unprofitable. A family would not, and an organism could not, do the same. When workers perceive a rift between pronounced ideals and practiced reality, they quickly come to the conclusion that all the talk about corporate ethics is merely a facade. Nothing is more damaging than first stimulating ethical sensibilities and then frustrating the persons so motivated. Moreover, this will also direct the moral energy of otherwise unaffected persons against the company.

The nemesis of business ethics

Corporations that do reflect critically upon the moral quality of their standards will feel the pulse of social expectations sooner. Hence, they are better positioned to practice a proactive values management. Accepting criteria beyond the realm of mere legality, they are prone to engage in a dialog with their stakeholders, and so they are more likely to recognize social change. Over time, a reputation for corporate social responsibility boosts productivity: it helps gain and retain motivated employees, attracts investors with long-term interests, creates customer loyalty, and establishes durable alliances with both business partners and governmental agencies. In the midst of conflicting religions, cultures, and traditions, moral management reduces the risks of conflict and litigation (Vinten 2002), and it also finds reward in the respect and trust it generates. Goodwill on the part of society, voluntary assistance by citizens, information sharing by the government, culture building in alliance with corporate partners and the like have, after all, budgetary impact. In sum, to cultivate morals is intelligent corporate policy. Unfortunately, this is precisely what neoclassical economics at best overlooks and at worst denies (Williamson 2000).

Traditional business ethics and conventional economic wisdom share a visionary deficit (Heilbroner and Milberg 1995). Without a concise vision of the future economy, and without coherent ideas about the amelioration of human life or the creation of more humane societies, customary business ethics offers no germane perspective for long-sighted corporate policies (Mongin 2006). Traditional case-based and/or rule-based management systems become less effective as the overall uncertainty about the future, and the degree of cultural diversity of today's business environments, increase. *Principle-oriented deliberation processes* that hold their ground even in drastically changing surroundings are, therefore, needed. A principle-based business ethics can help anticipate and tackle the problems that will confront the business world in coming years.

Philosophy is *the* discipline that scrutinizes the validity of guidance principles and their application in different cultural contexts. Long-term strategies must be based on an understanding of how people construct laws and create the various symbolic systems (religion, arts, science, etc.) in which they communicate and coordinate their ideas. Clarifying social value standards, interpreting symbolic communication, and identifying societal and individual needs have long been the mission of philosophers. Hence, we need a new business ethics grounding in a philosophical investigation into the nature and the qualitative goals of economic activity (Putnam 2003). Providing alternative thought models that are on par with the problems of the business world in the twenty-first century, economic philosophy could bring back visionary thinking to business ethics.

Instead, the neoclassical economic paradigm cements outdated business ethics as a result of its technical rationality that leaves no room for principled thinking or transdisciplinary ideas. Holding that any and all deviations from short-term profit maximization cause corporate death, conventional economic teaching misses the real latitude of corporate decision-making. When, however, one eliminates corporate freedom, corporate social responsibility must follow suit. Hence, neoclassical economics relegates most ethical considerations to the legal realm, which is neither always right nor always expedient. The legal route frequently offers merely second-rate solutions, and on the global level, enforcement problems block this option more often than not.

The theoretical assumptions upon which this misguided advice is grounded (i.e. that all moral efforts beyond what the law requires amount to economic suicide) collide manifestly with empirical evidence. Quite contrary to conventional economic wisdom, business can do well by doing good (Webley and More 2003). Frequently, moral ideals demand, as well as command, altruistic actions wholly unconceivable within the neoclassical matrix. Neglecting the internal realm of normative ideas and looking into externally observable factors alone, neoclassical economics predictably fails in its prognoses of human behavior (Bergmann 1989). Certainly, this harsh characterization leaves out many improvements that have been made on (and within) the neoclassical framework in the past three decades, and, to be sure, hardly any economist today endorses neoclassical economics without major stipulations (Solow 1997). Nonetheless, its fundamental premises still serve as the overarching paradigm of economics, and especially of business ethics.

This must change, because one of the major problems of business lies in the way the available theoretical models describe the corporation. For, inasmuch as academic thinking informs business, theoretical flaws translate into errors in practice; and neoclassical economics is prone to such flaws (Waligorski 1990). Since one cannot solve problems with the very model that generates them, and because the neoclassical paradigm proves quite resistant to internal revision, external efforts to transcend it must be made. Lest outdated conceptions block innovative solutions, we need to proceed toward a new economic thinking, one offered by economic philosophy.

What is economic philosophy?

Historically, economic philosophy dates back to Plato and Aristotle. After economics separated itself from moral philosophy in the late eighteenth century, as well as from political economics in the late nineteenth century, economic philosophy was largely abandoned in Western countries (Niehans 1980). In the East, it continued only under the aegis of Marxism-Leninism. Since the 1930s the West has produced some treatises on economic philosophy, but intensive debates did not surface before the 1970s (e.g. in the dispute over the "creation of wants" through consumer manipulation). Recently, the debate in and about economic philosophy has intensified (Dierksmeier 2003).

Institutionally, economic philosophy is at home in many academic realms. The critical theory of the early 1970s gave it shelter, and from the 80s onwards, cultural studies, inspired by French postmodernism and semiotics, grew hospitable toward it. From the early 90s, economic philosophy made headway in the social and political sciences, led in by public choice theory. At last, economic philosophy was reintroduced into some universities' departments of economics, mostly as an appendix or complement to meta-economics. All in all, economic philosophy is still a relatively young scientific discipline with a lot of unknown territory to be explored (Hausman 1994).

Systematically, economic philosophy comprises a philosophy of economics that serves as a meta-theory of economics: preparing the grounds for a normative critique of contemporary economics. Also, economic philosophy encompasses topics and methods neglected by, but relevant to, traditional economics. Through its unconventional approaches, methods, and interests, economic philosophy often generates novel insights into economic life. Aside from long-established approaches (metaphysics, ethics, and aesthetics) to socio-economic questions (e.g. on the symbolism in organizational communication, on theories of trust, social compact, and institutional justice, etc.), economic philosophy incorporates ideas from linguistics, *Systemtheorie,* and the cognitive sciences (Dierksmeier 2003).

Economic philosophy thus operates "above" and "below" conventional economics: "below," insofar as economic philosophy scrutinizes the legal frameworks and cultural preconditions of markets; and "above," in that it examines what lies beyond the scope of standard economic theory, including the cultural and moral impacts of business. Expanding the scope of investigation, the main objective of economic philosophy is to address questions concerning how the economy can best contribute to a humane way of life. For example, economic philosophy argues that only the introduction of "qualitative" standards into economic thinking can overcome the harmful "quantitative" tendency of the present economy to pursue infinite growth at any cost. For this reason, economic philosophy analyzes the long-shelved issues of the moral significance of wealth, the societal value of welfare, and, of course, distributive justice (Sen 2002). In order to specify in more detail the possible contributions of economic philosophy to the practical problems of business, let us consider three different levels: the realm of the individual (micro-level), the domain of the corporation (meso-level), and the sphere of macroeconomics (macro-level).

Micro-level

Economic philosophy regards the human being as an end in itself. Having the capability of (moral) self-critique, humans are able to change both their preferences and actions. This description stands in stark contrast to the *homo oeconomicus* model of neoclassical economics, which idealizes rationality, assumes optimal information, minimizes transaction costs, abstracts from community ties, disregards all irrational impulses, and operates from a clear, as well as forever fixed, set of preferences (Boulding 1969). Even proponents of the *homo oeconomicus* model admit that it cannot describe reality; but they continue to argue for its heuristic and prognostic use (Friedman 1953). Others are continuously modifying the model, moving away from its *maximizing* principle to *satisficing* principles, and so forth. None of these stipulations and modifications have, so far, come close to a true depiction of the human being. To employ a theory that misrepresents reality is, however, not as innocent an endeavor as the proponents of the model project.

The *homo oeconomicus* assumptions have provided the intellectual premises to numerous damaging economic policies such as a drive against any and all (transparency, safety, health, or environmental) regulations. Moreover, the *homo oeconomicus* model tends to decelerate ethical progress. Under this mode of thinking, economists dismissed, for example, the idea of fair-traded products, deeming it nonviable to market them whenever they were more costly than their generic counterparts. However, producers and customers proved the practicality of fair trade. Recognizing their success, the defenders of the old model decided to change strategy and suddenly equipped the *homo oeconomicus* with a new kind of preference – for ethical fairness. This is how followers of neoclassical economics are wont to react to adverse evidence; they allow for a myriad of exceptions, yet forever maintain the core paradigm. Economic philosophers hold that, instead, a new way of thinking is called for.

In economic philosophy, the complex nature of intrinsic motives (care, duty, virtue, etc.), the features of artistic productivity (innovation, creativity, spontaneity, etc.), and the important role of social values (conventions, customs, traditions, etc.), all play a vital role in explaining individual and social activity. Without cultural foundations, there is no human agency. We must, thus, stop treating what is essential to human agency as external to economic theory, and integrate cultural perspectives into economics (Boulding 1987). If we truly want to understand and foster economic productivity, artistic creativity and moral innovation, we must reach beyond the technical rationality of the *homo oeconomicus*.

Meso-level

In the past, corporate philosophies have often been chosen arbitrarily by self-proclaimed business gurus of dubious intellectual status. Most companies are obtusely following each corporate fad and their various prophets. Economic philosophy, however, knows – and shows – a better route. A company needs corporate philosophy in order to arrange its incentive structure, performance assessment, ethical guidelines, communication policies, and corporate symbolism into a well-ordered structure. Because economic philosophy does provide the requisite intellectual framework for a consistent corporate philosophy, the contribution of philosophy to corporate success cannot be overrated.

In stressing the autonomy and dignity of the individual, economic philosophy defends every employee's right to be respected as ends-in-themselves. Contrary to the alienating functionalism of neoclassical management theories that chiefly regard employees as mere means to corporate success, economic philosophy values individuals as human beings first: considerations of human capability precede the calculus of human capital (Sen 1999). Economic philosophy rejects, in consequence, all mechanistic incentive theories (e.g. more money = more effort). For example, in change management, "change" can never be introduced into corporate culture *ceteris paribus*. The mechanical assumptions of conventional economics fail because people simply do not react to change by leaving "all other things equal." Workers are not simplistic stimulus–response machines. Like every complex organism, they respond to outside impulses on the basis of a complex interpretation of their situation, and these interpretations differ from one corporate culture to another. Hence, it makes a huge difference whether a company's culture is oriented by a sound corporate philosophy.

Macro-level

Corporations are intertwined with the outside world through an intricate web of non-economic dimensions. In the past decade, stakeholder relations have risen on the corporate agenda, if mostly for tactical reasons. It is time for a more strategic perspective. Today's corporations will be able to establish sustainable relationships with society only if they sincerely acknowledge its concerns. Companies are likely to respond adequately to the needs of society only if they learn to see the world from the perspective of their various stakeholders. Thus, corporate philosophies can no longer be the spawn of managerial autism. Instead, they must develop in conversation with society. Adept in overcoming barriers of understanding and in elucidating outside perspectives, economic philosophy has a natural advantage. It provides the tools for productive dialogue across the social spectrum along with the normative principles of intercultural consensus.

Conventional economics proclaims that it advances the interests of business owners. By paying little attention to the nature of ethical commitments, traditional customs, religious systems, or community structures, however, neoclassical economics has long violated those interests. While experienced businesspeople always acknowledged the importance of societal and cultural institutions, economic theory for several decades dismissed such "messy" subjects (Summers 1991). Neoclassical economics directs business consequently to maximize its short-term profits ruthlessly, whereas economic philosophy directs corporate decision-making toward policies that are in a corporation's long-term interest. Neoclassical economics neglects external effects unless, and until, their internalization can be achieved through the law (von Mises 1960); economic philosophy, however, advises business to be proactive about the elimination of negative externalities. And while neoclassical economics treats corporations as strictly private entities, economic philosophy embraces the idea of corporate citizenship, therein affirming the "political" and "public" dimensions of corporate practice. It is, therefore, no accident that economic philosophy captures the pertinent topics of contemporary corporate social responsibility much better than traditional business ethics. The sharper perspective of economic philosophy is due to its investigations "below" and "above" the focus of conventional economics.

Foundations of economic philosophy

In centering on human agency, economic philosophy naturally gravitates around the notion of human freedom (Dierksmeier 2003). Yet, the acceptance of freedom as the foremost principle of the Western world is waning. To many, the worldwide impact of liberalized trade and production has made governance in the name of freedom suspicious. In fact, immense damage has been caused by an unrestrained realization of self-interest on the part of individuals, corporations, and nation-states. Although libertarian ideologues alone are to blame for the propagation and failure of *laissez-faire* policies all around the globe, it is quite understandable that the idea of freedom itself has come under attack. Many hold the principle of liberty accountable for the social, cultural, and ecological devastations caused by irresponsible neoliberal policies.

This crisis of liberalism also harbors a chance. The need to revamp the idea of liberty in light of its present challenges may well make for its rejuvenation. To be sure, we must have worldwide circumscriptions of business practices, governmental powers, and individual conduct in order to sustain human life on earth. People resent and resist, however, confinement by norms whose rationale they do not share. This problem swells to hitherto unknown proportions in our era of constant change and global interaction. Regional customs, traditional religions, and the conventions of the past no longer command unquestioned obedience. In order to conquer the problems of global governance, we must reform the idea of freedom in pursuit of a self-reflective and self-constraining notion of liberty.

It may appear paradoxical to align the limitation of individual liberty with the very notion of freedom. For decades, Anglo-American philosophy has favored an understanding of liberty centered on the protection of private autonomy and property. Important as the preservation of individual choice and personal possessions is, such theories overstate their goal. Presenting their tenets in the language of sacred human rights, these philosophies contribute, not always unwittingly, to the exclusion of any and all alternative understandings of liberty. Communitarian critics from within open societies, along with more extreme external voices, contend that the Anglo-American notion of freedom is a farce: a mask for commercialism, a threadbare cover for a hedonistic, as well as morally undemanding lifestyle. They inquire why traditional values should be restrained on behalf of a form of liberty that aspires merely to the maximization of profits at whatever cost, or to the reckless pursuit of individual pleasures. Why should this freedom be esteemed more highly than the values one is supposed to yield on its behalf?

In these debates, most defenders and adversaries alike identify freedom as a *quantitative* idea ("more choices"; "being unrestrained"; "infinite growth"; "profit maximization"). When, however, the idea of liberty is described in terms of quantity alone, its all-important *qualitative* components are lost. If freedom is to regain and retain respect, *qualitative* aspects that determine what kind of freedom we the people have reason to value must be recaptured (Dierksmeier 2007). The idea of *qualitative* freedom links personal liberty to universal freedom. The type of liberty we should defend becomes clear when we understand our right to liberty as encompassing the obligation to empower everyone with an autonomous life. This notion includes the poor within our societies, the destitute of foreign nations, and future generations. The idea of qualitative freedom thus defines and curtails the realm of both individual and societal liberties so that all can live in dignity and freedom.

Qualitative freedom (i.e. liberty in boundaries that are conducive to universal freedom) does not exclude anyone and has the capacity to extend itself across cultural and religious borders. That is why the principle of qualitative freedom ought to be central to any future ethics of global governance. Through this notion, we can understand the search for reasonable standards for the economic fairness and ecological sustainability as the obvious objective of every free society. Hence, the quest for a global framework to cease the "race to the bottom" (e.g. by the UN Global Compact) and to secure the socioeconomic participation of everyone (e.g. by the Global Marshall Plan) can be seen in a new light. The idea of qualitative freedom allows us to understand such endeavors as attempts to realize the true meaning of freedom – and not, as neoliberals obstinately clamor, as assaults upon it. For moral as well as for political reasons, therefore, we must undertake a reform of the idea and the politics of freedom.

As the principle of freedom has to limit itself, the critique of the free-market society must proceed from the very idea of economic liberty, and not from an adversarial external viewpoint. This is why the debate about the right concept of freedom is not just an academic skirmish, but instead an intellectual battle of truly global importance. Under the banner of qualitative liberty, a sustainable economy, based upon a humanistic business ethics, and rooted in a philosophically guided economics, is possible; with the business ethics and economics of old, however, it is not.

Conclusion

We must reform business ethics by dismissing the conceptual framework of conventional economic theory that cements the very kind of business practices we want to overcome. Hence, a philosophical critique of the teachings of conventional economics is indispensable. In place of neoclassical economics and neoliberal politics, this article advocates a socio-economic philosophy guided by the idea of "qualitative freedom" to achieve a more humane business society.

References

Bergmann, Barbara. 1989. "Why Do Most Economists Know So Little about The Economy?" in Samuel Bowles, Richard Edwards and William G. Shepherd (eds.), *Unconventional Wisdom: Essays on Economics in Honor of John Kenneth Galbraith*. Boston, MA: Houghton Mifflin, 29–37.

Boulding, Kenneth E. 1987. "The Economics of Pride and Shame," *Atlantic Economic Journal* 15(1): 10–19.

1969. "Economics as a Moral Science," *American Economic Review* 59(1): 1–12.

Chamberlain, Edward H. 1948. "An Experimental Imperfect Market," *Journal of Political Economy* 56: 95–108.

Colander, David and Klamer, Arjo 1987. "The Making of an Economist," *Journal of Economic Perspectives* 1(2): 95–111.

Cooper, Ruseel, DeJong, Doughlas, and Ross, Thomas. 1996. "Cooperation without Reputation: Experimental Evidence from Prisoner's Dilemma Games," *Games and Economic Behaviour*, 12:187–218.

Cornia, Giovanni Andrea. 2004. *Inequality Growth and Poverty in an Era of Liberalization and Globalization*. Oxford: Oxford University Press.

Dasgupta, Partha. 2005. "What Do Economists Analyze and Why: Value or Facts?" *Economics and Philosophy* 21:221–78.

Dierksmeier, Claus. 2003. "Über den gegenwärtigen Stand der Wirtschaftsphilosophie," *Archiv für Rechts- und Sozialphilosophie* 3: 551–61.

Dierksmeier, Claus. 2001. "Was heißt und zu welchem Ende studiert man Wirtschaftsphilosophie?" in *Arbeit und Lebenssinn. Wirtschaftsphilosophische Untersuchungen, Kritisches Jahrbuch der Philosophie*. Würzburg: Königshausen-Neumann, pp. 9–18.

2007. "Qualitative versus quantitative Freiheit," *Rechtsphilosophische Hefte* XII: 107–19.

Friedman, Milton. 1953. "The Methodology of Positive Economics," in Essays in Positive Economics. Chicago: University of Chicago Press.

Hausman, Daniel. 1994. "Why Look under the Hood?" in Daniel Hausman (ed.), The Philosophy of Economics: An Anthology (second edition). Cambridge: Cambridge University Press, pp. 17–21.

1998. Causal Asymmetries. Cambridge: Cambridge University Press.

Heilbroner, Robert L. and Milberg, William S. 1995. The Crisis of Vision in Modern Economic Thought. Cambridge: Cambridge University Press.

Hoover, Kevin. 2001. Causality in Macroeconomics. Cambridge: Cambridge University Press.

Keynes, John Maynard. 1931, "Economic Possibilities for Our Grand-children," in Essays in Persuasion. London: Norton, pp. 358–73.

Kirman, Alan. 1989. "The Intrinsic Limits of Modern Economic Theory: The Emperor Has No Clothes," The Economic Journal 99(395):126–39.

Marshall, Alfred. 1890. Principles of Economics, London: Macmillan and Co.

McCloskey, Donald. 1994. Knowledge and Persuasion in Economics. Cambridge: Cambridge University Press.

Menninger, Karl. 1969. Number Words and Number Symbols, a Cultural History of Numbers, Cambridge, MA: MIT Press.

Mongin, Philippe. 2006. "A Concept of Progress for Normative Econom-ics," Economics and Philosophy 22:19–54.

Niehans, Jurg. 1980. A History of Economic Theory: Classic Contributions 1720–1980. Baltimore: Johns Hopkins University Press.

Putnam, Hilary. 2003. "For Ethics and Economics without the Dichot-omies," Review of Political Economy 153:395–412.

Robbins, Lionell. 1932. An Essay on the Nature and Significance of Eco-nomic Science. New York: New York University Press.

Roth, Alvin. 1998. "Laboratory Experimentation in Economics: A Meth-odological Overview," The Economic Journal 98: 974–1031.

Sen, Amartya. 1999. Development as Freedom. Oxford: Oxford University Press.

2002. Rationality and Freedom. Cambridge, MA: Harvard University Press.

Skyrms, Brian. 1996. Evolution of the Social Contract. Cambridge: Cambridge University Press.

Solow, Robert. 1997. "How did Economics Get That Way, and What Way Did It Get?" Daedalus 134(4): 39–58.

Summers, Lawrence. 1991. "The Scientific Illusion in Empirical Econom-ics," Scandinavian Journal of Economics 93(2): 129–48.

Suppe, Frederick. 1989. The Semantic Conception of Theories and Scientific Realism. Chicago: Chicago University Press.

Ulrich, Peter. 2008. *Integrative Economic Ethics. Foundations of a Civilized Market Economy.* Cambridge: Cambridge University Press.

Vinten, Gerald. 2002. "The Corporate Governance Lessons of Enron," *International Journal of Business in Society* 2(4): 4–9.

Vitell, Scott J., Nwachukwu, Saviour L., and Barnes, James H. 1993. "The Effects of Culture on Ethical Decision-making: An Application of Hofstede's Typology," *Journal of Business Ethics* 12(10): 753–60.

von Mises, Ludwig. 1960. *Epistemological Problems of Economics.* New York: New York University Press.

Waligorski, Conrad. 1990. *The Political Theory of Conservative Economists.* Lawrence, KS: University of Kansas Press.

Webley, Simon and More, Elise. 2003. *Does Business Ethics Pay? Ethics and Financial Performance.* London: Institute of Business Ethics.

Williamson, Oliver E. 2000. "The New Institutional Economics: Taking Stock, Looking Ahead," *Journal of Economic Literature* 38(3): 595–613.

5 | The global economy from a moral point of view

STEPHEN B. YOUNG

There are many moral points of view and each one thinks it has a claim to our affections. In fact, the Chinese philosopher and jurist Mo Ti argued that each and every person has his or her own unique, particular, and completely idiosyncratic moral basis for judging the things of this world and the next. It is therefore impossible, Mo Ti argued, to arrive at a common standpoint for evaluation of something as complex and important as the global economy.

So, in the context of this book, it is initially difficult to decide upon which moral point of view has the most salience from which to offer a credible critique of the global economy. From which vantage-point should we sharpen the edge of our evaluative powers? Whose perspective should we embrace? Whose benefits should we endorse? A necessary preliminary observation points out that considerations regarding the economy are very much rooted in the material, non-transcendental reality of the life-world.[1] On the other hand, morality, from whatever point of view you take it, is not necessarily bound by the physical restraints and causal sequences that drive the life-world. Morality is open to the outer limits of human imagination, embracing all mental constructions about the workings of the life-world and all that which might be beyond the life-world.

I want to suggest in this chapter that, of all the possible moralities that could be brought to bear in analysis of the global economy, an aspect of humanism – stewardship – has a particular relevance. By stewardship I refer to an action orientation of human decision-making with respect to the life-world, that takes place only in the life-world, and that is outcome-determinative within the life-world.

---

[1] Habermas, Jürgen. 1984. *The Theory of Communicative Action.* Boston: Beacon Press.

Stewardship is intentional action seeking beneficial outcomes in material well-being that are more encompassing than selfish, personal enhancement. Stewardship is, therefore, partly utilitarian. But only partly. Stewardship integrates notions of duty, obligation, responsibility, of a larger whole, of a community of interest and purpose, into the decision-making calculus of what is prudentially right to do.

Turning now to an argument that of all possible moral points of view, something along the lines of stewardship makes great sense as a stance for evaluation of the global economy, let me begin by briefly and crudely setting forth a typology of moral points of view.

The options for moral grounding

It seems to me that all moral points of view can be placed within one of three categories depending on the origin of the truth that intellectually supports the point of view. I divide moral points of view among those originating with revealed truth, those reflecting principles of natural law, and those arising from community custom or mythic belief systems. The categories I have chosen are a bit arbitrary at the boundaries between them, as is the case with every attempt to place phenomena within set realms of linguistic definition. (See the Chinese Taoist argument that "the Tao that can be named is not the real Tao."[2])

Now from the perspective of believers, I fear that these distinctions will not carry much weight. A follower of community custom or a believer in a received myth may well feel that his or her moral point of view has some quality of truth so as to be seen as a natural law or as having been revealed by a higher power. This would especially be the case when the truth value of a perception comes to the advocate after a meditative or insightful experience with the transcendent. Under those circumstances, the relevant Godhead, human reason, natural law, myth, custom all interpenetrate a single stance towards the world, the truthfulness of which is not to be gainsaid in the mind of the believer.

But I am searching for a context in which the presentation of a humanist critique of the global economy might seem distinctive so,

---

[2] For an English version of the Tao Te Ching see e.g. Mitchell, Stephen. 1988. *Tao Te Ching*. New York: HarperCollins.

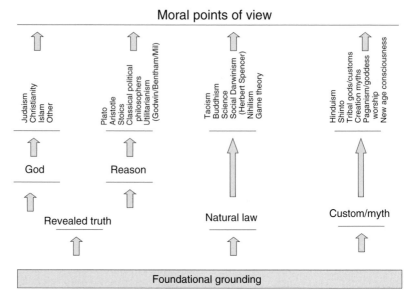

Figure 5.1 The variety of moral points of view

with your indulgence, I will outline how I would align the various foundations for moral advocacy. The following chart provides a summary, schematic outline of my presentation of a variety of moral points of view.

(1) The ground of revealed truth

From this perspective, the source of truth is taken to be a communication received by the mind from a higher directive power that demands our intellectual subservience.

(A) God

A principal source of revealed truth is the anthropomorphic supreme God, designer and maintainer of the cosmos. In all those approached, truth is communicated as an intellectual matter by one mind – a divine one – directly in conversation with or in writing to human minds.

i. Judaism – the Ten Commandments

In the Jewish tradition, Yahweh, the supreme God, provided the Ten Commandments as the moral code for devout and faithful descendants of Israel to follow. The Jewish scriptures expressly describe, for example, the personal and very intimate conversations between prophets such as Samuel and Isaiah and Yahweh.

ii. Christianity – St. Thomas Aquinas, Martin Luther, John Calvin

In the Christian tradition, it is Jesus, the son of God, who teaches us the holiness code that will bring us into God's grace, enable us to overcome sin, and permit us to reach heaven in the life hereafter. The authority of Jesus comes from his kinship with God the Father and his special knowledge of God's desires. For St. Thomas Aquinas, once he has proved God's existence, a quite finite structure of habits, virtues and vices is then established as a template for correct human conduct. Both Martin Luther and John Calvin, leaders of the Protestant Reformation of Christian teachings and liturgy, looked to a personal relationship with God through humility and prayer, a relationship sustained by right conduct as well as by knowing right from wrong. In addition, both Luther and Calvin accepted the written text of the Old and New Testaments as sufficient evidence of the knowable intentions and commandments of God.

iii. Islam – the Prophet Mohammad

In Islam, the supreme God, creator and sustainer of the cosmos, under the cognomen of Allah, revealed truth to Mohammad, who spoke it forth in the Arabic language. For faithful Muslims, submission of the will to these teachings provides a certain path to daily living under a mind that is rightly guided.

iv. Others: Zoroastrianism, Mormonism

For Zoroastrians prayer and insight reveal the option of leaving a sad and sinful world through the intercession of Ahura Mazda, the highest God. For Mormons, revelation of truth came to Joseph Smith through the help of the Angel Moroni and a reading of divine scripture in a sacred scripture that Smith unearthed in western New York State.

(B) Reason

I count reason as a second kind of revealed source of truth. The truth revealed by reason does not come after conversation with a god or by reading a sacred text that originated with a god. But the workings of reason take us out of our own minds to the contemplation of abstract principle, some perception universal, distant, and perfect – something like a godhead of the understanding. These abstractions which form in our minds are then reduced to words and grammatical constructions which shape our approach to the right and the good. The ideas speak directly to us and we highly value their truth content.

i. Plato

The Greek philosopher is justly famous for articulating a theory of ideas – conceptual forms with eternal life such as numbers and mathematical operations – that could ground not only our understanding of reality but also of right conduct.

ii. Aristotle

Aristotle used his powers of reason differently from Plato. Aristotle applied his mind to schemes of conceptualization where definitions were made to correspond to different aspects of reality. Then, Aristotle used the sequencing of language and grammar to move from one truth to a less obvious one until an entire intellectual structure was derived. The building of the truth edifice was both by the rigorous use of logic for scientific truths or the more subjective method of rhetoric to draw conclusions in the realm of practical wisdom. In his *Nicomachean Ethics* Aristotle elaborated a set of practical conclusions about how it is best to rule our actions with a view to avoidance of extremes.

iii. The Stoics

The Stoics, both Greek and Roman, extended Aristotle's method by using reason to piece out an understanding of natural processes. Stoic thought was the precursor of reliance on natural laws – causal connections and necessary linkages – that govern reality without recourse to any intending god or spiritual prime mover. Cicero's work on moral duties – *De Officis* – drew explicitly on Stoic teachings.

iv. The classical political philosophers: Thomas Hobbes, John Locke and Jean-Jacques Rousseau

Hobbes and Locke in England and, later, Rousseau in France used reason to derive recommendations for systems of just government. Hobbes argued from the premise that human nature could only be understood as depraved and so in need of restraint and authoritarian government. Locke attempted to prove that human nature had some redeeming and constructive qualities arising from labor and an ability for cooperative undertakings. Such a nature, argued Locke, could benefit most from wise and restrained government. Rousseau, to a different degree, created a set of premises and inferences that human beings undermined with social institutions and customs their natural rights and freedom to do as they please. He proposed a theoretical concept – the general will – to reconcile individual freedom with communal responsibilities.

v. Godwin, Bentham, John Stuart Mill, utilitarianism
William Godwin in England carried the deconstructive work of Rousseau further. He attacked social conventions and traditional political institutions for their limitations in not responding to the insights of reason, for irrationally denying opportunity to women, for example. Jeremy Bentham followed apace with the argument that reason leads to an appreciation of utility as the only substantial reality. Creation of social, economic, and political arrangements engineered to achieve the greatest good for the greatest number gave Bentham many grounds for seeking reform of English laws and practices. A proudly worldly philosophy, utilitarianism invokes reason as the sole and most sufficient navigational compass in the effort to achieve human happiness. John Stuart Mill, especially with his essay *On Liberty*, famously used such utilitarian justifications for his defense of a liberal social order and limited restriction of individual action and beliefs.

(2) The ground of natural law

The presence of natural law is discovered by our mental faculties, to be sure – reason, intuition, observation, inference, deduction from insights. But a natural law – a state of affairs prior to and over, above, beneath, and around human intention and willfulness – has more reality to it than do the revealed cognitions of reason alone. The operative moral dynamic in cases of natural law seems to be accommodation and adjustment of human actions to a higher and more powerful sense of purpose at work in the world. Most conclusions about the operative presence of natural laws do not ascribe their origins to an anthropomorphic intelligence at play in the universe.

(A) Taoism
This Chinese approach to first principles asserts that there is a way – a Tao – that leads to success and fitness for human actions. The key dynamic for finding the Tao and blending with its course is not to impose human passions, motivations, social conventions, ego needs, or moralistic pieties on our actions. Our stance, we are told, should be as water seeking its natural course in the low places.

(B) Buddhism
Buddhist teachings posit a human anthropology – a mindfulness inherent in our condition that leads to sorrow and unhappiness through a misunderstanding of reality. That which we see and feel, touch and desire, is only an illusory kind of existence – *Samsara* in Sanskrit – dragging us down emotionally and mentally. Open to the enlightened mind is a higher and better understanding of what is. Buddhist teachings and disciplines are designed to help us attain that higher and better understanding of what is.

(C) Science
Science, as it emerged in the modern era, explicitly seeks to find and publicize the mechanics by which the universe moves and seeks its being. Physics, biology, chemistry, and all their derivative intellectual implications and inter-combinations investigate the causes of things and posit rules and laws by which accurate predictions of outcomes can be made. The scientific orientation towards morality often is a meek acceptance of the material and the physically necessary, a kind of "what is, should be, because it must" state of mind.

(D) Herbert Spenser/social Darwinism
Writing his book *Social Statics* in 1851, Herbert Spencer founded the modern intellectual discipline of sociology. He used powers of observation and rational deductions from what he observed to advance a rule for human conduct: struggle to ensure survival of the fittest among us. Spencer reasoned simply that humans remained part of the carnivorous animal kingdom where each was for each and all were against all. To live well in the social mayhem of such unavoidable conditions, Spencer argued, individuals needed complete autonomy from others, a formidable sense of self, and a determined will to prevail.

(E) Nihilism

Philosophical nihilism might be considered an offshoot of science. It holds that power is the primordial and persistent existential reality and that, for morality, the will to power holds all life's trump cards. This state of affairs, nihilism posits, is the only possible state of affairs; it is the natural order in which we live. Jean-Paul Sartre and Albert Camus proffered versions of existentialism to help us shoulder the burden of choice in a world where all is open to choice and our will.

(F) Game theory

A natural law theory of motivation and choice within the limits of the possible is offered by the mathematicians and economists who work on equations of game theoretic outcomes of action. From the perspective of game theory, forms of utility – risk aversion, self-interest, rational calculation of costs and benefits – will lead to sustainable and predictable outcomes in human interaction. Morality here can be graphed as probabilities on a chart of possible alternatives. But the nature modeled by these equations is most often a cramped and narrow world of utility and interest, providing only a truncated range of human possibilities and enjoyments.

(3) The ground of custom/myth

The truths we accept based upon custom or myth require neither the revelation of a cosmically supreme deity or reasoned logic nor the observational foundation of a theory of natural law. The truth value offered by custom and myth is that of social legitimacy and cultural validation. Customary beliefs and myths are, if you will, the natural law perceived by a community tradition as true for itself and, for that reason, necessarily binding on its constituents. The mechanism of intellectual loyalty to what the community accepts and teaches as true works through the individual's identity with that community so that the norms and visions of the group become part of the individual's inner psychic world and self-concept.

(A) Hinduism

In the Upanishads, the *Bhagavad Gita*, and parts of the Rig Veda, Hinduism indeed presents cosmic understandings of the ego's relationship with reality in line with Buddhism and Taoism. But much of ordinary Hindu practice and worship – castes, the daily ritual of the Brahmin, shrine worship of Ganesh, Shiva, Parvati, Vishnu, and other deities, etc., strike me as most customary in their acceptance and justification.

(B) Shinto

Worship of the Kami or spirits in rocks, trees, waters – everything – is so local and set in legendary context that I consider it a form of customary worship. Shinto does not subscribe to any universal truth for humankind but relates its rituals and expectations to the protective totems of the Japanese only. Shinto origin myths, prayers, and rituals promote a calm and smooth mindfulness in the devotee who seeks protection from a particular Kami. One does not reason about the Kami; one only accepts offering the service they demand.

(C) Tribal gods and customs

From native Americans to Polynesian islanders and Australian aborigines, from African rituals to southeast Asian spirit worshipers, many live seeking the propitious compassion of tribal gods and totemic spirits.

(D) Creation myths

Creation myths – such as the origin of the Japanese emperor in the sun goddess, the Nazi myth of Aryan supremacy among the races of humanity, or the Aztec conviction that they had a divine right to rule the Valley of Mexico and its surrounding peoples – can powerfully structure our expectations of right and justice in the world.

(E) Paganism/goddess worship

The pagan ethic grants wider supernatural powers to gods and goddesses than more limited tribal traditions give local totems but the dynamic of worship and source of truth is similar in the two approaches. The pagan presence can reveal itself and its commands in a version of revelatory truth.

(F) New Age consciousness

A variety of contemporary faiths, beliefs, cults, and personal quests for meaning and more happiness in this world rest on a premise of changing the program content and default mechanisms of our consciousness. The recommendations do not, as a rule, rely on reasoned logic or the teachings of a revealed god; nor do they, as recently introduced conventions, rely on long-standing customs.

Morality and ethics

The second step in my argument here is to speculate on the informative connection between all the above levels of moral grounding and common themes of morality and ethics. I tend to associate morality more with teachings and doctrine and ethics more with actions. Both morality and ethics hope to align our actions with right ends. Morality tries to prescribe right actions in advance while ethics seeks to steer us away from abuse of power.

Of the above levels of moral grounding, some like the revealed religions more readily lend themselves to holiness codes of specific behaviors and conduct rules – such as the Ten Commandments provided by the Jewish Torah. Others are more inclined to social justice orientations where the outcomes of power are called into question. The understanding provided of what is right and just justifies some outcomes more than others and so sets up a critical stance vis-à-vis the life-world.

The experiences of the life-world can align with expectations of what is just or such lived experiences can be perceived as violating legitimate normative paradigms.

The critical stance taken towards contemporary global economic dynamics from the perspective of the revealed religions is the powerful tendency of the global economy to undermine the requisite holiness code with enticing consumerism, easily available sensuality, and the commodification of human dignity. Other levels of moral grounding look more to social justice criteria, where the favored group receives its just due in the distribution of wealth and economic opportunity. Or, to put the matter inversely, a disfavored group (greedy individuals) gets more than its fair share of goods and services.

The process of commodification of cultural values undermines concern for human dignity in several ways. First, a process of commodification looks to lowest-cost efficiency as the most desirable strategy for competition and success. This requires mass production, the loss of craft and attention to individuation in products and services in order to achieve lowest unit cost of production. Second, the arbiter of culture and taste is whatever will sell in volume. So the process demands a "dumbing down" of refinement and sensibility and increasing emphasis on coarseness and sensual pleasures – sexuality, hedonism, conspicuous consumption as a psycho-social medication provided to those who live alienated, self-referential lives. Third, when what we can purchase provides our personhood with identity so that the acquisition of commodities and consumer experiences gives our lives their deepest meanings, the dignity of humans has been cheapened both spiritually and intellectually.

In commodification, the instincts of the herd crowd out the judgments of those more attuned to angelic chimes. The "better angels of our nature" are listened to less and less. Leadership thereupon shrinks its sense of calling down to mere management of consumer demand; political argument becomes spin – whatever works to buy a little time is good enough; and politics becomes the manipulation of fear and greed, a Peronism writ large across the family of humankind.

In the business environment of commodification, rewards are reaped by those who, Enron-like, can "bring home the bacon," "hit the numbers," or "take the money and run." The mentality of the bazaar merchant intrudes where the long-term vision of the captain of industry should be guiding corporate decision-making.

And, third, some sources of moral grounding such as social Darwinism or game theory are quite accepting of the contemporary economic order, except to the degree that custom and government regulation restrict and limit maximization of rational efficiency in the production of goods and services and the allocation of finance capital around the world.

Social Darwinism, based largely on the mid-nineteenth century thought of Herbert Spencer, does not provide for the institutions of trust and reciprocity that are necessary for capital to be accumulated on a large scale and for long-term investments to be undertaken. In a most adversarial environment such as the war of all against all and survival of only the fittest that social Darwinism advocates, few will prosper over time. Under such conditions, risking one's well-being through dependence on others would be foolhardy. Yet, only such interdependencies facilitate the specialization of function and division of labor necessary to produce the wealth of nations. The secret to capital investment is not the assumption of risk, only the assumption of prudent risks where there is a reasonable chance of reward. The premises of social Darwinism alone will not foster robust social achievement. Spencer overlooked the anthropological fact, now confirmed by contemporary studies of evolution, that *homo sapiens* achieved an advance over the animal kingdom in the development of language, moral thinking, inventive teamwork, and a capacity for social constructions of reality. Humans are beings who must live in and for each other psychologically, economically, and politically.

Game theory in its classic formulations perpetuated the core insights of Social Darwinism. It assumes with each person a capacity for self-interested rational calculation of utilitarian advantage. Such oversimplification of human motivations, needs, and ingenuity leads to more zero-sum analysis of how market behavior will occur than is necessary. However, it is important to note that game theory does transcend Social Darwinism when it recognizes that individuals calculate their personal advantage in the context of others and with a view to the likely reactions of others, thus opening the theory to the embrace of a moral dimension of mutual dependencies. What is in our individual interest is not necessarily bad or deserving of stigmatization as being excessively selfish if our individual interest is broadly defined to include a range of values and desirable outcomes. Humans, we must never forget, have a multi-functional set of utility curves. Respect for their attempts to live with dignity requires that we also respect their various and variable utility curves.

Ends expected from the global economy

One can be more specific than seeking a generic critical moral or ethical stance vis-à-vis the global economy in looking at the moral points of view bearing upon our international economic arrangements. A list of such concerns would contain at least the following:

- justice in distribution of burdens and benefits, costs and opportunities
- wealth enhancement – bettering my condition
- no disruption of my truth, custom, or myth
- environmental risk/climate change
- tendency toward war or peace
- enhancement of national honor – China, South Korea, and Japan
- individualism/opportunity

- open immigration into more wealthy countries
- free trade in goods, services, and capital investment
- personal freedom.

How can such a variety of ends – each one able to sustain a moral point of view about the workings of the global economy – be reconciled into one agenda of concerns and remediation of shortcomings? Who is responsible for alignment of inputs, outcomes, and ends? And, more interestingly perhaps, is it necessary that there be a single moral stance vis-à-vis the global economy?

The issues here lie in the domain of political philosophy: do we impose ends and the means by which to reach them; or do we focus on a process with open architecture which does not foreordain such normative reductionism and such coercive engineering of results?

We do not have a world government, though we have many multi-national organizations. We do not have a meaningful parliament of religions. Many NGOs do, however, offer themselves as surrogates for the thinking of the global human community, especially on issues of human rights and environmental sustainability. Private corporations have selfish duties to their owners, and operate under the legal regimes specified by various national sovereign governments.

Under these structural conditions, the many moral points of view supporting a variety of end-games for the global economy co-exist in disharmony. The open architecture of the system is a given; a natural law of circumstance. Discourse ethics suggests itself as an appropriate way forward toward a more common moral stance vis-à-vis globalization.

The economy: a quintessential humanistic phenomenon

Achieving a felicitous melding of moral points of view via discourse becomes more likely once we focus on a truth feature of the global economy. I refer to the fact that the economy – of family, village, city, region, nation, the world – is a human product. It is a human response to the physical world in which we live – the life-world itself – and to human needs and desires, though reason can influence invention and reasoned persuasion does help make selling more successful. No god started it and no reasoned argument ever made or sold a good in commerce, though reason can influence invention and design and reasoned persuasion does help make selling more successful.

Economic activity proceeds from a natural condition that our species is *homo faber* as well as *homo sapiens*. We make as well as we think and we know. Universally, we have inventive, technical capacities to make what can be sold or exchanged. We can convert what is in our physical environment into what we want and need. Economic activity has to be more than the allocation of scarce goods, which gives analysis of investment, production, and exchange intellectual rigor; it must start with the fabrication of goods and the ability to provide service. These are uniquely human accomplishments.

Only then can the instinct to "truck and barter" kick in to drive economic activity ever onward and upward in complexity and sophistication.[3] We have indeed come a long way over the last several millennia from the first production of stone cutting tools and crude clay pots. But over all those years we have been engaged in materialism of a very non-transcendental nature. A humanistic perspective, accordingly, might be the best one to bring to bear on evaluation of the global economy.

Other very human traits have contributed to economic success as well. One is language – the means of social production and communal interaction supporting market arrangements. The second is the moral sense which promotes and protects trust. Long-term exchange relationships and the division of labor, necessary supports for any vigorous economy, are hard to come by in environments of low trust.[4]

A common alignment for human institutions

Our civilization stands on three institutional legs: public authority of government, private business, and the civil society sector of NGOs. Each leg provides a specialized social strength: government provides public goods; private business creates wealth; while the rest of civil society promotes and sustains norms, meanings, and sociability.

Each set of institutions has its particular strengths and weaknesses, but each remains vulnerable to abuses of power. The vice of humanism coincides with the dark side of human potential, just as the appeal of humanism lies in the promise of human ingenuity and moral imagination. Governments, private businesses, religions, schools, charities,

---

[3] Smith, Adam. 1776. *An Inquiry into the Nature and Causes of the Wealth of Nations*. London: Methuen and Co.

[4] Fukuyama, Francis. 1995. *Trust*. New York: Free Press.

etc., readily succumb to selfish manipulation of means and ends for unethical and unjust purposes.

Leadership and management philosophy can center on the just or on the dysfunctional with consequent benefit or costs to those subject to such power and authority. The common antidote to abuse of power in government, private business, and civil society is having power held only as an office in trust – not for oneself, but for beneficiaries.

The responsibilities of stewardship, namely the fiduciary duties of loyalty and due care, restrain the use of public power, profit-seeking endeavors in private economic activity, and management of civil society at large.

I conclude from this congruence of the need for one approach to the use of power in three sectors that good stewardship can be a common moral point of view from which to evaluate the norms and practices of the global economy.

The normative stance of stewardship does not resolve difference among viewpoints as to who should benefit from economic activity, what market risks are acceptable, what rewards are excessive, what products are objectionable, etc. But the fiduciary ideal does set up a common framework for assessment of each of those variables. From the fiduciary perspective we are to ask to be quite explicit in who we see as the beneficiaries of our work, what risks are salient to them, what benefits will lighten their life burdens, and what degree of care sits on our shoulders to be fair and just to them.

Guiding as it does every human use of power, the stewardship ideal has application on many levels: great social institutions of politics and government, business enterprises, individual ownership, family leadership.

Figure 5.2 illustrates the dynamic of the stewardship ideal as it impacts standards of social justice. When governments, NGOs, and businesses move outward towards the standard of abuse of power, they create respectively tyranny and conditions of corruption, breakdown of social capital, or negative externalities. But when each institution moves inward towards standards of fiduciary responsibility, they bring us closer to the target of social justice.

In the public sphere, the stewardship ideal demands that public office be held as a public trust, not as a fiefdom for personal exploitation or hubristic satisfaction of one's vanity. Public office should be sought for the right reasons – service of the common weal – and not for partisan and sectarian triumph or for economic advantage.

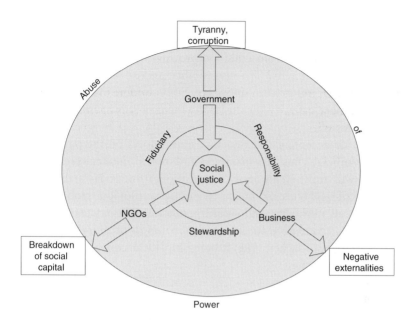

Figure 5.2 Dynamics of the stewardship ideal

In both government and business, the stewardship ideal demands respectful consideration of others. One is empowered to serve, not to impose. Senior positions of administrative command and control should, therefore, not provide their incumbents with a license to be harsh, inconsiderate, or brutish to those who report to them or who look to them for guidance and instruction.

In business the stewardship ideal demands showing respect, which can be motivated by some degree of self-interest to be sure, for stakeholders. Business can be said to hold a social office for the benefit of the larger society – to produce wealth and better living standards. The business is "paid" as it were with profits only when it performs satisfactorily its duty to improve society. Businesses that do not perform as expected are expendable. And one test of stewardship for every business is its responsible use of the environment.

The stewardship ideal may have its greatest impact at the level of the individual. It holds that even our personal powers and property – the dynamic heart of our freedom and morally grounded person-hood – should be used with restraint and respect for others. Since we have power and can therefore set in motion through our actions flows of effects and consequences – karma in other words – we can be held to standards of care in how we act and in what we set in motion. The growth of a person from childhood to maturity can be seen as the development of a sense of responsibility and an ability to act from the perspective of concern and duty. Since we are moral beings, we have an innate capacity for the deployment of stewardship standards in our actions.

The wide acceptance of fiduciary mindfulness on the part of government officials, business managers and owners, and cultural opinion leaders will most likely ease a transition from today's discordant plurality of rival ends and means to a more harmonious global process of enhanced mutuality and interdependence. The fiduciary mindset also is most conducive to discursive resolution of moral differences and ethical approaches. The stewardship ideal can be presented as humanism at its best.

References

Fukuyama, Francis. 1995. *Trust*. New York: Free Press.
Habermas, Jürgen. 1984. *The Theory of Communicative Action*. Boston: Beacon Press.
Mitchell, Stephen. 1988. *Tao Te Ching*. New York: HarperCollins.
Smith, Adam. 1776. *An Inquiry into the Nature and Causes of the Wealth of Nations*. London: Methuen and Co.

6 The implications of humanism for business studies

OMAR AKTOUF AND W. DAVID HOLFORD

Adopting a humanistic approach within business activities and inter-actions is of the utmost priority if society and, by extension, we as human beings both in the individual and collective sense are to sur-vive, flourish, and emancipate ourselves.

At first glance, mainstream management literature would appear to be showing encouraging signs of enlightenment across the myriad of leitmotivs that are discerned across such words as "humanism," "ethics," "corporate governance," "social responsibility for busi-ness," and "environmental responsibility." In fact, if there is a major point of convergence for the many streams of literature, it is the importance of the human person or personal attitudes and behaviors at work. No matter the trend or topic: whether it is about corporate 'culturalism' (Deal and Kennedy 1982; Ouchi 1981; Peters and Waterman 1982; Schein 1985 and 1991) or motivation and the val-orization of human resources (Archier and Serieyx 1987; Crozier 1989; Peters and Austin 1985; Waterman 1987); whether it is across total quality, the re-introduction of the meaning of work, "empowerment" (Juran and Gryna 1980; Michel 1989; Mintzberg 1989; Peters and Austin 1985; Serieyx 1989) or the realization of the workplace as an area of social interactions and sharing (DePree 1989; Peters 1987; Peters and Austin 1985; Weitzman 1984); or whether it is the various preoccupations with ethics, ethico-spirituality, or other management methods aiming towards cohesion, participation, ini-tiative and creativity at all levels, what stands out most clearly is the insistent call from all quarters to put the human element at the fore-front. *Yet let us not fool ourselves into thinking that these various streams reflect any significant attempt at creating business frameworks or management practices that embrace man's emancipation as a finality onto itself, or "man as the measure of all things."*

101

The deleterious dialectic

One of the telltale signs that makes us adhere to such a skeptical view involves a dialectical process working as a vicious circle, which when viewed from afar seems tautological: the endless pursuit of maximization of profits leads to a truncated understanding of the complex and profound nature of man, which in turn leads to the further quest for maximization of profits and monetary wealth, whereby cause and effect become interchangeable. But the various mechanisms behind the scenes of this process (of which we will only discuss a few) indicate to us that this process is far from being banal or tautological.

One half of this process (that is, the endless pursuit of maximization of profits leading to a reduced or truncated understanding of man) involves the very visible "global" context of unbridled capitalism, eagerly pursuing "maximum profits" in the shortest amount of time possible for shareholders, all the while seeking out infinitely exploitable labor. On a macroscopic level, adherents to such economic interests and passions (which Hirschman [1997] so eloquently described) attempt to paint these surrogate desires as being purely rational in nature, with more contemporary followers such as Baechler (1995) going to great pains to convince us that this is all about economic or corporate "efficiency" (that is, the striving to maximize profits while simultaneously trying to reduce economic costs to the barest minimum). But, as Godelier (1974) repeatedly pointed out, such an "efficiency" is merely a masked ideology, since the word "efficiency" by itself carries a neutral connotation that adheres to no specific objective. Furthermore, the choice of any output objective (whether it be a specific objective such as 50 percent, 200 percent or a generic one such as the maximization of "xyz") for any given input involves a decision on the part of an individual or collective subject having roots in a specific ideology. Such an ideology (or rationality) is also one of the prime motives for management's notion (and treatment) of the human being within the work environment as an instrument of production, a sort of "mechanical being with needs," a selfish maximizing and rational being, and as a cost to be controlled and minimized. Hence, all reference by mainstream management theory towards putting the human being in the forefront is (whether intentionally or not) a teleological conception of human activities and interactions whose end is simply the maximization of profits. Yet paradoxically, the attainment of this short-sighted (and often vulgar) objective has been a fleeting success at best for most Western businesses when measured through the lens of long-term profitability. Many, such as Agayo (1990), Albert (1992), Deming (1986), Liker (2004), Mintzberg (2005), and Pascale (1990, 1996), have noted that responsible management, productivity, and profitability has shifted towards areas such as Southeast Asia; and that North American industry has stagnated in comparison to the more dynamic Nordic, Japanese, and emerging Asian countries (we only have to look at the precarious financial situation of the US automotive companies over the last few years in comparison to the persistent, long-term profitabilities of Honda and Toyota throughout both the past and current decade – the reader can refer to CNN or Bloomberg over the past four years with reference to Ford and GM's losses in market share, bond de-ratings, negative profitabilities, or thin profit margins mostly sustained by extraordinary one-time events). At the same time, the degradation of nature and quality of life has only grown. Stuck in a theoretical gangue that is cemented by functionalism and an ideology of consensus, mainstream management theorists have failed to recognise that the root cause of the problem remains a question tied to the fundamental negation of humanist thought by a technocratic order striving for maximization of profits at all costs. Nonetheless, since the 1990s there has been an insistent call for bringing to the forefront a more "humane" corporate "ethic." But to what kind of human being are we referring? Unfortunately, it is a truncated human being reduced to his 'functional' dimension: dehumanized, instrumentalized, and reified.

A closer look at the first leg (in fact, there is no "first" or "second" leg in a hierarchical sense, but simply two complementary legs working together simultaneously) of our "deleterious dialectic" unearths further contradictions and paradoxes. For example, it has now been close to twenty-five years since *In Search of Excellence* (Peters and Waterman 1982) and its various derivatives have been circulating within academic and orthodox professional management circles, and we have yet to see members of corporations all working together, standing as one person, within an organization teeming with social interactions, enthusiasm, participation, and mutual support. Reflecting a simplistic and reductionist understanding of the human being, the vogue of "management by excellence" and "corporate culture" that followed in reaction to the German-Japanese corporate onslaught has always consisted of not only manipulating perceptions, but also personal values, beliefs, mental representations, symbols, self-image, identity, etc. with the aim of affecting the most intimate feelings and sentiments of the individual. All employees, including management and salaried workers, are, as a result, expected to confound their own ideal of the self with that of the organization that employs them. Yet all of this is doomed to failure, since the most elementary knowledge of anthropology shows us that subjectivity, ontology, and values cannot be manipulated or fabricated via the revamping of symbols, rituals, and ceremonies, since all of these are artificial and "dead" in the sense attributed by Branislaw Malinowski: a myth cannot be "operational" unless it is "alive," that is to say, actively integrated and based in mythology and the sacred as well as in the real-life experiences of individuals. Predictably, in trying to "motivate" workers, management's evacuation of the sacred and spiritual is most easily seen across their use of truncated versions of Maslow's (1959, 1969) pyramid, that is, without the use of the spiritual top level – a level, which when incorporated, sheds a very different light and perspective on the subsequent levels of the pyramid. Without attempting any "illuminated" journey on our part into "spiritualism," we can argue that part of man's spirituality involves an acceptance of his own mortality. For example, Sievers (1994: 56–7) explains that the fundamental split in corporations between those at the top (management) and those at the bottom (the workers) is due to a more fundamental split occurring in contemporary Western societies – namely "the split between life and death . . . the reality of death and mortality as constituent human qualities is neglected and denied in contemporary enterprises and in society in general. It seems that people are aberrantly preoccupied with the notion of life, and this can be correlated with our predominant organizational concerns for growth and survival. Through the fragmentation of work life and life, we have more or less succeeded in expatriating death and mortality from our institutions, and it seems that enterprises are exclusively devoted to an ongoing, permanent notion of life [immortality]." But as Sievers explains, the corporation does not provide "immortality" for all its members, but only in the Calvinistic sense: "immortality is a scarce resource, available only to the happy few; and immortality of the enterprise as well as its few members can only be achieved and maintained at the cost of many others and their lack of immortality." The infantilization of the worker becomes one of many consequences of the "management by excellence" movement, whereby management is deified simultaneously with the worker's' reification. Management's attempt to incite the worker to participate ends in a false interaction between the worker and the manager, based on a collusive quarrel over immortality which occludes any true participation based on equality: workers resent the fact that the managers become "immortal," while managers look at the workers as "mere mortals" (Sievers 1994). This also provides the basis for Western management's adoption of a theory of motivation based on the reification of the worker (Sievers 1994), whereby the worker is perceived as not being able to think or get involved in any *significant* decision-making. If we take Hegel's principle that "Man has no essence. His essence is within his action" (that is, when the human being is denied the opportunity to create he cannot emancipate his humanity and transcendence), then the worker, as an object, can no longer bring any meaning to his life. But management tries to convince the worker that what has no meaning still has meaning by using "motivation" as a surrogate for meaning. We now have a process whereby management has inhibited action on the part of the worker via his reification, while trying to motivate him at the same time. The resulting double-bind is nothing short of tragic.

Needless to say, such a situation renders many corporations vulnerable since machinism, robotization, and even the information age in themselves have failed to ensure sustained profitability. Product obsolescence has become ever more rapid, while the flexibility of the human mind is becoming more and more indispensable even if all we are aiming for is an impudent improvement in profitability. But is this the only goal? Before attempting to answer this question, per-haps we should first ask ourselves a question related to the "second" leg of our dialectical process: where does this truncated understanding of the human being lead? The quick and superficial answer to this was in effect highlighted in our analysis of the "first" leg, in that a trun-cated understanding of man paradoxically leads to lower profitability in the long run. Hence, we seem to be faced with a downward eco-nomic spiral: the quest for maximization of profits leads towards the adherence of a truncated understanding of man, which in turn leads to lower long-term profitability, which management, in their continued quest for maximization of profits, try to address via the "development" and use of further truncated notions of man, which, in turn, only exacerbates negative corporate performance. But far more alarming is the deep and irreparable damage that this truncated understanding of the human being wreaks on his own identity and *ego*. For example, a purely behavioral theory and understanding of the human being based on "measurable" empirical data ostracizes any of the human being's specificity not falling within established "norms" or "averages." Conversely, psychoanalytical and ethno-psychoanalytical approaches coupled with anthropological approaches have shown that any attempt to repress, as opposed to express/sublimate, one or more of the aspects of the self (be it the collective, the individual, the instrumental, the critical-rational, the emotional, the spiritual, the sexual, etc.) leads to schizoid or near-schizoid identities, emotions, values, "rationalities," and behaviors (Besançon 1974; Deveureux 1973; Erikson 1993; Laplantine 1973), which attempt to compensate these same initial repressions via obsessive addictions to surrogate substitutes. These surrogate substitutes, in turn, often have deleterious effects on both the subjects themselves as well as the environments in which they (and we!) subsist. Two of the major categories of such substitutes include the limitless accumulation of wealth and its close corollary, the quest for all-mightiness and immortality. Hence, we now have the "second" leg of the dialectical process we alluded to earlier on: a truncated understanding of the self (or the human being) leads to the quest for maximization of profits.

This modest examination on our part of both halves of the full dialectical process alluded to at the beginning of this section allows us to confirm a conservation of the status quo with respect to all that is related to power, managing of profits, division of labor, incessant operations of re-engineering, and fusion-acquisitions, whereby we can only conclude that all these management methods use humanism as a façade, humanism to deceive and carrying the seeds of its own destruction. To borrow the words of V. De Gaulejac at the World Congress of Sociology, Madrid, July 9–14, 1990: "Today it is as if the new management were trying to transform the psychic drives feeding the individual's narcissism into added work and an additional source of relative surplus value."

The need for a radical humanism

How does one break out of this endless impasse? We believe the answer lies in: (1) having managerial studies develop and adopt an understanding and theory of the human being that incorporates, as Rosaldo (1989) calls it, "the whole self" and embraces what we term "radical humanism"; and (2) adopting a concept of corporate governance that becomes a natural extension as well as a natural support for such an understanding of the human being (as opposed to the current situation of having man serve and support the corporate governance as we currently know it).

Various fundamental and radical shifts in management practices and their concepts of both work and the worker are part of the proposed agenda. For example, management, rather than relying on organizational behavior methods that try to find the secret of "how to" motivate employees, must try to understand *why* employees are not motivated. This means looking at things from the point of view of the employee. As such, three corollaries can be stated:

1. the outdated nature of orthodox management based on unilateral privileges, exclusive "rights," and authority (often concealed behind manipulations of perceptions, subjectivity, and symbols);
2. the outdated nature of "organizations" and "strategies" imposed by top management (often with the aid of outside management consultants);
3. the outdated nature of various "scientific" methods that have successively encroached upon the domain of management theory (scientific organization of work, behavioral science, science of decision-making, science of information management, econometric models, etc.).

Our proposed concept of radical humanism involves selections from each of today's major schools of thought that are convergent, complementary, and enlightening in the difficult and complex quest for a more humane conception of man. The humanism that we allude to involves a radical, in-depth re-introduction of the source and root of things related to historicism, diachrony, the social and economic structures at stake, and the sharing of power. And above all, it involves exploring the "nature" of what it means to be human:

To consider the human being as destined (owing his unique status to his "self-consciousness") to the pursuit of what will liberate him, emancipate him (from all forms of obstacles that we will analyze later in this chapter), and lead him towards fulfilling his inherent vocation: that is, a being endowed with consciousness, self-judgment, and free will who aspires to his own elevation. Thus, each person in humanity is a "generic being" who creates his own milieu, society, and, therefore, himself.

From authors such as Aristotle, Marx, Fromm, Sartre, Freud, and Evans-Pritchard we also retain the following essential points:

1. The humanism that is proposed here is one that is completely centered on the human being and the significance to the human being with regard to whatever activity is undertaken. The definition of humanism put forward by Erich Fromm (1961: 147) best summarizes this:

   [Humanism is] a system centered on Man, his integrity, his development, his dignity, his liberty. [It is based] on the principle that Man is
   not a means to reach this or that end but that he is himself the bearer
   of his own end. It is not just based on his capacity for individual
   action, but also on his capacity for participation in history, and on the
   fact that each man bears within himself humanity as a whole.

2. A long tradition, from Aristotle ("man is a political animal"), to Weber (the central idea of the passage from an organic society to a mechanical society; or from the *oikos* to bureaucracy) by way of Marx (on the importance of social relations and class phenomena), makes of man a being fundamentally defined by community, society, and his relations with others. Relations in and through which he lives, constructs and makes sense of himself (a sense-making which becomes the basis and condition for his self-realization). It is neither disparities nor similarities between Aristotle, Marx, or Weber as theorists that are of interest here, but rather, their shared understanding of the human being's nature as undeniably social and community-oriented.

3. Given that the main idea of this reflection has to do with men and women in the workplace, it would seem that the author that is most pertinent on this issue is Karl Marx. But it is not such an easy matter to position oneself simply and clearly amongst the infinite positions Marxist schools have previously established or retained with respect to humanism. For this reason, certain key theoretical clarifications are in order. Relying on the work of a few experts in the subject (Kołakowski, Mandel, Calvez, Lucács, Gramsci,

Fromm, and Heilbroner), and without minimizing the nuances or discrepancies between some of these authors, one must *consider the work of Marx as a whole,* including the works said to be "mature" and structural (*Capital*) while finding frameworks and roots from his more "youthful" anthropological and philosophical works (the *Manuscripts* of 1844). As Kołakowski (1987: 377) explains, "although Marx's terminology and mode of expression changed between 1844 and 1867 . . . the driving unity of Marx's thought can be found in the unrelenting search for the conditions dehumanizing man and for possible ways of restoring more humane conditions." Thus, a central element in radical humanism is the question of alienation and of alienated work. We will return to these terms shortly but, for the moment, let us remember that people are most in danger of "ruin" and "losing themselves" (alienation) through the very act by which they can express their generic essence: the act of work. In other words, *the heart of the process of dehumanizing the human being is alienation through work.* Hence, the reason for our first and foremost interest in what takes place, concretely, in the work process. In this process, the worker alienates himself by selling his capacity for work (and not his actual work, which is the expression of his creative act) while contributing to the development and consolidation of power (merchandise, profits, capital) which are exterior, foreign, and, in the final analysis, hostile to him, and thus even more "dehumanizing." The finality pursued is no longer the person and what is most human in him or her (e.g. satisfaction of needs through utility value) but the "unlimited growth of exchange value" (Kołakowski 1987: 280). It is within a "radical humanist" framework that this alienation must be addressed if we are to accede to a managerial conception that integrates a "re-humanized human" as well as an "ethic" in the communitarian-humanist-Aristotelian sense.

4. Finally, we also must consider a humanistic position which tends towards a theory of the subject. In this sense, Marx can be supplemented by Sartre (1948, 1966 and 1976) and by Marcuse (1964), whereby the notion of "bad faith" joins that of "false consciousness" and "alienation" and where the human being is, by definition and necessity, a being whose destiny is meaning, intentions, and projects – thus, by nature, a person is involved in his or her being and in his or her becoming (to which alienation is

an obstacle): a subject whose being is meaning and which has a need for meaning. Along these lines, we can also refer to a specific social anthropology, represented by people such as Evans-Pritchard (1950) who states that human beings are definitely not like mechanisms, machinery, or organisms. Rather, they are ruled by reasons, feelings, and choices – *not* "causes" or stimuli's (unless they are forced, other-determined, or alienated, in which case there is no longer a subject but something objectified and reified so as to become an instrument).

These are the main points of the humanistic position and concepts proposed in this chapter. We also propose other ideas in the field of management that can genuinely contribute towards a more human-istic path in one or more of the ways just discussed, by directly attacking specific problems seen as flagrantly disregarding human aspects within the corporate organization. A non-exhaustive thematic listing of such works includes:

1. A re-questioning of the established order, unilateral power, corporate monopoly of profits, instrumental conceptions of the employee, etc. as so many obstacles to collective creativity, adaptation, and innovation (Atlan 1972, 1985; Clegg 1975; DePree 1989; Morgan 1986; Orgogozo and Serieyx 1989; Varella 1980; Villette 1988; Weitzman 1984).
2. A call towards the struggle against the fragmentation of work, against the destruction of its meaning; or similarly against the overspecialization and sub-division of tasks which robs the worker of any sense of fulfillment and meaning; and against the disregard for the human being's need for symbols (whereby symbols reside in the human being's imagination/mind, thereby answering his need to think, his desire to create as well as his need to generate meaning), all reasons why work is becoming more and more alienating, de-motivating, uninteresting and source of suffering and tensions (Beynon 1973; Braverman 1974; Chanlat and Dufour 1985; Dejours 1980, 1990, 1998; Pfeffer 1979; Sievers 1986a,b Terkel 1972; Turner 1990).
3. A reflection on the relation between language and work, on the human being as a being of speech, the place and the role of dialogue, the possibility for self-expression, and on the pathologies of communication caused by violence to *homo loquens* in the

industrial world (Chanlat and Bédard 1990; Clegg 1990; Crozier 1989; Girin 1982, 1990).

4. A call to recognize that most managerial conceptions and practices foil any real possibility of giving the human being the status of subject, that of an actor personally and ontologically justified in identifying with and questioning the firm, re-appropriating the acts he or she is assigned to do, and experiencing them as an expression of his or her own desires (Chanlat and Dufour 1985; Crozier 1989; Dejours 1980, 1990; Pagès *et al.* 1984; Sainsaulieu 1983, 1987; Sievers 1986a,b).

5. A reconsideration of the relationship to time in the industrial workplace; and as such, the denunciation of the sufferings and violence (physical and symbolic) inflicted on workers via the imposition of a dehumanized pace and the fragmentation of time (Gasparini 1990; Hassard 1988 and 1990; Kamden 1990).

6. The denunciation of certain absences in ethics and honesty towards employees, of the damage done by monopolizing the fruits of worker commitment and productivity, and of the selfish and short-term behavior of management, all of which prevents employees from living and being treated as human beings (Etzioni 1989; Olive 1987; Packard 1989; Solomon and Hansen 1985).

7. The re-questioning of the narrow utilitarianism and economism with which prevailing managerial theories and practices are imbued, and which turn managers and corporations into cynical predators having little consideration or respect for nature, personal integrity, and dignity – whether of employees, consumers, or citizens having the right to a certain quality of life (Caillé 1989; Chossudovsky 2003; Etzioni 1989; Galbraith 1987; Mitroff and Pauchant 1990; Monthoux 1989; Pfeffer 1979; Rifkin 1980).

8. And finally, the growing and persistent call for a kind of epistemological and methodological radicalism highlighting the complex, systemic, and multi-dimensional nature of everything which has to do with individual human beings as well as groups, including, and above all, people at work and in organizational life. Contributions along these lines include multi- and inter-disciplinary approaches, dialectical and circular causality, the self-organization and general theory of systems (Atlan 1985; Chanlat and Dufour 1985; Chanlat *et al.* 1990; Maturana 1992; Morgan 1986; Morin 1993; Varela 1980; Vincent 1990).

These are the themes which can be considered as being of a more radical and humanistic tendency. Finally, there is a study of the human being, no longer through the sole eyes of profitability nor as simply an instrumental being, but through the lenses of more fundamental disciplines and human sciences (anthropology, linguistics, psychoanalysis, psychology, sociology, biology, etc.) which treat the human being not as a de-incarnated and isolated object of production, but for what he is, the entire him – the human being as a being of speech, of symbols, of senses, of society, of free will; and not just simply as a resource at the service of the company and of maximization of exchange value. This means the embracing and synthesis of the human being's inherent ambiguities and complexities, and not just limiting ourselves to the illusion of his so-called "rational side" (e.g. Levy 1997), which highlights the synthetical aspects of the human being's brain, across its various interconnections between the reptilian, limbic, and neo-cortex sections, whereby the human being cannot be viewed as being neither completely logical nor completely irrational. Equally, Damasio's (1995) past work and studies on the neurobiology of decision-making shows that the repression of emotions and intuition significantly decreases one's capacity for effective decision-making. Otherwise we risk falling into schizoid traps that not only truncate man's inherent richness, but often attempt to present various ideologies and passions of the dominant few as being completely "rational and reasonable."

This movement towards a more humanistic path within the firm is neither a romantic ideal, an *acte gratuit* of philanthropy, nor a Utopia, *but a necessity*. It is primordial to remember that it should be absolutely out of the question to conduct research in "productivism" for the sake of "productivism." Yet in simply trying to catch the advocates of maximized "productivism" within "their own trap", it is in their own interest, as selfish as they may be, to be more humanistic.

Towards a beneficial dialectic: the elimination of alienating work and the adoption of a humanistic governance

To attain the conditions that will give workers reason to be motivated in what they do, several radical changes must be implemented. But it is important to first arm ourselves with a conceptual framework that allows us to ask the right questions. And it is within this reasoning that we ask ourselves how can management thinking pretend towards radical change when it does not re-question its secular presuppositions and premises. When we look at reflections on man within other disciplines which place the understanding of man as central (e.g. Evans-Pritchard in anthropology), it is easy to understand why management theories of motivation fail abysmally in their quest to motivate people within the workplace: in that they merely consider humans beings as organisms ("termites," according to Herzberg 1980) which obey "causes," instinctive needs, and external stimuli. We must replace our behavioral sciences by a theory of man that allows the human subject *to find both by himself and for himself the reasons to make it his own what we ourselves would like him to do, all the while being a full partner in what is projected, planned, and intended.*

Marx's theory of alienating work is a solid framework from which to start our reflections on the synergies required for real productivity within traditional industry. Restoring a sense of meaning to work, as well as permitting the appropriation-commitment sought by "corporate culture" and "total quality," depends on nothing less than putting an end to the following four estrangements of alienated work:

1. Estrangement from the product (whereby the employee has no control over what, how, or for whom the final product is being produced, as well as no control over its destination, or the profits derived from it).
2. Estrangement from the act of work – a break perfected by Taylorism – whereby employees are reduced to muscular or mental stores of energy who accomplish tasks that are never their own but always dictated and imposed by bosses, assembly-line speed, and corporate goals and strategies.
3. Estrangement from nature – whereby working hours make time an artificial, saleable product as opposed to the natural time of the seasons, the cycle of day and night, and the biological clock; while substituting the satisfaction of natural needs with those dictated by money and capital.
4. Estrangement from the human element – whereby workers become estranged from their own generic essence, their capacity to create their own surroundings and themselves, as well as their own free will, while being placed in a situation of conflict with others who use and exploit them. Furthermore, the "exploiters" themselves are

in turn just as alienated by their subjugation to the laws of maximum fructification of capital.

There is not only a need to recognize that the meaning or the sense of work is the foundation for worker motivation and interest, but also a need to expand our reflection on all industrial, flexible, and virtual work that has essentially lost all meaning. Wanting to regain this sense of meaning is to also recognize, after a century of management that aimed towards negating or masking it, that work alienation is the heart of the problem of commitment and motivation. Within this perspective, there is only one possible solution for firms to surmount such problems: workers must experience their relation to their work as a real, rather than a formal, appropriation. What they do in the firm must be experienced as a real extension of themselves, as an occasion for self-expression as well as for the pursuit and satisfaction of personal desires and interests that converge with those of the firm. Thus, the firm would become a place for partnership and dialogue, and a workplace no longer run by the unilateral usage of force. The question must no longer be how to motivate the worker but rather why is he so little motivated within the current financial and socio-economic context. To question oneself on this aspect is, as Sievers (1986a,b, 1994) pointed out, to question the significance of work, the concept and organization of work, which in turn brings up the question of the status of the human being and his relationship with others. It is not hard to imagine that the functionalist-pragmatist conceptual framework of traditional management is rather ineffective in the face of such questions, as it has always rejected such questions as being outside of its field of preoccupations, claiming that they relate, at best, to philosophy, if not to a more or less subversive or leftist sociology.

The answer to the question of lack of motivation, interest, and implication of the employee within a traditional management also has to do with a reintegration of diachrony for which the anti-historicism of managerial functionalism has completely evacuated. One must remember that the modern, industrial, and postmodern company has been constituted – and continues to be constituted – most often on the basis of violence and suffering (in both the physical and symbolic sense). It has taken long struggles and terrible confrontations to attain, one by one, laws which require work conditions that are less unjust and more humane. We, via a return in history, can come to realize the pertinence of the element which Marxism has always put at the heart of its analysis of work relationships: the contradiction, which is very much "alive and well," between the interests of the owners and managers on the one hand, and those of the workers and nature on the other. For the former, it is always a matter of making the largest possible profits – which is synonymous with, amongst other things, having the lowest possible salaries and a continuously unchecked pollution; while for the latter, it has been an incessant battle and struggle in reaction to the former, so as to try and attain a better quality of life, better working conditions, and more decent salaries (regularly gouged away shortly after being attained).

In order to truly attain a company that is a place of consensus, partnership, and trusting relationships, one must also adopt one of the key and dear principles of Marx: *the abolition of wages* (salaried remuneration within the definition of it being a quantifiable remuneration completely dissociated from the true work value which the worker contributes). Highly performing economies such as those of Japan, Germany, and Sweden already practice several different forms of more equitable sharing and re-distribution of the produced riches. Many such as Weitzman (1984), Archier and Serieyx (1987), Orgogozo and Serieyx (1989), De Pree (1989), Crozier (1989), etc. speak of sharing – specifically profit sharing – as well as dialogue, listening, and community. They, whether explicitly or not, are advocating the abolition of wages, especially when they propose taking inspiration from the forms of remuneration found within these countries. For example, Peters (1987), calls for profit-sharing as part of remuneration; Perrow (1979) argues that control and coercion will be the only ways (more costly than profitable) to obtain maximum productivity as long as the salary system is the rule; while Etchegoyen (1990), sees salaries turning employees into mercenaries working in soulless enterprises (the "mercenary" element is seen here as an obstacle to individual commitment – a person no longer satisfied with doing what is asked, who has neither interest nor "soul"). Even if sharing of profits is not sufficient in itself to entrain a profound change in the nature of power and influence, to bring about de-alienation, and even less to mark the end of exploitation, it is certainly a significant step towards more equity (it is ironic that many corporate managers adhere to current "theories" which see salary increases as being mostly ineffective for worker motivation, yet rarely hesitate to award themselves astronomical salary increases, bonuses, and stock options in recognition for their individual "performances"). This, along with a true and concrete participation in management and orientation of the firm, as well as a larger degree of autonomy and multi-valency with respect to the worker, coupled with a basic level of security and quality of life are the necessary conditions for addressing stagnations in productivity (productivity in the original sense of the word, that is producing to satisfy "reasonable" needs, by reducing the amount of degradation and exploitation of nature and humans).

Hence, workers must no longer be viewed as a cost to reduce, but rather as an ally to convince. Conversely, managers must stop seeing themselves as the only people fit to think, decide, and manage. And while the pursuit of profit is a legitimate objective, it must no longer be maximalist or short-term in nature, and neither must it be managed in a selfish manner for the sole advantage of shareholders and managers, but rather, must be considered as the fruits of labor for all, whereby the rates, destination, and usage must be decided in common between the worker and managers, as well as between the business environment, the state, and society.

The price for this is the renunciation of numerous secular privileges by management and shareholders so as to be able to move towards a form of organization whereby flexibility, creativity, and quality can occur and evolve from the one and only source that must be respected at all times: the human individual. This is a necessary condition to address in order to improve the management capability of organizations in the face of growing complexities. It is also a difficult path, strewn with numerous forms of resistance, often deeply rooted in the unconscious, like the psychic prisons mentioned by Morgan (1986), or the delusions of immortality and grandeur referred to by Sievers (1986b, 1996) and Kets de Vries and Miller (1984). Yet the adoption of a radical humanism and conception of corporate governance which becomes a natural extension as well as a natural support for the profound nature of man not only breaks the vicious circle or dialectic we described much earlier, but introduces a virtuous one: the adoption of a fuller understanding and respect for man leads to the production and subsequent sharing of profits, which in turn reinforces the respect and understanding of man, leading to further profits (and its subsequent sharing), and so on. The exact starting or end point of this process is, as in all dialectical processes, non-existent, but its circularity implies long-term viability for man, nature, and, for the more financially minded amongst us, the corporation.

Key lessons

Numerous streams of management literature addressing the individual and his attitudes and behavior at work fail to create management frameworks and practices which embrace the human being's emancipation as a finality onto itself, or "man as the measure of all things." The dialectical nature of the current socio-economic process at work, namely, the endless pursuit of maximization of profits leading towards a truncated understanding of the human being, which in turn leads towards the further quest for maximization of profits, and so on, appears to pose an endless impasse. Within this cycle many interlinked negative paradoxes and contradictions can be identified, including: (1) management inhibiting creative action on the part of the worker via his reification, while at the same time trying to motivate him, produces the psychologically destructive "double-bind"; and (2) the downward economic spiral which consists of the quest for maximization of profits leads towards the adherence of a truncated understanding of the human being, which in turn leads to lower long-term profitability, which management, in their continued quest for maximization of profits try to address via the "development" and use of further truncated notions of the human being, which, in turn, only exacerbate negative corporate performance. Breaking this negative dialectic involves: (1) having managerial studies develop and adopt an understanding and theory of the human being that embraces a "radical humanism"; and (2) adopting a conception of corporate governance that aims to serve mankind in lieu of exploiting it. The radical humanism referred to in this chapter considers the human being no longer solely through the eyes of profitability and man as an instrumental being, but through the lenses of more fundamental disciplines and human sciences (anthropology, psychoanalysis, biology, linguistics, etc.) which treat the human being for what he is, the entire him – the human being considered as a being of speech, of symbols, of senses, of society, of free will, and not just simply as a resource at the service of the company and of maximization of profit. As such, *the heart of the process of dehumanizing mankind within our current socio-economies and corporations is alienation through work.* The theory of alienating work is a solid management framework from which to start in order to restore a sense and meaning to work. It also permits an appropriation-commitment on the part of individual workers by eliminating the sources of estrangement related to the product, the act of work, nature, and the human being (both as self and the other). In order to truly attain a company that is a place of consensus, partnership, and trusting relationships, one must also *abolish wages, and replace them with the sharing of profits.* Embracing a radical humanism, as well as a governance that aims to serve man rather than exploit him, introduces a virtuous dialectic: the adoption of a fuller understanding and respect for man and nature leads to the production and subsequent sharing of profits, which in turn reinforces the respect and understanding of man and nature, leading to further profits and subsequent sharing for all.

References

Agayo, R. 1991. *Dr. Deming: The American Who Taught the Japanese about Quality.* New York: Simon and Schuster.

Albert, M. 1992. *Capitalism against Capitalism.* London: Whurr Publishing.

Archier, G. and Serieyx, H. 1987. *The Type 3 Company.* Aldershot: Gower Publishing Limited.

Atlan, H. 1972. "Du bruit comme principe d'auto-organisation," *Communications* 18: 21–37.

   1985. "Ordre et désordre dans les systèmes naturels," in A. Chanlat and M. Dufour (eds.), *La Rupture entre l'entreprise et les hommes.* Paris: Les Editions d'organisation, pp. 119–37.

Baechler, J. 1995. *Le capitalisme,* vol. I, *Les origines.* Paris: Gallimard.

Besançon, A. 1974. *L'histoire psychanalytique. Une anthologie.* Paris: Mouton.

Beynon, H. 1973. *Working for Ford.* London: Penguin Books.

Braverman. H. 1974. *Labor and Monopoly Capital.* New York: Monthly Review Press.

Caillé, A. 1989. *Critique de la raison utilitaire, manifeste du MAUSS.* Paris: La Découverte.

Chanlat, A. and Bédard, R. 1990. "La gestion, une affaire de parole," in J.-F. Chanlat (ed.), *L'individu dans l'organisation. Les dimensions oubliées.* Québec: Presses de l'Université Laval, pp. 79–99.

Chanlat, A. and Dufour, M. 1985. *La rupture entre l'entreprise et les hommes.* Montreal: Quebec-Amérique.

Chanlat, J.-F. (ed.). 1990. *L'individu dans l'organisation. Les dimensions oubliées*. Québec: Presses de l'Université Laval.

Chossudovsky, M. 2003. *The Globalization of Poverty* (second edition). Oro, ON: Global Outlook.

Clegg, S. R. 1975. *Power, Myth And Domination*. London: Routledge & Kegan Paul.

  1990. "Pouvoir symbolique, langage et organization," in J.-F. Chanlat (ed.), *L'individu dans l'organisation. Les dimensions oubliées*. Québec: Presses de l'Université Laval, pp. 663–81.

Crozier, M. 1989. *L'entreprise à l'écoute*. Paris: InterEditions.

Damasio, A. 1995. *Descartes' Error: Emotion, Reason and the Human Brain*. New York: Avon.

Deal, T. E. and Kennedy, A. 1982. *Corporate Culture: The Rites and Rituals of Corporate Life*. Reading, MA: Addison-Wesley.

Dejours, C. 1980. *Le travail, usure mentale*. Paris: Le Centurion.

  1990. "Nouveau regard sur la souffrance humaine dans les organizations," in J.-F. Chanlat (ed.), *L'individu dans l'organisation. Les dimensions oubliées*. Québec: Presses de l'Université Laval, pp. 687–708.

  1998. *Souffrance en France*. Paris: Editions du Seuil.

Deming, W. E. 1986. *Out of the Crisis*. Cambridge, MA: MIT CAES.

DePree, M. 1989. *Leadership Is an Art*. New York: Doubleday.

Deveureux, G. 1973. *Essais d'ethno-psychiatrie générale*. Paris: Gallimard.

Erikson, E. 1993. *Childhood and Society*. New York: W. W. Norton.

Etchegoyen, A. 1990. *Les entreprises ont-elles une âme?* Paris: Francois Bourrin.

Etzioni, A. 1989. *The Moral Dimension: Toward a New Economics*. New York: Free Press.

Evans-Pritchard, E. 1950. *Social Anthropology*. London: Cohen & West.

Fromm, E. 1961. *Marx's Concept of Man*. New York: Frederick Ungar.

Galbraith, J. K. 1987. *Economics in Perspective. A Critical History*. Boston: Hougton Miflin.

Gasparini, G. 1990. "Temps et Travail en Occident," in J.-F. Chanlat (ed.), *L'individu dans l'organisation. Les dimensions oubliées*. Québec: Presses de l'Université Laval, pp. 199–214.

Girin, J. 1982. "Langage en actes et organizations," *Économie et Societé: The ISMEA Proceedings on Management Sciences* 3(16): 1559–91.

  1990. "Problèmes de langage dans les organizations," in J.-F. Chanlat (ed.), *L'individu dans l'organisation. Les dimensions oubliées*. Québec: Presses de l'Université Laval, pp. 37–78.

Godelier, M. 1974. *Rationality and Irrationality in Economics*. New York: Monthly Review Press.

Hassard, J. 1988. *Time, Work and Organization*. London: Routledge & Kegan Paul.

1990. "Pour un paradigme ethnographique du temps de travail," in J.-F. Chanlat (ed.), *L'individu dans l'organisation. Les dimensions oubliées*. Québec: Presses de l'Université Laval, pp. 215–30.

Herzberg, F. 1980. "Humanities: Practical Management Education," *Industry Week* 206(7): 69–72.

Hirschman, A. O. 1997. *The Passions and the Interests*. Princeton, NJ: Princeton University Press.

Kamdem, E. 1990. "Temps et travail en Afrique," in J.-F. Chanlat (ed.), *L'individu dans l'organisation. Les dimensions oubliées*. Québec: Presses de l'Université Laval, pp. 231–55.

Kets de Vries, M. and Miller, D. 1984. *The Neurotic Organization*. San Francisco: Jossey-Bass.

Kołakowski, L. 1987. *Histoire du Marxisme*, vol. I. Paris: Fayard.

Laplantine, F. 1973. *Ethnopsychiatrie générale*. Paris: Psychothèque.

Levy, J.-P. 1997. *La fabrique de l'Homme*. Paris: Éditions Odile Jacob.

Liker, J. K. 2004. *The Toyota Way*. New York: McGraw-Hill.

Marcuse, H. 1964. *One Dimensional Man: Studies in the Ideology of Advanced Industrial Society*. New York: Beacon Press.

Maslow, A. 1954. *Motivation and Personality*. New York: Harper.

1969. "Toward Humanistic Biology," *American Psychologist* 24: 724–35.

Maturana, H. 1992. *Tree of Knowledge*. Boston: Shambhala.

Michel, S. 1989. *Peut-on gérer les motivations?* Paris: PUF.

Mintzberg, H. 1989. *Inside Our Strange World of Organisations*. New York: Free Press.

2005. *Managers not MBA's: A Hard Look at the Soft Practice of Managing and Management Development*. San Francisco: Berrett-Koehler Publishers.

Mitroff, I. and Pauchant, T. 1990. *We're So Big and Powerful Nothing Bad Can Happen to Us*. New York: Birch Lane Press.

Morgan, G. 1986. *Images of Organizations*. Beverly Hills, CA: Sage.

Monthoux, P. 1989. "The Moral Philosophy of Management." Unpublished manuscript, Stockholm University.

Morgan, G. 1986. *Images of Organizations*. Beverly Hills, CA: Sage.

Morin, E. 1993. *Terre-patrie*. Paris: Éditions du Seuil.

Olive, D. 1987. *Just Rewards: The Case of Ethical Reform in Business*. Toronto: Key Porter Books.

Orgogozo, I. and Serieyx, H. 1989. *Changer le Changement*. Paris: Seuil.

Ouchi, W. G. 1981. *Theory Z: How American Business Can Meet the Japanese Challenge*. Reading, MA: Addison-Wesley.

Packard, V. 1989. *The Ultra Rich: How Much Is Too Much?* London: Little Brown.

Pages, M., Bonetti, V., and de Gaulejac, V. 1984. *L'emprise de l'organisation* (third edition). Paris: PUF.

Pascale, R. 1990. *Managing on the Edge*. New York: Simon & Schuster.

1996. "Reflections on Honda," *California Management Review* 38(4): 112–17.

Perrow, C. 1979. "Organizational Theory in a Society of Organizations." Paper presented at the symposium "L'administration publique: Perspectives d'avenir Public," Quebec, May.

Peters, T. and Waterman, R. 1982. *In Search of Excellence*. New York: Harper & Row.

Peters, T. 1987. *Thriving on Chaos*. San Francisco: Knopf.

Peters, T. and Austin, N. 1985. *A Passion of Excellence*. New York: Random House.

Pfeffer, R. 1979. *Working for Capitalism*. New York: Columbia University Press.

Rifkin, J. 1980. *The Entropy Law: A New World View*. New York: Bantam Books.

Rosaldo, R. 1989. "Subjectivity in Social Analysis," in *Culture and Truth. The Remaking of Social Analysis*, Boston: Beacon Press, pp. 168–195.

Sainsaulieu, R. 1983. "La regulation culturelle des ensembles organisms," *L'année sociologique* 33: 195–217.

1987. "Développement social et création institutionnelle en enterprise," in D. Desjeux (ed.), *Organisation et management en question(s)*. Paris: L'Harmattan, pp. 203–21.

Sartre, J.-P. 1948. *Existentialism and Humanism*. London: Methuen.

1966. *Being and Nothingness*. New York: Washington Square Press.

1976. *Critique of Dialectical Reason*, vol. I. London: New Left Books.

Schein, E. 1991. "The Role of the Founder in the Creation of Organizational Culture," in P. Frost, L. Moore, M. Louise, C. Lundberg, and J. Martin (eds.), *Reframing Organizational Culture*. Newbury Park, CA: Sage, pp. 14–25.

1985. *Organizational Culture and Leadership*. San Francisco: Jossey-Bass.

Serieyx, H. 1989. *Le zéro mépris*. Paris: InterEditions.

Sievers, B. 1994. *Work, Life and Death Itself*. Berlin and New York: Walter de Gruyter.

1986a. "Beyond the Surrogate of Motivation," *Organization Studies* 7: 335–51.

1986b. "Participation as a Collusive Quarrel over Immortality," *The Journal of SCOS* 1(1): 72–82.

Solomon, R. C. and Hanson, K. R. 1985. *It's Good Business*. New York: Atheneum.

Terkel, D. 1972. *Working*. New York: Avon Books.

Turner, B. A. (ed.). 1990. *Organizational Symbolism*. Berlin and New York: Walter de Gruyter.

Varela, F. J. 1980. *Principles of Biological Autonomy*. New York: Elsevier North Holland.

Villette, M. 1988. *L'homme qui Croyait au Management*. Paris: Seuil.

Vincent, J. C. 1990. *Des Systèmes et des Hommes*. Paris: Les Editions d'organisation.

Waterman, R. 1987. *The Renewal Factor*. New York: Bantam.

Weitzman, M. 1984. *The Share Economy: Conquering Stagflation*. Cambridge, MA: Harvard University Press.

7 | Current trends in humanism and business

DOMÈNEC MELÉ

Introduction

Familiarity with current trends in a field is not only interesting as an aid to understanding our world or as a form of erudition, but also helps to guide speculation about the future. Extrapolating a future based on current trends is often better than prophesying without considering the evidence at hand and the main historical drivers of the present. This is the case for all human activity and, more specifically, for humanism in business.

"Humanism," wrote Jacques Maritain (1996), "essentially tends to make man more humane and to manifest his original greatness by making him participate in everything in so far as it enriches him in nature and in history. It requires time that man develops virtues which he possesses, his creative strength and his rational life, and that man works to convert the forces of the physical world into tools of his freedom." These words contain provocative ideas, which lead us to question to what extent business and humanism cross paths. In this respect, some questions arise: Does business respect the sovereign human rights of people? Do business institutions or companies make the people who participate in them more human? Does business give people the possibility to participate in organizations in accordance with their humanity? Does business foster the growth of individuals as human beings? Does business favor aspects of human potential such as creativity, rationality, and character? Do companies contribute to creating an appropriate culture where people can exercise freedom, with a sense of responsibility and the awareness of making a real contribution to human well-being?

We can observe two mainstream tendencies in business, one humanistic, in which persons come first, and another, which can be called "economistic." In the latter priority is given to economic results, subordinating human dignity, rights, and growth to this end. While in the humanistic approach persons are central, in the economistic people become a mere part of the production or distribution processes, without full respect for their rationality, freedom, and capacity to grow as human beings.

The structure of this chapter is as follows: First, it presents the main tendencies in humanism and also in anti-humanism at the beginning of the twenty-first century. Second, it reviews how these two approaches – humanism and economism – are already present in the first stages of modern management. Third, it discusses some positive tendencies in favor of humanism in business, which are contrasted with some economistic views and practices still current in many businesses.

Humanism and anti-humanism at the beginning of the twenty-first century

At the beginning of the twenty-first century several quite diverse tendencies can be found in humanism itself. However, two streams of thought put forth specifically humanistic and anti-humanistic positions. Among the latter, there are those who are skeptical about or even clearly opposed to humanism, while others demand a renewed humanism. Among the former, there are some who feel disappointed with the results of certain notorious "humanisms" in the past, which were very influential, such as those associated with Marxism. More thoughtful is what is called *post-humanism*, a stream of thought whose proponents are relatively negative about humanism. One source of this tendency was structuralism, a school of thought developed in the second half of the twentieth century, which included thinkers as Claude Lévi-Strauss, Michel Foucault, Louis Althusser, and the psychoanalyst Jacques Lacan. Structuralism, in brief, was a movement that attempted to remove from the human subject his or her celebrated capacities of freedom, self-determination, self-transcendence, and creativity, substituting for them deep and unconscious structures, which are omnipresent and omnideterminant. The above-mentioned thinkers did not conceive of structuralism as a mere heuristic principle, or as only a method to categorize reality, or discover structures and sets of laws by which anthropological, economic, historical, and psychological phenomena are ruled. They went further and developed theories of human history which conceive of the human being as a free subject, conscious, self-determining, responsible, and creative. In this schema, individuals are no more than effects of the structure and a subject is a mere holder of production relationships. As far as structuralism is concerned, "man is dead," and, consequently, defending humanism makes no sense (Reale and Antiseri 1992: chapter 34).

Structuralism has been much criticized for its emphasis on deterministic structural forces rather than the efficacy of individual initiative. Structuralism is no longer lauded in the same manner as it was in the 1970s. However, another stream of thought against humanism has emerged from some ecologist ideologies, particularly from "deep ecology." This ideology maintains that the uncritical acceptance of anthropocentric values has abetted reprehensible practices with respect to the nonhuman world. Instead of considering the dignity and centrality of human beings in the world, this ideology sees humanity as one among many natural species. Although many agree that this is reprehensible, being a particularly short-term and narrow conception of human interests and concerns, this does not mean that we should reject anthropocentrism. Perhaps the challenge is to develop an enriched, fortified anthropocentric notion of human interest to replace the dominant short-term, sectional, and self-regarding conception (Grey 1993).

In recent years, another strong attack on humanism has come from Peter Singer (1994, 1996), a controversial moral philosopher. Basing his arguments on utilitarianism, Singer has proposed a model of ethics rooted in *quality of life* rather than in *identity*. What is of primary importance for him is not the *existence* of the being, but their *quality of life*. This approach leads to a process of dehumanization, which is clearly in opposition to the Judeo-Christian notion of sanctity of human life (Precee 2002) and to any other humanism which respects human life as an absolute.

Apart from these anti-humanistic positions, two main approaches, with some similarities and differences, can be distinguished in humanism at the turn of the twenty-first century: secular humanism and theistic humanism. The former is basically human-centered, and explicitly dissociated from any religious faith. The latter is also human-centered but complements rationality with faith. Since the Renaissance, some humanists have been trying to emphasize humans by moving away from God, while others found the greater guarantee of human dignity in God. Some secular humanisms have adopted an anti-religious position, while many others are not inherently anti-religious, except toward religions which deny human worth and dignity.[1]

Secular humanism rejects any reference beyond man himself. It is based on Protagoras' famous claim that "man is the measure of all things." In the words of the Humanist Manifesto III of 2003, (secular) humanism "affirms our ability and responsibility to lead ethical lives of personal fulfillment that aspire to the greater good of humanity." This breed of humanism presents itself as "guided by reason, inspired by compassion, and informed by experience" and "encourages us to live life well and fully."[2]

Secular humanism, an outgrowth of eighteenth-century enlightenment rationalism and nineteenth-century free thought, is centered on human interests or values, and stresses an individual's dignity and worth and capacity for self-realization through reason. Frequently, secular humanism has been presented as an alternative to religion and equally frequently it has been identified with atheism or agnosticism. Jean-Paul Sartre is one of the best-known philosophers to defend an atheistic humanism based on his particular existentialist philosophy. From a practical perspective, secular humanism has often been an attempt to function as a civilized society with the exclusion of God and of any moral principles derived from God.

In contrast, religious humanism finds the deeper roots of human worth and dignity in God (or in some divine transcendence). In some religious traditions, particularly in Christianity, reason and faith cannot be in contradiction. The question was posited no later than the thirteenth century, when Thomas Aquinas, in disagreement with Averroes, stated that there is no place for two truths. However, Aquinas added that there is a double order or horizon of truth. The first is achievable for human reason, either through scientific or philosophic method, the second exceeds it infinitely and is known through trust.

---

[1] Taken from "Definitions from *Webster's Ninth New Collegiate Dictionary.*" home.att.net/~tangents/data/rlgdef.htm (accessed November 29, 2006).

[2] Humanist Manifesto (Humanism and Its Aspirations). www.americanhumanist.org/3/HumandItsAspirations.htm (accessed November 29, 2006).

In the Judeo-Christian tradition there is a strong sense of human dignity and an essential equality among all human beings, since they are in the image and likeness of God, as is pointed out in the earliest pages of the Bible (Gen. 1:27). A number of thinkers in this tradition, including Søren Kierkegaard, Gabriel Marcel, Jacques Maritain, Martin Buber, and many others, have developed schools of thought on transcendent humanism. Recently, the Catholic Church, which has encouraged humanism for centuries, has published a *Compendium* of social doctrine (2004), in which "an integral and solidary humanism" is presented as crucial (paragraph 9). It is also said that this humanism is "capable of creating a new social, economic and political order, founded on the dignity and freedom of every human person, to be brought about in peace, justice and solidarity" (paragraph 19).[3]

In some respects secular and theistic humanism are quite different, but there are also some common points. For instance, in defending human dignity and human rights, both visions try to promote fulfillment, growth, and creativity for the individual and humankind in general. Although they frame human fulfillment in different ways, both views share a common concern for humanity. Humanism in business requires dealing with respect with every employee, fostering an ethical climate, and endeavoring to provide working conditions, which would favor, as much as possible, the psychological and physical well-being of employees.

Pope John Paul II particularly stressed humanism in business in the context of work. He condemns what he called "*the error of economism*, that of considering human labor solely according to its economic purpose. This fundamental error of thought," – he adds – "can and must be called *an error of materialism*; in that economism directly or indirectly includes a conviction of the primacy and superiority of the material, and directly or indirectly places the spiritual and the personal (man's activity, moral values and such matters) in a position of subordination to material reality." Consequently, the pope stressed the primacy of the worker over the working process, including instruments and conditions, because "we cannot assert that it (the

---

[3] "Compendium of the Social Doctrine of the Church." www.vatican.va/roman_curia/pontifical_councils/justpeace/documents/rc_pc_justpeace_doc_20060526_compendio-dott-socc_en.html (accessed June 4, 2008).

working process) constitutes as it were an impersonal 'subject' *putting man and man's work into a position of dependence"* (paragraph 13).[4]

Humanism and business: where we come from?

For quite some time the well-known expression "business is business" has enjoyed wide-spread acceptance, meaning that business put aside whatever ethical or humanistic consideration. In this way, it was emphasizing that profits – or maximizing the shareholder value – is the supreme end of the company and any other consideration, including humanism has to be subordinated to this goal. This mentality has not been completely overcome and we still come across it in many places and situations. But is it in fact a fallacy? Is it not possible to harmonize humanism with the production and distribution of economic goods that comes with the mission of increasing shareholder value? Is there any relationship between humanism and business?

Before Frederick W. Taylor wrote his influential book *Scientific Management* in 1911, the organization of factories and workshops was left in the hands of workers, leading to low productivity. Taylor's proposal was to substitute the experience and intuition of workers for an accurate analysis of manual activities and the subsequent planning of every operation with economy of movements. The main role of management was to prepare the workers' activity, including a detailed description of every task. In this way, management was understood as a "technical task," while workers were mere executors.

The positive side of this rationalization of work was that it brought about a substantial increase of productivity and, consequently, an appreciable rise in both profits and wages. Yield was even higher when later Henry Ford and the engineers in his car factories implemented the assembly line. Apparently, everybody had to be happy by applying these production methods with such economic rewards. However, *rationalization of work* had a dark side as well. Very soon, complaints against scientific management started to emerge. Workers and unions claimed that this kind of organization lead to a monotonous repetition of tasks during the whole day and the whole week,

---

[4] "Pope John Paul II: Encyclical on Human Work, promulgated 14 September 1981." www.ewtn.com/library/ ENCYC/JP2LABOR.HTM (accessed June 4, 2008).

and this produced boredom, stress, dissatisfaction, reduction of morale, absenteeism, and a greater risk of repetitive strain injuries. Beyond these problems, one can discover a strong "humanistic problem": "scientific management," while it increases productivity, leads to understanding management as simply a technique, lacking in any human consideration, apart from human capability to perform certain mechanical activities again and again.

In 1922, Henry Ford tried to justify his approach not only in terms of productivity but also for human reasons. In his own words: "The average worker wants a job in which he does not have to put much physical effort. Above all, he wants a job in which he does not have to think" (quoted in Carroll 1973: 41). Maybe some workers preferred this type of work to one which required more physical and mental effort. It is even possible that some workers may prefer routine jobs because they fit well with their capabilities and degree of education. But it is doubtful that this approach is the most appropriate for every worker. Ford was a genius responsible for many innovative developments in the car industry, but he will not be remembered for his humanistic vision of business. Taylorism and Fordism understood management as a mere technical function and its exercise as "giving order" to and control of worker performance. Their visions tend to reduce human beings to a sort of mechanism to move the whole productive machinery. Individual personality, personal talents, human relations, personal motivations (except the economic ones), and personal satisfaction are deemed irrelevant in these models.

However, while Taylorism obtained great success, in the second and third decade of the twentieth century Mary Parket Follet presented a more humanistic approach. Her concept of management differed substantially from Taylor's and from that of most of her contemporaries. In contrast to Taylor, Follett (1940, 1987, 1995) had no interest in the amount of energy expended or in the breaks that should be taken by the workers to avoid becoming too tired. Her interest was in how to get people to cooperate. Similarly, Chestor I. Barnard, another pioneer in management thought, insisted on cooperation as well. The centrality of persons in business and, above all, the necessity of knowing the human beings appeared especially clear to Barnard. "I have found it impossible," he wrote, "to go far in the study of organizations or of behavior of people in relation to them without being confronted with a few questions which can be simply stated. For example: 'What is an individual?' 'What is a person?' 'To what extent do people have power of choice or free will?' " (1968/1938: 8).

Soon, Elton Mayo (1933, 1946) stressed the importance of human behavior in organizations, and Abraham Maslow (1954) proposed the importance of human needs and motivations in behavior, which can be considered a certain humanistic approach, although limited. Mayo's tradition was followed, with significant contributions by McGregor (1960), Herzberg (1959, 1976) and Argyris (1957) among others. They stress the importance of developing a meaningful job, decentralization of power in organizations, and giving opportunities to workers for decision-making. They held that this humanistic approach would lead to more efficient organizations.

It could be questioned whether this first wave of humanism in business was actually humanism or a masked form of economism. Obviously, it depends on the intentionality. But we must not forget that business needs to make profits, and there is nothing wrong in considering how dealing with people in a more humane way can contribute, in certain conditions, to increased performance.

Humanistic tendencies in business

In the current business situation one can appreciate light and shadow in the consideration of persons within organizations. On one hand, the economistic view persists in a great variety of aspects in business life, but on the other, a humanistic tendency with old roots is also emerging in business and management. Let me review some of these aspects, emphasizing the humanistic tendencies.

A first point is the current emphasis on the "person–organization fit." We can start by going back to the Taylorist and Fordist approaches. In order to solve the problems of work monotony, it was proposed that innovations in job design be introduced. Among them were *job rotation*, a systematic shifting of employees from one job to another; *job enlargement*, in which the assignments to each worker are expanded to include additional or similar tasks; and *job enrichment*, in which there is variety in tasks assigned to employees and some responsibility for, and control over, their jobs. In essence, it was a matter of new techniques to solve the problems created by techniques. Such techniques were more humanistic, since the human condition is given fuller consideration than in Taylorism and Fordism, but in applying these techniques, management is still seen as a technical profession. However, the concept of "job enrichment" has opened the door to a wider consideration of persons and also to a better understanding of the richness and complexity of human nature and the uniqueness of each person. Thus, in "job redesign," which can be included within "job enrichment," work is restructured in ways that the employee skills, character, and attitudes fit with the needs of the organization. Cultivating a worker–job match can include combining tasks, forming work groups, or establishing closer customer association. In practice, it happens that while some workers are motivated by having a challenging job, taking more responsibility, dealing directly with clients, and therefore obtaining more rewards, others may prefer more specific and repetitive work. This latter can be the result of a lack of appropriate skills or character, or is perhaps due to lack of confidence, fear of failure, or distrust of management's intentions.

Today, the trend is to pay attention to "person–organization fit," which refers to a match in needs, desires, or preferences between employee and employer (organization) (Kristof 1996). A great challenge for many companies is to attract talented employees; their main concern is how to get the best employees. In this line of thought, it is argued that potential employees are going to be more attracted to companies if the individuals believe their own personal characteristics are aligned with organizational attributes (Cable and Judge 1994; Chatman 1989; Judge and Bretz 1992).

Both "job redesign" and concern for "person–organization fit", or person–environment fit – another, related concept – underline respect for the individual and the idea that every person is different and should be treated in accordance with his or her qualities and personality.

In contrast, in some countries, businesses are far from considering worker individuality and adapting the person to the organization. What is more, there are places and countries where the work is extremely repetitive, wages are inadequate, the hours too long, and the working conditions endanger safety or health. These "sweatshops," although they have almost disappeared in developed countries; still

exist in some developing countries. Sweatshops have received much
criticism around the world because of their inhumane conditions.
However, some economists argue in favor of sweatshops. This is
the case with Jeffery D. Sachs and Paul Krugman (1997) who, in the
New York Times, stated that Third World countries need more
sweatshops to relieve their poverty. One wonders whether it is not
possible to find other ways to overcome poverty in which human
dignity is respected. Sweatshops, rather than being a way to solve the
poverty problem, are an abuse of the situation of extreme necessity of
poor people.

A second tendency in management is to give an increased importance to people's involvement in organizations. In the Taylorist
approach, management is based on "giving orders." Managers have a
real power over workers, while these latter become mere executors of
managerial orders. Addressing this position, Mary Parker Follett
reacted by claiming that it was right for workers to resist management
having power over them, and also for employers to resist union efforts
to invert the situation and get power over them. She proposed changing "power over" for "power with." The distinction was humanistic,
as Follett herself explained with an example: "you have rights *over* a
slave; you have rights *with* a servant" (Follett 1940: 101). In addition,
she suggested that power over is not effective, because people resist,
do not want to be led, and do not want to be patronized (Follett
1940: 103).

Since that time, many other authors have insisted on participative
management and putting people first and trying to make sure that
people become more and more involved in business organizations.
Results obtained are much more satisfactory than using the old way of
"giving orders." Pfeffer and Veiga (1999) pointed out at the turn of
the twenty-first century: "Over the past decade or so, numerous
studies conducted both within specific industries and samples of
organizations that cross industries have demonstrated the enormous
economic returns obtained through the implementation of what
are variously called high involvement, high performance, or high
commitment management practices" (37). However, these scholars
immediately added something surprising: "trends in actual management practice are, in many instances, moving in a direction exactly
opposite to what this growing body of evidence prescribes" (37).
Some plain facts are evident to everybody: brutal downsizing,

delocalization of plants with scant consideration for the laid-off employees, and similar practices. Fortunately, this is not the case for many businesses, which not only consider people, but also try to involve them in managing business and try to foster the development of their creativity and willingness.

A third humanistic tendency is the consideration of business as a community of persons, contrasting with the vision of organizations only as dehumanized mechanisms, without any goal other than to enrich their owners. Companies are considered as a set of contracts, and nothing else. This is a premise assumed by some popular economic theories such as agency theory (Jensen and Meckling 1976) and transaction cost theory (Williamson 1975). In this economistic vision, people are presented as subjects with interests and preferences by which they make contracts.

Ordinary language also refers to the company as an object owned by shareholders. In mergers and acquisitions, companies are said to have been bought or sold. But companies are not a thing like a piece of land or a car. Companies are not only an amount of capital but, above all, they are human realities. Charles Handy has criticized the current language of business on this point. "The language of property and ownership no longer works as well as it should in modern society", he stated. The explanation is that "the idea of a corporation as the property of the current holders of its shares is confusing because it does not make clear where power lies." Speaking in these terms is inappropriate not only because some of the facts have changed, but also for ethical reasons: "It is an affront to natural justice in that it gives inadequate recognition to the people who work in the corporation and who are, increasingly, its principal assets. It might even be considered immoral for people to talk of owning other people, as shareholders implicitly do" (1999: 50).

The humanistic view is that companies are much more than mechanisms for profits and a mere set of contracts. Because humans have capacity for friendly and cooperative relationships it is limiting to conceive of their interaction as strictly contractual. As Solomon has written, what defines the organization "are relationships between people, whether of affection, friendship, loyalty, power, position or expertise," and "social contract theory only muddles this picture because it suggests, almost always falsely, that the primary relationship involved are predominantly contractual. This is a sure way to misunderstand that corporations are communities" (1994: 274). Individuals, with their personalities, interests, and personal goals, do not disappear within a corporation. However, business is not only a collection of self-interested individuals. "To see business as a social activity is to see it as a practice that both thrives on competition and presupposes a coherent community of mutually concerned as well as self-interested citizens" (Solomon 1992: 146).

Understanding business as a community of persons provides an explanation of organizational phenomena such as shared knowledge. The structure and quality of relationships within the firm is likely to be highly influential in creating and exchanging knowledge (Hansen 1999; Uzzi 1996). Through membership in a social community, including a business firm, identification with a community is developed; this identification process changes the character and quality of human behavior of its members (Kogut and Zander 1995). Another perspective which leads to understanding organizations and firms as communities comes from social capital theory, which assumes the existence of communities. Social capital theory provides a sound basis for explaining why organizations gain advantage by creating intellectual capital, and this could become a firm's most enduring source of competitive advantage (Moran 2005; Nahapiet and Ghoshal 1998).

A fourth humanistic tendency is in introducing values and ethics into corporations and what is called *values-based management*. In this latter approach, some values are introduced into the organization through the mission statement and subsequently into corporate plans and business plans.

Many companies now present a corporate values statement, although not many are seriously committed to a management by values. On the contrary, one can frequently notice attitudes which lack attention to moral judgments in making decisions. As Anderson points out, "despite discussion in the popular and academic press, the connection between value judgments and economic success is still unclear in the minds of many executives" (1997: 25); businesses are still managed according to the supreme criterion of maximizing value for the shareholders.

The humanistic approach emphasizes managing not along the lines of (economic) value but of (ethical and operative) values. This tendency can be traced back, at least, to C. Barnard, who published his influential book *The Functions of the Executive* in 1938. He wrote that effective managers "inspire cooperative personal decisions by creating faith: faith in common understanding, faith in the probability of success, faith in the ultimate satisfaction of personal motives, and faith in the integrity of objective authority, faith in the superiority of a common purpose as a personal aim of those who partake in it" (1968/ 1938: 259). Since then others have insisted on the necessity of managing by values (Anderson 1997; Blanchard and O'Connor 1996; and McCoy 1985, among others).

Related to values and business ethics is corporate social responsibility, which has been a major new emphasis in business worldwide. Many companies have institutionalized ethics through normative means, including: ethical codes, ethical offices, and ethical training. Such practices have been implemented by businesses of all sizes.

Leadership based on values or moral leadership has been also emphasized in recent decades. Burns (1978), in advancing the concept of transformational leadership, stresses that leaders have to inspire a sense of common purpose based on values. Several other authors have emphasized the importance of values for leadership. That is the case with Greenleaf (1977), who stressed the value of service for leadership; Ciulla (2004), who talks about ethics as the heart of leadership; Sison (2003), who pays special attention to the virtues of leaders and the moral capital which those habits confer, and many others.

A fifth tendency favorable to humanism is the increasing importance of personal competences, and particularly character, including the consideration of virtues and practical wisdom in management. This point is again in strong contrast to the Tayloristic view of management. In this, managers are basically technicians, that is to say, experts in organizing work scientifically. Now probably very few would accept this narrow view. However, there are more sophisticated approaches in which the character of managers is spurned. One is a certain "scientificism," which rejects everything, which cannot be measured as a source of knowledge. In this line of thought the paramount importance of social sciences, especially economics, in management is emphasized. As a consequence, it is held that managers basically have to acquire technical skills and analytical competences, while managers' character is seen as quite irrelevant.

The importance of personal virtues and putting people first has been highlighted by Collin (2001), studying companies which have gone from good to great, and the character and style of their leaders. Good-to-great leaders possessed a combination of personal humility and professional will. While one can expect that these kinds of leaders start with vision and strategy, actually they attended to people first, strategy second.

Conclusion

At the beginning of the twenty-first century, humanism is alive, in spite of some well-known streams of humanism, including those deriving from Comte, Marx, and Nietzsche (Lubac 1995) and some anti-humanistic visions derived from certain ecologistic ideologies. Two mainstreams of humanism are emerging, one secular and another religious, with some divergences but also with several convergent points.

Humanism is present in business and management. From their inception both business and management have evolved without humanistic principles, but with a strong economistic view. From the very beginning some voices have been heard demanding a greater consideration for people, both for the sake of human welfare and also because a humanistic approach can contribute to a better business or organizational performance.

Some encouraging trends can be noted in business and management, which show a certain movement towards more humanistic positions, and although it is happening slowly in many cases, some changes can be seen:

1. from rigid job designs and organizational structures to person–organization fit structures, although certainly some sweatshops still persist in too many places;
2. from organizations in which each person is just a cog of the business machine to organizations in which people are put first, with a greater degree of involvement, commitment, and participation;
3. from seeing firms as a set of contracts to considering the business as a community of people;
4. from a management aligned to maximization of shareholder value to management by values.

References

Adler, P.S. and Kwon, S. 2002. "Social Capital: Prospects for a New Concept," *Academy of Management Review* 27(1): 17–40.

Anderson, C. 1997. "Values-based Management," *Academy of Management Executive* 11(4): 25–46.

Argyris, C. 1957. *Personality and Organization. The Conflict between System and Individual.* New York: Harper.

Barnard, C. 1968/1938. *The Functions of the Executive.* London: Oxford University Press.

Blanchard, K. and O'Connor, M. 1996. *Managing by Values.* San Francisco: Berrett-Koehler.

Burns, J.G. 1978. *Leadership.* New York: Harper & Row.

Cable, D.M. and Judge, T.A. 1994. "Pay Preferences and Job Search Decisions: A Person-Organization Perspective," *Personnel Psychology* 47(2): 317–48.

Carroll, Swart J. 1973. "The Worth of Humanistic Management. Some Contemporary Examples," *Business Horizons* (June): 41–50.

Chatman, J.A. 1989. "Improving Interactional Organizational Research: A Model of Person-Organization Fit," *Academy of Management Review* 14(1): 333–49.

Cicerón. 1950. *El sueño de Escisión* [Scipio's Dream]. Madrid: Instituto A. Nebrija.

Ciulla, J. 1998. *Ethics, the Heart of Leadership.* London: Quorum Books.

Collins, J. 2001. *Good to Great: Why Some Companies Make the Leap and Others Don't.* New York: HarperCollins.

Collins, J. and Porras J. 1994. *Built to Last.* New York: Harper Business.

Follett, M.P. 1940. "Dynamic Administration," in H. Metcalf and L. Urwick (eds.), *The Collected Papers of Mary Parker Follett.* New York and London: Harper & Brothers.

1987. *Lectures in Business Organization.* New York and London: Longmans, Green and Co.

1995. *Prophet of Management.* Boston: Harvard Business School Press Classic.

Greenleaf, R.K. 1977. *Servant Leadership. A Journey into the Nature of Legitimate Power and Greatness.* Mahwah, NY: Paulist Press.

Grey, W. 1993. "Anthropocentrism and Deep Ecology," *Australasian Journal of Philosophy* 71(4): 463–75.

Hansen, M.T. 1999. "The Search-Transfer Problem: The Role of Weak Ties in Sharing Knowledge across Organization Subunits," *Administrative Science Quarterly* 44(1): 82–111.

Herrmann, P. 2005. "Evolution of Strategic Management: The Need for New Dominant Designs," *International Journal of Management Reviews* 7(2): 111–30.

Herzberg, F. 1959. *The Motivation to Work.* New York: Wiley & Sons.

1976. *The Managerial Choice: To Be Efficient and to Be Human.* Homewood: Dow Jones-Irwin.

Judge, T. A. and Bretz Jr., R. D. 1992. "Effects of Work Values on Job Choice Decisions," *Journal of Applied Psychology* 77(3): 261–71.

Kogut, B. and Zander, U. 1995. "Knowledge, market failure and the multinational enterprise: A reply," *Journal of International Business Studies* 26(2): 417–26.

Kristof, A. L. 1996. "Person-Organization Fit: An Integrative Review of Its Conceptualizations, Measurement, and Implications," *Personnel Psychology* 49(1): 1–49.

Maritain, J. and Bird, O. A. (eds.). 1996. *Integral Humanism. Freedom in the Modern World and a Letter on Independence.* Notre Dame: University of Notre Dame Press.

Maslow, A. H. 1954. *Motivation and Personality* (second edition). New York: Harper & Brothers.

Mayo, E. 1933. *The Human Problems of an Industrial Civilization.* New York: Macmillan.

1946. *The Social Problems of an Industrial Civilization.* Cambridge: Cambridge University Press.

McCoy, C. 1985. *Management by Values: The Ethical Difference on Corporate Policy and Performance.* Marchfield: Pitman.

McGregor, D. V. 1960. *The Human Side of Enterprise.* New York: McGraw-Hill.

Moran, P. 2005. "Structural vs. Relational Embeddedness: Social Capital and Managerial Performance," *Strategic Management Journal* 26(12): 1129–51.

Nahapiet, J. and Ghoshal S. 1998. "Social Capital, Intellectual Capital, and the Organizational Advantage," *Academy of Management Review* 23(2): 242–66.

Pfeffer, J. and Veiga J. F. 1999. "Putting People First for Organizational Success," *Academy of Management Executive* 13(2): 37–48.

Preece, G. R. (ed.) 2002. *Rethinking Peter Singer: A Christian Critique.* Downser Grove: InterVarsity Press.

Reale, G. and Antiseri, D. 1992. *Historia del Pensamiento Filosófico y Científico III. Del romanticismo hasta hoy.* Barcelona: Herder.

Sachs, J. D. and Krugman P. 1997. "Just What We Need – More Sweat Shops," *The New York Times, Dollars & Sense* 213: 4.

Singer, P. 1994. *Rethinking Life and Death: The Collapse of Our Traditional Ethics*. New York: St. Martin's Press.
   1999. *Practical Ethics* (second edition). Cambridge: Cambridge University Press.
Sison, A. J. G. 2003. *The Moral Capital of Leaders. Why Virtue Matters*. Cheltenham: Edward Elgar.
Solomon, C. R. 1992. *Ethics and Excellence: Cooperation and Integrity in Business*. New York: Oxford University Press.
   1994. *The New Word of Business. Ethics and Free Enterprise in the Global 1990s*. Lanham: Roman and Littlefield.
Taylor, F. W. 1911. *The Principles of Scientific Management*. New York: Harper.
Uzzi, B. 1996. "The Sources and Consequences of Embeddedness for the Economic Performance of Organizations: The Network Effects," *American Sociological Review* 61(4): 674–98.

PART 2

Towards an integration of humanism and business on a systems level

8 | Towards a civilized market economy: economic citizenship rights and responsibilities in service of a humane society

PETER ULRICH

A change of perspective: "It's not the economy, stupid – it's society!"

Everybody remembers Bill Clinton's slogan during his successful 1992 presidential campaign, "It's the economy, stupid!" My premise is that today this motto needs slight modernization. An up-to-date version would be: "It's *not* the economy, stupid – it's society!"

What is my point? We need to learn to make a clear distinction between economy and society and relate them in a sensible way, instead of confusing the two, as is common practice in neoliberal thinking, with its standard recipe for nearly all socio-economic problems: more market and more competition. The economic logic of competitive markets, productivity, and growth cannot be the whole answer to our societal problems, since these problems are simply a part of the success story of economic "liberalization" and "rationalization." Is it not the inherent *purpose* of that kind of development to set humans "free" from their workplaces in order to increase labor productivity and economic growth?

One of the core problems today could be that the social organization of our national economies – and of the developing transnational economy – lags behind their steadily rising productivity. What is increasingly needed is an overall reassessment and redesign of the *societal* relationships between all involved; this could be a prerequisite for an *economic* development that makes sense with regard to our quality of life. After all, economic activities are not an end in themselves but only a *means* to "the good life" and the just coexistence of humans in society. The confusion of ends and means also brings about

143

a symptomatic confusion of problems and solutions. Precarious labor market conditions are a *humane problem* for a growing share of the population (jobs near or even beneath the minimum living wage, or even getting a "red card" and being eliminated from the labor market). Nevertheless, this problem is usually alleged to be a necessary part of the *systemic solution* (whose solution?) to what is considered "economic progress": economic growth. While growth may be qualitative, in the sense of sustainability, it primarily has to be quantitative. Moreover, mainstream economic policy is interested in the development of the gross national product but not in its distribution, because its normative background is rooted in a utilitarian calculus that presumes a precedence of the collective aggregate over individual claims. Obviously, this kind of economic "rationalization" does not include *economic reason* as a whole. Conventional "pure" economic rationality runs the risk of conflicting with the basic *ethical rationality* of a well-ordered society of free and equal citizens.

A brief critique of (not quite) pure economic rationality

One of the core axiomatic elements of the neoclassical concept of economic rationality is that economic agents are strictly concerned with maximizing their own advantage and are mutually unconcerned. No moral obligation influences their interactions. The clever, but one-dimensional, homunculus who corresponds to this narrow rationality is called *homo oeconomicus*. Pure economics develops nothing but the general logic of the success-oriented rational action of individuals only "busy" with the pursuit of their own interests, even in their social relationships beyond the marketplace. Every kind of human interaction and cooperation can be interpreted under the *normative logic of mutual advantage*. Therefore, pure economics conceives itself as a systematic rationalization perspective for all areas of life and action (economic imperialism).

Modern philosophical ethics develops a completely different *normative logic of human interaction* as its specific idea of practical reason or ethical rationality (Ulrich 2003, 2008: 13ff.). This idea of ethical rationality develops nothing but the humane grammar of interpersonal relations. Benefit-oriented *conditional* interaction and cooperation between agents have an economic perspective. Conversely, deontological ethics, or moral philosophy, is exclusively

Economic rationality: normative logic of mutual advantage	Ethical reason: normative logic of human interaction
Power-based (what can be asserted is what counts)	Justice-based (what is legitimate is what counts)
Interest in maximization of private success	Intersubjective moral obligations
Benefit-oriented *conditional* cooperation between self-interested, mutually unconcerned individuals	*Unconditional* reciprocal respect and recognition of human beings as persons of equal dignity
Market principle	Moral principle

Figure 8.1 Ethical reason vs. economic rationality

concerned with the substantiation of interpersonal obligations associated with the *unconditional* mutual recognition of persons as beings of equal dignity and the resulting reciprocal moral rights and duties: "An attitude which is not integrated in the intersubjective structure of moral demands is not moral at all" (Tugendhat 1994: 64).

Not surprisingly, there is a considerable difference between economic rationality and the ethical idea of reason (Figure 8.1). In the first case, the "given" interests of the individuals already form what is regarded as a sufficient proviso for a rational "balancing of interests" among the participants. In the second case, however, those interests are merely the object of an ethical-critical examination from the viewpoint of their legitimacy under the terms of the moral rights of everyone affected and the protection of those rights. In short, economic rationality is power-based while ethical reason is justice-based. At best, "efficient" market exchange reproduces the "given" power relations.[1] The market principle of the mutual exchange of benefits can therefore in no way be equated with the moral principle. Instead, the primacy of (political) ethics over market logic is the fundamental economic-ethical principle.

A comprehensive concept of economic reason will include the *legitimacy proviso*, i.e. the categorical subordination of private benefit or profit seeking to the normative precondition of societal legitimacy.

[1] For this fundamental criticism, see Ulrich 2008: 166 ff.

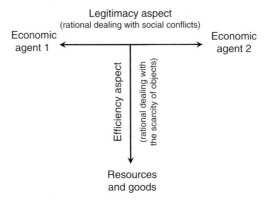

Figure 8.2 The two-dimensional concept of socio-economic rationality

This means that reasonable economic agents will not separate their private business ends from their self-understanding as good citizens. They want or should want to realize only those private benefits that they perceive as justifiable in respect of those concerned. The corresponding regulative *integrative idea of socio-economic rationality* can be defined as follows: Any action or institution is socio-economically rational which free and mature citizens can – through deliberation between all concerned – consensually justify as a legitimate way of creating value. This integrative idea of reasonable economic activity is the "civilized" perspective of (upright) citizens who regard themselves as persons of *integrity* (as we will see in the next section). Figure 8.2 symbolizes this ethically integrated or "embedded" idea of socio-economic rationality, which includes the precedence of legitimacy over efficiency.

The horizontal dimension of this T-model of integrative economic rationality represents the essential problem of a rational *societal* order of free and equal citizens, whereas the vertical dimension represents the "pure" *economic* rationality (or efficiency) of "free markets." The first dimension of socio-economic rationality has systematic priority, because the good life and just coexistence of free citizens is an end in itself. However, as we have already seen, the efficient use of scarce resources and goods is only a means. There is no "efficiency" as such – we have to determine *for whom*, and *in regard to which of his/her life plans*, something is to be used efficiently. A self-determined life script is not only the constitutive moment of free citizenship; it is also an indispensable moment of any rational economic activity.

Thus, free citizenship is a universal precondition of a fair market economy, as well as the guiding principle of modern civil society. As a logical consequence, we have to plead for a two-level concept of liberalism: free citizens take priority over "free" markets. Therefore, *market liberalism* has to be embedded into a political or, more precisely, a *republican* concept of *liberalism*: its focus is on the *res publica* of the equal freedom and fair coexistence of all citizens.

The republican spirit of true liberalism and the business ethos of responsible citizens

Properly understood, freedom is, of course, not "natural liberty" (as usually seen by libertarians) but politically constituted freedom – constituted by a universal set of inviolable civic rights laid down in the constitution of a free and democratic society and supported by citizens who have a corresponding civic mind. This is the basic insight of political liberalism according to John Rawls (1993). Its core is certainly the idea of the constitutional role of strong and equal civic rights as the central mode of social integration. In contrast, neoliberal doctrine regards the mutual exchange of advantages in the market as the central mode of social order, and the communitarians assume that the community spirit, i.e. the shared values of a specific cultural tradition, fulfills this constitutive role. While this is not the place for a thorough critique of these two pseudo-alternatives (see Ulrich 2008: 276ff.), political liberalism appears to be the best option.

The Rawlsian conception of justice in a liberal society is, however, not strong enough to tackle the socio-economic challenges that we face today. This concept lacks a thorough and all-encompassing delimitation from market liberalism, as Rawls does not fully consider the *structural partiality of the free market* (Ulrich 2008: 131ff., 239), which is incompatible with his supposition that the basic political order of a liberal society has to be neutral with regard to different concepts of a good life (Rawls 1993: 190ff.). Consequently, Rawls does not reflect enough on the importance of social and economic citizenship rights as a precondition of a well-ordered society. The established basic personality and political citizenship rights are not good enough under the competitive constraints of our time. In line with Thomas Marshall's classical distinction (1963), we need a third group of socio-economic citizenship rights as the basis of *real* freedom for all (Van Parijs 1995). This completion of civic rights could be a crucial point in granting or saving the principles of a humane society in our current "economic life." Let us examine the indispensable motivational basis of such an undertaking before returning, in the next section, to the institutional side of the problem.

Both political liberalism (in the Rawlsian sense) and radical market-based neoliberalism (libertarianism) hardly provide any *motives* for individuals to be interested in a just and unified, or at least a "decent," society (in the sense of Margalit 1996), rather than in the sole pursuit of private interests. However, it is impossible to establish a better societal order without citizens who really want it, who understand it, and who are able to recognize their resulting self-responsibility as well as their co-responsibility for the *res publica*. In this regard, the tradition of political *republicanism* has always been a decisive moment of civil society, as Pocock (1975) and many other political philosophers have demonstrated. What is important, however, is to integrate the republican spirit within a liberal order – which means not sacrificing the constitutive role of civic rights – in order to synthesize a *republican liberalism.*[2] The core idea of republican liberalism – in the republican tradition – is that civic virtue is essential but, according to political liberalism and contrary to classical republicanism, it should focus on nothing but the general and real freedom of the citizens. This *republican-liberal ethos* deeply affects the self-image of the citizens: They desire to live as free citizens among others, not against them. Consequently, they *participate* mentally and politically in the public matters of a well-ordered society and *integrate* their private interests into this political self-understanding. That is why they are, in principle, willing to bind themselves to the ethical principles of harmoniously living together in a free and fair society.

When applied to business life, this civic spirit takes the form of a *republican business ethos*: even as economic agents, the citizens are ready to integrate their "acquisitive intentions" (or "capitalist spirit" as explained by Max Weber 1930) into their civic sense and be co-responsible for a well-ordered *res publica* of truly free citizens. As a result, they are interested in personal success or profit only as far as

---

[2] See Ulrich 2008: 278ff. (first German edition, 1997) and (independently) Dagger 1997, who does not, however, consider the socio-economic side of the concept.

they, as citizens, can accept this as ethically and politically legitimate. *Business integrity* therefore means quite literally that a business person is not willing to behave as an economic agent only – by separating private financial and business interests from his/her civic identity. The same applies to a company or corporation. Accordingly, *corporate citizenship* would mean significantly more than "corporate giving," *after* making the greatest possible profit with an unquestioned business model. It would, furthermore, mean more than community involvement separated as far as possible from the inherent normative content of the business model itself. Rather, corporate citizenship involves a basic integration of the declared principles of business integrity into one's own business model along with a republican co-responsibility for public concerns: especially for a "civilizing" regulatory framework of the markets – including all the implications for a company's own business policy.

The contrast is obvious between this integrated republican-liberal identity, on the one hand, and "possessive individualism" (Macpherson 1962), as conceived by Thomas Hobbes, on the other. The latter is nothing other than the concept of economic man behind pure market liberalism. The primary task of all concerned with the socio-economic and political foundations of a truly liberal society (instead of a liberal economy only) is to support the project of such a republican liberalism by integrating the institutional concept of political liberalism with the civic spirit of economic agents who are ready to understand and to acknowledge their societal responsibilities.

One of the central concerns of citizens with a republican business ethos certainly focuses on social and economic citizenship rights as a means of "civilizing" the market economy. Civic rights are, after all, understood as the constitutive mode of social integration in a well-ordered society of free and equal citizens. The systematic consequence is that citizens will sympathize with and become actively involved in a *rights-based* approach to a humane socio-economic order, instead of a *needs-based* approach to "humanistic economics" (Lutz and Lux 1988).

The core of a civilized market economy: rights and responsibilities of economic citizenship

The self-determined conduct of an individual life is central to citizenship status; and this status has to be guaranteed for all citizens regardless of their socio-economic conditions. Lord Dahrendorf made the following point: "Citizenship is a non-economic concept. It defines people's standing independent of the relative value attached to their contribution to the economic process. The elements of citizenship are thus unconditional" (Dahrendorf 1994: 13). It is precisely the function of strong economic and social citizenship rights to guarantee this order of precedence.

The fundamental consequence is an *emancipatory* conception of social or welfare policies, instead of an only *compensatory* one. More specifically: a social state that *ex post* compensates individuals who are not in a situation to compete and assert themselves in the market as a result of a lack of real freedom is not enough. In the republican liberalism perspective an *ex ante* approach is essential: citizens who are really free can help themselves and do not need "social welfare," except in circumstances of heavy blows of fate. Hence, the *social progress* of a civil society should not manifest itself in the growth of compensating social transfers, but in the enlargement of universal economic citizenship rights that give all citizens a fair chance to live a self-determined life. In brief: social progress is first a question of civic rights, not of money.

At this point, we detect the inherent social demand of a truly liberal society. Or to put it in a programmatic formula: a *more emancipatory socio-economic citizenship status* is the best way toward *less need for compensatory social welfare*. The old debate on social welfare policy (in the sense of compensatory social transfers) can and should be replaced with a debate on the socio-economic preconditions of universal and real civic freedom.

Republican liberalism is not directed against open and competitive markets. The contrary is true: the social integration of everybody, regardless of their success or failure in their economic life, should be regarded as the legitimate precondition for market pressure on people who need to earn their living in the (labor) market. The Danish concept of *flexicurity* – i.e. flexible labor markets *within* social security – demonstrates that a clear vertical order and combination of social integration and economic competition may be advantageous on both levels. Competitive markets can be a means in service of the common good, which increases when the people's citizenship status, in its full meaning of inviolable personal, political, and socio-economic rights, is guaranteed. Consequently, *first* the markets have to be literally "civilized" by new economic citizenship rights and *then* the intensification of market competition will be both legitimate and life-serving.

The importance of this from civil society's point is clear. For the sake of the greatest possible real freedom for all citizens, "civilizing" the market economy is as vital as civilizing the state. Liberals of all schools have always postulated civilizing the state, but some of them are still blind with regard to markets. Now, a civilized market economy has to be understood as regulated by the civic rule of law as well. Inherent market necessities are no longer an accepted reason for limiting the real freedom and equal opportunities of citizens and the justice of the rules of the game. The opposite priority is actually crucial.

Concretizing economic citizenship rights in the different dimensions of a "civilized" economic life is obviously an epochal project that has to be tackled democratically by mature citizens. Distributing economic and social rights, and no longer merely material goods, is essential for the emancipatory goal. Economic citizenship rights clearly aim at the material improvement of the conditions of disadvantaged persons. However, they do this indirectly, primarily by strengthening the chances of self-determination and self-assertion, and thus civil status, in "economic life." Access to education and know-how, capital, and credit – especially micro credits for the poor (Yunus 1999) – are the prerequisites of entrepreneurship for everyone; they therefore deserve the status of basic rights that expand the options of autonomous economic activity. Individual and collective rights to information, hearing, and participation, at least in decisions regarding jobs and working conditions, are also important for citizens working as employees.

While these economic activity rights help guarantee the status of full citizens *within* the market economy, a second dimension of economic civil rights will be increasingly vital in future. This second dimension aims at a fair chance for the partial emancipation of all citizens *from* the pressure of competing as "entrepreneurs" of (nothing but) their labor power at almost any price in the market. This is not a contradiction. Rather, a balance of integration in the working life and emancipation from the constraints of the "free" market corresponds to the very normal balance sought by free citizens between autonomy (in the sense of inviolable privacy) and social integration (in the sense

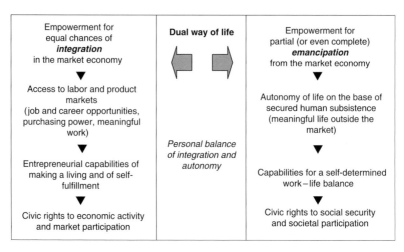

Figure 8.3 The dual empowerment function of (socio-) economic citizenship rights

of full participation in the *res publica*). We have probably not yet fully understood that this is also the prerequisite of a truly free "economic life." For the sake of this balance, the rights to economic activity need the complement of the emancipatory rights to social participation and protection (Figure 8.3).

The social rights of protection and participation are now under-stood as rights that partly liberate people from the "merciless" dependence on their success at self-assertion in the market. These rights grant a reasonable possibility of a non-humiliating form of existence outside the normal working life to those who, for whatever reasons, cannot or will not become integrated into the market. "Non-humiliating" means being spared the stigmatization as failures and "welfare cases" and not being subjected to "special treatment" as a social problem group but, rather, claiming a universal, normal civil right without having to demonstrate a special justification or need. Thus, the universal character of social citizenship rights is essential in the emancipatory perspective of real civic freedom. In the long term, this might be reflected in the goal of an unconditional basic income for all citizens as the liberal Belgian social philosopher Philippe Van Parijs (1995) convincingly explained.

Such approaches to a fully developed civil society demonstrate how meaningful socio-economic progress is still possible in our hyper-dynamic, late-industrial society, which is fixed on endlessly increasing productivity and growth and rather disoriented with regard to the practical meaning of the whole. These integrated approaches reveal that all the countries of the world, even the advanced OECD countries, are still civilisatory "developing countries." These ideas can also be corroborated with recent findings on the global development problematic. Without money, nothing happens in development policy; however, money alone does not promote good socio-economic development. The empowerment of people for both integration into and partial emancipation from the market is essential if we regard the enlargement of real freedom for all citizens as the essence of *human development*. This is precisely why Amartya Sen (1999: 87) regards poverty and underdevelopment as expressions of a "capability deprivation," which is the lack of "substantive freedoms he or she enjoys to lead the kind of life he or she has reason to value."

However, as discussed above, human and civic development imply the republican ethos of responsible and reasonable citizens. Such a civic ethic is based on the normative logic of human interaction and substantiated in mutual respect and solidarity. Hence, the flipside of all citizen rights is the citizen's shared responsibility for the *res publica* of a civilized socio-economic order and all able citizens' fair contribution to social cooperation. Both guaranteed economic citizenship rights and responsibilities are, of course, essential subject matters of public deliberation by mature citizens. Responsibility might include fair tax paying and/or accepting a (lifetime's) minimum workload (White 2003: 202ff.). However, it seems to be important for a liberal society that such moral obligations do not become preconditions for the recognition of socio-economic citizenship rights, since this would simply undermine the emancipatory sense of rights like an *unconditional* basic income for all citizens (van der Veen 1997; Van Parijs 1997).

Conclusion

In conclusion, there are three core elements of a republican-liberal political order (Ulrich 2008: 242): first, as a motivational base, an appropriate *civic virtue* with its resulting republican business ethos; second, as the constitutive order principle, fully established *civic rights* including (instead of excluding, as to date) the socio-economic preconditions of a really free and decent living; and third, as an economic-ethical consequence, a truly *civilized market economy*. Civilizing the market economy is an idea as constitutive of a humane society as that of the civilizing of the state. It is time to acknowledge that the traditional, "purely" economic recipes (as represented by neoliberal doctrine) are no longer sufficient to meet today's socio-economic challenges. The core problem, at least of advanced countries, is not a lack of productivity and competitiveness but, on the contrary, an inconvenient awareness and handling of the societal consequences of a highly productive market economy. "It's not the economy, stupid – it's society!" The conception of a fully developed civil society, including a truly civilized market economy, might open new vistas of human development all over the world.

References

Dagger, R. 1997. *Civic Virtues: Rights, Citizenship, and Republican Liberalism*. New York and Oxford: Oxford University Press.

Dahrendorf, R. 1994. "The Changing Quality of Citizenship," in B. Van Steenbergen (ed.), *The Condition of Citizenship*. London: Sage, pp. 10–19.

Lutz, M. A. and Lux, K. 1988. *Humanistic Economics: The New Challenge*. New York: Bootstrap.

Macpherson, C. B. 1962: *The Political Theory of Possessive Individualism*. Oxford: Clarendon Press.

Margalit, A. 1996. *The Decent Society*. Cambridge, MA: Harvard University Press.

Marshall, T. M. 1963. "Citizenship and Social Class," in *Sociology at the Crossroads and Other Essays*. London: Heinemann, pp. 67–127.

Pocock, J. G. A. 1975. *The Machiavellian Moment: Florentine Political Thought and the Atlantic Republican Tradition*. Princeton, NJ: Princeton University Press.

Rawls, J. 1993. *Political Liberalism*. New York: Columbia University Press.

Sen, A. 1999. *Development as Freedom*. Oxford: Oxford University Press.

Tugendhat, E. 1994. *Vorlesungen über Ethik*. Frankfurt: Suhrkamp.

Ulrich, P. 2003. "Ethics and Economics," in L. Zsolnai (ed.), *Ethics in the Economy: Handbook of Business Ethics* (second edition). Berne and Oxford: Peter Lang, pp. 9–37.

2008. *Integrative Economic Ethics: Foundations of a Civilized Market Economy*. Cambridge: Cambridge University Press [first published in German language, 1997, fourth edition 2008].

van der Veen, R. J. 1997. "Real Freedom versus Reciprocity: Competing Views on the Justice of Unconditional Basic Income," *Political Studies* XLV: 140–63.

Van Parijs, P. 1995. *Real Freedom for All: What (If Anything) Can Justify Capitalism?* Oxford: Oxford University Press.

1997. "Reciprocity and the Justification of an Unconditional Basic Income. Reply to Stuart White," *Political Studies* XLV: 327–30.

Weber, M. 1930. *The Protestant Ethic and the Spirit of Capitalism*, trans. T. Parsons. London: Unwin Hyman.

White, S. 2003. *The Civic Minimum: On the Rights and Obligations of Economic Citizenship*. New York and Oxford: Oxford University Press.

Yunus, M. 1999. *Banker to the Poor: Micro-Lending and the Battle against World Poverty*. New York: Public Affairs.

9 | Development as freedom: individual freedom as a social commitment

AMARTYA SEN[1]

Bertrand Russell, who was a firm atheist, was once asked what he would do if, following his death, he were to encounter God after all. Russell is supposed to have answered, "I will ask him: God Almighty, why did you give so little evidence of your existence?"[2] Certainly the appalling world in which we live does not – at least on the surface – look like one in which an all-powerful benevolence is having its way. It is hard to understand how a compassionate world order can include so many people afflicted by acute misery, persistent hunger, and deprived and desperate lives, and why millions of innocent children have to die each year from lack of food, or medical attention, or social care.

This issue, of course, is not new, and it has been a subject of some discussion among theologians. The argument that God has reasons to want us to deal with these matters ourselves has had considerable intellectual support. As a nonreligious person, I am not in a position to assess the theological merits of this argument. But I can appreciate the force of the claim that people themselves must have responsibility for the development and change of the world in which they live. One does not have to be either devout or nondevout to accept this basic connection. As people who live – in a broad sense – together, we cannot escape the thought that the terrible occurrences that we see around us are quintessentially our problems. They are our responsibility – whether or not they are also anyone else's.

---

[1] Excerpted with permission from the last chapter of Amartya Sen. 1999. *Development as Freedom*. New York: Alfred A. Knopf, Inc.

[2] I heard this account from Isaiah Berlin. We have now lost Berlin, and I take this opportunity of paying tribute to his memory and recollecting how very much I have benefited over the years from his gentle critique of my rudimentary ideas on freedom and its implication.

As competent human beings, we cannot shirk the task of judging how things are and what needs to be done. As reflective creatures, we have the ability to contemplate the lives of others. Our sense of responsibility need not relate only to the afflictions that our own behavior may have caused (though that can be very important as well), but can also relate more generally to the miseries that we see around us and that lie within our power to help remedy. That responsibility is not, of course, the only consideration that can claim our attention, but to deny the relevance of that general claim would be to miss something central about our social existence. It is not so much a matter of having exact rules about how precisely we ought to behave, as of recognizing the relevance of our shared humanity in making the choices we face.[3]

Interdependence between freedom and responsibility

That question of responsibility raises another. Shouldn't a person herself be entirely responsible for what happens to her? Why should anybody take responsibility for influencing her life? That thought, in one form or another, seems to move many political commentators, and the idea of self-help fits well into the mood of the present times. Going further, some argue that dependence on others is not only ethically problematic, it is also practically defeatist in sapping individual initiative and effort, and even self-respect. Who better to rely on than oneself to look after one's interests and problems?

The concerns that give force to this line of reasoning can indeed be very important. A division of responsibility that places the burden of looking after a person's interest on another person can lead to the loss of many important things in the form of motivation, involvement, and self-knowledge that the person herself may be in a unique position to have. Any affirmation of social responsibility that *replaces* individual responsibility cannot but be, to varying extents, counterproductive. There is no substitute for individual responsibility.

The limited reach and plausibility of an exclusive reliance on personal responsibility can best be discussed only after its essential role has first been recognized. However, the substantive freedoms that we respectively enjoy to exercise our responsibilities are extremely

[3] On this subject, see also Sen (1982, 1985a, 1990b).

contingent on personal, social, and environmental circumstances. A child who is denied the opportunity of elementary schooling is not only deprived as a youngster, but also handicapped all through life (as a person unable to do certain basic things that rely on reading, writing, and arithmetic). The adult who lacks the means of having medical treatment for an ailment from which she suffers is not only prey to preventable morbidity and possibly escapable mortality, but may also be denied the freedom to do various things – for herself and for others – that she may wish to do as a responsible human being.

The bonded laborer born into semi-slavery, the subjugated girl child stifled by a repressive society, the helpless landless laborer without substantial means of earning an income are all deprived not only in terms of well-being, but also in terms of the ability to lead responsible lives, which are contingent on having certain basic freedoms. Responsibility *requires* freedom.

The argument for social support in expanding people's freedom can, therefore, be seen as an argument *for* individual responsibility, not against it. The linkage between freedom and responsibility works both ways. Without the substantive freedom and capability to do something, a person cannot be responsible for doing it. But actually having the freedom and capability to do something does impose on the person the duty to consider whether to do it or not, and this does involve individual responsibility. In this sense, freedom is both necessary and sufficient for responsibility.

The alternative to an exclusive reliance on individual responsibility is not, as is sometimes assumed, the so-called nanny state. There is a difference between "nannying" an individual's choices and creating more opportunity for choice and for substantive decisions for individuals who can then act responsibly on that basis. The social commitment to individual freedom need not, of course, operate only through the state, but must also involve other institutions: political and social organizations, community-based arrangements, nongovernmental agencies of various kinds, the media and other means of public understanding and communication, and the institutions that allow the functioning of markets and contractual relations. The arbitrarily narrow view of individual responsibility – with the individual standing on an imaginary island unhelped and unhindered by others – has to be broadened not merely by acknowledging the role of the state, but also by recognizing the functions of other institutions and agents.

Justice, freedom and responsibility

Central to the challenges we face in the contemporary world is our idea of an acceptable society. Why are some social arrangements hard to cherish? What can we do to make a society more tolerable? Underlying such ideas lie some theories of evaluation and – often implicitly – even some basic understanding of social justice (see Sen 1980, 1985b, 1990a, 1992).

First, I argue for the primacy of substantive freedoms in judging individual advantage and in evaluating social achievements and failures. The perspective of freedom need not be merely procedural (though processes do matter, *inter alia*, in assessing what is going on). The basic concern, I have argued, is with our capability to lead the kind of lives we have reason to value.[4] This approach can give a very different view of development from the usual concentration on GNP or technical progress or industrialization, all of which have contingent and conditional importance without being the defining characteristics of development.[5]

Second, the freedom-oriented perspective can accommodate considerable variations within that general approach. Freedoms are inescapably of different kinds, and in particular there is the important distinction between the "opportunity aspect" and the "process aspect" of freedom. While these different constituent components of freedom often go together, sometimes they may not, and much will then depend on the relative weights that are placed on the different items.[6] Also, a freedom-oriented approach can go with different emphases on the relative claims of efficiency and equity. There can be

[4] The principal issues in characterizing and evaluating freedom – including some technical problems – are considered in my Kenneth Arrow lectures, in Sen (forthcoming).

[5] Development is seen here as the removal of shortfalls of substantive freedoms from what they can politically achieve. While this provides a general perspective – enough to characterize the nature of development in broad terms – there are a number of contentious issues that yield a class of somewhat different exact specifications of the criteria of judgments. On this, see Sen (1985a, 1992) and also my forthcoming book *Freedom, Rationality, and Choice*. The concentration on the removal of shortfalls in some specific dimensions has also been used in UNDP's annual *Human Development Report*, pioneered in 1990 by Mahbub ul Haq. See also some far-reaching questions raised by Ian Hacking in his review of *Inequality Reexamined* (Hacking 1996). See also Tilly (1998).

[6] On this, see Sen (1985a, 1992, 1993).

conflicts between (1) having less inequality of freedoms and (2) getting
as much freedom as possible for all, irrespective of inequalities.
The shared approach permits the formulation of a class of different
theories of justice with the same general orientation. Of course, the
conflict between equity-oriented and efficiency-oriented considerations is not "special" to the perspective of freedoms. It arises no
matter whether we concentrate on freedoms or on some other way of
judging individual advantage (for example by happiness or "utilities,"
or by "resources" or "primary goods" that the persons respectively
have). In standard theories of justice this conflict is addressed by
proposing some very specific formula, such as the utilitarian require-
ment to maximize the sum total of utilities irrespective of distribution,
or the Rawlsian difference principle that requires maximizing the
advantage of the worst off, no matter how this may affect the advantages of all others (Rawls 1971, and see Dworkin 1981; Harsanyi 1976;
see also Roemer 1996).

In contrast, I do not argue for a specific formula to "settle" this
question, and have concentrated instead on acknowledging the force
and legitimacy of both aggregative and distributive concerns. That
acknowledgment itself, along with the need to pay substantial attention to each of these concerns, draws our attention forcefully to the
relevance of some basic but neglected issues in public policy, dealing
with poverty, inequality, and social performance *seen in the perspective of freedom*. The relevance of both aggregative and distributive
judgments in assessing the process of development is quite central to
understanding the challenge of development. But this does not require
us to rank all development experiences in one linear order. What is, in
contrast, indispensably important is an adequate understanding of the
informational basis of evaluation – the kind of information we need to
examine in order to assess what is going on and what is being seriously
neglected.

In fact, at the level of pure theory of justice,[7] it would be a mistake
to lock prematurely into one specific system for "weighting" some of
these competitive concerns, which would severely restrict the room
for democratic decision-making in this crucial resolution (and more

---

[7] This is discussed in Sen (1992), and more fully in Sen (1997), which is a part of
my Rosenthal lectures at Northwestern University Law School, given in
September 1998.

generally in "social choice," including the variety of processes that relate to participation). Foundational ideas of justice can separate out some basic issues as being inescapably relevant, but they cannot plausibly end up, I have argued, with an exclusive choice of some highly delineated formula of relative weights as being the unique blueprint for "the just society."[8] For example, a society that allows famines to occur when prevention is possible is unjust in a clearly significant way, but that diagnosis does not have to rest on a belief that some unique pattern of distribution of food, or of income, or of entitlements, among all the people in the country, will be maximally just, trailed by other exact distributions (all completely ordered vis-à-vis one another). The greatest relevance of ideas of justice lies in the identification of *patent injustice*, on which reasoned agreement is possible, rather than in the derivation of some extant formula for how the world should be precisely run.

Third, even as far as patent injustice is concerned, no matter how inescapable it may look in terms of foundational ethical arguments, the emergence of a shared recognition of that "injustice" may be dependent in practice on open discussion of issues and feasibilities.

Extreme inequalities in matters of race, gender, and class often survive on the implicit understanding – to use a phrase that Margaret Thatcher made popular (in a different but somewhat related context) – that "there is no alternative." For example, in societies in which antifemale bias has flourished and been taken for granted, the understanding that this is not inevitable may itself require empirical knowledge as well as analytical arguments, and in many cases, this can be a laborious and challenging process.[9] The role of public discussion to debate conventional wisdom on both practicalities and valuations can be central to the acknowledgment of injustice.

Given the role that public debates and discussions must have in the formation and utilization of our social values (dealing with competing claims of different principles and criteria), basic civil rights and political freedoms are indispensable for the emergence of social values.

---

[8] There is a similar issue relating to competing ways of judging individual advantage when our preferences and priorities diverge, and there is an inescapable "social choice problem" here too, which calls for a shared resolution (discussed in Sen 1999).

[9] On this see Sen (1995). There are a number of other papers in this collection that bear on this issue.

Indeed, the freedom to participate in critical evaluation and in the process of value formation is among the most crucial freedoms of social existence. The choice of social values cannot be settled merely by the pronouncements of those in authority who control the levers of government. We must see a frequently asked question in the development literature to be fundamentally misdirected: do democracy and basic political and civil rights help to promote the process of development? Rather, the emergence and consolidation of these rights can be seen as being *constitutive* of the process of development.

This point is quite separate from the *instrumental* role of democracy and basic political rights in providing security and protection to vulnerable groups. The exercise of these rights can indeed help in making states more responsive to the predicament of vulnerable people and, thus, contribute to preventing economic disasters such as famines. But going beyond that, the general enhancement of political and civil freedoms is central to the process of development itself. The relevant freedoms include the liberty of acting as citizens who matter and whose voices count, rather than living as well-fed, well-clothed, and well-entertained vassals. The instrumental role of democracy and human rights, important as it undoubtedly is, has to be distinguished from its constitutive importance.

Fourth, an approach to justice and development that concentrates on substantive freedoms inescapably focuses on the agency and judgment of individuals; they cannot be seen merely as patients to whom benefits will be dispensed by the process of development. Responsible adults must be in charge of their own well-being; it is for them to decide how to use their capabilities. But the capabilities that a person does actually have (and not merely theoretically enjoys) depend on the nature of social arrangements, which can be crucial for individual freedoms. And there the state and the society cannot escape responsibility. It is, for example, a shared responsibility of the society that the system of labor bondage, where prevalent, should end, and that bonded laborers should be free to accept employment elsewhere. It is also a social responsibility that economic policies should be geared to providing widespread employment opportunities on which the economic and social viability of people may crucially depend. But it is, ultimately, an individual responsibility to decide what use to make of the opportunities of employment and what work options to choose. Similarly, the denial of opportunities of basic education to a child, or of essential health care to the ill, is a failure of social responsibility, but the exact utilization of the educational attainments or of health achievements cannot but be a matter for the person herself to determine. Also, the empowerment of women, through employment opportunities, educational arrangements, property rights, and so on, can give women more freedom to influence a variety of matters such as intrafamily division of health care, food and other commodities, and work arrangements, as well as fertility rates. However, the exercise of that enhanced freedom is ultimately a matter for the person herself. The fact that statistical predictions can often be plausibly made on the ways this freedom is likely to be used (for example, in predicting that female education and female employment opportunity would reduce fertility rates and the frequency of childbearing) does not negate the fact that it is the exercise of the women's enhanced freedom that is being anticipated.

What difference does freedom make?

The perspective of freedom must not be seen as hostile to the large literature on social change that has enriched our understanding of the process for many centuries. While parts of the recent development literature have tended to concentrate very much on some limited indicators of development such as the growth of GNP per head, there is quite a long tradition against being imprisoned in that little box. There have indeed been many broader voices, including that of Aristotle, whose ideas are of course among the sources on which the present analysis draws (with his clear diagnosis in *Nicomachean Ethics*: "wealth is evidently not the good we are seeking; for it is merely useful and for the sake of something else").[10] It applies also to such pioneers of "modern" economics as William Petty, the author of *Political Arithmetick* (1691), who supplemented his innovation of national income accounting with motivating discussions on much broader concerns.[11] Indeed, the belief that the enhancement of freedom is ultimately an important motivating factor for assessing economic and social change is not at all new. Adam Smith was

---

[10] See Aristotle, translated by Ross (1980).
[11] On the relevance of freedom in the writings of pioneering political economists, see Sen (1987).

explicitly concerned with crucial human freedoms.[12] So was Karl
Marx, in many of his writings, for example when he emphasized the
importance of "replacing the domination of circumstances and chance
over individuals by the domination of individuals over chance and
circumstances."[13] The protection and enhancement of liberty supplemented John Stuart Mill's utilitarian perspective very substantially,
and so did his specific outrage at the denial of substantive freedoms to
women (see Mill 1859, 1869). Friedrich Hayek has been emphatic in
placing the achievement of economic progress within a very general
formulation of liberties and freedoms, arguing: "Economic considerations are merely those by which we reconcile and adjust our different
purposes, none of which, in the last resort, are economic (except those
of the miser or the man for whom making money has become an end
in itself)" (Hayek 1960: 35).

Several development economists have also emphasized the importance of freedom of choice as a criterion of development. For example,
Peter Bauer, who has quite a record of "dissent" in development
economics (including an insightful book called *Dissent on Development*) has argued powerfully for the following characterization of
development:

I regard the extension of the range of choice, that is, an increase in the range
of effective alternatives open to the people, as the principal objective and
criterion of economic development; and I judge a measure principally by its
probable effects on the range of alternatives open to individuals. (Bauer
1957: 113–14; see also Bauer 1971)

W. A. Lewis also stated, in his famous opus *The Theory of Economic Growth*, that the objective of development is increasing "the
range of human choice." However, after making this motivational
point, Lewis decided, ultimately, to concentrate his analysis simply on
"the growth of output per head," on the ground that this "gives man
greater control over his environment and thereby increases his freedom" (Lewis 1955: 9–10, 420–1). Certainly, other things given, an
increase in output and income would expand the range of human

---

[12] This applies to his *Wealth of Nations* (1776) as well as to *The Theory of Moral
Sentiments* (revised edition, 1790).
[13] This particular statement is from Marx and Engels (1846), the English
translation is from McLellan (1977: 190). See also Marx's *The Economic and
Philosophical Manuscripts of 1844* and *Critique of the Gotha Programme*.

choice – particularly over commodities purchased. But, as was discussed earlier, the range of substantive choice on valuable matters depends also on many other factors.

Why the difference?

It is, in this context, important to ask whether there is really any substantial difference between development analysis that focuses (as Lewis and many others choose to do) on "the growth of output per head" (such as GNP per capita), and a more foundational concentration on expanding human freedom. Since the two are related (as Lewis rightly points out), why are the two approaches to development – inescapably linked as they are – not substantively congruent? What difference can a focal concentration on freedom make?

The differences arise for two rather distinct reasons, related respectively to the "process aspect" and the "opportunity aspect" of freedom. First, since freedom is concerned with *processes of decision-making* as well as *opportunities to achieve valued outcomes*, the domain of our interest cannot be confined only to the outcomes in the form of the promotion of high output or income, or the generation of high consumption (or other variables to which the concept of economic growth relates). Such processes as participation in political decisions and social choice cannot be seen as being – at best – among the means to development (through, say, their contribution to economic growth), but have to be understood as constitutive parts of the ends of development in themselves.

The second reason for the difference between "development as freedom" and the more conventional perspectives on development relates to contrasts within *the opportunity aspect* itself, rather than being related to the process aspect. In pursuing the view of development as freedom, we have to examine – in addition to the freedoms involved in political, social and economic processes – the extent to which people have the opportunity to achieve outcomes that they value and have reason to value. The levels of real income that people enjoy are important in giving them corresponding opportunities to purchase goods and services and to enjoy living standards that go with those purchases. But as some of the empirical investigations presented in my book *Development as Freedom* showed, income levels may often be inadequate guides to such important matters as the freedom to live long, or the ability to escape avoidable morbidity, or the opportunity to have worthwhile employment, or to live in peaceful and crime-free communities. These non-income variables point to opportunities that a person has excellent reasons to value and that are not strictly linked with economic prosperity.

Thus, both the *process* aspect and the *opportunity* aspect of freedom require us to go well beyond the traditional view of development in terms of "the growth of output per head." There is also the fundamental difference in perspective in valuing freedom *only* for the use that is to be made of that freedom, and valuing *it over and above* that. Hayek may have overstated his case (as he often did) when he insisted that "the importance of our being free to do a particular thing has nothing to do with the question of whether we or the majority are ever likely to make use of that possibility" (Hayek 1960: 31). But he was, I would argue, entirely right in distinguishing between (1) the *derivative* importance of freedom (dependent only on its actual use) and (2) the *intrinsic* importance of freedom (in making us free to choose something we may or may not actually choose).

Indeed, sometimes a person may have a very strong reason to have an option precisely for the purpose of rejecting it. For example, when Mahatma Gandhi *fasted* to make a political point against the raj, he was not merely *starving*; he was rejecting the option of eating (for that is what fasting is). To be able to fast, Mahatma Gandhi had to have the option of eating (precisely to be able to reject it); a famine victim could not have made a similar political point.[14]

While I do not want to go down the purist route that Hayek chooses (in dissociating freedom from actual use altogether), I would emphasize that freedom has many aspects. The *process* aspect of freedom would have to be considered in addition to the *opportunity* aspect, and the opportunity aspect itself has to be viewed in terms of *intrinsic* as well as *derivative* importance. Furthermore, freedom to participate in public discussion and social interaction can also have a constructive role in the formation of values and ethics. Focusing on freedom does indeed make a difference.

---

[14] These and related issues in "the evaluation of freedom" are discussed in my Kenneth Arrow lectures included in Sen (forthcoming). Among the questions that are addressed there is the relation between freedom, on the one hand, and preferences and choices, on the other.

Human capital and human capability

I must also briefly discuss another relation which invites a comment, to wit, the relation between the literature on "human capital" and the focus in this work on "human capability" as an expression of freedom. In contemporary economic analysis the emphasis has, to a considerable extent, shifted from seeing capital accumulation in primarily physical terms to viewing it as a process in which the productive quality of human beings is integrally involved. For example, through education, learning, and skill formation, people can become much more productive over time, and this contributes greatly to the process of economic expansion.[15] In recent studies of economic growth (often influenced by empirical readings of the experiences of Japan and the rest of East Asia as well as Europe and North America), there is a much greater emphasis on "human capital" than used to be the case not long ago.

How does this shift relate to the view of development – development as freedom – presented here? More particularly, what, we may ask, is the connection between "human capital" orientation and the emphasis on "human capability" with which this study has been much concerned? Both seem to place humanity at the center of attention, but do they have differences as well as some congruence? At the risk of some oversimplification, it can be said that the literature on human capital tends to concentrate on the agency of human beings in augmenting production possibilities. The perspective of human capability focuses, on the other hand, on the ability – the substantive freedom – of people to lead the lives they have reason to value and to enhance the real choices they have. The two perspectives cannot but be related, since both are concerned with the role of human beings, and in particular with the actual abilities that they achieve and acquire. But the yardstick of assessment concentrates on different achievements.

Given her personal characteristics, social background, economic circumstances and so on, a person has the ability to do (or be) certain things that she has reason to value. The reason for valuation can be *direct* (the functioning involved may directly enrich her life, such as

---

[15] On this and related issues, see Barro and Lee (1993), Sala-i-Martin (1994) and Barro (1996).

being well-nourished or being healthy), or *indirect* (the functioning involved may contribute to further production, or command a price in the market). The human capital perspective can – in principle – be defined very broadly to cover both types of valuation, but it is typically defined – by convention – primarily in terms of indirect value: human qualities that can be employed as "capital" in *production* (in the way physical capital is). In this sense, the narrower view of the human capital approach fits into the more inclusive perspective of human capability, which can cover both direct and indirect consequences of human abilities. Consider an example. If education makes a person more efficient in commodity production, then this is clearly an enhancement of human capital. This can add to the value of production in the economy and also to the income of the person who has been educated. But even with the same level of income, a person may benefit from education – in reading, communicating, arguing, in being able to choose in a more informed way, in being taken more seriously by others and so on. The benefits of education, thus, exceed its role as human capital in commodity production. The broader human-capability perspective would note – and value – these additional roles as well. The two perspectives are closely related but distinct.

The significant transformation that has occurred in recent years in giving greater recognition to the role of "human capital" is helpful for understanding the relevance of the capability perspective. If a person can become more productive in making commodities through better education, better health, and so on, it is not unnatural to expect that she can, through these means, also directly achieve more – and have the freedom to achieve more – in leading her life.

The capability perspective involves, to some extent, a return to an integrated approach to economic and social development championed particularly by Adam Smith (both in the *Wealth of Nations* and in *The Theory of Moral Sentiments*). In analyzing the determination of production possibilities, Smith emphasized the role of education as well as division of labor, learning by doing, and skill formation. But the development of human capability in leading a worthwhile life (as well as in being more productive) is quite central to Smith's analysis of "the wealth of nations."

Indeed, Adam Smith's belief in the power of education and learning was peculiarly strong. Regarding the debate that continues today on the respective roles of "nature" and "nurture," Smith was an uncompromising – and even a dogmatic – "nurturist." Indeed, this fitted in well with his massive confidence in the improvability of human capabilities:

The difference of natural talents in different men is, in reality, much less than we are aware of; and the very different genius which appears to distinguish men of different professions, when grown up to maturity, is not upon many occasions so much the cause, as the effect of division of labor. The difference between the most dissimilar characters, between a philosopher and a common street porter, for example, seems to arise not so much from nature, as from habit, custom, and education. When they came into the world, and for the first six or eight years of their existence, they were, perhaps, very much alike, and neither their parents nor play-fellows could perceive any remarkable difference. (Smith 1776: 120)

It is not my purpose here to examine whether Smith's emphatically nurturist views are right, but it is useful to see how closely he links *productive* abilities and *lifestyles* to education and training and presumes the improvability of each (see Rothschild 1998). That connection is quite central to the reach of the capability perspective (see e.g. Earls and Carlson 1993, 1996).

There is, in fact, a crucial valuational difference between the human-capital focus and the concentration on human capabilities – a difference that relates to some extent to the distinction between means and ends. The acknowledgment of the role of human qualities in promoting and sustaining economic growth – momentous as it is – tells us nothing about *why* economic growth is sought in the first place. If, instead, the focus is ultimately on the expansion of human freedom to live the kind of lives that people have reason to value, then the role of economic growth in expanding these opportunities has to be integrated into that more foundational understanding of the process of development as the expansion of human capability to lead more worthwhile and more free lives.[16]

The distinction has a significant practical bearing on public policy. While economic prosperity helps people to have wider options and to lead more fulfilling lives, so do more education, better health care, finer medical attention, and other factors that causally influence the effective freedoms that people actually enjoy. These "social

---

[16] I have tried to discuss this issue in Sen (1983) and also in Sen (1985a).

developments" must directly count as "developmental," since they help us to lead longer, freer, and more fruitful lives, in *addition* to the role they have in promoting productivity, or economic growth, or individual incomes.[17] The use of the concept of "human capital," which concentrates on only one part of the picture (an important part, related to broadening the account of "productive resources"), is certainly an enriching move. But it does need supplementation. This is because human beings are not merely means of production, but also the end of the exercise.

Indeed, in arguing with David Hume, Adam Smith had the occasion to emphasize that to see human beings only in terms of their productive use is to slight the nature of humanity:

it seems impossible that the approbation of virtue should be of the same kind with that by which we approve of a convenient or a well-contrived building, or that we should have no other reason for praising a man than that for which we commend a chest of drawers. (Smith 1759: 188)

Despite the usefulness of the concept of human capital, it is important to see human beings in a broader perspective (breaking the analogy with "a chest of drawers"). We must go beyond the notion of human capital, after acknowledging its relevance and reach. The broadening that is needed is additional and inclusive, rather than, in any sense, an alternative to the "human capital" perspective.

It is important to take note also of the instrumental role of capability expansion in bringing about social change (going well beyond economic change). Indeed, the role of human beings even as instruments of change can go much beyond economic production (to which the perspective of "human capital" standardly points), and include social and political development. For example, as was discussed earlier, expansion of female education may reduce gender inequality in intrafamily distribution and also help to reduce fertility rates as well as child mortality rates. Expansion of basic education may also improve the quality of public debates. These instrumental achievements may be

---

[17] To a considerable extent the annual *Human Development Report* of the United Nations Development Programme, published since 1990, has been motivated by the need to take a broader view of this kind. My friend Mahbub ul Haq, who died in 1998, played a major leadership role in this, of which I and his other friends are most proud.

ultimately quite important – taking us well beyond the production of conventionally defined commodities.

In looking for a fuller understanding of the role of human capabilities, we have to take note of:

1. their direct relevance to the well-being and freedom of people;
2. their indirect role through influencing social change; and
3. their indirect role through influencing economic production.

The relevance of the capability perspective incorporates each of these contributions. In contrast, in the standard literature human capital is seen primarily in terms of the third of the three roles. There is a clear overlap of coverage, and it is indeed an important overlap.

But there is also a strong need to go well beyond that rather limited and circumscribed role of human capital in understanding development as freedom.

A final remark

I have tried to present, analyze, and defend a particular approach to development, seen as a process of expanding substantive freedoms that people have. The perspective of freedom has been used both in the evaluative analysis for assessing change, and in the descriptive and predictive analysis in seeing freedom as a causally effective factor in generating rapid change. I have also discussed the implications of this approach for policy analysis as well as for the understanding of general economic, political and social connections. A variety of social institutions – related to the operation of markets, administrations, legislatures, political parties, nongovernmental organizations, the judiciary, the media, and the community in general – contribute to the process of development precisely through their effects on enhancing and sustaining individual freedoms. Analysis of development calls for an integrated understanding of the respective roles of these different institutions and their interactions. The formation of values and the emergence and evolution of social ethics are also part of the process of development that needs attention, along with the working of markets and other institutions. This study has been an attempt to understand and investigate this interrelated structure, and to draw lessons for development in that broad perspective.

It is a characteristic of freedom that it has diverse aspects that relate to a variety of activities and institutions. It cannot yield a view of development that translates readily into some simple "formula" of accumulation of capital, or opening up of markets, or having efficient economic planning (though each of these particular features fits into the broader picture). The organizing principle that places all the different bits and pieces into an integrated whole is the overarching concern with the process of enhancing individual freedoms and the social commitment to help to bring that about. That unity is important, but at the same time we cannot lose sight of the fact that freedom is an inherently diverse concept, which involves – as was discussed extensively – considerations of processes as well as substantive opportunities. This diversity is not, however, a matter of regret. As William Cowper puts it:

> Freedom has a thousand charms to show,
> That slaves, howe'er contented, never know.

Development is indeed a momentous engagement with freedom's possibilities.

References

Aristotle. 1980. *The Nicomachean Ethics* (revised edition), trans. D. Ross. Oxford: Oxford University Press, I (6): 7.

Barro, R. 1996. *Getting It Right: Markets and Choices in a Free Society.* Cambridge, MA: MIT Press.

Barro, R. and Lee, J-W. 1993. "Losers and Winners in Economic Growth." Working Paper 4341. Cambridge, MA: National Bureau of Economic Research.

Bauer, P. 1957. *Economic Analysis and Policy in Underdeveloped Countries.* Durham, NC: Duke University Press.

1971. *Dissent on Development.* London: Weidenfeld & Nicolson.

Dworkin, R. 1981. "What is Equality? Part 2: Equality of Resources," *Philosophy and Public Affairs* 10: 283–345.

Earls, F. and Carlson, M. 1993. "Toward Sustainable Development for the American Family," *Daedalus* 122: 93–121.

1996. *Promoting Human Capability as an Alternative to Early Crime.* Cambridge, MA: Harvard School of Public Health and Harvard Medical School.

Hacking, I. 1996. "In Pursuit of Fairness," *New York Review of Books* 43(14), September 19, 40–4.

Harsanyi, J. 1976. *Essays in Ethics, Social Behavior and Scientific Explanation.* Dordrecht: Reidel.

Hayek, F. 1960. *The Constitution of Liberty.* London: Routledge and Kegan Paul.

Lewis, W. A. 1955. *The Theory of Economic Growth.* London: Allen & Unwin.

Marx, K. 1844. *The Economic and Philosophical Manuscripts of 1844.* Reprinted 1959. Moscow: Progress Publishers.

   1875. *Critique of the Gotha Programme.* Reprinted 1970. Moscow: Progress Publishers.

Marx, K and Engels, F. 1846. *The German Ideology.* Reprinted 1932. Moscow: Progress Publishers.

McLellan, D. 1977. *Karl Marx: Selected Writings.* Oxford: Oxford University Press

Mill, John S. 1859. *On Liberty.* Republished 1974, Harmondsworth: Penguin Books.

   1869. *The Subjection of Women.*

Rawls, J. 1971. *A Theory of Justice.* Cambridge, MA: Harvard University Press.

Roemer, J. 1996. *Theories of Distributive Justice.* Cambridge, MA: Harvard University Press.

Rothschild, E. 1998. "Condorcet and Adam Smith on Education and Instruction," in A. O. Rorty (ed.). *Philosophers on Education.* London: Routledge, pp. 209–26.

Sala-i-Martin, X. 1994. "Regional Cohesion: Evidence and Theories of Regional Growth and Convergence." Discussion Paper 1075. London: CEPR.

Sen. A. (forthcoming). *Freedom, Social Choice, and Responsibility: Arrow Lectures and Other Essays.* Oxford: Clarendon Press.

   1980. "Equality of What?" in S. McMurrin (ed.), *Tanner Lectures on Human Values*, vol. I. Cambridge: Cambridge University Press. Reprinted in Sen, A. 1982. *Choice, Welfare and Measurement.* Oxford: Blackwell and Cambridge, MA.: MIT Press; republished 1997 Cambridge, MA: Harvard University Press, pp. 352–72.

   1982. "The Right Not to Be Hungry," in G. Floistad (ed.), *Contemporary Philosophy 2.* The Hague: Martinus Nijhoff, pp. 343–60.

   1983. "Development: Which Way Now?" *Economic Journal* 93: 745–62. Reprinted in Sen, A. 1984/1997. *Resources, Values and Development.* Cambridge, MA: Harvard University Press.

   1985a. *Commodities and Capabilities.* Amsterdam: North-Holland.

   1985b. "Well Being, Agency, and Freedom: The Dewey Lectures 1984," *Journal of Philosophy* 82(4): 169–221.

1987. "The Standard of Living," in G. Hawthorn (ed.). *Tanner Lectures on Human Values*. Cambridge: Cambridge University Press, pp. 1–38.

1990a. "Justice: Means versus Freedoms," *Philosophy and Public Affairs* 19(2): 111–21.

1990b. "Individual Freedom as a Social Commitment," *New York Review of Books* 37(10): June 16, 49–55.

1992. *Inequality Reexamined*. Oxford: Clarendon Press; Cambridge, MA: Harvard University Press.

1993. "Capability and Well Being," in M. Nussbaum and A. Sen (eds.), *The Quality of Life*. Oxford: Clarendon Press, pp. 30–53.

1995. "Gender Inequality and Theories of Justice," in M. Nussbaum and J. Glover (eds.), *Women, Culture and Development: A Study of Human Capabilities*. Oxford: Clarendon Press, pp. 259–73.

1997. "Justice and Assertive Incompleteness." Mimeograph, Harvard University.

1999. *Development as Freedom*. Oxford: Oxford University Press.

Smith, A. 1759. *The Theory of Moral Sentiments*. Revised edition, 1790. Republished 1976, D. Raphael and A. Macfie (eds.). Oxford: Clarendon Press.

1776. *An Inquiry into the Nature and Causes of the Wealth of Nations*. Republished 1976, R. H. Campbell and A. S. Skinner (eds.). Oxford: Clarendon Press.

Tilly, C. 1998. *Durable Inequality*. Berkeley, CA: University of California Press.

10 | On corporate responsibility for human rights

KLAUS M. LEISINGER

> The recognition of the inherent dignity and of the equal and inalienable rights of all members of the human family is the foundation of freedom, justice and peace in the world.
>
> Preamble, Universal Declaration of Human Rights

Accepting a conceptual challenge

The debate on "business and human rights" has become a central theme on the international corporate responsibility agenda. Two processes in particular have contributed to this: the discourse on the practical consequences of the two UN Global Compact principles that are specific to human rights and the work of a sub-commission of the Human Rights Commission under the chairmanship of American law professor David Weissbrodt. The result of this work, a set of "Draft Norms on the Responsibilities of Transnational Corporations and Other Business Enterprises," was considered to contain "useful elements and ideas" but was not accepted by the Human Rights Commission as a document with legal standing. One factor that evoked concern and disapproval for some observers was a generally negative undertone regarding the impact of corporate activities on human rights as well as impractical monitoring and verification mechanisms "already in existence or to be created".[1]

To overcome the deadlock that evolved from incompatible positions of different stakeholders vis à vis the draft norms, on April 20, 2005, the UN Commission on Human Rights adopted a resolution on "Human Rights and Transnational Corporations and Other Businesses," which

---

[1] See ECOSOC E/CN.4/2005/91 (15 February 2 2005) pp. 9–11. Despite that, a group of enlightened companies took the material content of the "Draft Norms" as a basis for a Business Leaders Initiative on Human Rights and looked for practical ways to implement *minima moralia*; see www.blihr.org.

requested the secretary-general to appoint a "Special Representative on the Issue of Human Rights and Transnational Corporations and Other Businesses." On July 28, 2005, Secretary-General Kofi Annan appointed Professor John Ruggie as the special representative and asked him to submit a report in 2007 that would identify corporate responsibilities with regard to human rights and elaborate the role of states in regulating and adjudicating business on such issues, to clarify ambiguous concepts such as "complicity" and "sphere of influence," to develop materials and methodologies for undertaking human rights impact assessments of business activities, and to compile a compendium of best practices.

In his first "Draft Interim Report," John Ruggie notes that "some companies have made themselves and even their entire industries targets by committing serious harm in relation to human rights, labor standards, environmental protection, and other social concerns." And he cites this as one of three distinct drivers behind the increased attention paid to transnational corporations and their non-financial performance.[2] The fact is that 8 out of 10 people in an opinion poll conducted among 21,000 respondents in 20 industrial countries and emerging markets assign to large companies at least part of the duty to reduce the number of human rights abuses in the world (Globescan 2005). While this public opinion – at least in the short run – will not have legal consequences for companies, it is a strong indicator of the perceived legitimacy of corporate activities.

In view of the complexity of the matter under debate here, a few fundamental preliminary remarks are necessary.

Bearers of rights need corresponding bearers of obligations

Since all human beings are born free and equal in dignity and rights, everyone – simply by virtue of being human – is entitled to all the rights and freedoms enshrined in the Universal Declaration of Human Rights. This entitlement applies without discrimination, whether by race, skin color, sex, language, religion, political or other views, national or social origin, property, birth, or any other criteria. The

---

[2] "Draft Interim Report of the Secretary-General's Special Representative on the Issue of Human Rights and Transnational Corporations and Other Business Enterprises," Boston, February 2006, available at www.ohchr.org/english/bodies/chr/docs/62chr/E.CN.4.2006.97.pdf, p.4.

almost universal recognition of the idea that all people have inalienable rights that are not conferred or granted by the state, a party, or an organization but that are non-negotiable principles is one of the greatest achievements of civilization.

However, it is also implicit in the very first article of the Declaration of Human Rights that freedoms and rights may not be exercised and realized without corresponding responsibilities and obligations: human beings are not only born free and equal in dignity and rights but are also endowed with reason and conscience and should act towards one another in a spirit of brotherhood. Rights and responsibilities are to be seen as a package, and whenever we talk of rights, it ought to be clear on whom the relevant obligations fall. Otherwise the discourse remains what Max Weber described as "sterile excitation," "romanticism of the intellectually interesting, running into emptiness devoid of all sense of objective responsibility" (Weber 1980: 545). A notable approach to the assignment of responsibilities in line with human rights is the Universal Declaration of Human Responsibilities proposed by the InterAction Council under the chairmanship of former German Chancellor Helmut Schmidt (InterAction Council 1997).

Without a doubt, the state and its institutions bear primary responsibility for ensuring that human rights are respected, protected, and fulfilled: not only must they refrain from subjecting citizens to tyranny and inhumane treatment; they also have a number of legal obligations towards them. The fact that these obligations are not met in the real world is illustrated by the annual reports of Amnesty International – even in the twenty-first century, many countries show terrible human rights deficits.[3] Again, civil societies agree that tolerance and openness to other cultures have their limits in those instances where human rights abuses are excused with (misunderstood) ethical relativism. Governments bear at least three distinct human-rights-related duties:

- to create a clear and reliable legal framework and hence a level playing field for the respect and support of human rights;
- to enforce existing law; and
- to sanction violations consistently and coherently.

These duties cannot be delegated to any other organ of society. The reference to the state and its institutions as primary bearers of

---

[3] See www.amnesty.org.uk.

responsibility does not mean that other actors have no obligations. The preamble to the Universal Declaration of Human Rights of the UN General Assembly in 1948 states that "every individual and *every organ of society*, keeping this Declaration constantly in mind, *shall strive by teaching and education to promote respect for these rights and freedoms and by progressive measures, national and international, to secure their universal and effective recognition and observance*" (emphasis added).

Increasingly, human rights groups have seen this statement as a basis for numerous far-reaching demands on companies. This often arose from a view of things in which globalization critics tar all the usual suspects – that is, transnational companies – with the same brush: namely, that they are generally driven by pure greed for profits and do not care one bit about human rights. Some groups go so far as to present companies that operate on the international stage as "major violators of human rights" and as the principal rogues in a *chronique scandaleuse* showing nothing but contempt for humanity.[4] In doing so, they usually point to the worst-case examples from the extractive sector, which – regardless of the specifics of the individual cases – present unique human rights issues that do not always apply to other sectors (such as textiles, leather processing, the construction and electricity generating sector, or pharmaceuticals).

Accusations based on such crude generalizations can quickly and readily be disproved through serious empirical analysis. The intellectual challenge therefore does not lie in pointing to the selective nature of the generalizations on which these accusations are based. The challenge – both intellectually and politically – lies in working out a meaningful and broadly accepted package of corporate human rights responsibilities and implementing them in the day-to-day business of different sectors through appropriate management processes.

Different generations of human rights

Despite the fact that the human rights community insists that *all* rights are of the same significance, it makes sense in the context of the task

---

[4] For example in *New Academy Review* 2(1) (spring 2003): "Business interests . . . have been antagonistic to human rights" (p. 50) or "MNCs can now pose a significant threat to human rights, and also undermine the ability of individual states to protect people from human rights abuses" (p. 92).

of assigning human rights obligations to companies, to distinguish between different "generations" of human rights. The differentiation of human rights according to their generational status helps to focus on corporate human rights obligations that are in line with a fair societal distribution of responsibilities. This distinction does not call into question the fact that all human rights together represent an indivisible whole and an integral, indissoluble unity.

The first generation: rights of defense against state tyranny

Civil and political rights (such as the protection of life and freedom from bodily harm, nondiscrimination, personal freedom, and legal and political rights) form the first-generation rights. They are defensive rights that are intended to protect individuals from infringements by the state – and they are matters of course that typically require little in the way of financial resources beyond simply good governance and responsible public servants. It is therefore to be expected of even the poorest countries that the prohibition of torture, slavery, and even genocide be fully implemented without any need for a transitional period. Where this is not done, political officials place their country outside the community of civilized nations. Today, governments or government-supported actors are unequivocally responsible for the overwhelming majority of violations of human rights – particularly the most basic rights, such as the right to life and freedom from bodily harm.[5] As we will see later, the overriding obligation for companies with regard to the first generation of human rights is to respect and support them in their sphere of influence and make sure that the company is not benefiting from violations of third parties.

The second generation: rights of entitlement to a life of dignity

Economic, social, and cultural rights (such as the right to an appropriate standard of living that guarantees health and well-being for a family, including food, clothing, accommodation, and medical care) form the second generation. These are positive rights that usually require resources in order for them to be fulfilled – resources, for

[5] See the detailed reports at www.state.gov/g/drl/hr/c1470.htm.

example, to ensure nondiscriminatory access to basic medical care and to guarantee a living standard that allows all people to exercise these rights. Sometimes, of course, they merely require refraining from interference with the enjoyment of such rights.

Since poor countries cannot immediately guarantee these rights in view of a shortage of resources, it is expected that governments make measurable progress with the increasing availability of resources – or, in the words of the UN High Commission for Human Rights (UNHCHR)'s International Covenant on Economic, Social and Cultural Rights, "to take steps, individually and through international assistance and co-operation, especially economic and technical, to the maximum of its available resources, with a view *to achieving progressively the full realization of the rights* recognized in the present by all appropriate means, including particularly the adoption of legislative measures" (emphasis added).

In view of such shameful realities as 2.5 billion or so people facing a daily struggle for survival on $2 a day or less, more than 10 million children dying every year before they reach their fifth birthday, and 500,000 women dying annually as a result of pregnancy and birth complications, it is obvious that not only do the state and the international community have a legal duty to do all in their power to promote human development but also that other organs of society have a moral obligation to support such endeavors (UN Development Programme 2005: 24). Corporate contributions to respect, promote, protect, and fulfill human rights of this generation become reality mainly through doing business with good management principles.

The third generation: rights to development in peace and justice

The third generation of human rights encompasses collective rights, such as the right to peace, to development, or to a social and international order in which the rights and freedoms proclaimed in the Universal Declaration can be fully realized. This generation of rights remains the most debated one and is least covered by legal or political means.

The state of the human rights and business debate

The "Human Rights and Business" debate was initiated by Mary Robinson in her term as High Commissioner for Human Rights

(1997–2002) and amplified by the two human rights principles of the UN Global Compact. In order to answer the question "What do the two principles mean for concrete corporate action or omission?" a group of (mainly political, academic and NGO) experts worked on "Draft Norms on the Human Rights Responsibilities of Transnational Corporations and Other Business Enterprises." Their final recommendation was designed to impose on companies, directly under international law, human rights duties that were hitherto formulated exclusively for states. This was rejected in 2005 by all the major industrial countries. In contrast, most developing countries and the relevant UN bodies supported the "Draft Norms."

To overcome the political deadlock, a position for a "Special Representative on the Issue of Human Rights and Transnational Corporations" was created, and John Ruggie of Harvard University was appointed in July 2005. His 2008 report, "Promotion and Protection of All Human Rights, Civil, Political, Economic, Social and Cultural Rights Including the Right to Development," constitutes a new benchmark against which companies will be assessed in the "court of public opinion."[6]

The conclusions of the "Ruggie report"

The most significant outcomes of the "Ruggie report" are that:

- the state has a duty to protect human rights
- the corporate sector must respect human rights
- access to remedy in cases of violations of human rights must be facilitated and improved
- ambiguous terms such as "sphere of influence" and "complicity" have been defined in a more concrete manner.

The state duty to protect

In so far as governance gaps are most often at the root of the business and human rights predicament, effective responses must aim to reduce those gaps. International law provides that states have a duty to protect against human rights abuses by non-state actors, including businesses, that affect persons within their territory or jurisdiction.

---

[6] See http://www.reports-and-materials.org/Ruggie-report-7-Apr-2008.pdf.

Thus states are expected to take all necessary steps to protect against such abuse, including to prevent, investigate, and punish abuse and to provide access to redress. States have discretion to decide what measures to take; both regulation and adjudication of corporate activities vis-à-vis human rights are appropriate. This duty applies to the activities of all types of businesses – national and transnational, large and small – and it applies to all rights that private parties are capable of impairing. The rights referred to here cover those set forth in the Universal Declaration of Human Rights, its associated covenants, and other international agreements (such as the UNICEF Convention on the Rights of the Child).

The corporate responsibility to respect

The "Ruggie report" defines a corporate responsibility to respect human rights and thus took broader NGO requests off the table that – especially big and supposedly powerful – corporations must "promote" and "fulfill" human rights.

The corporate responsibility to respect human rights is already recognized in soft law instruments such as the Tripartite Declaration of Principles Concerning Multinational Enterprises and Social Policy or the OECD Guidelines for Multinational Enterprises. This responsibility is also acknowledged by the largest global business organizations, which state that companies "are expected to obey the law, even if it is not enforced, and to respect the principles of relevant international instruments where national law is absent."[7] It is also one of the commitments that companies undertake in joining the Global Compact. The "responsibility to respect" is basically an obligation to "do no harm" – and exists independently of the state's duties.

In addition to compliance with national laws, the baseline responsibility of companies is to respect the principles of relevant international law where national law is below or silent on a specific standard. Where local law conflicts with the relevant principles of international law, companies should strive to uphold the spirit of internationally recognized human rights. Failure to meet this responsibility can subject companies to the court of public opinion – the

---

[7] See http://www.reports-and-materials.org/Letter-IOE-ICC-BIAC-re-Ruggie-report-May-2008.pdf.

opinions of employees, communities, consumers, civil society, as well as investors – and occasionally to charges in courts of law.

Because the responsibility to respect human rights is a baseline expectation, a company cannot compensate for human rights harm in one area by performing good deeds elsewhere. "Doing no harm" is not merely a passive responsibility for firms but may entail positive steps – for example, a workplace anti-discrimination policy might require the company to adopt specific recruitment and training programs.

In order to properly discharge the responsibility to respect human rights, the "Ruggie report" demands *due diligence* procedures, i.e. conscious efforts a company must take to become aware of, prevent, and address adverse human rights impacts. Companies should consider three sets of factors. The first is the *country contexts* in which their business activities take place and the specific human rights challenges they may pose. The second is the human rights impacts their *own activities* may have within these contexts – for example, in their capacity as producers, service providers, employers, or neighbors. The third is whether they might *contribute to abuse* through the relationships connected to their activities, such those as with business partners, suppliers, state agencies, and non-state actors. How far or how deep this process must go will depend on circumstances.

Defining "sphere of influence" and "complicity"

Sphere of influence remains a useful metaphor for companies in thinking about their human rights impacts beyond the workplace and in identifying opportunities to support human rights. The "Ruggie report" complains, however, that it conflates two very different meanings of "influence": one is *impact*, where the company's activities or relationships are causing human rights harm; the other is whatever *leverage* a company may have over actors that are causing harm. The first (impact) falls squarely within the responsibility to respect human rights; the second (leverage) may only do so in particular circumstances.

Companies cannot be held responsible for the human rights impacts of every entity over which they may have *some* influence, because this would include cases in which they were not a causal agent, direct or indirect, of the harm in question. Nor is it desirable to have companies act whenever they have influence, particularly over governments. Asking companies to support human rights voluntarily where they have influence is one thing, but attributing responsibility to them on that basis alone is quite another.

The emphasis on *proximity* in the sphere of influence model can, so Ruggie claims, be misleading. Companies need to be concerned with their impact on workers and surrounding communities. But their activities can equally affect the rights of people far away from the source – for example, violations of privacy rights by internet service providers can endanger dispersed end-users.

Complicity refers to indirect involvements of companies in human rights abuses, that is, the actual harm is committed by another party, including governments and non-state actors. Due diligence can help a company avoid complicity. Claims of complicity can impose reputational costs and even lead to divestment, without legal liability being established. In this context, allegations of complicity have included indirect violations of the broad spectrum of human rights – political, civil, economic, social, and cultural.

It is not possible to specify definitive tests for what constitutes complicity in any given context. But companies should bear in mind the following considerations:

- *Mere presence* in a country, paying taxes, or silence in the face of abuses *is unlikely* to amount to the practical assistance required for legal liability. However, acts of omission in narrow contexts have led to legal liability of individuals when the omission legitimized or encouraged the abuse.
- *Deriving a benefit* from a human rights abuse *is not likely on its own* to bring legal liability. Nevertheless, benefiting from abuses may carry negative implications in public perception for companies.
- Legal interpretations of "having knowledge" vary. When applied to companies, it might require that there be actual knowledge, or that the company "should have known," that its actions or omissions would contribute to a human rights abuse. Knowledge may be inferred from both direct and circumstantial facts. The "should have known" standard is what a company could reasonably be expected to know under the circumstances.
- Complicity does not require knowledge of the specific abuse or a desire for it to have occurred, as long as there was knowledge of the

contribution. Therefore, it may not matter that the company was merely carrying out normal business activities if those activities contributed to the abuse and the company was aware or should have been aware of its contribution. The fact that a company was *following orders*, fulfilling contractual obligations, or even complying with national law *will not guarantee its legal protection.*

In short, the relationship between complicity and due diligence is clear and compelling: companies can avoid complicity by using the due diligence processes described above – which, as noted, apply not only to their own activities but also to the relationships connected with them.

Access to remedies

As judicial mechanisms are often under-equipped to provide effective remedies for corporate abuse, victims face particular challenges when seeking personal compensation or reparation as opposed to more general sanctions of the corporation through a fine or administrative remedies. States should strengthen the judicial capacity to hear complaints and enforce remedies against all corporations operating or based in their territory, while also protecting against frivolous claims.

Currently, the primary means through which grievances against companies play out are litigation and public campaigns. For a company to take a bet on winning lawsuits or successfully countering hostile campaigns is at best optimistic risk management. Companies should identify and address grievances early, before they escalate. An effective grievance mechanism is part of the corporate responsibility to respect human rights. A company can provide a grievance mechanism directly and be integrally involved in its administration. This could include the use of external resources – possibly shared with other companies – such as hotlines for raising complaints, advisory services for complainants, or expert mediators.

Generally accepted essentials

The generally accepted essential standards after the "Ruggie report" can be described as follows:

- compliance with applicable local and national law, whether or not it is enforced;

- respect for the principles of relevant international law where national law is lower than a specific standard or is silent on it;
- when local law conflicts with the relevant principles of international law, striving to uphold the spirit of internationally recognized human rights.

The most important practical areas of deviation between local law and international law will probably also in future be labor standards (not only remuneration but also discrimination that might be culturally justified and therefore not questioned in some countries) and environmental law.

Potentially evolving requirements

The human rights and business debate is likely to continue after "Ruggie I." The mandate was extended in June 2008 by three more years with the specific focus "to elaborate further on the scope and content of the corporate responsibility to respect all human rights and to provide concrete guidance to business and other stakeholders . . . in coordination with the efforts of the human rights working group of the UN Global Compact."[8]

Companies will be expected to have policies and respective corporate guidelines as well as to take all necessary measures to ensure that actual and potential human rights violations are detected and illegitimate practices abandoned. The Human Rights Compliance Assessment of the Danish Institute for Human Rights and IBLF's Human Rights Impact Assessment (in development) are potential diagnostic tools.

It is to be expected that the debate will become less general, more sector-specific, and more focused on economic, social, and cultural human rights. Whereas governments will continue to define the scope of legal compliance, the broader scope of the responsibility to respect human rights will continue to be defined by *public expectations*.

Corporate human rights commitment as values management

A company is a social (sub-)system that has a specific mission and purpose and that is committed to achieving specific results. Where the

---

[8] See http://ap.ohchr.org/documents/E/HRC/resolutions/A_HRC_RES_8_7.pdf.

corporate purpose is not focused solely on the level of the next quarterly financial result but is also concerned with attaining the highest possible social and ecological quality in the pursuit of its economic interests, the managers of that company have to engage in "values management," defined as the use of "company-specific instruments designed to define the moral constitution of a team or organisation and its guiding values and to live them in all day-to-day practices" (Wieland 2004). A value management system embraces all the process variables that a company has at its disposal in this respect.

With regard to corporate human rights achievements, this means defining what the company considers to be in keeping with its values in terms of human rights. For statements of practical relevance on normative requirements, a distinction should be drawn in the context of human rights between:

- non-negotiable *"must" norms* – these demand compliance with relevant national laws and regulations in all cases as an *ethical minimum*;
- *"ought to" norms* – these are not stipulated by law but are *morally expected* of a company competing with integrity (De George 1993) (for instance, living up to reasonable social or environmental standards even if local law would allow a "race to the bottom"); and
- *"can" norms* – these allow the assumption of additional responsibilities not covered by the first two dimensions and let companies that conform to them focus particular attention on their role as excellent corporate citizens (for example, through corporate philanthropy programs, pro bono research, community programs, and other not-for-profit endeavors).[9] The assumption of "can" norms is *desirable* from a human development point of view.

Responsibility for the implementation of these norms in corporate activities may be direct or indirect in nature.

According to these distinctions (not corresponding with the three generations of human rights), corporate instructions are formulated on what to do and what not to do (codes of conduct and corporate guidelines) to put the basic value-specific decisions into practice in

---

[9] For this distinction according to different degrees of obligation for social norms, see Dahrendorf 1959: 24ff.

day-to-day business operations. Apart from serving as a catalogue of what not to do, these "moral guidelines" also have the function of providing employees with a positive reference framework that they can invoke when they are confronted in their work environment with unreasonable demands that violate the spirit of the principles and guidelines for action.

With numerous methods and instruments – corporate communications programs, agreements on individual business objectives and performance targets, performance dialogues and appraisals of achieved results, compliance monitoring, ombuds institutions, and auditing – the implementation phase encompasses all the other components of the management processes used in the company for the achievement of financial, technical, or other objectives.

By acting in this informed and structured way and by being able to justify the portfolio of corporate responsibility-related activities in a coherent and consistent manner, a company avoids the pitfall of making opportunistic concessions to the most vociferous demands and finding itself at the mercy of variable external interests and constantly increasing demands from, for example, nongovernmental organizations (NGOs).

The decision-making process on corporate commitment to human rights

As with all decisions on complex issues, in the case of issues touching on human rights it is necessary to do one's "homework" first in terms of both fact-based and value-based knowledge. Part of this homework is to identify the stakeholders essential to the company and to address their concerns and demands. For this purpose, it is also useful to enter into dialogue with competent human rights institutions and to take part in "learning forums" such as those offered by the UN Global Compact and the Novartis Foundation for Sustainable Development,[10] because they inspire ideas that go beyond one's "own backyard" and help ensure that, as far as possible, all relevant aspects of a complex issue have been identified.

---

[10] See the symposium reports at www.novartisfoundation.com/de/symposium/ 2003/index.htm and www.novartisfoundation.com/de/symposium/2004/ index.htm.

It is on the basis of the potential for reason and the knowledge that exists within a company and in society that the internal corporate decision is made with regard to the nature and scope of human rights obligations accepted by the company, thus setting itself apart from others. A landmark decision of this kind should, for example, be that the company is not only committed to the relevant national principle of legality but that it goes beyond this and, through a voluntary commitment to higher standards, ensures as far as possible that it does not profit from any gaps in the law or "freedom of interpretation."

The "midwife function" of internal and external dialogue

Socrates pointed out that "truth" lies in all people, they simply need help in seeing it. In view of what in most cases is a huge knowledge potential within companies and the ability of companies to mobilize resources to buy in any knowledge that is lacking, there is no doubt that the "truth" about company-specific human rights obligations is also present in every company – they simply need help in seeing it. The points of intersection between human rights and corporate responsibilities are regarded as "chaotic and contested": on the one hand, there are those who regard companies (especially multinationals) as the "source of all evil"; on the other hand, there are those who have a touching faith in the ability of companies, economic growth, and the laws of the market to solve all human rights problems (Sullivan 2003). Yet reality is more complex and indeterminate than these extreme views: the expectations directed at companies remain unclear.[11]

"Obstetric help" for the birth of "truth" is provided in the first instance by the self-critical study of materials produced by competent institutions, such as Amnesty International UK Business Group, the Business & Human Rights Resource Centre, or the Business Leaders Initiative on Human Rights.[12] Debates with constructive lateral thinkers, such as Mary Robinson, Irene Khan, or Sir Geoffrey Chandler, help in the identification of risks that normally lie beyond

---

[11] A notion that also shines clearly through the "Draft Interim Report."
[12] For example, Amnesty International UK/Prince of Wales International Business Leaders Forum, *Business & Human Rights. A Geography of Corporate Risks* (London, 2002); see also the excellent websites www.business-humanrights.org/Home and www.blihr.org.

the boundaries of corporate perception. Although by far not all demands put forward in such discussions are to be understood as "corporate obligations," anyone who wants to be successful in product markets in the long term has to be familiar with the most important "opinion markets." A midwife function for deeper insights in terms of corporate responsibility for human rights is thus served by management engaging in an informed discussion of critical questions such as:

- What are the human-rights-related risks of our business operations? If there are any, in what priority should we approach them? Are there human-rights-related opportunities?
- Is there, to the best of our knowledge and belief, any reason to change our business practices in the context of the human rights principles laid down in the UN Global Compact?
- In what areas of activity do those things we consider morally imperative and reasonable differ from what influential human rights groups demand of companies?
- Where and on the basis of what special circumstances (such as market failures or failing states)[13] do we recognize particular demands for the fulfillment of economic or social human rights (such as the offer of life-saving medicines on special terms), and what concrete deliverables result from this?
- In what areas of activity and in which countries does a corporate policy aimed only at meeting basic legal requirements create vulnerabilities, such as not meeting the expectations of civil society?
- Are there priority arrangements in place for overcoming such conflicts?
- Which actors of civil society (NGOs, media, Churches, etc.) do we want to include in our internal analysis of the problem to ensure that the information (fact-based and value-based knowledge) on which we base our decision is appropriate to the complexity and the many-layered context of the issue under debate?

---

[13] On the special problem of "failing states" and "failing markets", see K. M. Leisinger, "The Right to Health: A Multi-Stakeholder Task," in Novartis Foundation for Sustainable Development, *The Right to Health: A Duty for Whom? International Symposium Report 2004* (Basel, 2005) (available at www.novartisfoundation.com). With its voluntary commitments to action, Novartis far exceeds the obligations stipulated by law.

- Where do we draw the limits of our responsibility for the respect, support, and fulfillment of human rights – in other words, how do we define our sphere of influence?
- What do we understand by "complicity"?

Such questions need to be discussed to uncover the "truth" about corporate responsibilities for human rights and allow for informed decisions on the nature, scope, and depth of the sustainable corporate contributions in this regard. The distinction between "must," "ought to," and "can" norms helps to distinguish what is essentially *good management practice* and what constitutes *corporate responsibility excellence*, partly having a "nice to have" character.

All responsibilities in the context of first-generation human rights are an integral part of the "must" dimension and hence an essential ingredient of good management practices. Although one could find evidence that illegitimate practices have a positive impact on doing business in a country with deficits in good governance, companies competing with integrity will not put first-generation rights in the negotiation basket with economic goods. On the contrary, as far as these rights are concerned, a company must do all in its power to ensure that there are no violations within its own sphere of influence and that it also does not benefit from human rights abuses by other parties. This implies the obligation to strive for all relevant knowledge in this respect as far as is reasonably possible.

As far as second-generation human rights are concerned, the normal business operations of a company form the main corporate contribution to the preservation of these rights: it is the basic social function of companies to produce products and services in a legal way and to sell these on the market. To this end, they hire employees of an adult age who work of their own volition in exchange for pay as defined in legally binding contracts or collective bargaining agreements. In addition, companies pay contributions into the social security system. In this way, they enable their employees to secure their own economic human rights. Companies purchase goods and services, pay market prices for them, and thereby engender economic linkage effects. Last, but not least, companies make a financial contribution towards the community through taxes and duty. This enables the state to carry out its tasks.

All activities subject to the criterion of "legality" are part of the "must" dimension. Activities that go beyond what is legally required

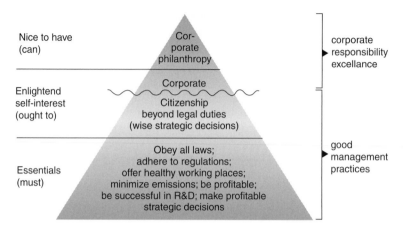

Figure 10.1 The hierarchy of corporate responsibilities

fall under the "ought to" dimension. Most of them are moral obligations but nevertheless constitute good management practice. This includes, for example, activities in the context of a remuneration system that ensures that basic needs can be met even for those people at the lowest levels of qualification in developing countries (a "living wage"), affirmative efforts for greater gender justice, training beyond a person's immediate needs (improvement of "employability"), corporate pension funds, and more.

Delivering on moral obligations is to be seen in terms of corporate responsibility excellence – that is, accepting ambitious challenges that are mainly located in the "can" dimension. Companies – seeing themselves as good corporate citizens – may provide additional services of their own volition. They may, for example, offer products in special cases at special conditions (such as differential pricing of medicines for poverty-related and tropical diseases or product donation programs), finance philanthropic foundations, do pro bono research, make donations, and, on a case-by-case basis, contribute to the fulfillment of economic, social, and cultural rights in other ways.[14]

With regard to third-generation human rights, it is too early to apply the "must," "ought to," and "can" grid. As essential questions – such as who exactly is entitled and who is under obligation?; on the basis of what criteria and to what extent? – remain for the time being

---

[14] See, e.g., www.novartisfoundation.com and www.nitd.novartis.com.

unanswered, these are treated by companies as aspirations, albeit aspirations whose fulfillment is in the interest both of the international community and of the companies themselves. The UN Global Compact, which serves here as a platform for clarification efforts and provides with its 10 principles a reference framework, explicitly is on record that one of its objectives is to help meet the UN millennium goals with "fair globalization."

While the rational justification of normative maxims of behavior is an essential step in values management, the justification and formulation alone do not inevitably lead to their implementation. For this reason, appropriate management processes and standard operating procedures must be put in place.

Implementation through management processes

While it is true that no further-reaching process can be set in motion without value-based management decisions, such decisions are only the first step. Once they have been made, then principles of action and behavior resulting from these decisions, as well as corporate guidelines for dealing with human rights, have to be formulated and communicated both inside and outside the company. They often have to be "practiced" as well, by using e-learning modules, for example, or case studies. Personal model behavior and visible commitment at management level, as well as an attractive launch campaign addressing imperative and prohibited modes of behavior, are the first important steps.

Further management elements are the appointment of someone at management level with responsibility for human rights issues, the development of measurable benchmarks, and the setting of concrete, bonus-relevant goals and corresponding performance appraisals. Finally, compliance with self-declared commitments must be monitored in a manner similar to the way in which compliance with legal requirements is checked.[15] A useful support for internal learning and cognitive processes is the Human Rights Compliance Assessment tool developed by the Danish Institute for Human Rights.[16]

[15] See also BLIHR/UN Global Compact, *A Guide for Integrating Human Rights into Business Management* (New York, 2006) and UN Global Compact/Office of the United Nations High Commissioner for Human Rights (UNHCHR), *Embedding Human Rights in Business Practice* (New York, November 2004).
[16] See www.humanrightsbusiness.org/040_hrca.htm.

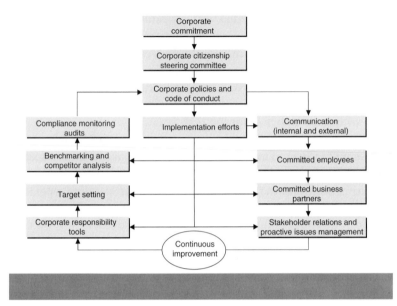

Figure 10.2 Corporate human rights management cycle

There are different approaches to measuring and reporting on corporate human rights performance (CSR Europe/Business for Social Responsibility 2001). It is hoped that the new set of Global Reporting Initiative indicators provides a widely accepted basis so that corporate performances become comparable between companies and over time. Since both the legal state of the art and the sense of what constitutes legitimate action changes with time, the corporate guidelines and recommendations for action derived from these guidelines have to be reviewed from time to time and adjusted, if necessary. As there are "good practices" available, companies willing to make a difference but not knowing how to can refer to what has been done so far by others.[17]

However, not all challenges can be satisfactorily met in the long term by means of "standard operating procedures." To face up to

---

[17] For diverse corporate experiences, see the excellent website of Christopher Avery and his colleagues at www.business-humanrights.org, as well as BP's "position on difficult issues involving human rights", at www.bp.com/liveassets/bp_internet/globalbp/STAGING/global_assets/downloads/H/Human_rights_guidance.pdf.

unexpected or structurally new problems in the spirit of the same sense of responsibility, a corporate culture has to be developed in which moral insights mature into self-stabilizing convictions that are invested with life out of an inherent motivation and not adhered to "as specified" because of some compliance monitoring procedure. Especially in the context of human rights issues, sensitivity and keen intuition are needed to recognize ambivalent situations and to assess them critically in the light of the existing guidelines. Help desks, clearinghouses, and ombuds institutions can provide further assistance if requested.

When designing appropriate management processes and standard operating procedures, it is important to understand the corporate human rights engagement not a "project" that on command is started and then finishes once the objective has been achieved. It is more of an open-ended process that, once launched, may provoke changes in basic corporate practices. Companies – especially large multinational conglomerates – are increasingly faced with questions of responsibility that lie beyond the conservatively defined "normal" day-to-day business routine. Examples include particular claims related to the economic, social, and cultural human rights realm, such as the "right to health" claim against the pharmaceutical industry.[18] Against the background of persistent mass poverty and the associated diseases, successful companies will see themselves increasingly confronted with new demands that amount to an ever-growing substitution of the obligations of the state and the international community.

It will be one of the great tasks of values management in the future to adopt a credible approach in finding the right balance between the extremes of a basic refusal to accede to such demands, citing the obligations of the primary bearer of responsibility (the state), and a general acceptance of obligations attributed by pressure groups. Both "fundamentalisms" would lead in the long term to competitive dis-advantages that would be detrimental to business as well as society. In this context, it might be useful to refer to Peter Drucker's state-ment many years ago: successful companies are those that focus on responsibility rather than power, on long-term success and societal reputation rather than piling short-term results one on top of the other (Drucker 1993: 57).

[18] See www.novartisstiftung.com.

Credible verification

Although the verification of corporate responsibility achievements is an integral part of the management process in the context of human rights, this issue is examined separately here because of its enormous political sensitivity. Credible corporate activity calls for independent jurors – this is also, if not especially, the case in the context of corporate human rights commitments. But who can be considered an independent juror? Most companies prefer verification processes they are familiar with from other business areas – financial auditors or consultants, such as PriceWaterhouseCoopers or KPMG, for example. Although those firms have the professional skills and tools to assess the human rights performance of companies, they do not enjoy the same credibility as, for example, Amnesty International or Human Rights Watch. Nor would institutions such as these latter ones necessarily recognize the results of commercial auditor firms. At the same time, however, no human rights defense group is available to provide such verification services. This is commonly explained by a fear of becoming "involved" and thereby – at least in the perception of critical human rights stakeholders – losing their critical distance and thus their most important asset, their own credibility.

Since there is little hope that such fears might be allayed in the short term, innovative solutions are called for. This could entail, for example, multi-stakeholder projects in which several actors with different competencies and experience collaborate. A project of this kind would undoubtedly show the development of the "human rights impact assessment" that is currently under way. Its country-specific results could be discussed with human rights experts and the auditors and then published in the company's annual report. The outcome of such work and the use of human rights indicators of the Global Reporting Initiative would have the advantage of providing a basis for comparing results between companies as well as measuring progress over time.[19] Finally, a human-rights-specific "Richter scale" (like the scale used to measure earthquakes) would help give the broader public a better idea of how to weigh reports on human rights abuses (Leisinger 2004: 72–100).

[19] See www.globalreporting.org.

Economic, social, and cultural human rights issues

What corporate activities can be reasonably expected in order to appropriately address economic, social, and cultural human rights issues? As mentioned earlier, companies mainly contribute to the safeguarding and fulfillment of second-generation human rights in the course of their usual business activities. But renowned human rights champions demand substantially more – and the expectations of society in some cases also go far beyond what managers regard as business duty. A survey carried out in Germany shows among other things that a large majority of people expect pharmaceutical companies, for example, to distribute medicines free of charge or at massively reduced prices if patients cannot afford them because they lack the necessary purchasing power (Lunau and Wettstein 2004: 140). John Ruggie mentions in his interim report that major pharmaceutical companies are "widely perceived to abuse their power" and quotes as examples "overpricing and patents of AIDS treatment drugs in Africa".[20]

Most managers of pharmaceutical companies would be astonished to hear that patent rights are equated with abuse of power – they would probably quote Article 17 of the Universal Declaration of Human Rights, which states that "everybody has the right to own property" and "no one shall be arbitrarily deprived of his property." Some of them would also put forward the argument that it is completely clear that governments are the primary bearers of responsibility and have a duty to give priority to ensuring that their resources are used to satisfy basic needs – and that the international community should be assisting those countries whose lack of resources renders them vulnerable despite having "good governance" in place. And yet, even business schools debate answers to such questions as whether there is a "morally right price" for drugs in the developing world.[21]

But then, issues like this bring in the distinction between what is a "legal" entitlement and what is perceived to be a legitimate handling of an extraordinary social catastrophe. In view of persistent mass poverty and the human suffering that goes with it, and also as a reaction to what in many cases are evident shortcomings in the

---

[20] "Draft Interim Report."
[21] Brennan and Baines (2006) answer the question affirmatively by advocating for enlightened self-interest.

engagement of the primary bearers of responsibility, many concerned people turn to the private sector for help. How are companies – especially profitable ones – to cope with the fact that the expectations of society are growing on a scale that is incompatible with a reasonable definition of a fair societal distribution of responsibility?

The only possibility for establishing a credible corporate standpoint on this issue is through informed decisions based on the "homework" and dialogue with stakeholders described earlier. There will never be complete agreement in society on the breadth and depth of the activities under discussion here. But the uncompromising rejection or opportunistic acceptance of demands in this regard is always a worse solution than the self-confident presentation of the scale and limits of economic, social, and cultural human rights engagements that are felt by corporate management to be reasonable. It is obvious that, while all companies must avoid direct or indirect involvement with human rights abuses, large profitable companies in the upper section of the "corporate responsibility pyramid" can, and should, do more to exceed the minimum standard than small to medium-size enterprises or those with fewer resources. Companies that strive to show leadership in corporate responsibility are also prepared to do more in this regard – and not only to provide resources but also to offer potential innovation and knowledge, as well as management processes, for new and better solutions. Avoiding human rights problems is one thing. Affirmative action with benefits for the safeguarding of human rights is another – namely, the more positive and constructive alternative.

Conclusion: the business case for corporate human rights engagement

Those who are in breach of the most important consensus of the international community place themselves outside the corridor of legitimate activities. For companies of integrity, there can therefore be no rational justification for sacrificing other people's human rights to achieve corporate profits. This observation applies in the first place to all obligations enshrined in law. Hence, all efforts have to be undertaken nationally – if necessary, with international support – so that national laws with regard to human-rights-specific items are compatible with what most governments have ascribed to by explicitly recognizing the International Bill of Human Rights.[22] But where national laws are not in harmony with what is defined by enlightened consensus of the international community, moral obligations come into play, the scope of which is subject to considerable differences of opinion.

However, there are a number of good reasons for assuming corporate responsibility in order to support and respect human rights if national law is either not state of the art or is only a "paper tiger" that is not consistently implemented:

- Companies that critically reflect on the quality of standards relating to human rights, that feel the pulse of society's expectations through dialogue with stakeholders, and that are prepared to be measured by criteria of legitimacy and not just those of legality reduce their legal, financial, and reputational risks.[23] Any increased costs that may be incurred as a result of responsible human rights commitment must be seen as an "insurance premium" against such risks becoming reality.
- Companies that reduce the potential for friction with society on human rights issues by taking a proactive approach informed by their sense of integrity tend to be seen as "part of the solution" rather than as "part of the problem." This provides a company with its "social licence to operate" and safeguards it from calls for a boycott or from "shaming" campaigns.[24]
- Companies with a reputation for integrity tend to have better motivated employees because they look at their company with pride

---

[22] See www.ohchr.org/english/law/index.htm.

[23] For a discussion of these risks see Leisinger and Schmitt 2003: 154ff. Given that for companies listed on the stock exchange, reputation accounts for at least 50 percent of total value, the scale of potential damage inherent in such risks becomes clear; see *Business Week*, 2 August 2004. For new developments of consequence the context of failure to comply with human rights *minima moralia*, see I. Schwenzer and B. Leisinger, "Ethical Values and International Sales Contracts," in Jan Ramberg *et al.* (eds.), *Commercial Law Challenges in the 21st Century*, Jan Hellner in Memoriam (Stockholm: forthcoming).

[24] According to figures published by the Prince of Wales International Business Leaders Forum, calls for boycotts alone cause economic damage of almost 4 billion euros; see IBLF, *Human Rights: It Is Your Business* (London, 2005), p. 4.

and identify with its objectives; this kind of company is also more attractive to highly qualified talents. And both trends tend to increase productivity.

- Companies whose performance is regarded as exemplary in terms of human rights tend to be preferred by ethical investment funds and ethically sensitive customers (provided other performance conditions remain unchanged). And this ethical distinction can lead to advantages in the valuation of the company and in the competitive environment of established markets (especially with products that are subject to high competitive pressures).
- Sustainable responsible corporate performance creates a greater reliability and thus better cooperation opportunities for all potential cooperation partners (business partners, joint ventures, and mergers and acquisitions).
- Finally, the acceptance of responsibility that is credible by virtue of the fact that it is verifiable is the best argument against political demands for additional regulation: freedom, including corporate freedom, is always tied to responsibility for the common good – and here human rights have absolute priority.

Companies are increasingly being assigned moral responsibility. While the dimension and complexity of these expectations often makes it difficult to satisfy all stakeholders, the human-rights-related expectations should be dealt with in a constructive and positive way. No company competing with integrity can justify "collateral human rights damage" in its endeavors to achieve its profit targets. Enlightened companies will therefore take a "rights-aware approach" – that is, be willing to accept that its stakeholders have universally accepted human rights and take appropriate action to strive to respect these.

While many of the deliverables that result from a "rights-based approach" can be seen as part of good management practices – and thus make management a "force for good" (Birkinshaw and Piramal 2005) – the corporate human rights commitment (for instance, in the context of economic, social, and cultural human rights) could be extended if and when judgments by civil society actors (NGOs, media, political parties) were more differentiating. Today, companies that behave in an exemplary way in terms of their human rights commitment (but also in social and ecological terms and in efforts to combat corruption) are tossed into the same discussion basket with the worst cases of aberrant behavior. The moral reputation capital that would be conferred upon a company by differentiating it from those that chose not to take an appropriate approach towards human rights would reward additional efforts. Through this, the discretionary freedom of management could be guided into the acceptance of doing more – in the best of all cases, a new level of corporate competition could be established. This would be in the interest of everyone who is concerned about human rights.

As Secretary-General Annan expressed it: "Wherever we lift one soul from a life of poverty, we are defending human rights."[25] Economic deprivation is a standard feature of most definitions of poverty, and no social phenomenon is as comprehensive in its assault on human rights as poverty. Economic development is the single most important element to alleviate poverty. The private sector contributes to poverty alleviation by contributing to economic growth, job creation, and poor people's income. Thus, encouraging corporate activities and unleashing entrepreneurship is so important.[26]

Sustainable responses to the many facets of poverty do not violate human rights in the pursuit of economic growth. On the contrary, sustainable responses to poverty alleviation involve securing[27] and enlarging freedom,[28] increasing choices, and enabling empowerment. The promotion of human development and the fulfillment of human rights share, in many ways, a common motivation and reflect a fundamental commitment to promoting the freedom, well-being, and dignity of individuals in all societies.[29] Good companies are part of the solution of filling these aspirations with living content.

---

[25] www.unhchr.ch/development/poverty-01.html.
[26] UNDP Commission on the Private Sector & Development, *Unleashing Entrepreneurship. Making Business Work for the Poor* (New York, 2004).
[27] UNDP, *Human Development Report 2000: Human Rights and Development* (New York: Oxford University Press, 2000).
[28] "Report of the Secretary-General of the United Nations for Decision by Heads of State and Governments," in *Larger Freedom. Towards Security, Development and Human Rights for All* (New York, September 2005); see www.un.org/largerfreedom.
[29] UNDP, *Human Development Report 2000*, p. 19, n. 46.

References

Birkinshaw, J. and Piramal, G. (eds.). 2005. *Sumanthra Goshal on Management. A Force for Good*. London: Prentice Hall/Financial Times.

Brennan, R. and Baines, P. 2006. "Is There a Morally Right Price for Antiretroviral Drugs in the Developing World?" *Business Ethics: A European Review*, 15(1): 29–43.

Business and Human Rights Seminar Report. 2005. *Exploring Responsibilities and Complicity*. London: Business & Human Rights Seminar Ltd.

CSR Europe/Business for Social Responsibility. 2001. *Measuring and Reporting Corporate Performance on Human Rights*. San Francisco.

Dahrendorf, R. 1959. *Homo Sociologicus*. Cologne: Opladen.

De George, R. T. 1993. *Competing with Integrity in International Business*. New York: Oxford University Press.

Drucker, P. 1993. *Post Capitalist Society*. New York: Harper Business.

GlobeScan. 2005. "CSR Monitor." www.EnvironicsInternational.com/sp-csr.asp.

InterAction Council. "Universal Declaration of Human Responsibilities. September 1997." www.interactioncouncil.org/udhr/declaration/udhr.pdf.

Leisinger, K. M. 2004. "Business and Human Rights," in M. McIntosh, S. Waddock, and G. Kell (eds.), *Learning to Talk: Corporate Citizenship and the Development of the UN Global Compact*. London: Greenleaf Publications.

Lunau, Y. and Wettstein, F. 2004. *Die Soziale Verantwortung der Wirtschaft. Was Bürger von Unternehmen erwarten*. Berne: Haupt Verlag.

Novartis Foundation for Sustainable Development. 2003. "Symposium Report." www.novartisfoundation.com/de/symposium/2003/index.htm.

Novartis Foundation for Sustainable Development. 2004. "Symposium Report." www.novartisfoundation.com/de/symposium/2004/index.htm.

Novartis Foundation for Sustainable Development. 2004. "The Right to Health: A Duty for Whom?" International Symposium Report 2004. Basle: Novartis.

OHCHR Briefing Paper. 2004. "The Global Compact and Human Rights: Understanding Sphere of Influence and Complicity," in UN Global Compact/UNHCHR, note 20.

Sullivan, R. (ed.). 2003. *Business and Human Rights. Dilemmas and Solutions*. Sheffield: Greenleaf.

The *Corporate Lawyer*. 2004. "Lawyers, Corporations and the International Human Rights Law," *The Corporate Lawyer*, 25(10): 298–302.

UN Development Programme (UNDP). 2005. *Human Development Report 2005. International Cooperation at a Crossroads.* New York: Oxford University Press.

Watchman, P. 2005. "Complicity: Charting a Path through the Conceptual Minefield," in Business and Human Rights Seminar Report. 2005, note 29.

Weber, M. 1980. "Politik als Beruf," in J. C. B. Mohr (ed.), *Gesammelte Politische Schriften.* Tübingen: Paul Siebeck.

Wieland J. (ed.). 2004. *Handbuch Wertemanagement.* Hamburg: Murmann Verlag.

11 | *The value shift: merging social and financial imperatives*[1]

LYNN SHARP PAINE

The turn to values

Business has changed dramatically in the past few decades. Advances in technology, increasing globalization, heightened competition, shifting demographics – these have all been documented and written about extensively. Far less notice has been given to another, more subtle, change – one that is just as remarkable as these more visible developments. What I have in mind is the attention being paid to values in many companies today.

When I began doing research and teaching about business ethics in the early 1980s, skepticism about this subject was pervasive. The whole enterprise, said critics, was misguided and based on a naive view of the business world. Back then, accepted wisdom held that "business ethics" was a contradiction in terms. The most generous view was that business ethics had something to do with corporate philanthropy, a topic that might interest executives *after* their companies became financially successful. But even then, it was only a frill – an indulgence for the wealthy or eccentric.

Today, attitudes are different. Though far from universally embraced – witness the scandals of 2001 and 2002 – ethics is increasingly viewed as an important corporate concern. What is our purpose? What do we believe in? What principles should guide our behavior? What do we owe one another and the people we deal with – our employees, our customers, our investors, our communities? Such

[1] Excerpted with permission from: Lynn Sharp Paine. 2003. *Value Shift: Why Companies Must Merge Social and Financial Imperatives to Achieve Superior Performance*. New York: McGraw-Hill.

questions of ethics are being taken seriously in many companies around the world.

A thoughtful observer might well ask: "What is going on? Why the upsurge of interest in ethics and values?" In discussing these questions I have learned that motivating concerns are varied:

- An Argentine executive sees ethics as integral to transforming his company into a "world-class" organization.
- A group of Thai executives want to protect their company's reputation for integrity and social responsibility from erosion in the face of intensified competition.
- Two Nigerian entrepreneurs want their company to become a "role model" for Nigerian society.
- A US executive believes that high ethical standards are correlated with better financial performance.
- An Italian executive wants to make sure his company stays clear of scandals that have embroiled others.

As these motivations show, the paths to values are many and varied. Some companies arrive by way of crisis or scandal. Others come by way of executives' personal conviction or a process of logical reasoning and reflection. Some are problem-driven. Others are opportunity-driven. Most arrive through a mix of both positive and negative factors.

Whatever the path, though, more and more companies are rejecting traditional ideas of management as a "value-free" science and business as an "ethics-free zone." Executives are coming to see attention to values not as a frill or an indulgence but as an integral part of effective management, touching all aspects of a company's operations. Many now believe that adhering to the core principles found in virtually all the world's ethical traditions is neither naive nor a sign of weakness, but rather smart and a source of organizational strength. And some are coming to view moral judgment as a help rather than a hindrance in doing business.

What accounts for this shift in attitudes? Is it a passing fad or a symptom of fundamental change? Are the driving forces financial, or are other factors at work? To answer these questions, we must look more deeply at the themes introduced in this chapter and place the turn to values in a larger context.

Ethics pays

Many argue that ethics pays. In addition to savings from reduced misconduct and benefits from an enhanced reputation, studies have shown that:

- Trust, helpfulness, and fairness in rewarding creative work are associated with higher levels of work group creativity. Less creative work groups are more likely to have experienced dishonest communications, destructive competition, and political problems (Amabile 1997, 1998).
- Employees are more likely to support management decisions that have been reached through a fair process. By the same token, employees are more likely to subvert decisions that benefit particular groups at the expense of the organization as a whole (Kim and Mauborgne 1993).
- Employees are more likely to engage in discretionary behavior (that is, beyond the defined requirements of the job) to benefit the organization if they trust their supervisors to treat them fairly and perceive that the organization operates fairly (Moorman 1991; Organ and Konovsky 1989).
- Partnerships between manufacturers and retailers are more profitable when they are based on high levels of mutual trust. High-trust partnerships emerge when the parties are honest, dependable, and mutually attentive to one another's welfare (Kumar 1996).[2]

A recent review of some 95 academic studies of the relationship between corporate financial and social performance found that only 4 of the 95 studies reported a negative relationship between the two. Fifty-five studies found a positive correlation between better financial performance and better social performance. Twenty-two found no relationship; and 18 found a mixed relationship (Margolis and Walsh 2001).

Although no study has convincingly measured corporate ethical competency and shown its positive relation to financial performance, one thing is quite clear. Ethics and financial self-interest are no longer the implacable enemies they have sometimes been thought to be.

---

[2] This study covered 1,500 manufacturer–retailer relationships.

In this respect the growing acceptance of "ethics pays" is a remarkable shift from the "ethics costs" stance of only a few decades back.

In many situations, however, the ethically preferable course of action is not financially beneficial and may not even be financially feasible. We must acknowledge that the link between ethical commitment and economic advantage is both fragile and ever-changing. Whether the relationship tends towards harmony or hostility reflects the financial and moral standards to which companies are held and the context in which they operate. But even under favorable conditions, the financial case for ethics goes only so far. Although the financial case is stronger than has often been thought, it does not fully explain the turn to values. For that, we must look to changes in the business environment.

The corporation's evolving personality

According to the Millennium Poll on Corporate Social Responsibility, a 1999 survey of more than 25,000 individuals across 23 countries on six continents, two in three people say that companies should go beyond their traditional functions of making a profit, paying taxes, creating jobs, and obeying the law. In addition, respondents said, companies should also try to set a higher ethical standard and contribute to broader societal goals. In other words, companies should achieve profitability in ways that help build a better society. In all but three of the countries surveyed, 50 percent or more of the respondents took this position. Among those who expressed this view, about half defined the corporation's role as "exceeding all laws, setting a higher ethical standard, and helping build a better society for all." The remainder of this subset said companies should operate "somewhere between" the traditional definition of the corporation's role and this more demanding one (GlobeScan 1999).

In attributing a capacity for moral judgment to the corporation, these respondents go against an orthodoxy whose lineage is both long and venerable. The doctrine of corporate amorality has ancient roots in corporate law, and it has played a central role in the thinking of many economists and management theorists up to this day. This doctrine found perhaps its most colorful expression in the comment of an eighteenth-century English jurist who railed at the corporation for lacking either "pants to kick" or "a soul to damn" (Stone 1975: 3).

Though forcefully put, the thought itself was not original. In a seminal legal case decided early in the preceding century, another eminent English jurist, Sir Edward Coke, had declared that corporations, because they had no souls, could neither commit treason nor be outlawed or excommunicated (Coke 1613). To Coke and many who came before him, it made no sense to attribute moral responsibility to a corporation. How could such a manifestly "artificial" and "intangible" entity be a moral agent? This logic, which is also known as the "fiction theory" had been spelled out almost four centuries earlier by Pope Innocent IV, for ecclesiastical corporations (Dewey 1926). The "fiction theory," shorn of its overt religious origins, was carried forward and reaffirmed in 1819 by the US Supreme Court in the well-known case of *Dartmouth College* v. *Woodward*.[3]

In the late nineteenth century, the fiction theory underwent a makeover reflecting the changing time. With the proliferation of "general incorporation statutes," beginning around mid-century, the government's role in forming corporations receded into the background. Under these statutes, corporations could be formed without a special charter from a state legislature (Horwitz 1992). By 1875, special charters had become largely a thing of the past, and virtually anyone could form a corporation simply by filing the appropriate forms and paying the required fee (Heberton Evans 1948). Many did so: The latter half of the century saw a phenomenal increase in the number of incorporations across the United States. A similar expansion occurred in England as freedom of incorporation took hold and the joint stock company, with the advantage of limited liability, became a form available as of common right (Heberton Evans 1948: 35).

The new conception of the corporation as a fictional umbrella for a private association of shareholders strengthened the argument against government control over corporations and enlarged their sphere of authority. Nevertheless, the corporation's moral status, or lack thereof, remained unchanged.

Of course not everyone bought into the idea of the corporation as a fiction. By the dawn of the twentieth century, with the spectacular growth of corporations in the United States and Europe, academics on both sides of the Atlantic had begun to challenge this characterization.

---

[3] Trustees of Dartmouth College v. Woodward, 17 US (4 Wheat) 518, 636 (1819).

They insisted that the corporation was a "natural" or "real" entity, thereby drawing attention to the sociological fact of growing corporate power and influence as seen in the great railroad and manufacturing corporations as well as the immensely powerful oil trusts of the time.

The "natural entity" theory found an audience among both critics and supporters of the corporation's growing influence. Critics saw it as justifying their concerns about increasingly large concentrations of capital and its impact on community life. Supporters, on the other hand, saw it as legitimating new rights for corporations and enhancing the authority of officers and directors in relation to shareholders.

For legal purposes, the corporation had been declared a citizen, contrary to Justice Marshall's earlier insistence that this was not the case. Moreover, US law had unequivocally embraced the doctrine of limited shareholder liability. Shareholders were now safely shielded from personal accountability for the corporation's debts and other liabilities incurred in carrying out corporate activities (Hovenkamp 1988).

By the 1930s, the corporation had attained sufficient stature to be counted among the ranks of society's essential institutions. According to one leading authority on corporations writing at the time, "it was apparent to any thoughtful observer that the American corporation had ceased to be a private business device and had become an institution" (Berle 1932: v).

The institutional view of the corporation thus moved into the mainstream and became the dominant framework for legal thinking. With this move came suggestions that the corporation, as such, had responsibilities not just to stockholders but to other parties as well – a position that would seem to imply a moral personality for the corporation.

Meanwhile the fiction theory of the corporation had not entirely died off. In certain economic circles, this old bottle was being filled with new wine. Unlike the English jurist who had seen in the corporation's fictional nature a cause for frustration, the theory's new proponents viewed it as a shield against the period's increasingly strident calls for corporate responsibility (Baldwin 1984). "Only people can have responsibilities," wrote a leading economist in 1971, in a coolly reasoned argument against corporate social responsibility (Friedman 1970).

This argument, with its eerie echoes of Sir Edward Coke and even Pope Innocent IV, can only ring hollow to the contemporary ear. The size and influence of today's corporations far exceed anything even remotely imaginable to the authors and early proponents of the corporate fiction doctrine. Indeed, as the size and the importance of corporations have increased, so has the general propensity to view their activities through a moral lens.

New standard of performance

As many have by now observed, corporations today are not just tools we use to organize economic activity. They have become the environment we live in. The moralization of the corporation provides the key to understanding the recent turn to values. The growing acceptance of the moral actor premise has affected how companies are expected to behave and has raised the bar for their performance.

As companies have become pervasive and powerful actors in the world, society has endowed them with a new kind of character. More and more, they are being evaluated as if they were responsible human beings whose functional task must be carried out in a moral framework. Evidence of this "ethico-nomic" standard is abundant. Corporate reputation studies, best company rankings, employee commitment surveys, public opinion polls, stock price movement – these are a few of the more telling indicators. Like the survey respondents mentioned earlier, those who say that companies should set a higher ethical standard and contribute to broader societal goals in addition to performing their traditional functions, other constituencies are injecting moral criteria into their evaluations of corporations. We can see this in the expectations and concerns different groups such as employees, customers, investors, or suppliers bring to their dealings with companies. Whether they are deciding where to work, where to buy, where to invest, or what companies they want in their communities, significant numbers of people are including moral considerations with financial ones in their deliberations.

The new standard is also seen in the "most admired" and "most respected" company surveys that have proliferated in recent years. Although each survey is different, most include criteria that pertain to companies' overall functioning, as well as their appeal to investors, employees, customers, and communities.

The doctrine of corporate amorality was always a parasitic idea. It presupposed that society's moral order would be tended and maintained by families, schools, churches, governments, and other civic organizations. So long as the rest of society looked after that

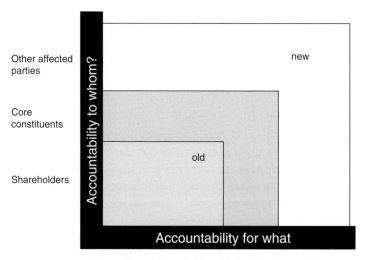

Figure 11.1 Accountability matrix

moral framework, corporations could be treated as an exception. But just as liberalization has shifted the boundaries between business and government, it has broken down old distinctions between for-profit and not-for-profit organizations. It has also blurred familiar boundaries between home and work. The walls that separated the sphere of domesticity from the sphere of commerce have crumbled as women have entered the corporate world and men and women alike have sought to combine work and family.

In the past it might have been possible to think of business as a separate realm exempt from the ethics of hearth, home, and community. As late as 1968, a consultant writing in the *Harvard Business Review* defended business practices that were of "questionable morality" if judged by "ordinary standards" on the grounds that business had its own "rules of the game." He advised executives, moreover, that failure to draw a sharp distinction between the ethical systems of the home and those of the office could be deleterious to their health (Carr 1968).

Today such an argument cannot stand. So intertwined is business with every aspect of life that it has become impossible to distinguish, let alone disentangle, these different threads. Corporations are routinely judged by ordinary standards of morality. The rise of the corporation, liberalization around the globe, advances in knowledge and technology made the emergence of a new and more demanding standard of corporate performance almost inevitable. That, however, does not mean that companies have fully grasped the new standard or that meeting it is easy. For many, the very idea will require a radical shift in mindset – not to mention fundamental changes in management practice.

Rather than responding to every possible objection to this argument, let's just ask one simple question: what is the most likely future? Do we foresee a world in which companies are expected to behave as moral actors or a return to the corporate amorality doctrine? So long as corporations continue to play a pervasive and central role in society, a return to the past is unlikely. In the more probable future, companies will be expected to show a moral face to the world while at the same time fulfilling their functions as wealth creators, producers, and employers.

Performing at a higher level

To meet the new standard, companies need a moral center. By a moral center I don't mean just a code of conduct or list of aphorisms inscribed on a Lucite plaque, but rather a set of answers to fundamental questions that every moral actor, whether individual or corporate, must address. For companies, the questions cluster around four main themes:

- *Purpose:* what is the company's purpose? Besides creating wealth and using resources efficiently, what is the company's contribution to society? How do its products and services add value to people's lives?
- *Principles:* what are the company's guiding principles? What precepts guide the conduct of its people in carrying out its purpose? What are its nonnegotiable standards, its ideals and aspirations?
- *People:* what is the company's concept of the person? Who counts as a member of its moral community? Whose interests are considered in its decision making?
- *Power:* what is the scope of the company's power and authority? To whom and for what is the company accountable? How is decision-making authority to be allocated within the organization?

These themes suggest a simple framework that managers can use to assess the ethics of their decisions. The framework consists of four questions, each associated with a distinctive mode of analysis and a long tradition of ethical thought.

Purpose: will this action serve a worthwhile purpose?

This mode of analysis has to do with the ethics of ends and means, or "pragmatic analysis." "Pragmatic" is sometimes used to mean "expedient rather than moral," but I am using the term in its more general sense to mean "goal-directed" or "purposeful." Pragmatic analysis examines the quality of our goals and the suitability of the means we choose for attaining them.

This mode of analysis thus calls for clarity about both the ends and means, but the ends must be judged worthwhile and the means found to be effective as well as efficient (James 1948).

The central question is whether a proposed course of action will serve a worthwhile purpose. But an answer to this question will normally require answers to a cluster of subsidiary questions calling for facts as well as judgment:

- What are we trying to accomplish? What are our short- and long-term goals?
- Are these goals worthwhile? How to they contribute to people's lives?
- Will the course of action we're considering contribute to achieving these goals?
- Compared to the possible alternatives, how effectively and efficiently will it do so?
- If this is not the most effective and efficient course, do we have a sound basis for pursuing the proposed path?

Principle: is this action consistent with relevant principles?

A second mode of analysis examines actions from the standpoint of applicable principles and standards. Its roots lie in the ethics of duty and ideals. Let's call it "normative analysis" since it references various norms of behavior, those entailed by self-imposed ideals and aspirations as well as those found in bodies of standards such as law, industry codes, company codes, and the emerging body of generally accepted ethical principles for business. In contrast to pragmatic analysis, which uses instrumental or means–end reasoning, normative analysis relies on reasoning from general principles to specific instances – what has sometimes been called "formal reasoning."

The central question is whether a proposed course of action is consistent with the relevant principles. Among these may be principles that express duties or obligations whose fulfillment is required as well as principles that express ideals or voluntary standards associated with good practice. Normative analysis involves subsidiary questions such as:

- What norms of conduct are relevant to this situation, including those found in law, customary practice, industry codes, company guidelines, or the emerging body of generally accepted ethical principles?
- What are our duties under these standards?
- What are the best practices under these standards?
- Does the proposed action honor the applicable standards?
- If not, do we have a sound basis for departing from those standards?
- Is the proposed action consistent with our own espoused standards and ideals?

People: does this action respect the legitimate claims of the people likely to be affected?

A third mode of analysis focuses on the expected consequences of a proposed course of action for the people likely to be affected by it. Will they be injured? Will they benefit? Will their rights be violated or infringed? This mode of analysis is sometimes called "stakeholder analysis" or "stakeholder impact analysis" because it takes the vantage-point of those with a stake in the outcome. The central question is whether a proposed course of action respects the legitimate claims of the parties affected by it (Freeman 1984; Donaldson and Preston 1995).

Stakeholder analysis is useful for identifying opportunities to mitigate harms as well as to pursue mutual gains. Skill in social reasoning is essential for carrying out this kind of analysis, since understanding others' perspectives and circumstances is the starting-point for evaluating their concerns, interests, and expectations. However, formal reasoning is also involved insofar as norms play a role in assessing the claims presented. Key questions in stakeholder analysis include:

- Who is likely to be affected, both directly and indirectly, by the proposed action?

- How will these parties be affected?
- What are these parties' rights, interests, expectations, and concerns as derived from law, agreement, custom, past practice, explicit norms, or other sources?
- Does our plan respect legitimate claims of the affected parties?
- If not, what are we doing to compensate for the infringement?
- Have we mitigated unnecessary harms?
- Are there alternatives that would be less harmful or more beneficial on balance?
- Have we taken full advantage of opportunities for mutual benefit?

Power: do we have the power to take this action?

A fourth mode of analysis stems from the ethics of power. In a sense, this is the most fundamental question because it concerns the actor's authority and ability to act. Unless a proposed action is within the scope of the actor's legitimate authority and unless the actor actually has the ability – the skills, resources, clout, energy – to carry out the proposed plan, all the previous questions are moot. Following the ancient dictum that "ought implies can," this analysis might be termed a "capacities" or "wherewithal" analysis. It examines both the actor's moral right and his material resources to act. From this perspective, then, the central question is whether the proposed action is within the actor's legitimate power. This question leads to the following subsidiary inquiries:

- What is the scope of our legitimate authority in view of relevant laws, agreements, understandings, and stakeholder expectations?
- Are we within our rights to pursue the proposed course of action?
- If not, have we secured the necessary approvals or consent from the relevant authorities?
- Do we have the resources, including knowledge and skills as well as tangible resources, required to carry out the proposed action?
- If not, do we have the ability to marshal the needed resources?

These questions are not a set of moral precepts or standards of behavior in any conventional sense but rather a set of analytical frames or "lenses" that managers can use to identify ethical issues and test their decisions. Taken together, the four lenses may be thought of as a metaphorical "manager's compass."

For both moral and financial reasons, today's companies need a methodology for integrating the moral point of view into their decision-making. In a restless sea of moral and financial expectations, managers cannot navigate with financial perspectives alone. To meet new financial, legal, and ethical accountabilities, companies will need to integrate the moral point of view into their decision-making. The manager's compass is one framework for doing this. Undoubtedly there are others that could work just as well, or perhaps even better, so long as they raise the core questions. Just as important as the framework is the care and rigor with which it is applied. What is essential is to have some way of engaging the moral perspective at the moment of decision. Otherwise, companies will find it very difficult to meet the new standard of performance on a sustained basis.

Conclusion

The new standard of performance is likely to remain in effect for the foreseeable future. Whether we anticipate prosperity or recession, peace or war, it is hard to imagine the corporation's importance to society diminishing or its functions being transferred to other institutions. In the years ahead, we are thus likely to see continuing calls for companies to be more efficient and more profitable, and at the same time more responsive to their constituencies, more accountable for the impact of their activities, and more respectful of law and generally accepted ethical standards. In this environment, we can also expect many more companies to recognize the benefits of honoring human values and presenting a moral face to the world as they carry out their business. The capacity to merge financial and social imperatives will become increasingly important for companies worldwide.

References

Amabile, T. M. 1997. "Mobilizing Creativity in Organizations," *California Management Review* 40(1): 39–58.
    1998. "How to Kill Creativity," *Harvard Business Review* (September–October): 77–87.
Baldwin, F. D. 1984. *Conflicting Interests: Corporate-Governance Controversies*. Lexington, MA: D. C. Heath and Company.
Berle, A. A. and Means, G. C. 1932. *The Modern Corporation and Private Property*. New York, NY: Commerce Clearing House, Inc.

Carr, A. Z. 1968. "Is Business Bluffing Ethical?" *Harvard Business Review*, 68102: 5–7.

Coke, E. 1613. "The Case of Sutton's Hospital," 10 Coke Report 1a, 77 Eng. Rep. 937 (Exchequer Chamber).

Dewey, J. 1926. "The Historic Background of Corporate Legal Personality," *Yale Law Journal*, XXXV(6) (April 1926): 655–73.

Donaldson, T. and Preston, L. E. 1995. "The Stakeholder Theory of the Corporation: Concepts, Evidence, and Implications," *Academy of Management Review*, 20(1): 65–91.

Freeman, E. R. 1984. *Strategic Planning: A Stakeholder Approach.* Boston, MA: Pitman Publishing.

Friedman, M. 1970. "The Social Responsibility of Business Is to Increase Its Profits," *New York Times Magazine*, September 13, p. 33.

GlobeScan. 1999. "The Millennium Poll on Corporate Social Responsibility," in cooperation with the Prince of Wales Business Leaders Forum and the Conference Board, http://www.globescan.com/news_archives/MPExec Brief.pdf (accessed August 22, 2008).

Heberton Evans, G. 1948. *Business Incorporations in the United States 1800–1943.* New York, NY: National Bureau of Economic Research, pp. 3, 10, 35.

Horwitz, M. J. 1992. "Santa Clara Revisited: The Development of Corporate Theory," in *The Transformation of American Law 1870–1960.* New York, NY: Oxford University Press, pp. 65–107.

Hovenkamp, H., 1988. "Classical Corporation in American Legal Thought," *Georgetown Law Journal*, 76(5): 1593–689.

James, W. 1948. "What Pragmatism Means," in A. Castell (ed.) *Essays in Pragmatism.* New York, NY: Hafner Publishing Company, p.146.

Kim, C. and Mauborgne, R. 1993. "Making Global Strategies Work," *Sloan Management Review* (Spring): 11–27.

Kumar, N. 1996. "The Power of Trust in Manufacturer-Retailer relationships," *Harvard Business Review* (November–December): 92–106.

Margolis, J. D. and Walsh, J. P. 2001. *People and Profits? The Search for a Link between a Company's Social and Financial Performance.* Mahwah, NJ: Lawrence Erlbaum Associates.

Moorman, R. H. 1991. "Relationship Between Organizational Justice and Organizational Citizenship Behaviors: Do Fairness Perceptions Influence Employee Citizenship?" *Journal of Applied Psychology* 76(6): 845–55.

Organ, D. W. and Konovsky, M. 1989. "Cognitive Versus Affective Determinants of Organizational Citizenship Behavior," *Journal of Applied Psychology* 74(1): 157–64.

Stone, C. D. 1975. *Where the Law Ends: The Social Control of Corporate Behavior*, 2nd edn. New York, NY: Harper & Row Publishers.

12 | *The ugly side of capitalism: what the young generation needs to combat*

ULRICH STEGER

Introduction

Just as the last Marxists are disappearing from the globe, capitalism has shed the "soft" face it developed during its struggle with communism after the Second World War. Currently, capitalism resembles Karl Marx's description of it: harsh, cold, uncompassionate, anti-humanistic, crisis-prone, relentlessly exploiting every country and opportunity for the sake of profit – with the resultant huge collateral damage in terms of people, cultures, and traditions. Greed is omnipresent and even seems to have halted the mechanism that has been driving prosperity and – to some extent – humanistic advances since the Second World War. The failure of the Doha round appears to have been the end of a shared responsibility for an increasingly integrated globe.

This book does not, however, indulge in scare mongering; the focus is therefore not on doomsday scenarios, but on practical alternatives, which are relevant for young academicians. Consequently, this chapter describes what has happened since the collapse of communism and why (section 2 below) as well as the priorities of the required change. The latter focuses particularly on the finance sector dominance of the economy and companies (section 3), resource waste (especially energy [section 4]), and the reminder that life is more than consumption (section 5). In conclusion, some recommendations regarding what young academicians can do to stem these negative trends are provided.

Globalization–technology–US supremacy: the turning of the tide?

The collapse of communism was the most visible historical event for Europe at the end of the millennium. Not only did it drastically change the security landscape – especially in Europe, where military confrontation has become a remote memory – but also indirectly in Third World countries, where local conflicts no longer become the superpowers' proxy battles. It also changed Europe's economic land-scape, as developed but low-wage countries were suddenly competing on the EU's doorstep. We often also overlook the fact that the decline of centrally planned economies had far-reaching consequences for the emergence of developing countries. Whereas the dominant paradigm in the 1960s and 70s was building domestic industries to ensure "import substitution" through state intervention, opening up the economy and deregulation have been the name of the game since the mid-80s. The spectacular success of the "four tigers" in South East Asia – Hong Kong, Singapore, Taiwan, and South Korea – convinced many coun-tries around the world to shift their economic policy towards integra-tion into the world economy. Between 1985 and 2005 the membership of the World Trade Organization (WTO) (formally GATT) grew significantly. This changed the pattern of trade dramatically. Whereas the traditional pattern was raw material and cheap mass products exchanged for high-tech and luxury goods, these countries built their export capacity and international reach on a broad range of industrial and consumer goods, which are now competing quite successfully on the world market. A role model is Thailand, which today provides more than a quarter of the world's SUVs and light trucks. An additional new feature emerged as well. More than one third of world trade no longer takes place between different firms in different countries but are intra-company flows as a result of interlocked supply chains across borders.

Global economic integration was heavily fostered by technological developments, notably information and communication technology, and their rapid managerial applications. Global procurement and supply chain management, with their underlying complex logistics, are specific examples of activities that would be impossible if they were not IT-based. The same holds true for financial markets, examined in section 3 of this chapter. Distances and time seem to shrink continually. As the value of an export good from the other side of the world increases, the volume decreases, making transportation costs less relevant. Another example is the cement industry (the incarnation of the "local" bulk industry), which is now dominated by three global companies. Web-based management and logistics were sufficient incentives to build global companies.

The political umbrella for this development was provided by the US, the only military, economic, and political superpower left. Although difficult to grasp today, in the 1990s, bookshops were flush with titles such as *The American Millennium* by Nick Yapp (1998) and *The End of History* by Francis Fukuyama (1992), because – to exaggerate only a bit – everybody was becoming like the US. The finalization of the Uruguay trade round with the creation of a World Trade Organization was probably the most remarkable success. What is now in hindsight called the "dotcom bubble" was at that time the "New Economy" that led to books like *Dow 100,000* by Charles Kadlec (1999), which basically argued for stock prices to increase tenfold as a result of the new IT cornucopia.

The "Washington Consensus" – deregulation, free trade and capital movements, fiscal austerity combined with tax cuts – permeated national institutions and many national government policies. Globalization was, however, never a linear process. First, there were winners and losers, and the losers organized themselves by pushing for more sophisticated means of protectionism. Second there was a vocal, but politically ineffective "anti-globalization" movement. A fairer label would be "current-globalization critics," as they have raised awareness of some of the negative impacts of globalization: a growing income inequality both between and within nations (unskilled and semi-skilled labor in particular is losing out in developing countries), increasing environmental degradation, loss of diversity (ecologically, culturally, and economically), and a more hectic, stressful life.

This skeptical attitude, which started as a minority view, appears to be the dominant paradigm today. The Doha round, which was supposed to be a new trade and service liberalization round, failed. The US Congress no longer has a free trade majority, a trait it shares with many other parliaments – even in the deeply integrated European Union, nationalistic and protectionist attitudes are on the rise. The US is no longer providing leadership as it is too tied up in Iraq and very few would people would today regard the US as a role model for the "society of the future" despite its out-pacing consumption growth.

What went wrong? Was globalization a passing fad and is capitalism on the decline again? Or do they have certain inbuilt features that could turn self-destructive if not managed better?

I would argue for the latter, which does not involve a fundamental critique of capitalism, and identify three issues – the dominance of the financial sector, resource waste, and the emptiness of the consumption and career ideology – as the key negative dynamics that the young generation needs to combat.

Dominance of the financial sector

The financial service industry (FSI) has been one of the fastest-growing industries and the biggest profiteer from globalization and related developments like the privatization of pension systems. Its assets are measured in trillions of dollars. In the US it accounts for 8 percent of GNP, while the figure for Europe is about half. By one estimate, approximately half of the profits generated by the 100 largest companies in the US are from financial institutions. As money, which can currently be slotted around the world within seconds, is the ultimate commodity, it is no surprise that financial asset bubbles are rapidly growing larger and will burst simultaneously. In the late 1980s, the bursting of an FSI bubble nearly ruined Latin America. In the late 1990s, another strongly affected Asia, while there was a strong risk that the world economy could be contaminated. If there is something like an "average 10-year" rule in which the herd behavior of traders creates a speculative bubble, then expect something in the years to come. Next to these more global risks, a number of local and regional asset markets also went from boom to bust.

Besides the macro impact, financial institutions' impact on companies is of great concern. Pitches by investment banks and their finance capabilities fuel the mergers and acquisitions cycle as companies try to ensure that, as always, less value is ultimately destroyed. The private equity industry is so awash with cash that no company is safe from a takeover. The line between legitimate restructuring and raiding corporations has too often become blurred. Although stock trading has been electronically rationalized, the entire system of financial analysts, specialized media, and institutionalized investors – increasingly bloated, noisy, and ridden with conflicts of interest – is pushing companies to maximize shareholder value. In principle, there is nothing wrong with creating shareholder value. The problem starts if this goal is reduced to analysts' quarterly earnings per share estimates, which are always higher than the real economy can deliver. In the US, profits grew by around 7 percent, over the last cycle, but analyst estimates were rarely below double digits, mostly around

15 percent. The intentions are clear: to present a bright stock market outlook in order to lure more buyers for stocks, hoping to create a self-fulfilling prophecy. As deviations from estimates are punished by a declining share price and, consequently, a decline in executives' income, this pressure is not only the root cause of all kinds of "massaging the numbers," but is also pushing companies towards riskier strategies. This in turn increases the risk premium on equity and the required profit margins, etc.

Criticism of the financial service industry's dominance of the real economy is not new. Scholars of economic history might remember Rudolf Hilferding's *Das Finanzkapital* (1923), in which he analyzed the role of big bangs as the real masters of corporate capitalism. However, according to all meaningful indicators, the financial service industry's influence has never been so high. In addition, the ability of national regulators to supervise the system risks has never been so low. Nevertheless, as the financial service industry has become increasingly detached from its original service function and "making money with money" has become the only game in town, the limits of development are also becoming more visible. Public mistrust – fueled by a never-ending series of scandals – is growing. It is irony indeed. To add insult to injury, the academic literature is experiencing an avalanche of demands for corporate social responsibility (CSR) and sustainable development even as the short-term pressure of the financial service industry, real economic development, and the behavior of companies and their leaders move in exactly the opposite direction. Some attempt has been made to disguise reality through a huge number of CSR reports that confuse reporting and performance, which only fools those who do not know how companies tick. Given the framework conditions under which management has to operate today, this should be no surprise. There are strong dynamics against humanism in business. It is, after all, a rational response to the prevailing business environment and its framework conditions.

Waste of resources

Even though the cyclicality of energy prices has disguised long-term trends to some extent, it has now become clear that our natural resources cannot support our intensive lifestyle. This is truer than ever, now that a significant part of the world is catching up. Although this applies to many raw materials, it is most significant in respect of fossil fuel, as our whole economy depends on its permanent availability and accessibility. Although the first writing on the wall appeared more than 30 years ago with the first oil price crisis, little has changed. Even in Europe, a master of energy saving compared to the US and the rapidly growing emerging economies, the promotion of energy efficiency and renewable energy resources could only compensate for approximately half of what economic growth added. We are therefore facing a new Cold War: one in which nations try to secure scarce energy resources. It is no wonder that Asian energy companies compete aggressively with Western multinationals and more often than not ignore all the progress that has been made in terms of corporate respect for human rights, environmental safeguards, and biodiversity.

I stress this struggle for resource distribution more than global warming. Although awareness of the fundamental risks of climate change has increased, the readiness to act is still strongly underdeveloped. This is, for example, demonstrated in the difficulty in reaching a follow-up agreement to the Kyoto Protocol. The shorterterm probability of an oil price of $100 per barrel, which translates into approximately $5 per gallon for gasoline in the US, will hit harder and exert more pressure for behaviors to change. Thirty years ago, a lack of technology may have been the strongest barrier to change, but now we have the technologies to decouple growth, energy, and resource consumption, although their wider diffusion is dramatically slow. It is deeply ingrained behavior that is the main obstacle today and will be so in the foreseeable future, on both the individual and societal level. One hopes for more rational enlightenment, but there is ample evidence that it is mostly pressure that changes behavior. As this comes rather late, the frictions and social cost of a turnaround can be immense.

Life is more than consumption

The background of new video games can be tailored to simulate the player's commercial neighborhood and thus target the advertising message more sharply – probably a new height in the advertising intensity (and intrusiveness) with which we are confronted. More homogenous consumption patterns have become more dominant in the course of globalization. They are the common patterns that define the similarities of our economies and, partly, that of our societies. The many global consumption options do, however, create new stress: how can the maximum opportunities be realized? As we no longer believe much in an eternal afterlife, we try to pack two lives into one. The IT-generated pressure of permanent availability and immediate response match the psychological stress caused by consumption. Then add travel, coordination across time zones, and, last but not least, growing job insecurity, even in professions requiring high qualifications. Whereas the income of the better educated is growing in the globalization process, their quality of life is clearly deteriorating. The poorest countries such as Bangladesh constantly score higher on global happiness indices. Their integral families and social cohesion are significant reasons for their happiness. Consequently, the world risks losing even more of its humanistic side with regard to this fifth dimension – over-consumption can never be a panacea for happiness.

There is an additional interesting contradiction between the two stressful parts of life. The marketing director's ideal consumer – hedonistic, looking for instant gratification, a bit of a hypochondriac, and egocentric – is the HR director's nightmare. The latter is looking for resilience, social competences as team player, etc. In short, the role models transmitted via advertising and entertainment are eroding the very work ethic on which capitalism has always been built.

All these issues are of course at least partly linked. The dominance of consumption is driving the resource-intensive lifestyle, as well as the growth of the financial service industry – US consumers especially are accumulating massive debts to maintain that level of consumption. Don't blame them – they have saved the world from a recession more than once.

What can the younger generation of academics do?

The purpose of this short introduction is not to develop a comprehensive action plan to address the weakness, if not the illness, of capitalism, but to examine the role that young academicians can play in creating more transparency and a clear understanding of the impacts of certain trends. It is not about becoming political agitators, which is one of the main problems with the entire academic CSR community: "too many priests, too few believers" (as Michael Porter

put it – I have nothing to add). Rather, upholding the highest professional standards is the key to credibility and to creating effective
findings.

The main purpose of social science is to create new knowledge
through the analysis of situations, the impacts of contingencies, and
the available options to solve specific problems. This is what I refer to.
We don't need more chairs for ethics or CSR, but we do need more
sober analysis and empirical evidence of what is happening, why it is
happening (or who makes it happen), and what the direct and indirect
consequences are. Another key question is, of course: who is paying
the full bill?

Just to highlight some examples of what needs to be done in
research and transferred to effective teaching and publications to a
wider audience:

- Where is the marketing expert who, with new approaches and
  sophistication, will examine the plausible assumption that advertising in all its facets has rapidly diminishing returns, and will then
  communicate the evidence effectively?
- For the logistics freaks: what are the real total costs and impacts of
  global supply chains with all their long-term financial, environmental, and social impact?
- For the finance guys: what role have investment bankers played in
  so many M&A failures?

Again, breaking new ground with evidence has to be the job of
those who specialize in a field, but are also capable of seeing the
broader and, hopefully, more humanistic picture. Of course it needs
more efforts, courage, and thinking to pioneer and go in against the
mainstream. But isn't this how progress in science has been achieved
ever since Galileo's time? What is the justification for the freedom and
resources that science enjoys in our society if we remain stuck in
conventionality? Do only dead fish swim with the mainstream? Can
the creativity of the smartest part of a generation be washed away in a
meaningless correlation by data warehouses? Is it really the purpose of
very sophisticated methods to find answers to questions nobody is
asking, or to answer yesterday's questions?

The only correlation in which I believe is: the better you are at your
scientific profession, the more relevant you have to be. And believe
me, the world needs it.

References

Fukuyama, Francis. 1992. *The End of History and the Last Man*. London: Penguin Books.

Hilferdings, Rudolf. 1923. *Das Finanzkapital*. Vienna: Verlag der Wiener Volksbuchhandlung.

Kadlec, Charles. 1999. *Dow 100,000: Fact or Fiction*. New York: Prentice Hall.

Yapp, Nick. 1998. *The American Millennium*. New York: Konemann.

PART 3

Humanistic management

13 | *Democratizing the corporation*[1]

ALLEN L. WHITE

As the economic, environmental, and social footprints of multi-national corporations MNCs have expanded, this influence has become a fact of life in the twenty-first century global economy. For champions of globalization, the rise of the MNC is cause for cele-bration. Job creation in poor countries, spreading innovation across borders, and building indigenous managerial talent are some of the rewards of MNC activity. For globalization skeptics, the picture, at best, is mixed. In their view, the borderless economy has intensified income disparities across and within countries, favored Northern firms at the expense of local entrepreneurs in part because of global trade rules, and accelerated the destruction of critical marine, forest, and atmospheric ecosystems as the culture of consumerism has fueled relentless demand for goods and services.

Within this unsettled landscape, the question of governance of MNCs has emerged as a pivotal issue among investors, civil society and government, and within MNCs themselves. The incongruity between the continued expansion of MNC scale and influence and the absence of a generally accepted governance framework is becoming increasingly evident. In a world where MNCs collectively are as economically and socially consequential as many national govern-ments, what are the rules of accountability to harness MNC interests such that they serve the long-term public interest?

This core question has spawned a multitude of frameworks, prin-ciples, and norms to bring MNCs into alignment with societal expectations, including: the OECD Guidelines for MNCs, the OECD Principles for Corporate Governance, the World Bank's Global Cor-porate Governance Forum, the UN Global Compact, specialty organizations such as the Global Reporting Initiative (sustainability

[1] The author gratefully acknowledges the research and editorial assistance of Anna Fleder.

reporting) and AccountAbility (assurance standards), and investor-led initiatives such as the International Corporate Governance Network (corporate governance principles). All of these initiatives, and many more, represent the first wave of efforts to align MNC governance with emerging global norms.

Beginning in 2001, a second wave of governance-related initiatives took shape, spurred by the revelation of governance failures by individual companies such as Enron, WorldCom, Royal Ahold, and Parmalat. These cases largely centered on fraudulent accounting practices, leading to misrepresentations in financial reporting that sent ripples through the investment, employee, and retiree communities. Virtually overnight, tens of billions of dollars of market capitalization evaporated, CEOs and other top executives were dismissed, and governments in North America and Europe scrambled to fashion legislation to prevent future occurrences of such egregious violations of the public trust. The result was a spate of legislative, regulatory, and voluntary initiatives that lead to new standards for internal control systems, auditing, reporting, and oversight of the professional accounting community as well as the expansion of independent directors on corporate boards.

Beyond containment

Taken as a whole, it is fair to say that the plethora of corporate governance initiatives during the last decade have achieved significant strides toward containment of harms without altering the fundamental obligations and duties of corporations to broader societal interests. Corporate directors are more vigilant, managers are more attentive, and shareholders are better protected against losses linked to breakdowns in corporate governance.

At the same time that progress in protecting shareholder interests has been achieved, the governance reforms have left intact the fundamental primacy of shareholders as the centerpiece of the "duty of loyalty" exercised by directors and executives. Shareholders remain the only stakeholder with the power to elect directors and bring lawsuits against corporations for violations of fiduciary duty, i.e. failure of the organization to protect shareholder interests. Requirements for independent directors, mandatory assessment of internal control systems, audits, and virtually every other component of pre- and post-Enron governance reforms reinforce the core doctrine of contemporary governance; that is, the interests of capital providers trump the interests of all other constituencies of the corporation. While cursory reference to employees, communities, the environment, and other stakeholders may appear in voluntary governance principles such as those promulgated by the International Corporate Governance Network (ICGN) and OECD, such principles and norms leave no doubt whose interests are paramount when directors and management make decisions. This is the case as much for capital allocation and mergers and acquisitions decisions as it is for cost and asset management and share buy-back and dividend payments.

To be sure, containment of harms through stronger controls against accounting and reporting misconduct is not without its benefit to stakeholders other than shareholders. The last decade has witnessed enormous costs to employees (who themselves are often shareholders) in terms of lost jobs, pensioners whose retirement funds suddenly evaporate, and communities whose social fabric is torn apart by abrupt plant and office closures. It is no coincidence that pension funds have been among the most aggressive champions of higher governance standards. Their beneficiaries wear multiple hats – they may simultaneously be shareholders, employees (active or retired), and members of the community.

Few would question that corporate governance today, just a few years after the dramatic misconduct and, in some cases, financial collapse of a number of US and European companies, has achieved significant improvements from the investor standpoint. But far less clear is whether such progress has been achieved in aligning governance structures with twenty-first-century societal needs and expectations of all stakeholders with legitimate claims on the conduct and performance of the firm.

The scale, complexity, and reach of MNCs is transforming the corporation from an entity of primarily localized consequences to one whose impacts are felt transnationally. Yet despite this shift from the local to the transnational, the fundamentals of governance norms remain remarkably stable, seemingly stuck in frameworks that bear less and less relevance to contemporary global realities. Changes that have occurred, e.g. in the number of independent directors, the role of audit committees, and the implementation of new standards for internal control systems, fall well short of altering the core accountability relationships between the corporation and its stakeholders. If governance norms are going to continue to evolve and align with twenty-first-century expectations, then future changes must become more systemic than those witnessed in the last few years. And the critical dimension of such systemic shifts is democratic control: the empowerment of all stakeholders with legitimate interests in the enterprise to exercise influence over key decisions of the enterprise which affect their lives.

Why democratize governance?

Democracy signifies accountability of an institution to those affected by its actions. In democratic nations, citizens hold their elected authorities accountable for providing goods and services, e.g. legal and regulatory structures to ensure public order and justice, physical infrastructure in the form of roads and canals, public education and health systems, and relations with other nations to create fair global trade and security. Public officials through the electoral process are periodically judged on their success in meeting citizen expectations. When they fail, they are replaced. When they succeed, they are re-elected.

The principles of political democracy applied to the corporation should yield comparable accountability. Since the corporation is granted its license to exist by sovereign governments, it should be held, subject to reasonable adjustments for its commercial character, to the same standards of accountability as political democracies – standards that hold it accountable to all parties with a legitimate stake in its activities. However, to adopt such a perspective, as we do in this article, requires departure from conventional wisdom, which defines the corporation in terms of property – owned, controlled, and accountable only to shareholders. This property-centric view of the corporation is the pillar of corporate law, regulation, and practice (Greenfield 2007). It is not, however, intrinsic to the concept of the corporation. Instead, the corporation-as-property view is the outcome of centuries of historical domination of capital owners (originally land, now financial capital) in the evolution of global economic systems and institutions (Kelly 2002).

Loosening the property-centric definition of the corporation opens up an array of alternatives that, many would argue, more aptly describe how corporations do and should behave in a globalizing economy. One such alternative is the concept of the corporation as a "team production" entity, comprising a group of individuals linked to others through complex supply networks, all of whom contribute jointly and inseparably to the wealth-creation process (Blair and Stout 1999). Another alternative, a variant on the team production concept, is the corporation as a community of individuals and institutions – workers, communities, suppliers, customers – who contribute various types of assets to the organization for the purpose of creating goods and services (Post *et al.* 2002). Still another alternative is the corporation as a living organism, given life by the convergence of human, natural, and financial capital, evolutionary from early-stage formation to mature organization and capable of reorganizing, reinventing, and refocusing its activities using the human intelligence of its constituents as external opportunities and threats come and go.

All of these alternatives to the property-centric definition share common roots in the notion of multiple resource providers as the essence that enables corporations to create wealth. Figure 13.1 depicts the various contributions of different resource providers to the corporation and to the wealth-creation process.

Eight parties, often referred to as "stakeholders," provide different types of resources, all of which are essential to the corporation's existence, operations and prosperity (White 2006a). For example, shareholders and lenders provide financial capital that helps transform labor, natural capital, and technology into the production of goods and services. Employees provide human capital, unions provide workforce liaison, and governments contribute a stable and predictable legal/regulatory infrastructure. Customers provide markets and, over time, brand loyalty and reputation to the organization. Communities provide a local license to operate, as well as access to air, water, and land resources. Suppliers are providers of networks and technologies essential to the corporation's own production activities.

Finally, future generations lend common assets to the corporation for temporary use, much like communities do on a shorter-term basis. Biodiversity, clean air and water, and productive land are "common assets" inherited by present generations with the understanding that contemporary users will be stewards of such assets, protective of both their quality and quantity, such that the stock is preserved for future generations (Barnes 2006). The corporation that exploits and

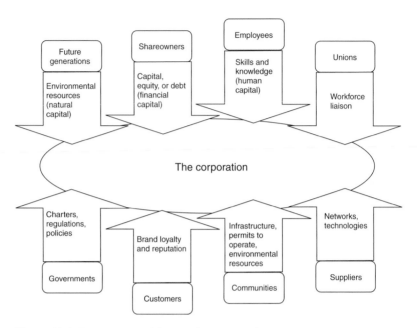

Figure 13.1 Resource providers to the corporation

undermines a common asset is, in effect, a delinquent borrower. Such is the case, for example, of those that have produced carbon emissions for generations which now threaten to undo climate stability owed to future generations.

In exchange for the resources provided, each party merits a return to its contribution (Figure 13.2). As in the case of resource providers, returns vary with regard to type and value. Future generations expect the firm to act as a trustee of the environmental resources, leaving the stock of resources undiminished. Shareowners expect dividends and growth in share price. Employees expect, at minimum, wages and benefits commensurate with their contribution. Unions expect a safe working environment and a place at the negotiating table. For governments, taxes and compliance with the law constitute some of the expected returns. Customers expect quality goods and services, while communities expect taxes, jobs for residents, and an uncompromised natural environment. For suppliers, long-term relationships that produce a steady revenue stream and timely payment of invoices are anticipated returns.

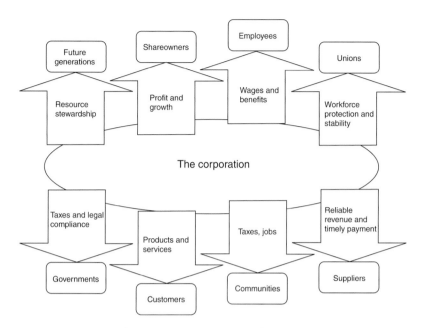

Figure 13.2 Expected returns to resource providers

Framing the corporation as the beneficiary of multiple resource providers opens new horizons for the role of democratic governance. Seeing the organization through the lens of multiple contributors to wealth creation repositions shareholders as one among many worthy recipients of the residual. It suggests that "stakes, not shares" (Cowe 2001) is the appropriate paradigm through which we view corporate accountability. Why, one may ask, are shareholders the sole stakeholder group to elect corporate directors and to bring lawsuits in cases of alleged breach of fiduciary duty? Indeed, why is fiduciary duty of directors defined, either *de jure* or *de facto*, as a duty of loyalty only to shareholders?

Once these property- and shareholder-centric strictures are removed, democratization becomes not only possible, but compelling. If the corporation is conceived as a team production entity, a community of individuals or a living organism, then control of its activities logically expand from the few to the many, from the capital providers and their agents – directors and managers – to the full array of legitimate claimants, ranging from employees and communities to suppliers and future generations. The licensing function of the state as a basis for democratic control is amplified by the reality that *all* corporations, and especially MNCs, are social entities with complex economic, ecological, and social footprints. This reality is the foundation for shifting from shares to stakes, and from shareholder-centric to stakeholder-based forms of corporate oversight, governance, and accountability.

Unbundling democratization

Bringing democratic principles to the corporation may occur along multiple pathways, not only through strengthening stakeholder influence and/or control of the organization.[2] Democratization of ownership, for example, is a form of economic democratization, and employee ownership is one of the most prominent examples of this concept. Distributing shares among employees has occurred in countries and regions as diverse as Britain, Chile, Egypt, Jamaica, the United States, Zimbabwe, Central and Eastern Europe, the former Soviet Union, and the People's Republic of China (Groban 2001). An estimated 10,000 employee stock option plans (ESOPs) are operative worldwide, and an estimated 15 percent of public companies in the US, with a disproportionate concentration in the technology sector, offer employees ESOPs. However, the vast majority of ESOPs in the US are found in unlisted companies; majority employee ownership structures among publicly traded companies are still highly exceptional (Gates 1998).

Among ESOPs, a small fraction – probably less than 10 percent – are entirely employee-owned. In many of these cases, economic democratization was not firmly implemented during the creation of the organization, but evolved slowly over time. Gradualism is common because the responsibilities and duties of ownership are learned skills that require nurturing among those not accustomed to stewardship responsibilities. For the last two centuries, as corporations have become increasingly complex and reliant on passive investors to meet capital needs, shareowners (some would say share-renters) have become increasingly detached from the organizations whose stock they hold. Though its consequences are largely adverse to workers, the

---

[2] I use the terms "democratization of the corporation" and "stakeholder governance" interchangeably while recognizing that the former is an outcome and the latter is a means toward that end.

notion that capital rents labor is one of the most enduring and deeply ingrained conventional wisdoms in modern management theory and practice. The result is the entrenchment of the work-for-paycheck mentality as opposed to work-as-investment mentality.

ESOPs are not the only form of economic democratization of corporations. Of equal or greater importance is the rise of the "new capitalists" (Davis *et al.* 2006), or individuals who assign their assets to institutional investors such as pension and mutual funds. The resources represented by these pooled assets are vast. In the US, the top 1,000 pension funds control US$5 trillion. The largest among these, including California, New York, and Florida public employee pension funds, each controls over $100 billion. Similarly in Europe, the Dutch ABP, the Danish ATP, and the UK telecommunications and mineworkers represent tens of billions of euros in assets. Overall, more than half of all equity holdings are in the hands of these large institutional investors, whose assets represent the accumulated wealth of millions of actual or eventual retirees.

This dramatic shift from highly concentrated ownership of corporate shares by a few wealthy individuals to a highly dispersed pattern of ownership is a phenomenon of the last three decades. It represents a sea change in ownership patterns and, with it, the empowerment of individuals to influence behavior of corporations in which they hold shares. It is having, in other words, a profound effect on corporate governance by giving voice to the multitude of citizen investors who are demanding a say in how the corporation is run.

The mechanisms by which this influence is wielded vary across countries and companies, but in general, all are intensifying as citizen investors become increasingly emboldened to seek change in boards or management. Shareholder resolutions in the US on issues such as climate change and employee diversity occur by the score every year, spearheaded by investor activists led by groups both ad hoc (e.g. groups of shareowners within companies) and permanent (e.g. issue-focused civil society groups and faith-based organizations concerned with human rights or labor practices). In recent years, such activism has been fueled by investor displeasure with certain conduct – e.g. soaring executive compensation or backdating stock options to maximize payouts to executives – reminiscent of the Enron-era ethical lapses.

In short, from the perspective of shareholder democracy, the age of citizen-investor activism is gradually democratizing the corporation by introducing new forms of accountability between shareholders, boards, and managers. While progress is impressive, many changes that would deepen shareholder democracy have yet to occur (Ray 2005). These include, for example: making board positions competitive by having two candidates for each vacant position; enabling investors and employees to co-nominate candidates for board positions; and creating a mechanism for full disclosure as well as for input to and/or approval of executive compensation by shareholders.

Most changes of this nature represent steps in the direction of shareholder democracy. But shareholder democracy must not be confused with stakeholder governance, a transformation of corporate accountability more fundamental – and more threatening to the status quo – than measures focused on strengthening the rights of shareholders.

Toward deeper democratization

Democratizing the corporation beyond the boundaries of shareholder-centric governance reforms toward stakeholder governance does not come easily to the contemporary MNC. Neither prevailing management nor governance culture creates a propitious environment for bringing diverse voices and perspectives into the decision-making process.

On the management side, traditional perspectives become entrenched early on in a manager's career owing to mainstream business education that schools managers in a certain organizational mindset. Within this traditional framework, the task of management is to establish the optimal hierarchical structure by which a company's leadership retains most decision-making authority and mid- and lower-level employees are agents for implementing such decisions. Underlying this perspective is a worldview deeply rooted in the belief that employees must be controlled and supervisors must be constantly vigilant to ensure they are properly executing the dictates from above (Ghoshal 2005). The enduring impact of such beliefs sustains what Senge and colleagues call "machine age" concepts: control, predictability, standardization, and "faster is better," even as such concepts are largely responsible for disharmony between modern, growth-at-any-cost corporate culture and "the need of all living systems to evolve" (Senge *et al.* 2004).

On the side of corporate boards, practices are changing in the wake of the Enron-era scandals. Indeed, more than a decade before Enron, there were calls for changes in corporate boards. Authoritative sources concluded that board composition and duties were misaligned with the realities of the modern corporation. On the basis of interviews with nearly 1,000 corporate directors in the late 1980s, Harvard Business School Professor Jay W. Lorsch observed:

Corporations exist to provide more than a return to their owners – they also provide goods and services, and employment, which in turn produces taxpayers and contributes to the nation's economic well-being. Their conduct affects a wide range of national interests . . . it makes no sense to instruct their governors to rule only for investors, especially now when so many investors are short term institutional holders . . . Thus, we believe that wider adoption of broad-constituency laws would reduce the ambiguity facing directors. (Lorsch 1989)

Despite such calls for enlarging the range of constituencies to which directors are accountable, remarkably little has changed either in law or practice (Springer 1999). At the turn of the twenty-first century, governance reforms that followed the Enron scandal made some inroads in democratizing boards with regard to mandating a higher proportion of independent directors. Independence, it was assumed, would strengthen the arms length relationship between directors and top executives such that the corporation's financial affairs would be scrutinized more systematically and without undue influence on the part of executives. The audit and control measures introduced by the Sarbanes-Oxley legislation ("SOX") of 2002 intensified pressure on boards to sharpen their duty of care in overseeing the financial affairs of the organization.

But for all the attention given to SOX, the law has had minimal effect on democratizing either the election or behavior of corporate directors. Election rules in most corporations still decidedly favor nominees of the board and management rather than shareholders, who in most cases may not vote "no," but, rather, may only abstain or vote "yes" to candidates on the ballot. Access to board members is normally tightly controlled and often limited to perfunctory interaction with shareholders at the annual general meeting. Thus, despite the rhetoric, progress toward at least shareholder democracy – much less stakeholder democracy – has been remarkably slow (Minnow 2006). This successful resistance of boards and management to even narrowly construed shareholder democracy attests to how deeply entrenched power structures are in the American corporate governance culture.

Prototypes for the future

Changing boards is not the only pathway toward corporate democracy. Already, though rarely couched in terms of democratization, a number of mechanisms provide access for different stakeholders to weigh in on key decisions of the corporation. In the chemical industry, for two decades Community Advisory Panels (CAPs) provided advice to facilities in managing local environmental, economic, and social issues associated with plant operations. Though lacking legal muscle, CAPs have become an example of best practice in the international chemical industry.

In the US electric utility industry, most states have mechanisms for public – especially consumer and community – input into major decisions regarding electricity rates and the siting of new generation facilities. For example, Offices of Consumer Advocates have long challenged utility companies to justify rate increases proposed to the Public Utility Commissions of various states. Facility Siting Councils play a parallel role by providing access for community interests in major new facility development projects. Though electricity deregulation has tended to weaken the role of Consumer Advocates and Siting Councils, they remain among the few instruments for non-shareholder influence in the pricing and capital investment decisions of energy companies.

While institutional arrangements such as those mentioned above are longstanding and moderately consequential in terms of introducing stakeholder interests into corporate decision-making, they fall far short of the deeper changes in management and governance that are preconditions for serious democratization of the corporation. To achieve this objective, one must imagine substantially modified or even entirely different accountability structures than those characteristic of the contemporary corporation. Some organizations have begun to move in this direction (Cramer and Hirschland 2006). Board

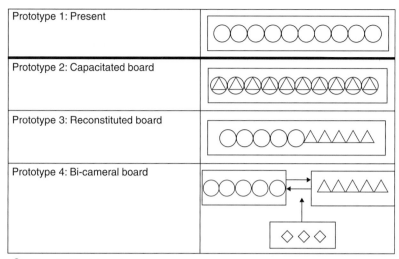

○ Shareholder interests
△ Non-shareholder interests
◇ Mediators

Figure 13.3 Models of corporate boards

committees on public policy and social/environmental issues are becoming increasingly commonplace, as in the cases of MNCs such as Merck, Rio Tinto, and McDonald's. An estimated 20 percent of the Standard and Poor's 500 companies have some type of committee of this nature. In a similar vein, British American Tobacco, General Mills, and Unilever disperse oversight of corporate responsibility across a number of directors, typically those identified as "independent."

While these developments represent modest steps toward broader accountability, deeper changes in the fiduciary duty, election, and composition of boards await a next wave of governance reforms. To illustrate, consider three prototype board structures for the future (White 2006b). These prototypes, depicted in Figure 13.3, are simplified portraits of the possible, designed to draw reasonably clear distinctions between each other and the present board. As a benchmark, assume the generic **present board** (Prototype 1) comprises 10 members operating under conventional rules of fiduciary duty in which shareholder interests are pre-eminent. It is a self-perpetuating board, with a nominating committee that selects candidates to succeed departing members, and shareholders vote on the proposed slate. The extent of direct nominations new board members may make varies by country, but in no case are explicit competencies or representation of other stakeholder interests incorporated in the selection process.

Prototype 2, the **capacitated board,** depicts a modest but noteworthy step in the direction of stakeholder governance. Here the contemporary rules of governance remain unchanged in terms of the rules of fiduciary duty. The capacitated board is formally trained and credentialed in relation to stakeholder issues such as environment, human rights, labor standards, and sustainability reporting. In this scenario, business groups, associations of corporate directors, and academic institutions that already offer board training have expanded their offerings to include the standard menu of corporate responsibility topics. Such training has emerged as a standard practice based on the generally accepted belief that corporate directors – no less than physicians, accountants, pilots, and educators – should be held to a standard of professional competency in their role as corporate directors. Training institutions offer various levels of credentials. Directors of MNCs are required to obtain the highest level of certification; those who serve smaller enterprises are held to a somewhat less demanding standard. In all cases, maintaining one's credential requires periodic updating of competencies in corporate responsibility.

Prototype 3, the **reconstituted board,** is a more aggressive step toward stakeholder governance. Here, three key changes have occurred relative to the current board. First, multilateral and national governance principles have evolved to the point where parity between shareholder and non-shareholder interests is universally recognized as a best practice. The rules of governance, both mandatory and voluntary, share language that asserts that the purpose of corporations is to serve the public interest by harnessing the private interests in growth, innovation, and wealth generation.

Second, reflecting this revised mandate, the board in this scenario is split between those with backgrounds and competencies in shareholder matters versus those with backgrounds and competencies in various aspects of environment, social issues, and governance. The duty of both clusters is the same – to promote the corporation's capacity to produce long-term wealth – and the composition of the reconstituted board mirrors this new mandate.

Third, the method for board selection has been democratized. Mechanisms for direct election by various stakeholder groups are now in place, replacing the earlier indirect and incumbent-dominated system in which slates of nominees were put forward by existing board members and shareholders were asked to either approve or abstain. The combination of a redefined corporate purpose, a reconstituted board, and new procedures for board selection represents a substantial advancement in changing the rules of accountability to bring greater democratic control to the organization.

Prototype 4, **the bi-cameral board**, rests on the same assumptions as the reconstituted board, except in this case power is divided into shareholder and stakeholder chambers. In this scenario, the shareholder chamber is similar to the conventional board, with some combination of audit, ethics, compensation, and strategy committees. The stakeholder chamber, in contrast, has the explicit mandate to identify and advocate for the interests of non-shareholders.

The preferred outcome, over time, is a convergence of the shareholder and non-shareholder interests based on the principle of "enlightened shareholder interest." This concept posits that shareholders' long-term interests are best protected when the corporation integrates stakeholder interests into its decision-making, thereby strengthening reputation, reducing risks, and identifying commercial opportunities through continuous dialogue with stakeholder groups. However, recognizing that the preferred outcome may not materialize, a standing mediatory body adjudicates disagreements between the chambers when major decisions are under review and consensus cannot be achieved, e.g. an acquisition or merger that benefits shareholders but occasions major disruptions in the workplace and community. The bi-cameral board configuration relies on checks and balances in much the same way that political democracies do. The mediatory body is analogous to the judicial branch, in this case, as an adjudicator of shareholder and non-shareholder interests when they cannot be reconciled by the two chambers of the board.

All three alternatives to the current board – capacitated, reconstituted, and bi-cameral – have their strengths and limitations, and the implementation of each would vary widely in terms of complexity and transaction costs. The capacitated board represents the most modest departure from current practice – capacity building of board members already is commonplace in many countries. Prototype 2 would build on these practices by introducing social and environmental content into such training and formalizing the process through a credentialing mechanism.

Reconstituting boards requires a combination of changes in fiduciary duty, board selection, and board composition. Together, they represent a dramatic departure, not from who serves on boards, but from the definition of directors' duty of loyalty. It represents a departure from shareholder-centric fiduciary rules, and reconfigures accountability by ensuring the presence of non-shareholder voices.

Finally, the bi-cameral board is most likely to produce high transaction costs, as any checks-and-balances structure tends to do. It is an approach that connotes skepticism that a unitary board, no matter how diverse and how democratically elected, can ever escape the pressure of top management to weight decisions in favor of shareholders. Its message is that the higher transaction costs of a bi-cameral structure is an acceptable, reasonable price to pay for ensuring that stakeholder interests are elevated securely and unequivocally to a level equal to that of shareholder interests. It may be a "messy" structure, but no less so than other structures seriously committed to democratic process.

Reflections

Turbulent times lie ahead for global corporations. Continuation of the momentum toward open markets driven by breakthroughs in communications and information technology and free movement of capital and technology markets is by no means assured during the coming decades (Abdelal and Segal 2007). Persistent protectionism of agricultural goods, sluggish progress in international trade negotiations, growing barriers to transboundary movement of labor, and deepening resource nationalism all loom large as potential blockages to free markets that have yielded enormous benefits to MNCs. The public appetite for unfettered globalization may be waning with the perception that its benefits are inequitably concentrated in the hands of corporate and financial interests while its costs are inequitably concentrated among the world's most vulnerable people.

It is these conditions that give urgency to the question of democratization of the corporation. If the MNCs are to prosper in the new century, they must move beyond traditional shareholder-centric governance structures to ones better aligned with twenty-first-century societal expectations. To date, governance initiatives undertaken by multilateral organizations such as OECD, national governments, e.g. US SOX and the UK Company Law Review, and coalitions such as ICGN have demonstrated remarkably little readiness to move beyond the dominant shareholderism as the central organizing framework for corporate governance. Indeed, by focusing on marginal improvements without revisiting core tenets, such initiatives have further ingrained the very flaws in the prevailing governance models that make them increasingly misaligned with societal expectations.

This must change if corporations are to build public trust for the long term. Fortunately, the case for democratization of the corporation is compelling on three fronts: ethical, political, and economic. From an ethical perspective, shareholder-centric governance is incompatible with the notion that a multiplicity of resource providers enables the corporation to succeed in a globalizing world. To subordinate the interests of employees, communities, suppliers, future generations, and other stakeholders is a violation of the principle of fairness as applied to corporate activity. Those that contribute to wealth creation should have a voice in the governance of the organization that depends on such stakeholders for its wealth-creating capacity.

From a political perspective, democratization is integral to obtaining and maintaining the license to operate. Corporations that empower stakeholders make a statement to national and local authorities that they understand their existence is part of a social contract that is more encompassing than the legal document that grants such license. Corporations that assign real authority to community panels at their operating sites, that seriously involve employees in merger and acquisition decisions, and that allocate stock to community environmental trust funds demonstrate in a concrete form their commitment to the principles of democratic decision-making. Such commitment, in turn, strengthens their legitimacy in the eyes of those empowered to grant their license to operate.

From a business case perspective, the rewards of transitioning toward stakeholder governance lie in both risk management and opportunity exploitation. In an increasingly borderless world, diversity associated with stakeholder governance elevates the capacity of boards and management to see the world through the lens of the customers and communities they serve. The capacity of corporations to anticipate social changes material to their operations is as indispensable to risk management as it is to identifying new technologies and markets. Stakeholder engagement is a step in this direction. Stakeholder governance goes further. It is a recognition that business-relevant knowledge is possessed not by a few experts within the confines of the organization but by stakeholders that span a broad array of constituencies and geographies. By bringing such knowledge-holders into the governance structure, the organization positions itself to access on a continuing basis the best ideas that build the foundation for long-term prosperity.

Peter Senge and his colleagues have observed that any life form, including corporations, has the potential to grow, learn, and evolve. "As long as our system is governed by habit . . . we will continue to re-create institutions as they have been, despite their disharmony with the larger world" (Senge *et al.* 2004: 9).

Democratizing the corporation promises a different future. Whether through the voluntary actions of corporations themselves or mandatory actions imposed by governments, transitioning to stakeholder governance will help end the "disharmony" that stands in the way of corporations reaching their full potential as agents of sustainable development. In the end, this above all is the most compelling reason for pursuing the pathway toward democratization.

References

Abdelal, R. and Segal, A. 2007. "Has Globalization Passed Its Peak?" *Foreign Affairs* January/February: 103–14.
Barnes, P. 2006. *Capitalism 3.0. A Guide to Reclaiming the Commons.* San Francisco: Berrett-Koehler Publishers.
Blair, M. and Stout, L. 1999. "A Team Production Theory of Corporate Law," *Virginia Law Review* 85: 247–313.
Cowe, R. 2001. *Stakes, Not Shares.* London: New Economics Foundation.
Cramer, A. and Hirschland, M. 2006. "The Socially Responsible Board," *The Corporate Board* November/December: 20–4.
Davis, S, Lukomnik, J., and Pitt-Watson, D. 2006. *The New Capitalists: How Citizen Investors are Reshaping the Corporate Agenda.* Boston: Harvard Business School Press.
Gates, J. 1998. *The Ownership Solution: Toward a Shared Capitalism for the 21st Century.* Reading, MA: Perseus Books.

Ghoshal, S. 2005. "Bad Management Theories Are Destroying Good Management Practices," *Academy of Management Learning & Education* 4(1): 75–91.

Greenfield, K. 2007. *The Failure of Corporate Law: Fundamental Flaws, Progressive Possibilities.* Chicago: University of Chicago Press.

Groban, D. O. 2001. "Introduction: Why Owernship for All?" Capital Ownership Group. http://cog.kent.edu/PapersMay2001/COGPapers. PDF.

Kelly, M. 2002. *The Divine Right of Capital.* San Francisco: Berrett-Koehler Publishers.

Lorsch, J. W. 1989. *Pawns or Potentates: The Reality of America's Corporate Boards.* Boston: Harvard Business School.

Minnow, N. 2006. "Substance Over Style," in *International Corporate Governance Network (ICGN) 2006 Yearbook.* London: ICGN, pp. 28–9.

Post, J. E., Preston, L. E., and Sachs, S. 2002. *Redefining the Corporation: Stakeholder Management and Organizational Wealth.* Stanford: Stanford University Press.

Ray, D. M. 2005. "Corporate Boards and Corporate Democracy," *Journal of Corporate Citizenship* 20 (Winter): 105.

Senge, P., Sharmer C. O., Jaworski J., and Flowers, B. S. 2004. *Presence: An Exploration of Profound Change in People, Organizations, and Society.* New York: Currency Books.

Springer, J. D. 1999. "Corporate Law, Corporate Constituency Statutes: Hollow Hopes and False Fears," *Annual Survey of American Law*: 85–124.

White, A. L. 2006a. "Transforming the Corporation." Great Transition Initiative (GTI) Paper Series No. 5. www.gtinitiative.org/documents/ PDFFINALS/5Corporations.pdf.

2006b. "The Stakeholder Fiduciary: CSR, Governance and the Future of Boards." Business for Social Responsibility Occasional Paper. www.bsr.org/meta/BSR_AW_Corporate_Boards.pdf.

14 | Social entrepreneurship: a blueprint for humane organizations?

MICHAEL PIRSON

Introduction

"Business as usual" has come under intense scrutiny. Public outrage over crooked corporate officers, the looting of pension funds, the defrauding of stockholders, and the wholesale firings of hardworking employees has reached a new high (see e.g. Jackson and Nelson 2004; Pirson 2007). Not only the anti-globalization movement of the far left but also more traditional thinkers and the public are increasingly uncomfortable with corporate power and influence. In September 2000 (even before Enron's collapse), over 70 percent of Americans surveyed said that business had too much power over too many aspects of their lives and too much political influence. Only 4 percent agreed that companies should have only one purpose, namely to make the most profit for shareholders. Ninety-five percent agreed that American corporations should have more than one purpose and, additionally, that they owe something to their workers and the communities in which they operate (Bernstein 2000; Paine 2003). International surveys on trust in corporations also demonstrate that trust in big business continues to decrease. According to GlobeScan (World Economic Forum 2006), in 2006, trust in multinational and global companies reached its all-time low. In the eyes of bestselling author William Greider (2003), the avatars of capitalism are meeting deeply rooted anger and are blamed for the erosion of family life, the decreased sense of personal and professional security, corroded communities, impoverished spiritual lives, and a devastated natural environment. Overall, the criticism leveled at current capitalism is that it fails to be life-conducive. It is not set up to fulfill authentic human needs (Diener and Seligman 2004), or, in humanistic terms, it fails to make "humans the measure of all things" (Protagoras).

As a result current business organizations are facing a predicament that Jackson and Nelson (2004: 19) compare to a "perfect storm." They argue that "despite the ongoing pressures of relentless competition, and the need to deliver short-term financial performance, no major company can ignore and fail to respond to the following threats to long-term corporate success and viability:

- the crisis of trust;
- the crisis of inequality; and
- the crisis of sustainability."

This chapter examines how organizations can weather the "perfect storm" by learning from a newly emerging field called social entrepreneurship.

The evolution of social entrepreneurship

Anticipating the crises of the private and public sectors, Etzioni (1973) suggested that neither the market nor the state alone could "catalyze the necessary innovations and reforms of society but rather that the source would be "a third alternative" that could combine the efficiency of the entrepreneurial market place with the welfare orientation of the state. Bill Drayton (2006: 45) argues that over the last two and a half decades, the "operating half of the world that deals with social issues has gone through an historical transformation of unprecedented speed and scale." The third alternative that has developed features a wide range of non-governmental organizations (NGOs). Social entrepreneurs, "a new breed of pragmatic, innovative, and visionary social activists" (Nicholls 2006: 2), are largely credited with having transformed and developed the third sector to become entrepreneurial and competitive in precisely the same sense as businesses are (Drayton 2006).

Leadbeater (1997) views social entrepreneurs as similar to business entrepreneurs in the methods they use, but different in being motivated by social goals rather than material profits. "(T)heir great skill is that they often make something from nothing, creating innovative forms of active welfare, health care, and housing which are both cheaper and more effective than the traditional services provided by the government."

While there have been extraordinary social change-makers throughout history, such as Florence Nightingale or Friedrich Wilhelm

Raiffeisen, the scale and reach of the new social impact being generated as well as the extraordinary variety of approaches being employed are different today (Nicholls 2006: 2–3). Over the last ten years there has been an unprecedented wave of growth in social entrepreneurship globally. "Social" start-ups are emerging at a faster rate than traditional commercial ventures (Harding and Cowling 2004: 5; Nicholls 2006: 3). More single social entrepreneurs and their organizations are bringing about systematic change by influencing social behavior for the good on a global scale in areas such as the environment, education, economic development, human rights, health, and civic engagement.

Social entrepreneurship has many facets and represents an umbrella term for a considerable range of innovative and dynamic international ventures (Nicholls 2006: 5). Borrowing and mixing approaches from business, charity, and social movements, it represents a new force in the social and environmental sectors. It reconfigures solutions to community problems to deliver sustainable social value, thus contributing to the solution of inequity and sustainability problems, building trust with stakeholders on a larger scale.

Social entrepreneurship – a fundamentally humanistic endeavor?

So, does social entrepreneurship serve as a promising model for human-centered, life-conducive business organizations? While many proponents such as Bill Drayton would claim that it does, other observers view social entrepreneurship more critically. Such critics (e.g. Dart 2004) view it as a manifestation of the usurping supremacy of business models across all aspects of life.

To answer the question of whether social enterprises serve as a model for humanistic organizations, we need to look into the constitutive elements of social entrepreneurship and determine under what conditions social entrepreneurship is indeed humanistic. Nicholls and Cho (2006) argue that social entrepreneurship comprises three main elements: market orientation, innovation, and sociality.

Market orientation

Market orientation is a key feature that differentiates social entrepreneurship ventures from other social organizations. Market orientation entails rationalizing strategic operations in response to exogenous variables traditionally conceived as competitive market pressures. Even though many social purpose organizations are located in dysfunctional or non-existent markets, social entrepreneurs nevertheless recognize the value of market orientation. They give primacy to the most effective deployment of resources towards achieving a social goal. Market orientation is present in descriptions of social entrepreneurship employing a "double or triple bottom line," cost or full cost recovery, or the development of independent profit-making ventures such as social enterprises. With its implicit focus on efficiency and effective use of resources, market orientation distinguishes many social entrepreneurship ventures from traditional models of not-for-profit social service delivery or advocacy, as well as much of the public sector (cf. Nicholls and Cho 2006: 107).

Innovation

Innovation is another major distinguishing feature of social entrepreneurship. The Schumpeterian narrative of entrepreneurship emphasizes the role of the entrepreneur as an innovator. The social entrepreneur distinguishes himself through his ability to disrupt stable systems. He uses originality, creativity, and imagination, and he pragmatically implements innovative solutions to unresolved social issues. It is the pattern-breaking change, the disruptive creation of new models and techniques, that differentiates the social entrepreneur from other social actors (Nicholls and Cho 2006).

Sociality

The real difference between social entrepreneurs and classic business entrepreneurs is the domain in which they operate. Both employ market orientation and innovation, but social entrepreneurs apply them in the areas traditionally considered to be public goods. The qualification of entrepreneurship as "social" raises two questions (Nicholls and Cho 2006).

   The first is conceptual and asks which objectives can legitimately be called social. Social objectives are not necessarily homogenous, but can be deeply contested (see the pro-life/pro-choice struggle with regard to abortion). The heterogeneity of social interests depends on societal values, culture, religion, and ideology. The question of what is *social* is as difficult to determine as what is *good*. It can never be conclusively answered and has to be continuously negotiated. The more a goal is universally applicable, the more support it is likely to garner. That support can only be gauged through a discursive process, which includes all stakeholders, and thus secures the legitimacy of social entrepreneurship. For humanists there are some non-negotiable values such as human rights and the promotion of human dignity. At the moment, the legitimacy of business organizations' social engagement will depend on how life-conducive it is and how much business will contribute to poverty alleviation, inequity reduction, the promotion of sustainability, and the restoration of overall societal trust (Jackson and Nelson 2004; Porter and Kramer 2006).

The second question is empirical in nature and concerns the extent to which a given organization actually advances social objectives. This is largely a question of measurement; many researchers are currently struggling to conceive useful social impact metrics. These metrics will have to enable everyone interested to better evaluate whether a social entrepreneurial venture makes society indeed better off. Financial metrics have failed to do so, as wealth is not a comprehensive and adequate predictor of well-being anymore (see also Diener and Seligman 2004).

Overall social entrepreneurship by its very definition puts humans at its focal point. This is its advantage over traditional financially driven entrepreneurship. It thus provides a very interesting perspective for humanistic organizations. The challenge of social entrepreneurship lies in the measurement of its impact, the proof that society is better off than before. Counting money is fairly simple; accounting for increases in societal well-being is more challenging and will require increased efforts in the future. Given the current situation, however, businesses might well benefit by learning from social entrepreneurs on "how to put people first."

Models of social entrepreneurship

Despite its challenges, the hallmark of social entrepreneurship remains its ability to combine social interests with business practices to effect social change (cf. Alter 2006: 205). The distinctive feature of each of the respective social enterprises lies in how it approaches its dual objectives – the depth and breadth of social impact to be realized and

Figure 14.1 Types of social enterprises
Adapted from Alter (2006).

the financial returns to be achieved (Alter 2006: 206). In the social enterprise, the pursuit of financial gains and social missions are inextricably intertwined. Even though a wide range of social enterprises have emerged, Alter (2006) suggests there are three main categories defined by the emphasis and priority given to financial and social objectives: embedded, integrated, and external social enterprises (cf. Alter 2006). All of these can be models for current financially driven businesses.

Embedded social enterprise

The embedded social enterprise describes a model in which business activities and social programs are synonymous. The enterprise activities are "embedded" within the organizations' operations and social programs (Alter 2006: 212). The social activities are based on earned income strategies. The relationship between business activities and social programs is therefore comprehensive as financial and social benefits are achieved simultaneously. The Grameen Bank model of micro loans serves as an example for embedded social enterprise. These micro loans are paid back by the borrowers with a high interest rate, but serve the poorest of the poor, who do not have access to normal credit, as they are lacking collateral. Other models that serve the bottom of the pyramid (see Prahalad 2005) could also be valid approaches.

Integrated social enterprises

The integrated social enterprises describes a model in which social programs overlap with business activities, but are not synonymous. Social and financial programs often share costs, assets, and program attributes. The integrated type of social enterprise often leverages organizational assets such as expertise, content, relationships, brand, or infrastructure as the foundation for its business (Alter 2006: 212). The Aravind Eye Hospital in Madurai, India, is an example of an integrated social enterprise. It serves cataract patients in a main hospital, where wealthy patients pay a market fee for their surgery. These fees are then used to pay for the surgery of poor patients in the free hospital (Rangan 1993). The relationship between the business activities and the social programs is hence synergistic, adding financial and social value to one another. These mixed or shared value models have largely been unexplored by traditional businesses, but could serve well as a blueprint for future shared value creation.

External social enterprise

The external social enterprise illustrates a model in which social programs are distinct from business activities. The financial activities are "external" to the organization's social programs and/or operating costs. In this model it is not a prerequisite that social mission and financial activities are congruent or symbiotic (Alter 2006: 13). An example of external social enterprises are licensing programs (e.g. WWF, Save the Children) in which products are sold using the brand name of the NGO to create a stable financial influx. The relationship between the business activities and social programs is supportive, providing unrestricted funding to the non-profit parent organization. The option for the partnering of businesses with NGOs has been increasingly used (see the alliance of Timberland and City Year), but there seems to be a yet-untapped potential.

How can social entrepreneurship serve as a model for humane business organizations?

Milton Friedman's paradigm of "the business of business is business," meaning creating the highest shareholder value, can only hold when financial value creation will not exacerbate the sustainability crisis, the inequity crisis, and the trust crisis. Mohammad Yunus (in this volume) claims that the separation of economic and social dimensions has always been nonsensical, and even the managing partner of McKinsey & Co., Ian Davis, agrees that the continued separation of the social and the economic is strategically unsustainable for big business (Nicholls 2006: 24). Good businesses understand that a proactive reduction of the sustainability, inequity, and trust crises is also good strategy.

While traditionally businesses were responsible for financial value creation, and NGOs or the government for social value creation, social entrepreneurship allows the conceptualization of new value propositions to effectively deal with the sustainability and inequity crises. Shared value propositions are much more likely to instill public trust, as simple profit maximization is seen as opportunistic (Pirson 2007).

Corporate social entrepreneurship

At this point current business organizations and most large corporations have made use of the external model of social value creation. Many have set up external foundations that are independently managed and share only the name with its founder (e.g. Alcoa Foundation, Ford Foundation, Gates Foundation, etc.). While this model can certainly create social value and enhance the brand image, these models are often criticized for simply "cleaning up the mess" that the economic organizations have left. The overall impact on sustainability and inequity is questioned. The external model will not suffice to deal effectively with the current crises, and corporations will have to go beyond traditional charity and get more involved in a strategic value blend.

Corporations will benefit by being more proactive and moving more towards the integrated and even the embedded model. Porter and Kramer (2006) argue that the creation of shared value will be a major factor for competitive advantage in the future. They argue that each company can identify the particular set of societal problems that it is best equipped to help resolve and from which it can gain the greatest competitive benefit.

Austin *et al.* (2005; 2006) propose the concept of "corporate social entrepreneurship" to more closely align social and financial integration. They define the concept of corporate social entrepreneurship (CSE) as the "process of extending the firm's domain of competence ... through innovative leveraging of resources, both within and outside its direct control, aimed at the simultaneous creation of economic and social value" (Austin *et al.* 2006: 170) When implementing CSE in corporations, several areas need to be considered: the capacity of the organizational leadership, the quality of the strategy, the organizational structures to support the strategy, and the systems which are designed to support the implementation.

Leadership

When implementing CSE in corporations, the role of leadership is crucial. That said CSE cannot be a one-man show, but needs to be lived throughout the organization. A successful leader hence provides vision, legitimization, and empowerment.

Following Austin *et al.* (2006: 176) the leader needs to have the capacity to envision a company in which the social dimension is a core element of the corporation's identity. The leader also needs to create a culture in which the appropriateness and the desirability of the CSE process is demonstrated. And third, the leader needs to empower others to become leaders and change agents in the company to build and execute that process (see also Maak and Pless, and Badaracco, this volume).

Strategy

Austin *et al.* (2006: 177) further suggest three key strategic elements for CSE: alignment, leveraging core competencies, and partnering. With regard to alignment, both the social dimensions and the business dimensions of the company's strategy must be aligned with each other; the closer they are aligned, the greater the possibility of a shared value creation. Concerning leveraging core competencies, CSE focuses on discovering creative ways to mobilize and deploy the company's key assets such as technology, talent, image, infrastructure, procurement and distribution systems, and communications. The third strategy is partnering. While many CSE actions can be performed internally, creating alliances with external entities can be particularly effective at carrying out innovative strategies.

Structure

Structure needs to follow strategy and innovative structures will be needed to accommodate CSE-based strategies (Austin *et al.* 2006: 177).

In traditional corporate structures we often find separate social responsibility departments which do get marginalized and in turn function sub-optimally. The key here is to integrate social responsibility in the core corporate structure and in its daily operations. It is crucial to find new ways for interdepartmental collaboration to truly embed social commitment in the organization.

Systems

The process of social value creation requires operational support. The decision-making process has to integrate social and financial considerations and needs to include all stakeholders to ensure legitimacy. A top-down approach to decision-making is often detrimental, while a discursive stakeholder dialog seems more promising. The organization also needs to provide a combined learning and performance-oriented measurement and management system, such as a balanced scorecard. It should hold managers accountable and support their learning to achieve set goals. Another useful support system is an effective economic and social value communication process, which is required to build continuous support internally and externally based on stakeholder dialog.

Conclusion

As Porter and Kramer (2006) argue, corporations are not responsible for all the world's problems, nor do they have the resources to solve them all; governments and citizens will have to do their share. That, however, does not excuse businesses from acting responsibly or having a co-responsibility to act. In fact, businesses will actively have to address social and environmental needs, not only for the benefit of society but also for their own benefit. Social entrepreneurship and its dual-value objective can serve as an interesting model for traditional corporations to meet increasing societal expectations (see Paine 2003). It also serves as a blueprint for organizations that actively want to serve authentic human needs. By reducing the inequities and decreasing their environmental impact, such organizations can become more life-conducive and better enable our system to address issues relevant to human survival. Efforts to find shared value in operating practices and in the social dimensions of competitive context have the potential not only to foster economic and social development but to change the way companies and society think about each other. The current dichotomy, with business on one side and society on the other can be overcome. Business is part of society, and a more integrated view will serve business as it becomes more competitive (cf. Porter and Kramer 2006) and society as it becomes more humane.

References

Alter, S. K. (2006). "Social Enterprise Models and Their Mission and Money Relationships," in A. Nicholls (ed.), *Social Entrepreneurship – New Models for Sustainable Social Change*. Oxford: Oxford University Press, pp. 411–79.

Austin, James E., Leonard, H. B., Ezequiel, R., and Wei-Skillern, Jane. 2005. "Corporate Social Entrepreneurship: A New Vision for CSR," in Marc J. Epstein and Kirk O. Hanson (eds.), *The Accountable Corporation*, vol. III. Oxford: Praeger Publishing.

   2006. "Social Entrepreneurship: It's for Corporations, Too," in A. Nicholls (ed.), *Social Entrepreneurship – New Models for Sustainable Social Change*. Oxford: Oxford University Press, pp. 169–80.

Bernstein, A. 2000. "Too Much Corporate Power?" *BusinessWeek* September 11: 145–9.

Dart, R. 2004. "The Legitimacy of Social Enterprise," *Nonprofit Management and Leadership* 14(4): 411–24.

Diener, E. and Seligman, M. E. P. 2004. "Beyond Money: Toward an Economy of Well-being," *Psychological Science in the Public Interest* 5: 1–31.

Drayton, W. 2006. "The Citizen Sector Transformed," in A. Nicholls (ed.), *Social Entrepreneurship – New Models for Sustainable Social Change*. Oxford: Oxford University Press, pp. 45–55.

Etzioni, A. 1973. "The Third Sector and Domestic Missions," *Public Administration Review* 33: 314–23.

Greider, W. 2003. *The Soul of Capitalism – Opening Paths to a Moral Economy*. New York: Simon & Schuster.

Harding, R. and Cowling, M. 2004. *Social Entrepreneurship Monitor: United Kingdom*. London: Global Entrepreneurship Monitor.

Jackson, I. and Nelson, J. 2004. *Profits with Principle – Seven Strategies for Delivering Value with Values*. New York: Currency Doubleday.

Leadbeater, C. 1997. *The Rise of the Social Entrepreneur*. London: Demos.

Nicholls, A. 2006. "Introduction," in A. Nicholls (ed.), *Social Entrepreneurship – New Models for Sustainable Social Change*. Oxford: Oxford University Press, pp. 1–36.

Nicholls, A. and Cho, A. H. 2006. "Social Entrepreneurship: The Structuration of a Field," in A. Nicholls (ed.), *Social Entrepreneurship – New Models for Sustainable Social Change*. Oxford: Oxford University Press, pp. 99–118.

Paine, L. Sharp. 2003. *Value Shift: Why Companies Must Merge Social and Financial Imperatives to Achieve Superior Performance*. New York: McGraw-Hill.

Pirson, M. 2007. *Facing the Trust Gap: How Organizations Can Measure and Manage Stakeholder Trust*. St. Gallen: University of St. Gallen.

Porter, M. and Kramer, M. 2006. "Strategy and Society: The Link between Competitive Advantage and Corporate Social Responsibility," *Harvard Business Review* December: 78–92.

Prahalad, C. K. 2005. *The Fortune at the Bottom of the Pyramid: Eradicating Poverty through Profits*. Philadelphia: Wharton School Publishing.

Rangan, K. 1993. "The Aravind Eye Hospital, Madurai, India: In Service for Sight." Harvard Business School Case Study No. 593098. Cambridge, MA: Harvard Business School Publishing.

World Economic Forum. 2006. "Decline in Trust." www.weforum.org/site/homepublic.nsf/Content/Trust+in+Governments,+Corporations+and+Global+Institutions+Continues+to+Decline.

15 Humanism at work: crucial organizational cultures and leadership principles

CLAUDIA PEUS AND DIETER FREY

Globalization, technological developments, and insecurity regarding the stock market pose considerable challenges for today's organizations. In light of these challenges many managers argue that, in principle, they would like to give employees more room for development and creativity, but must focus on efficiency and cost-cutting. But do humanistic principles and superior business performance really contradict each other? This chapter presents organization cultures that are based on humanistic principles and have been implemented by numerous successful organizations.

In the first part of this chapter we briefly present the philosophical foundations of our approach. Subsequently, we describe how the philosophers' claims can be met in modern organizations. Specifically, we present organizational cultures – the center of excellence cultures – that can be used to implement humanistic principles and have been realized by many exceptional organizations. To illustrate these organizational cultures we provide examples of ways in which well-known business organizations have implemented these organizational cultures. Finally, we present guidelines for managers on how to create the center of excellence cultures in their own organizations, i.e. the principle-based model of leadership.

1. Philosophical foundations

Fundamental for creating humane organizations are the philosophies of Immanuel Kant (1724–1804), Gotthold Ephraim Lessing (1729–81), and Karl Popper (1902–94).

Kant, a major philosopher of the Enlightenment, stressed man's emergence from his self-imposed immaturity. He emphasized that humans have to "dare to know" (Latin: *sapere aude*), to think autonomously, i.e. free of the dictates of external authority, to free themselves from immaturity and dependence. Successful business organizations have clearly recognized that employee empowerment, emancipation, and autonomy are imperative and that organizational cultures and leadership principles have to be designed in a way that promotes autonomy and participation. Managers are responsible for demanding and facilitating these. However, a prerequisite for demanding and facilitating autonomy, participation, and critical thinking is the manager's willingness and ability to adopt his/her employees' perspectives. For example, managers have to ask themselves what they would expect of a good manager and how they would feel if in the employee's situation. Overall, managers and employees should follow Kant's imperative: act in a way you would like others to act; treat people in a way you would like to be treated; lead in a way you would want to be led.

Another important philosopher of the Enlightenment whose focus was on reason as a means to gain freedom was Gotthold Ephraim Lessing. Lessing's philosophy – although it dates back more than 200 years – is highly relevant to modern organizations and societies as a whole. In his drama *Nathan the Wise* (1779), he emphasized that the three monotheistic religions can and should learn from one another, instead of looking down on and even battling each other. Lessing propagates tolerance for people who are different from oneself and have different ideas, and underlines that people should embrace the opportunity to learn from each other. Applied to modern organizations this means that diversity of talent, background, culture, ideas, etc. should be regarded as an opportunity for learning and the development of new innovative ideas. In addition, Lessing was an advocate of the individual's right to freedom of thought, which parallels Kant's teachings.

A more modern philosopher who emphasized reason and criticized dogmatism was Karl Popper. In his so-called "critical rationalism" he argued that the main problem of science in the past had been that it was too strongly oriented towards verification and that it was necessary to be oriented towards falsification, i.e. to look for the shortcomings of a theory or model, to ask how the model can be improved or even falsified and to develop a model that explains the existing findings better. Furthermore, in his book *The Open Society and its Enemies* (Popper 1966), he emphasized how dangerous all kinds of dogmatism are – dogmatism being the open society's enemy. We argue that Popper's ideas regarding both science and society can and should be applied to create humane organizations.

They point to the fact that members of an organization should not aim at verifying established policies and procedures, but rather create an open culture of discussion where they ask themselves and each other which new approaches have to be considered in response to alterations in the market or changes regarding the needs of employees and customers. The main feature of Popper's thinking – the constant questioning of procedures and the creation of an open culture in which dogmatisms are taboo and every individual can freely express his or her ideas – not only follows humanistic principles. It also facilitates innovation and thus sustains business performance.

2. Organizational cultures based on humanism: center of excellence cultures

The center of excellence model (see Frey 1996; Frey, Peus, and Jonas 2004; Frey, Osswald, Peus, and Fischer 2006) describes organizational cultures that are based on the philosophies described above and at the same time have been found to be characteristic of exceptionally successful organizations, as will be illustrated below. We call these organizations or divisions centers of excellence since they are outstanding with respect to criteria such as business performance, innovativeness, or quality of service. Among the widely recognized cultures that characterize outstanding organizations are customer orientation, benchmarking, entrepreneurial, and implementation cultures. Whereas all of the above are important for the functioning of an organization, they are not sufficient for the creation of a center of excellence. Crucial to this is the implementation of organizational cultures that facilitate critical thinking, tolerance, and constant questioning, as called for in the teachings of Kant, Lessing, and Popper. Table 15.1 gives an overview of the organizational cultures that are based on the works of these three philosophers.

1. Problem-solving culture

In Popper's last book, *All Life is Problem Solving* (Popper 1999), he emphasized that science as well as individual living is problem solving.

Table 15.1 *Center of excellence cultures*

1. Problem solving
2. Mistakes as learning opportunity
3. Constructive confrontation and conflict
4. Questioning and curiosity
5. Creativity and fantasy

Either one is part of the solution or one is part of the problem. In application to modern organizations this means that every member of the organization has to view himself as a problem solver rather than as someone who simply states problems. Problems are to be regarded as challenges and opportunities for further development. Every employee should be held responsible for not only stating a problem, but also solutions to it. The ultimate goal is to develop a common conviction that "we are world-champions in problem solving."

A mentality of this sort has direct effects on the likelihood that certain problems will be solved. For example Dweck (1991) reported that persons of the same levels of intelligence are able to solve problems substantially better if they display cognitions of accomplishment ("I can do it"; "Even in the face of failure I will continue") as compared to persons whose cognitions are dominated by helplessness ("I won't even try this"; "I will fail anyway"). This finding demonstrates that mental focus is crucial for the solution of problems. If all members of an organization think in terms of cognitions of accomplishment, the focus is no longer on problems but rather on their solutions. A great practical example of an organization that has embraced a problem-solving culture is Toyota, where "employees are encouraged to see problems not as something undesirable, but to view them positively as a way to help them improve their performance further" (*Economist* 2006b).

2. Mistakes-as-learning-opportunity culture

Popper (2002) pointed out that scientific progress will only take place where one views mistakes as learning opportunities. This notion can be applied to modern organizations as well. A mistakes-as-learning-opportunity culture is characterized by the fact that mistakes are not ignored, hidden, or associated with blame. On the contrary, mistakes are regarded as a chance to critically reflect on wrong decisions and to develop better solutions in the future. Within a center of excellence mistakes are seen as chances for continuous improvement so that the recurrence of the same mistake is prevented. Complaints by employees, customers, or contractors are regarded as a warning sign and a chance for improvement at the same time. Therefore, every top organization will develop tools to learn from the complaints and grievances expressed.

One important aspect of dealing with mistakes is the realization that people often react defensively when they are made aware of their mistakes. In order to prevent this sort of behavior, it is wise to state issues positively, e.g. "I have an idea for improvement" or "How about doing it this way?" rather than saying "You made a mistake," which leads people to defend themselves. Here are several examples of techniques that are instrumental in establishing a mistakes-as-learning-opportunity culture in organizations:

- *Lists of deficits:* Every employee carries with him/her a notepad that he/she uses permanently to list grievances, sources of interference, duplication of work, customer complaints, etc. and addresses them during monthly meetings and provides possible solutions. This constructive form of dealing with mistakes and complaints has been implemented successfully at Audi.

- *Pin boards:* Employees note deficits and suggestions for improvement on a pin board which is available to everyone, as at Gore-Tex. A modern version of this tool has been implemented at IBM, where employees can post their ideas on an online suggestions box called "Think Place." Of the first 4,500 suggestions that were posted, 300 have already been adopted (*Economist* January 2006a).

- *Team reflection* (West 1997): Employees are encouraged to reflect on the things that went well within their team in a certain project/ period of time on both the relational and the factual level; afterwards reflection on what did not go well and should be improved is stimulated. When using this method it is important to start out with the positive aspects so that people open themselves up to deficits once they are in a position of strength. No improvement without reflection!

- *Five why? questions when mistakes happen:* Toyota has established an effective method to get to the root of the underlying problem and to avoid the hunt for scapegoats in the face of mistakes: its employees use five consecutive *why?* questions to reveal the various causes that led to a mistake.

By reflecting on the underlying causes, mistakes can be used as triggers for learning and development. As Senge (1994) points out, the constant analysis of mistakes as well as of positive experiences and their incorporation into one's own store of knowledge are prerequisites for the realization of a learning organization. Another important characteristic is the fact that the new ideas and solutions to problems an employee develops are made available to all employees shortly afterwards. That means all techniques to support the dissemination of information have to be used.

A true mistakes-as-learning-opportunity culture comprises the willingness to accept the fact that today's success is the first step to tomorrow's failure if the organization and all its employees stop improving. As Lester Thurow (1999: 59) has stated, "Businesses must be willing to destroy the old while it is still successful if they wish to build the new that will be successful. If they don't destroy themselves others will destroy them."

3. Constructive confrontation and conflict culture

Pivotal for Popper's model of critical rationalism is the assumption that progress in science and society overall can only be achieved by means of exchanging arguments and critique. That is, critique leads to a productive conflict, but only when open communication and dialogue are possible. This requires tolerance, as argued by Lessing. Applying these principles to modern organizations we note that it is not the occurrence of conflicts but rather the way they are dealt with that impedes or facilitates an individual's development and is critical for the overall success of the business. Conflicts of interest can result in product or process innovations, rather than stagnation and withdrawal.

However, this is only true when they are carried out constructively and cooperatively and thereby serve as change engines. That also means people who are criticized without sound reason have to be given the chance to reject the allegations without facing negative consequences. Rigid confrontation as well as false harmony leads to ignorance of warning signals for erroneous trends. In line with this, based on his analyses of detrimental decisions that were made in groups, Janis (1982) warns that groups which do not engage in constructive criticism and discussion are likely to develop "groupthink," which leads to serious false estimations and wrong decisions.

Therefore, a constructive confrontation and conflict culture has to incorporate the demand for and encouragement of thinking outside the box, constructive stubbornness, and speaking up. It is evident that an organizational culture of this sort allows employees to freely express their views and therefore follows humanistic principles as well as enables organizational innovation and thus long-term business success. Although all employees are responsible for the establishment of such a culture, top management is especially accountable for it.

4. Questioning and curiosity culture

In order to be innovative and successful in the long run, one has to be curious and to ask questions – as Popper stressed for science and as Kant argued was the only way for humans to free themselves from their self-imposed immaturity. Applied to modern organizations this means that employees should be encouraged and called upon to ask questions. No question is out of bounds; the manager who has been asked decides freely if he/she wants to answer and in how much detail. It is thereby important that (s)he provides a reason for his/her answer or for not answering particular questions. A questioning and curiosity culture also implies that managers "lead by asking questions," as managers at Porsche are taught (Wiedeking 2007).

The manager asks the employee about his/her reality (Where are impediments to motivation and creativity? What would you do differently if you were in my position?). The consequences of these questions and answers have to be corresponding improvements. However, in many organizations the culture is more characterized by a mentality of "do your work and do not ask unnecessary questions." This mentality impedes humans' innate curiosity and prevents employees from becoming entrepreneurs within their organization.

5. Creativity and fantasy culture

Flexibility regarding thoughts and behaviors is essential – inflexible striving for perfection kills creativity and innovation. Thinking outside the box, fantasy, and creativity are wanted; creative chaos has to be supported. No new theories or methods (see Popper), no new products or procedures can come into being without creativity. The imperative is to minimize rules and regulations, allow exceptions to the rule, and to give more attention to people who are visionary or think outside the box. The search for new solutions incorporates unknown ways, the willingness to take risks, inventive talent, and unconventional ideas. Trial and error, experimenting, fantasizing, and the creation of the necessary room for development are crucial factors of success. They are the prerequisites for the development of innovative products, processes, and services: ideas evolve into innovations. The basis is Einstein's opinion that we are not lacking knowledge but rather fantasy. It is a managers' duty to not merely tolerate fantasy but to actively encourage it.

A prime example of the realization of a creativity and fantasy culture in practice comes from Semco, a Brazilian machinery manufacturer and service provider whose growth increased by 900 percent in ten years. As Ricardo Semler (2000: 58), the company's president, points out, Semco is characterized by "a respect for individuals and their ideas, a distrust of bureaucracy and hierarchy, [and] a love for openness and experimentation."

As our research on corporations from various branches of industry and many of the examples cited above show, the center of excellence cultures not only allow employees to freely express their opinions, develop new ideas, and realize their full potential – all of which are humanistic claims; these organizational cultures are also essential for superior business performance. In the next section we discuss what an individual manager can do to facilitate the implementation of the center of excellence cultures in his/her organization. Specifically, we present leadership principles that can serve as guidelines.

3. Guidelines for implementing center of excellence cultures: principle-based leadership

Fundamental for the lasting implementation of the Center of Excellence Cultures in any organization is the leadership style of its managers. Only if the predominant leadership style recognizes employees' fundamental needs and grants opportunities for their fulfillment can a true center of excellence be established. Empirical evidence shows that

Table 15.2 *Principles of leadership*

Principle of:

1. Providing meaning and vision
2. Transparency through information and communication
3. Participation and autonomy
4. Justice
5. Constructive feedback
6. Optimal stimulation by means of goal-setting
7. Personal growth
8. Being a role model

a leadership style that empowers employees, inspires them to develop their own solutions, and facilitates their development, has a significant positive effect on objective measures of business performance (see Frey, Jonas, and Greitemeyer 2002). For example, this type of leadership predicted objective performance of business units in a Canadian financial institution (Howell and Avolio 1993), Austrian bank branches (Geyer and Steyrer 1998), or for American sales agents (MacKenzie, Podsakoff, and Rich 2001). We call a leadership style that facilitates employee development by meeting fundamental human needs, for example a need for sense, a need for transparency, and a need for fairness, principle-based leadership.

The principle-based model of leadership

The principle-based model of leadership (Frey 1996; Frey et al. 2004) provides a framework that integrates different models of leadership and presents ways of meeting employees' needs in their workplace. Underlying the model is a principle that Hans Jonas (1903–93) emphasized in his teachings: responsibility for human dignity. Managers have to be aware that they are responsible for the team and the individual team members they lead, but also for the organization and for the future of society. Managers' striving for economic success and self-realization are bounded by their responsibility for other humans and the environment they live in. The principles presented in this chapter (see Table 15.2) can serve as practical guidelines for managers on how to meet their responsibilities and realize the center of excellence culture in their organizations. Table 15.2 gives an overview of the principles of leadership.

With the assumption that the manager should grant the employee vast opportunities for participation and facilitate his/her development as a coach and mentor, the model does justice to research on the change in values: since the 1960s the importance of values of duty and acceptance have decreased significantly, in favour of values of self-development and self-actualization (Pearlin and Kohn 1966). This implies that employees are increasingly interested in their self-development in the workplace; the mere earning of a living is no longer the driving force of motivation.

1. The principle of providing meaning and vision

Employees who do not understand the meaning of their work and its broader implications, who do not have a vision, will mentally resign from their jobs (internal withdrawal) sooner or later. On the contrary, where employees experience their job as meaningful, they will be willing to contribute new ideas and engage themselves for the goals of the team and thereby add to the establishment of a creativity and fantasy culture. Meaningful work content is more important to many employees than status and mere career advancement. This is a direct consequence of the "principle of meaning" (Schulz-Hardt and Frey 1997), which is a specification as well as generalization of the ideas by Frankl (1997): humans are endowed with a yearning for meaning; they always ask "why?" when the meaning of certain things is not evident to them. Thus, providing meaning and vision as a leader serves an important humanistic principle. In addition, there is empirical evidence for the fact that the communication and dissemination of a vision has an impact on objectively measured organizational per-formance (Baum, Locke, and Kirkpatrick 1998): the existence of an inspiring vision as well as the communication of this vision had a significant effect on the development and revenues of entrepreneurial firms.

2. The principle of transparency through information and communication

Closely related to the principle of providing meaning and vision is the principle of transparency: the manager has to provide information to his/her employees that goes beyond their work area, because only employees who are well informed can be forward looking and responsible and thereby become entrepreneurs within their organization. In order to achieve this it is not sufficient to rely on one-way communication where the manager informs the employee; rather it is necessary to engage in a permanent dialogue with employees.

Drastic evidence regarding the importance of transparency within an organization comes from Enron. An analysis of the conditions that were crucial for its collapse comes to the conclusion that "the enacted values that most shaped behaviors within Enron were high arrogance and low transparency" (Spector 2003: 215). In contrast, Semco provides a positive and progressive example for the realization of the principle of transparency, where board meetings are completely open and all employees are welcome to attend.

3. The principle of participation and autonomy

Since the longing for autonomy is a fundamental human need (Deci and Ryan 1985), transparency by itself will not motivate employees in the long run, if they are not given any kind of opportunities for participation and autonomous actions. As research on reactance theory (Brehm 1966) shows, employees who have not been involved in a decision-making process but have to carry out the consequences, often react with a mindset of blockade. The findings underline the importance of integrating employees in projects as soon as possible and inviting their opinions, even if the decision ultimately has to be made by the manager. These behaviors encourage employees to question procedures that have become a habit and to constantly develop new ideas; in short, to realize a questioning and curiosity as well as a problem solving culture.

A practical example of the realization of the principle of participation comes from one of the most successful American firms. When restating its core values in 2003 IBM held a 72-hour online real-time chat session with its employees in order to incorporate their ideas and opinions (*Economist* 2006a).

As research by Tom Tyler (1994) shows, even if a decision is contrary to employees' interests, their identification with it is greater when they have participated in the decision-making process and believe that the process was fair. This is of great importance, since the implementation of a decision is dependent on the employees and their commitment to it. Hence it is also necessary to explain the underlying rationale of decisions the employees have not been involved in (certain situations may require this).

4. The principle of justice

The research literature on justice distinguishes between four different types of justice: distributive, procedural, interpersonal, and informational justice. The term distributive justice refers to the question whether an outcome is fair, e.g. if all the team members have received equal shares of a good. Procedural justice, in contrast, is only concerned with the process, not the outcome; e.g. is the rule by which the resources have been distributed, fair? Especially in situations where distributive justice cannot be accomplished, it is very important to realize procedural justice. That means managers should communicate the rules by which decisions are made as well as the rationale underlying previous decisions. Even if an employee is not directly involved in a decision, it is important that (s)he is granted a "voice", i.e. that (s)he can articulate his/her opinion and is taken seriously.

Empirical evidence shows that if leaders act in procedurally fair ways, they are not only viewed as more legitimate and more competent, but employees are more accepting of organizational change such as a "hostile merger"(see Tyler and DeCremer 2005). In addition to procedural justice, interpersonal justice plays a central role, i.e. is the employee treated fairly and respectfully or is (s)he deceived and not taken seriously? Empirical research shows unambiguously that the perception of interpersonal justice is crucial for employees' trust and ultimately their performance (Cohen-Carash and Spector 2001). For example, in a study by Simons and Roberson (2003) in 97 hotels the procedural and interpersonal fairness perceived by the employees was a significant predictor of customer satisfaction – a crucial variable in the service industry. Finally, informational justice plays an important role. As stated under the heading of the principle of transparency, it is important to provide employees with sufficient information. Especially when the realization of distributive justice and procedural justice is sub-optimal, the employee has to be convinced that he/she has been informed authentically, honestly, and comprehensively.

Another important topic with regard to fairness is employees' financial compensation. As we know from Hertzberg's (1966) model of job satisfaction, remuneration is a "hygiene factor," i.e. adequate reimbursement does not cause job satisfaction by itself; however, if compensation is not adequate, this leads to dissatisfaction. Clear and transparent standards for the measurement of performance and the distribution of rewards are therefore indispensable, when leaders want to be regarded as fair.

5. The principle of constructive feedback

The fact that praise and correction are crucial motivators is strongly supported by empirical evidence from theories of learning, particularly operant conditioning. However, both managers and employees must have certain skills at their disposal in order to be able to provide constructive feedback. This applies both to praise (praise as the most important motivator) and to criticism which supports the adherence to goals previously agreed upon. The guideline for giving feedback can be summarized as "tough on the issue, soft on the person." Many managers give too little praise and criticize too little or too destructively. However, the provision of constructive feedback is a crucial factor for success. Feedback is critical for development since every person knows only his/her limited perspective of the world and may miss facts that are important to others. Another aspect that is highly relevant for the implementation of center of excellence cultures is the fact that praise and criticism are not only given to the employees by their managers, but also vice versa, particularly regarding the aspects that have a great impact on their motivation and creativity (see Useem 2002).

A good example for the realization of the principle of constructive feedback is the "real time reporting" system at Nokia which ensures that all employees and managers receive feedback about their performance. Periodical meetings of employees with their manager ensure that goals are adhered to; bottom-up feedback and the annual employee survey complete the reporting system by providing feedback to all managers.

6. The principle of optimal stimulation by means of goal-setting

The joint agreement upon the goals to be achieved serves several purposes: it prevents a chronic over-stretching of the employee as well as under-challenge, and facilitates employees' productivity and development. The research findings regarding goal-setting theory (Locke and Latham 2002) show that goals have to be challenging and specific in order to yield top performance. This implies that employees and their managers have to jointly agree upon very specific, measurable goals. Leading by goal agreement means that every employee knows the standards (s)he will be evaluated against and that the superordinate goals of the organization are transformed into specific goals for every division, team, and individual. These principles have been put into practice at Xerox Corporation by means of the "performance excellence process," which incorporates agreement upon qualitative and quantitative goals for every employee, both regarding their performance and their personal and professional development. This process has been proven to be crucial for the company's success (Schoenauer and Jessenberger 2005).

7. The principle of personal growth

The notion that personal growth is a fundamental concern for humans was first stated in humanistic psychology (Rogers 1959). In an organizational context this means that employees do not always want to simply fulfill goals; they also want to develop their competencies further and, if they fulfill their goals, they want to be given opportunities for advancement. Therefore, every employee should be given the opportunity to advance in accordance with his/her skills, talents, and interests. If an employee is endowed with the necessary competencies, his/her advancement within the organization – or an expansion of his/her responsibilities – should be facilitated. The principle of personal growth points to the realization of criteria that were demanded by Hackman and Oldham (1980): work should be organized in a way that allows for personality development and the realization of holistic and versatile thriving. In the end the employees will be both more satisfied and more productive.

8. The principle of being a role model

Managers have to be aware of their function as a role model in respect both of their expertise and their personal integrity. This is imperative for the creation of trust and thus for a culture of constructive confrontation and conflict as well as a culture of mistakes as a learning opportunity. Sincerity and the concordance of words and actions are necessary characteristics of a good and authentic leader (see George 2003). Only where the leader is a role model will the employees be really involved in their work in the long run. As Walumbwa *et al.* (2008) have shown empirically, authentic leadership is significantly and positively related to follower performance. That means leaders who are self-aware, present their authentic self, analyze data as objectively as possible before making decisions, and are guided by internal moral standards not only facilitate employees' efficacy beliefs (i.e. the conviction that they can achieve the things they want to achieve), but also their performance as rated by their supervisor. But are all leaders aware of the impact their beliefs, values, and actions have on possible followers? Leaders who want to be role models should ask themselves several times a year: do I practice what I preach? Are my behaviors in concordance with the values advertised by my organization? What would I do if I were in my employees' position? Where do I impede innovation and motivation?

When adopting the leadership principles described above to create a more humane organization it is important to first reflect on the status quo. Where is the organization at the moment? To what degree is the current organizational culture in concordance with the center of excellence cultures? Which of these cultures should be implemented first? In short, the implementation of the center of excellence cultures should not follow the motto "the more, the better," rather it has to follow the specific circumstances of the organization and its employees and managers. A useful first step is to examine to what degree each center of excellence culture has been implemented so far and which cultures should be improved. The next step is to ask which principles of leadership seem most useful for the implementation of the desired cultures. It is necessary to keep in mind that the realization should be adjusted in accordance with the skills of the leader, the characteristics of the employees, and the particularities of the organization. Since different personalities are receptive to different types of leadership and some situations require extensive discussion, whereas others necessitate quick decisions, leaders have to employ "situational leadership" in order to transform their organization into a center of excellence.

4. Conclusion

This chapter has argued that principles emphasized by occidental philosophers such as Immanuel Kant, Gotthold Ephraim Lessing, and in particular Karl Popper are the basis of organizational cultures that encourage constructive criticism, creativity, employee participation and development and thereby follow humanistic principles.

Furthermore, we have presented numerous examples highlighting the fact that the implementation of these organizational cultures may provide a competitive advantage for organizations. The principles formulated by philosophers centuries ago facilitate the superior business performance of modern organizations.

Crucial for the implementation of such center of excellence cultures is a leadership style that meets the fundamental needs of the employees and thereby enables them to bring their full self to work. The philosophy underlying the principles of leadership is that top performance always has to be coupled with human dignity. Where organizational cultures and leadership styles do not reward employees' performance, or where human dignity is violated, employees' ability to work under pressure and their overall performance is substantially limited. Based on empirical evidence we believe that the implementation of center of excellence cultures is an effective way to create more humane organizations.

References

Baum, R., Locke, E., and Kirkpatrick, S. 1998. "A Longitudinal Study on the Relation of Vision and Vision Communication to Venture Growth in Entrepreneurial Firms," *Journal of Applied Psychology* 83 (February): 43–54.

1966. *A Theory of Psychological Reactance*. New York: Academic Press.

Cohen-Charash, Y. and Spector, P. 2001. "The Role of Justice in Organizations: A Meta-Analysis," *Organizational Behavior and Human Decision Processes* 86 (November): 278–321.

Deci, E. and Ryan, R. 1985. *Intrinsic Motivation and Self-Determination in Human Behavior*. New York: Plenum.

Dweck, C. 1991. "Self Theories and Goals: Their Role in Motivation, Personality, and Development", in K. Dienstbier (ed), *The Nebraska Symposium on Motivation*. Lincoln: University of Nebraska Press.

Economist. 2006a. "Big and No Longer Blue," January 21: 15.

Economist. 2006b. "Inculcating Culture," January 21: 11.

Frankl, V. 1997. *Man's Search for Ultimate Meaning*. New York: Plenum Press.

Frey, Dieter. 1996. "Notwendige Bedingungen für dauerhafte Spitzenleistungen in der Wirtschaft und im Sport: Parallelen zwischen Mannschaftssport und kommerziellen Unternehmen," in A. Conzelmann, H. Gabler and W. Schlicht (eds.), *Soziale Interaktionen und Gruppen im Sport: Parallelen zwischen Mannschaftssport und kommerziellen Unternehmen*. Cologne: bps Publishers, pp. 3–28.

Frey, D., Jonas, E., and Greitemeyer, T. 2002. "Intervention as a Major Tool of a Psychology of Human Strength: Examples from Organizational Change and Innovation," in L. G. Aspinwall and U. M. Staudinger (eds.), *A Psychology of Human Strength: Perspectives on an Emerging Field*. Washington, DC: American Psychological Association, pp. 149–64.

Frey, D., Osswald, S., Peus, C., and Fischer, P. 2006. "Positives Management, ethikorientierte Führung und Center of Excellence: Wie Unternehmenserfolg und Entfaltung der Mitarbeiter durch neue Unternehmens- und Führungskulturen gefördert werden können," in M. Ringlstetter, S. Kaiser, and Müller-Seitz, G. (eds.), *Positives Management*. Wiesbaden: Gabler: Edition Wissenschaft, pp. 237–65.

Frey, D., Peus, C., and Jonas, E. 2004. "Soziale Organisationen als Centers of Excellence mit Menschenwürde – Zur Professionalisierung der Mitarbeiter- und Unternehmensführung," in B. Maelicke (ed.), *Personal als Erfolgsfaktor in der Sozialwirtschaft*. Baden-Baden: Nomos, pp. 27–52.

George, W. 2003. *Authentic Leadership: Rediscovering the Secrets to Creating Lasting Value*. San Francisco: Jossey-Bass.

Geyer, A. and Steyrer, J. 1998. "Transformational Leadership and Objective Performance in Banks," *Applied Psychology: An International Review* 47: 397–420.

Hackman, J. and Oldham, G., 1980. *Work Redesign*. Reading, MA: Addison-Wesley.

Hertzberg, F. 1966. *Work and the Nature of Man*. Cleveland, OH: World.

Howell, J. M. and Avolio, B. J. 1993. "Transformational Leadership, Transactional Leadership, Locus of Control, and Support for Innovation: Key Predictors of Consolidated Business-unit Performance," *Journal of Applied Psychology* 78: 891–902.

Janis, I. 1982. *Groupthink* (second edition). Boston: Houghton Mifflin.

Locke, E. and Latham, G. 2002. "Building a Practically Useful Theory of Goal Setting and Task Motivation," *American Psychologist* 57 (September): 705–17.

MacKenzie, S. B., Podsakoff, P. M., and Rich, G. A. 2001. "Transformational and Transactional Leadership and Salesperson Performance," *Journal of the Academy of Marketing Science* 29(2): 115–34.

Pearlin, L. and Kohn, M. 1966. "Social Class, Occupation, and Parental Values: A Cross-National Study," *American Sociological Review* 31: 466–79.

Popper, K. 1966. *The Open Society and Its Enemies*. Princeton University Press.

1999. *All Life is Problem Solving*. London: Routledge.

2002. *The Logic of Scientific Discovery*. London: Routledge Classics.

Rogers, C. 1959. "A Theory of Therapy, Personality, and Interpersonal Relations as Developed in the Client-centered Framework," in S. Koch (ed.), *Psychology, a Study of a Science*. New York: McGraw-Hill.

Schoenauer, M. and Jessenberger, J. 2005. "Xerox GmbH – From Good to Great," In D. Kudernatsch and P. Fleschhut (eds.), *Management Excellence*. Stuttgart: Schaeffer-Poeschel.

Schulz-Hardt, S. and Frey, D. 1997. "Das Sinnprinzip: Ein Standbein des homo psychologicus," in H. Mandl (ed.), *Bericht über den 40. Kongress der Deutschen Gesellschaft für Psychologie*. Goettingen: Hogrefe, pp. 870–6.

Semler, R. 2000. "How We Went Digital without a Strategy," *Harvard Business Review* September: 51–8.

Senge, P. 1994. *The Fifth Discipline Fieldbook*. New York: Currency Doubleday.

Simons, T. and Robertson, O. 2003. "Why Managers Should Care About Fairness: The Effects of Aggregate Justice Perceptions on Organizational Outcomes," *Journal of Applied Psychology* 88: 432–43.

Spector, B. 2003. "HRM at Enron: The Unindicted Co-Conspirator," *Organizational Dynamics* 32 (May): 215.

Thurow, L. C. 1999. *Building Wealth: The New Rules for Individuals, Companies, and Nations in a Knowledge-Based Economy*. New York: HarperCollins.

Tyler, T. 1994. "Psychological Models of the Justice Motive: Antecedents of Distributive and Procedural Justice," *Journal of Personality and Social Psychology* 67: 850–63.

Tyler, T. and DeCremer D. 2005. "Process-based Leadership. Fair Procedures and Reactions to Organizational Change," *Leadership Quarterly* 16: 529–54.

Useem, M. 2002. "When Your Boss Needs Help: Leading Up and Voicing Concerns," *Personalfuehrung* 4: 34–8.

Walumbwa, F., Avolio, B., Gardner, W., Wernsing, T., and Peterson, S. 2008. "Authentic Leadership: Development and Analysis of a Multidimensional Theory-based Measure," *Journal of Management* 34 (February): 89–126.

West, M. 1997. *Developing Creativity in Organizations*. Leicester: BPS Books.

Wiedeking, W. 2007. *Don't Follow the Crowd*. Munich: Piper.

16 Positive organizational scholarship: embodying a humanistic perspective on business

MIGUEL PEREIRA LOPES, MIGUEL PINA E
CUNHA, STEPHAN KAISER, AND GORDON
MÜLLER-SEITZ

"What a man can be, he must be"
(Maslow 1970: 46)

Positive Organizational Scholarship (POS) is an umbrella label that includes theory and research concerned with the study of positive outcomes, processes, and attributes of both organizations and their members (Cameron, Dutton, and Quinn 2003; Roberts 2006). As such, POS embraces the study of topics such as gratitude, resilience, appreciative inquiry, energizing relationships, happiness, and others that involve the pursuit of human growth and self-development.

POS was initially based on the positive psychology movement. According to the proponents of positive psychology, instead of only accentuating the dysfunctional and negative aspects of human life, with a deficit framework in mind, researchers and practitioners alike should start to look more into identifying and nurturing people's strongest qualities, and focus on understanding those things that make life worth living (Seligman and Csikszentmihalyi 2000). Those who support POS are likewise committed to understanding how organizations and institutions can help individuals devise their best selves and delineate how they can best accomplish them (Roberts *et al.* 2005). This resembles the contributions of humanistic scholars such as Maslow, quoted above, in their emphasis on the need for the self-actualization of the human being, and attests to the humanistic roots of POS.

There is a clear continuity of POS with humanism. However, POS constitutes more than just another humanistic approach. It represents an accentuation of the humanistic values, strengthening both the humanistic claims and their impact on the business world. As such, in the positive and appreciative spirit of POS, in this chapter we outline three contributions that the POS movement is offering to help bolster a humanistic perspective on business. First, POS is accentuating the need to look for the most positive aspects of business and organizations, leading the revival of a humanistic stance toward the world of business. Second, POS seems able to create "real world" change in the direction of humanistic assumptions, because of its focus on the business level, the level at which we can cause dramatic social change. Third, because POS is grounded in sound empirical research, there is the strong possibility that it might create a more humane society in real-world applications, because it raises the legitimacy of humanistic claims. We believe POS offers concrete and pragmatic management insights that can translate humanistic ideals into substantive real-world business change.

We begin this chapter by making a brief point about what a humanistic perspective on business can mean, and then introduce the character and historical roots of the POS movement. After this, we discuss the three major contributions that POS is offering toward more humanistic management and society. We conclude by appealing to all those identified with humanistic assumptions to follow the benefits of the POS approach.

A humanistic perspective on business

The term "humanism" is believed to be derived from the Latin *humanitas*, which meant the development of human virtue to its fullest extent, and included the development of human qualities such as benevolence, compassion, and love (Grudin 1989). The epigenesis of a humanistic tradition can be traced back to the writings of Greek philosophers such as Socrates, Aristotle, and Protagoras that explicitly concentrated on differentiating human beings from all other objects in the world.

Humanism has been represented by the leading thinkers in philosophical approaches throughout the succeeding centuries. These include the influential writings of John Stuart Mill and Wilhelm von Humboldt as they sought to create a society of well-developed individuals (Valls 1999), as well as the later manuscripts of Georg Wilhelm Hegel and Karl Marx with their accent on the possible ways of restoring ideal human conditions, free from the alienation of work and the dehumanized exploitation of labor (Aktouf 1992).

Throughout the twentieth century, influential philosophers continued to voice their humanistic concerns. This is the case with Martin Heidegger and Jean-Paul Sartre. For Heidegger (1982), philosophers should focus their insights on the "totality" of human existence, a recurrent call in every humanistic theory. Taking this focus on the whole of human existence as a method, Sartre (1943) came to defend the view that freedom is a basic human tenet, which confronts human beings with the responsibility of their choices, i.e. by assuming their own choices, humans are propelled to construct a meaning for their existence. Meaning-making becomes, in fact, a human need, and is at the core of most humanistic theories.

In the business literature, humanism early on established a constant presence, representing "a philosophy that asserts the dignity and worth of people and their capacity for self-realization through reason" (McFarland 1977). Melé (2003) identifies three major sets of humanistic approaches to management.

The first concerns the humanistic assumptions of leading authors in the middle of the twentieth century, such as Elton Mayo and Abraham Maslow, who were mainly interested in understanding how human behavior could be motivated to improve outcomes through self-actualization. The second set of approaches is linked to the cultural movement in organizational studies that emerged in the second half of the last century, originated by scholars such as Deal and Kennedy (1982), Peters and Waterman (1982), and Schein (1992). These approaches were based on the assumption that culture is part of human life, as well as the best way to understand the human condition. Melé (2003) considers still another, more contemporary set of humanistic management theories, built around the concept of *community*. The notion of community is used here to refer to the social structures of people with specific actions, relations, and a sense of unity, which allows the existence of a supra-personal character without removing from individuals their own personality and idiosyncrasies.

POS represents a leading humanistic approach in management studies. Sharing similar concerns with past humanistic authors, a group of scholars in management and associated research fields are laying the institutional foundations of POS. In addition, there is also a vivid discussion in POS discussion forums, symposiums, conference sessions and tracks that have taken place in recent years, such as the Academy of Management and the European Academy of Management annual conferences.

The same is true in the related fields of organizational behavior and organizational psychology (Wright 2003). A positive stance has been adopted by widely recognized authors such as Luthans (2002a,b) and Avolio (Avolio and Luthans 2006). These authors' research repeatedly demonstrates that business benefits by investing in humane, positive psychological capabilities, such as hope, optimism, and resilience (Luthans, Youssef, and Avolio 2007). It is thus clear that POS is gaining *momentum* in scholarly environments. But what is POS? What are POS' core constructs and concerns? What are its tenets and foundational roots?

What is positive organizational scholarship?

Positive organizational scholarship (POS) is a movement in organizational sciences that focuses on the dynamics leading to exceptional individual and organizational performance such as developing human strength, producing resilience and restoration, and fostering vitality, along with improved employee satisfaction/retention and increased worker happiness combined with better company performance (Cameron and Caza 2004). Mainly derived from the influence of the positive psychology movement, POS focuses on positive outcomes, processes, and attributes of organizations and their members. This positive bias does not mean, however, that the study of negative states, such as stress, depression, and other dysfunctional behavior and performance is not of prime importance. In POS, the emphasis is upon the importance of the usually forgotten part of the phenomena – the life giving, generative, and ennobling human factor. As stated by Cameron, Dutton, and Quinn (2003: 5): "Whereas POS does not reject the examination of dysfunctions, or dynamics that disable or produce harm, it does tend to emphasize the examination of factors that enable positive consequences for individuals, groups, and organizations." This is a new framework for studying organizational phenomena, which departs from mainstream organization studies.

Furthermore, positive enabling factors are approached within POS studies in the context of organizations, focusing on the processes and conditions that occur in organizational contexts that trigger

Table 16.1 *Main research topics in POS*

Research topic	Content
Appreciative inquiry	Appreciative inquiry is "a process of search and discovery designed to value, prize, and honor . . . The objective of Appreciative Inquiry is to touch the "positive core" of organizational life" (Cooperrider and Sekerka 2003: 226). Research has long shown that a focus on opportunities rather than on threats leads employees to an increased organizational understanding (Jackson and Dutton 1988).
Authentic leadership	Authentic leadership is "a process that draws from both positive psychological capacities and a highly developed organizational context, which results in both greater self-regulated positive behavior on the part of leaders and associates, fostering positive self-development" (Luthans and Avolio 2003: 243). Research has shown that a leader's support of this kind leads to positive outcomes both for employees (job satisfaction, positive mood) and for organizations (commitment, reduction in withdrawal behavior, performance) (Gardner and Schermerhorn 2004).
Compassion	Dutton *et al.* (2006) have defined compassion as noticing, feeling, and responding to another's suffering. Compassion is important for business organizations because it influences the activation of people's attention to pain, empathetic concern, and action, to extract and coordinate resources from an organizational system, especially in crisis situations.
Energizing networks	Energy is a type of positive affective arousal which people can experience as emotion (Dutton 2003). In social networks, high energizing people are better at getting others to act on their ideas, in gathering support for their initiatives, and persuading clients to purchase their services and products (Cross, Baker, and Parker 2003; Cross and Parker 2004).
Gratitude	Park and Peterson (2003: 36) define gratitude as "being aware of and thankful for the good things that happen; taking time to express thanks." There is evidence from experimental research that gratitude positively relates to individual levels of well-being (Emmons and Shelton 2002) and more prosocial behavior and collaboration (Baron 1984).

Table 16.1 (*cont.*)

Research topic	Content
High-quality connections	According to Dutton and Dukerich (2006), high quality connections are ties between individuals in which the individuals in them feel a sense of mutuality, positive regard, and vitality. They contrast with corrosive and toxic relationships also described in organizational research (Frost 2003). High quality connections have both individual positive effects on health and well-being, and organizational impacts on outcomes such as intra- and inter-organizational collaboration and organizational learning and resilience (Dutton and Heaphy 2003).
Meaning and meaningfulness	Meaning can be defined as "a subjective kind of sense that people make of their work" (Wrzesniewski 2003: 297). Meaning is a basic human tenet related to the need to find some way of interpreting the deeper purpose of what they do. Meaning is an important organizational topic because of the assumption that it is related to positive job and organizational attitudes, motivation and performance (Roberson, 1990).
Positive psychological capital	PsyCap (Positive Psychological Capital) is an individual's positive psychological state of development, characterized by high levels of self-confidence, optimism, hope, and resilience, which are the four main positive psychological capabilities (Luthans, Youssef, and Avolio 2007). There is now significant evidence that PsyCap strongly relates to organizational performance outcomes (Luthans *et al.* 2005).
Resilience	Resilience refers to the maintenance of positive adjustment under challenging conditions (Sutcliffe and Vogus 2003). As Sutcliffe and Vogus (2003: 104) assert, "organizational resilience results from enhancing particular competences, such as processes that encourage mindfulness as well as processes that enhance capabilities to recombine and deploy resources in new ways."
Strengths	A strength is "the ability to provide near-perfect performance in a given activity" (Clifton and Harter 2003). They can relate both to individual performance (e.g. the ability to manage several activities at the same time) and the organizational level (e.g. continuous

Table 16.1 (*cont.*)

Research topic	Content
	innovation) and are positively related to employee engagement and performance.
Virtues	Virtues are positive traits that contribute to individual fulfillment. Park and Peterson (2003) have developed a classification of virtues – the values in action classification (VIA) – including wisdom and knowledge, courage, love, justice, temperance, and transcendence.
Virtuousness	Virtuousness in organizations refers to transcendent, elevating behavior of the organization's members (Cameron *et al.* 2004). At the organizational level, virtuousness refers to features of the organization that engender virtuousness on the part of members. Research has shown that virtuousness and organizational performance, as measured by innovation, customer retention, employee turnover, quality, and profitability, are positively related.

appreciation, collaboration, vitality, and fulfillment, and where creating abundance and human well-being are the key indicators of success (Cameron, Dutton, and Quinn 2003). Consequently, to achieve its mission, POS scholars attempt to understand, explain, and predict the occurrence of positive organizational phenomena as well as to better understand its causes and consequences in existing organizational theories and those under development (Cameron *et al.* 2003, 2004). An outline of the main research areas covered by POS is seen in Table 16.1.

POS is not a movement without outside influence. In fact, it springs from insight in other research areas where many scholars and professionals have preceded POS in the study of positive organizational dynamics. These include community psychology and its emphasis on the prevention of illness and on wellness enhancement (more than on illness treatment), managerial studies of organizational citizenship behavior with its focus on extra-role discretionary behaviors, and corporate social responsibility and its emphasis on the value and urgency of organizations in addressing societal problems and ills (Cameron, Dutton, and Quinn 2003).

Table 16.2 *Contributions of POS to a humanistic perspective on business*

The three contributions of POS

1. Accentuating the positive
2. Impacting the real world
3. Strengthening legitimacy

All these roots of POS testify to the humanistic nature of the movement. However, POS is more than just another humanistic approach. It brings a new perspective on the possibility of integrating economic business goals and humanistic concerns. We now turn to an explanation of how POS is contributing to the development of a new humanistic foundation of business and society.

Contributions of POS to a humanistic perspective on business

While addressing the roots of POS, Cameron *et al.* (2003) exposed the reasons for the *positive organizational scholarship* label. In their argument, POS is *positive* because it strives to understand positive states, dynamics, and outcomes; it is *organizational* given its focus on positive phenomena that exist within organizational contexts; and it is *scholarship-driven* since it is founded on the rigorous, systematic, and theory-based practices that ground the scientific method, which are fundamental to gaining empirical credibility and societal impact. We realize that these three proclivities of POS also constitute its main contributions to a humanistic perspective on business. Based on these three distinctive features of POS, in the following sections we elaborate on how POS represents a robust and pragmatic humanistic perspective on management (Table 16.2).

Accentuating the positive

POS is about accentuating the positive in organizational functioning (Roberts 2006). The positive here refers to an orientation toward the human fulfillment and social betterment that characterizes the most ennobling human behaviors (Cameron *et al.* 2003). As such, we can see POS as a movement in management studies that embodies the deepest assumptions of humanistic theories. Accentuating the positive is also an affirmation of a more humanistic approach to management. For this reason, some humanistic theorists, such as Held (2001), have maintained that the recent emergence of these positive scholarly movements is no more than the resurgence of the humanistic tradition.

This thesis can be further grounded within the framework of Barley and Kunda (1992), who view the development of the American managerial discourse as alternating in cycles between a rational efficiency and a normative rhetoric, where the first stresses the efficient use of structures and technologies, and the second stresses employee relations and well-being. These authors found evidence that these cycles in managerial ideologies were contingent upon the cycles of economic expansion and contraction proposed in the Kondratieff waves. They found data consistent with the idea that rational rhetoric surges when economies are expanding, while normative rhetoric is associated with economic contractions. In light of this, POS can be considered the embodiment of such a new resurgence of a normative humanistic wave in business, linked to an economic contraction phase. As such, POS represents a movement on the cutting edge, with a rational-efficiency-driven model that has characterized management ideologies since the end of the twentieth century (e.g. business process re-engineering).

Whether this humanistic resurgence is the output of a managerial rhetoric to cope with certain socio-economic environments and attain organizational productivity (Barley and Kunda 1992; Alvesson 1982) or is really concerned with the pursuit of employee happiness, health, and personal betterment as an end in itself (Wright 2003) is still a question of debate, one that we address at the end of this chapter. Still, one cannot deny that POS represents a breakthrough concerning the need to accentuate the positive on the human side of business and organizations. Thus, it is clearly an outstanding contribution of POS to the humanistic aims.

In this humanistic quest, POS is also expanding our knowledge of what constitutes an effective human functioning and how we can enable its emergence. Subjects such as meaning-making at work (Wrzesniewski and Dutton 2001), resilience (Masten and Reed 2002), and psychological strengths (Clifton and Harter 2003) are now topics whose function we understand much better. This knowledge production will ultimately lead to a better comprehension of what the basic tenets of human welfare are, and what we can do to achieve them.

Besides extending research and our scientific understanding of positive human functioning, POS also extends the study of human affairs beyond the individual level. As Jane Dutton has pointed out (interviewed in Bernstein 2003), "POS is not just about looking at topics like self-actualization. It is about structures, cultures, processes, leadership and other organizational conditions that foster positive states and positive dynamics in human communities". This is precisely the point we now turn to in discussing the next major contribution of POS to humanism – making an impact on the real world.

Impacting the real world

A second contribution from POS to humanism has to do with the real-world impact of humanistic values. Positive organizational scholars are concerned with the creation of positive organizational and business environments. They are focused on the individual realm at the level of positive individual traits (strengths and virtues), but they also bear on the institutional realm, which includes the study of both positive institutions and positive communities and societies, embracing such units as families, work organizations, and schools (Peterson and Seligman 2003; Seligman 2003).

As such, POS adopts an inclusive and broad perspective that goes beyond the individual level, to consider the relationships among these levels – individual, organizational, institutional, and societal – and focus on how some institutional characteristics can enable the emergence of positive strengths and virtues (Cameron *et al.* 2003; Seligman 2002). This feature of POS is very important, because some humanistic authors have often been criticized for adopting an individual view of personal growth while de-emphasizing the importance of humanistic issues at other levels (Hanley and Abell 2002). This does not mean that both past (e.g. Humboldt 1969) and contemporary authors (e.g. Despain 2004) have not shown concern for the supra-individual aspects of humanism. However, these authors have not found a vehicle to significantly craft humanistic values in the business world.

Given its accent on the organizational level, POS is at the forefront of creating a body of knowledge which is able to contribute to real-world change. Take the example of appreciative inquiry (Cooperrider and Whitney 1999). Appreciative inquiry is "a process of search and discovery designed to value, prize, and honor. It assumes that organizations are networks of relatedness and that these networks are 'alive'. The objective of appreciative inquiry is to touch the "positive core of organizational life" (Cooperrider and Sekerka 2003: 226). It is grounded in the idea that asking positive questions draws out the positive spirit in a self-organized way. The operational net value of appreciative inquiry methodologies has been proved to be significantly positive for organizational change and development efforts (Bushe and Kassam 2005), by helping people to trigger their best qualities and engaging them in outstanding performances. Through this change of continuous betterment, business organizations are able to affect society in a positive way and drive the emergence of positive organizational and individual (i.e. humanistic) welfare. As such, POS is proving to be an appropriate vehicle to create the real humanistic change in the world of business. POS scholars are developing the correct methodologies and finding the appropriate management practices that enable a more humanized society, with more authentizotic organizations (Kets de Vries 2001).

Humanistic scholars have long argued that good theory and research is that which impacts real life (Giordi 2005). They are working at a level where a humanistic concern can be seen not only as an idealistic philosophy, but as real business practice.

Strengthening the legitimacy

A final contribution of POS to humanism is related to POS' scholarly foundation. POS advocates a bias toward scholarship which is based first on scientific method, and on following methods rooted in a "careful definition of terms, a rationale for prescriptions and recommendations, consistency with scientific procedures in drawing conclusions, and grounding in previous work" (Cameron, Dutton and Quinn 2003: 6). This scholarly-based character has contributed heavily to asserting POS assumptions among the core concerns of both the business research community (Cameron and Caza 2004; Roberts 2006) and a larger business audience.[1]

---

[1] POS was considered by the *Harvard Business Review* one of the "Breakthrough Ideas for 2004."

The legitimacy that the POS movement has attained in less than half a decade is largely due to this empirical and scientific basis, and constitutes a landmark in the assertion of a human-centered perspective on business. In this regard, POS contrasts with some humanistic approaches to business that rely on purely philosophical work (e.g. Melé 2003). In the words of Kim Cameron:

> One explanation for the lack of attention to POS phenomena is that they have often been associated with philosophy, religious or moral dogmatism, and scientific irrelevance. We are serious, however, about the word "scholarship". We are firmly committed to investigating positive phenomena scientifically. (interviewed in Bernstein 2003)

Grounding a management perspective in careful scientific evidence has long been recognized as contributing to the establishment of a new management fashion (Abrahamson 1996). The presentation of empirically validated scientific theories leads a management rhetoric to create the belief that a management technique or assumption is a rational one. But why is this so? Why is solid scientific research so important for POS and humanistic approaches to gain the legitimacy they need to make a real-world contribution?

We know from neo-institutional theories that prevailing social templates can help to legitimize certain practices (Meyer and Rowan 1977; Scott 1987). As POS researchers base their assumptions and recommendations on the well-established template of the scientific institution, they are raising social acceptability and legitimacy for humanistic claims. This clearly constitutes a major contribution from POS to a humanistic approach to business.

This reliance of POS on such a "scientific" approach to positive human functioning is not without its critics, however. Some authors stress that this constitutes evidence of the insolence of the positive movement towards a more traditional humanistic research that is aligned with the work of pioneering humanists (Held 2004). Some humanistic psychologists, for instance, have demonstrated some reluctance regarding this scholarly character of POS and have, instead, advocated an existential and phenomenological approach to the study of human issues. In the words of Maslow (1968: 9), humanistic psychology should "stress on starting from experiential knowledge rather than from systems of concepts or abstract categories or *a priori*s. Existentialism rests on phenomenology, i.e. it uses personal,

subjective experience as the foundation upon which abstract knowledge is built."

Some authors have seen this as a divisive debate, but it does not
have to be so. As pointed out by Rathunde (2001), the debate on what
constitutes "good empirical research" should be more of a unifying
one, and studies within the POS approach should adopt a wide variety
of research methods (Cameron, Dutton, Quinn, and Wrzesniewski
2003; Caza and Caza in press; Dutton and Dukerich 2006), some of
them resembling the phenomenological approaches championed by
humanistic psychologists. As such, POS researchers do not deny the
importance of research methods grounded in existentialism, nor do
they exclude it from POS' scope. Instead, they accept a diversity of
research methods that include many other traditions (including positivism) that may help POS and its humanistic view to gain legitimacy
in academia and in the world of business.

Concluding remarks: POS as pragmatic humanism

Some researchers are raising legitimate concerns regarding the goals of
humanistic and positive theories and their impact on the *real* business
world on both human resources management (McGuire, Cross, and
O'Donnell 2005) and POS (Fineman 2006). These authors argue,
under the label of critical management theory, that humanistic
approaches assume (whether intentionally or not) a naive perspective
on humanistic business practices and usually provide idealistic theories that do not take into account the real world of business and
work. In fact, management can misappropriate humanistic and positive discourses in order to promote its own totalitarian and exploit-
ative practices. This would ultimately impose strong limits on the aims
of humanistic business theories (Alvesson 1982), and explain why the
espoused humanistic ideals are incongruent with widespread cost-
cutting and market-oriented management practices.

Despite the truth in this criticism, it is conceivable that there are
still other situations where a humanistic management philosophy
genuinely exists. Even while not denying that humanistic premises can
sometimes be used in a misleading way and have the effect of
reinforcing the dominant power structures, it is also reasonable to
assume that humanistic management practices can be seen as promoting employee motivation along with taking into account the need

for people to nurture their human virtues (Melé 2003). Furthermore, by admitting that positive management philosophies can help management achieve its business goals, but at the same time do it in a more "humane" and socially responsible way, POS theories advocate a perspective on business that is neither idealistic nor naive.

Take the example of positive organizational behavior (POB) as proposed by Luthans (2002a). A leading author in the field of organizational behavior and father of POB, Luthans (2002b: 59) has defined it as "the study and application of positively oriented human resource strengths and psychological capacities that can be measured, developed, and effectively managed for performance improvement in today's workplace." This implies that the promotion of positive psychological states in organizations must go hand in hand with high performance levels to be considered as a positive phenomenon, an association that existing research already demonstrates (Luthans *et al.* 2005).

In line with this evidence, the perspective set forth by scholars of POS is much more aligned with a pragmatic view of positive organizational phenomena in that it holds a broader vision of what is positive, striving to include a multi-stakeholder countenance. As such, POS scholars have been able to distinguish themselves from other perspectives, by focusing solely on the positive phenomena that are seen as positive by all the stakeholders, contrary to other perspectives that have over-inflated the value of some stakeholders in their analysis (Figure 16.1). In fact, whereas critical management theorists focus on making explicit the negative results of many "positive" management practices, and humanistic approaches stress the positive for people regardless of whether they are negative for organizations, POS accentuates the need to explore how we can bring out relationships that are humane and more productive at the same time, a stance that is not far from past research on the happy-productive worker hypothesis (Staw 1986; Wright and Staw 1999).

A good example of this pragmatic view of POS is the research conducted by Cameron and his colleagues on the topic of organizational downsizing (Cameron 1994, 1998; Cameron, Bright, and Caza 2004). The context of downsizing is a very negative one, usually not conducive to positive outcomes in terms of either the financial or the human side of business. Cascio, Young, and Morris (1997) found that, after controlling for the industry variable, downsizing companies had

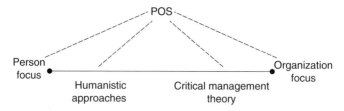

Figure 16.1 Focus of analysis of critical management theory, humanistic approaches, and POS

a return on assets (ROA) of 12.92 percent while upsizing companies had a ROA of 16.74 percent, a significant difference. Cascio (1993) also reported a study showing that only 46 percent of the companies in a sample of 1,005 firms said that cuts reduced expenses enough over time and fewer than one third said that profits increased as much as expected. Despite these results regarding downsizing, research has found that some organizations have been able to respond with success to downsizing – the common ground of these few organizations being their genuine commitment to virtuousness. In these organizations, virtuousness is recognized by management, but mainly by employees who identify in their managers virtues such as compassion, humility, and love, and reciprocate with their forgiveness for management action (Cameron and Caza 2002). This abundant virtuousness from all the stakeholders is what makes these organizations effective with respect to both people issues and financial affairs.

Taken together, these studies show that virtuousness and financial performance may go hand in hand in the real world of business. Whether virtuousness is only an end in itself or also serves as a means toward better financial performance is a secondary question, because only organizations genuinely committed to creating employee well-being and positiveness are able to benefit from these synergies. For this reason, we should be concerned by the warnings of critical management scholars that "positive speeches" can often be used in a perverted way to actually maintain inhumane employee conditions (Alvesson 1982; Fineman 2006), but we should welcome the fact that empirical data suggest that these "masked" organizations and managers will not get far with their fraudulent positiveness.

All in all, the message from POS to other humanistic scholars is twofold. First, adopt a multi-stakeholder viewpoint on what is considered humanistic management, instead of centering humanistic claims on working and living conditions only. Management action should not be seen as inhumane or self-interested without a deep examination of their reasons. Second, search for evidence that shows that only genuinely true concerns about treating people grounded in the fundamental human values can lead to business success and development. This will ultimately discourage everyone from adopting opportunistic behaviors, and engage people in productive and genuinely virtuous relationships at work.

We call this a *pragmatic humanistic* perspective because it maintains the idealistic nature of humanistic theories, while admitting to the need to take a broader perspective. It requires us to look into the world of business and pragmatically search for a manner through which core humanistic assumptions can find their way to make a real difference in our world. This requires pragmatic attention to the positive relationships between humanistic management practices and business success, even more as research points to the existence of few situations where we can have one without the other.

In conclusion, we see POS as a vehicle for implementing pragmatic changes in today's management styles (Ghoshal and Moran 2005) and fulfilling our hope of having a more humanized business society.

References

Abrahamson, E. 1996. "Management Fashion," *Academy of Management Review* 21(1): 254–86.

Aktouf, O. 1992. "Management and Theories of Organizations in the 1990's: Toward a Critical Radical Humanism?" *Academy of Management Review* 17(3): 407–31.

Alvesson, M. 1982. "The Limits and Shortcomings of Humanistic Organization Theory," *Acta Sociologica* 25(2): 117–31.

Avolio, B. J. and Luthans, F. 2006. *The High Impact Leader: Moments Matter in Accelerating Authentic Leadership Development*. New York: McGraw-Hill.

Barley, S. R. and Kunda, G. 1992. "Design and Devotion: The Ebb and Flow of Rational and Normative Ideologies of Control in Managerial Discourse," *Administrative Science Quarterly* 37(3): 1–30.

Baron, R. A. 1984. "Reducing Organizational Conflict: An Incompatible Response Approach," *Journal of Applied Psychology* 69: 272–9.

Bernstein, S. D. 2003. "Positive Organizational Scholarship: Meet the Movement," *Journal of Management Inquiry* 12: 266–71.

Bushe, G. R. and Kassam, A. F. 2005. "When is AI Transformational? A Meta-Case Analysis," *Journal of Applied Behavioral Science* 41: 161–81.

Cameron, K. S. 1994. "Strategies for Successful Organizational Downsizing," *Human Resource Management Journal* 33: 189–211.

  1998. "Strategic Organizational Downsizing: An Extreme Case," *Research in Organizational Behavior* 20: 185–229.

Cameron, K. S., Bright, D., and Caza A. 2004. "Exploring the relationships between organizational virtuousness and performance," *American Behavioral Scientist* 47: 766–90.

Cameron, K. S. and Caza, A. 2002. "Organizational and Leadership Virtues and the Role of Forgiveness," *Journal of Leadership and Organizational Studies* 9(1): 33–48.

  2004. "Contributions to the Discipline of Positive Organizational Scholarship," *American Behavioral Scientist* 47: 731–9.

Cameron, K. S., Dutton, J., and Quinn, R. E. 2003. "Foundations of Positive Organizational Scholarship," in K. S. Cameron, J. E. Dutton, and R. E. Quinn (eds.), *Positive Organizational Scholarship: Foundations of a New Discipline*. San Francisco: Berrett-Koeller, pp. 3–13.

Cameron, K. S., Dutton, J., Quinn, R. E., and Wrzesniewski, A. 2003. "Developing a Discipline of Positive Organizational Scholarship," in K. S. Cameron, J. E. Dutton, and R. E. Quinn (eds.), *Positive Organizational Scholarship: Foundations of a New Discipline*. San Francisco: Berrett-Koeller, pp. 361–370.

Cascio, W. F., Young, C. E., and Morris J. R. 1997. "Financial Consequences of Employment Change Decisions in Major U.S. Corporations," *Academy of Management Journal* 40: 1175–89.

Caza, B. B. and Caza, A. (in press). "Positive Organizational Scholarship: A Critical Theory Approach," *Journal of Management Inquiry*.

Clifton, D. O. and Harter J. K. 2003. "Investing in Strengths," in K. S. Cameron, J. E. Dutton, and R. E. Quinn (eds.), *Positive Organizational Scholarship: Foundations of a New Discipline*. San Francisco: Berrett-Koeller, pp. 111–21.

Cooperrider, D. L., and Sekerka, L. E. 2003. "Toward a Theory of Positive Organizational Change," in K. S. Cameron, J. E. Dutton, and R. E. Quinn (eds.), *Positive Organizational Scholarship: Foundations of a New Discipline*. San Francisco: Berrett-Koeller, pp. 225–240.

Cooperrider, David L. and Whitney D. 1999. *Appreciative Inquiry*. San Francisco: Berrett-Koehler.

Cross, R., Baker, W., and Parker A. 2003. "What Creates Energy in Organizations?" *MIT Sloan Management Review* 44: 51–7.

Cross, R. and Parker, A. 2004. *The Hidden Power of Social Networks: Understanding How Work Really Gets Done in Organizations.* Boston, MA: Harvard Business School Press.

Deal, T. E. and Kennedy A. A. 1982. *Corporate Cultures: The Rites and Rituals of Corporate Life.* Harmondsworth: Penguin Books.

Despain, H. G. 2004. "Taking Radical Responsibility to Create a Humanized World," *The Humanist* 64(5): 26–30.

Dutton, J. E. 2003. *Energize Your Workplace: How to Create and Sustain High Quality Connections at Work.* San Francisco: Jossey Bass.

Dutton, J. E. and Dukerich, J. 2006. "The Relational Foundation of Research: An Underappreciated Dimension of Interesting Research," *Academy of Management Journal* 49(1): 21–6.

Dutton, J. E. and Heaphy, E. D. 2003. "The Power of High-quality Connections," in K. S. Cameron, J. E. Dutton, and R. E. Quinn (eds.), *Positive Organizational Scholarship: Foundations of a New Discipline.* San Francisco: Berrett-Koeller, pp. 263–78.

Dutton, J. E., Worline, M., Frost P. J., and Lilius J. 2006. "Explaining Compassion Organizing," *Administrative Science Quarterly* 51(1): 59–96.

Emmons, R. A. and Shelton C. S. 2002. "Gratitude and the Science of Positive Psychology," in C. R. Snyder and S. J. Lopez (eds.), *Handbook of Positive Psychology.* Oxford: Oxford University Press, pp. 459–71.

Fineman, S. 2006. "On Being Positive: Concerns and Counterpoints," *Academy of Management Review* 31(2): 270–91.

Frost, P. J. 2003. *Toxic Emotions at Work: How Compassionate Managers Handle Pain and Conflict.* Cambridge, MA: Harvard Business School Press.

Gardner, W. L. and Schermerhorn, J. R. 2004. "Unleashing Individual Potential: Performance Gains through Positive Organizational Behavior and Authentic Leadership," *Organizational Dynamics* 33: 270–81.

Ghoshal, S. and Moran, P. 2005. "Towards a Good Theory of Management," in J. Birkinshaw and G. Piramal (eds.), *Sumantra Ghoshal on Management.* London: FT-Prentice Hall, pp. 1–27.

Giordi, A. 2005. "Remaining Challenges for Humanistic Psychology," *Journal of Humanistic Psychology* 45(2): 204–16.

Grudin, R. 1989. "Humanism," in *The New Encyclopaedia Britannica.* Chicago: Encyclopaedia Brittanica, vol. XX.

Hanley, S. J. and Abell, S. C. 2002. "Maslow and Relatedness: Creating an Interpersonal Model for Self-actualization," *Journal of Humanistic Psychology* 42(4): 37–57.

Heidegger, M. 1982. *The Basic Problems of Phenomenology*, trans. A. Hofstadter. Bloomington: Indiana University Press.

Held, B. S. 2004. "The Negative Side of Positive Psychology," *Journal of Humanistic Psychology* 44: 9–46.

Humboldt, W. 1969. *The Limits of State Action.* Cambridge: Cambridge University Press.

Jackson, S. and Dutton, J. E. 1988. "Discerning Threats from Opportunities," *Administrative Science Quarterly* 33: 370–87.

Kets de Vries, M. 2001. "Creating Authentizotic Organizations: Well-functioning Individuals in Vibrant Companies," *Human Relations* 54(1): 101–11.

Luthans, F. 2002a. "The Need for and Meaning of Positive Organizational Behavior," *Journal of Organizational Behavior* 23: 695–706.

  2002b. "Positive Organizational Behavior: Developing and Managing Psychological Strengths," *Academy of Management Executive* 16: 57–72.

Luthans, F. and Avolio, B. J. 2003. "Authentic Leadership Development," in K. S. Cameron, J. E. Dutton, and R. E. Quinn (eds.), *Positive Organizational Scholarship: Foundations of a New Discipline.* San Francisco: Berrett-Koeller, pp. 241–58.

Luthans, F., Avolio, B. J., Walumbwa, F. O., and Li, W. 2005. "The Psychological Capital of Chinese Workers: Exploring the Relationship with Performance," *Management and Organization Review* 1(2): 247–69.

Luthans, F., Youssef, C. M., and Avolio, B. J. 2007. *Psychological Capital: Developing the Human Competitive Edge.* Oxford: Oxford University Press.

Maslow, A. 1968. *Towards a Psychology of Being* (second edition). New York: Van Nostrand.

  1970. *Motivation and Personality.* New York: Harper and Row.

Masten, A. S. and Reed, M.-G. J. 2002. "Resilience in Development," in C. R. Snyder and S. J. Lopez (eds.), *Handbook of Positive Psychology.* Oxford: Oxford University Press, pp. 74–88.

McFarland, D. E. 1977. "Management, Humanism, and Society: The Case for Macromanagement Theory," *Academy of Management Review* 2(4): 613–23.

McGuire, D., Cross, C., and O'Donnell, D. 2005. "Why Humanistic Approaches in HRD Won't Work," *Human Resource Development Quarterly* 16(1): 131–7.

Melé, D. 2003. "The Challenge of Humanistic Management," *Journal of Business Ethics* 44(1): 77–88.

Meyer, J. and Rowan, B. 1977. "Institutionalized Organizations: Formal Structures as Myth and Ceremony," *American Journal of Sociology* 83: 340–63.

Peters, T. J. and Waterman, R. H. 1982. *In Search of Excellence*. New York: Harper Row.

Peterson, C. M. and Seligman, M. 2003. "Positive Organizational Studies: Lessons from Positive Psychology," in K. S. Cameron, J. E. Dutton, and R. E. Quinn (eds.), *Positive Organizational Scholarship: Foundations of a New Discipline*. San Francisco: Berrett-Koeller, pp. 14–28.

Rathunde, K. 2001. "Toward a Psychology of Optimal Human Functioning: What Positive Psychology Can Learn from the 'Experimental Turns' of James, Dewey, and Maslow," *Journal of Humanistic Psychology* 41(1): 135–53.

Roberson, L. 1990. "Functions of Work Meanings," in A. Brief and W. Nord (eds.), *Meanings of Occupational Work*. Lexington, MA: Lexington Books, pp. 107–34.

Roberts, L. M. 2006. "Shifting the Lens on Organizational Life: The Added Value of Positive Scholarship," *Academy of Management Review* 31(2): 292–305.

Roberts, L. M., Dutton, J. E., Spreitzer, G. M., Heaphy, E. D., and Quinn, R. E. 2005. "Composing the Reflected Best Self-Portrait: Building Pathways for Becoming Extraordinary in Work Organizations," *Academy of Management Review* 30(4): 712–36.

Sartre, J.-P. 1943. *Being and Nothingness*, trans. Hazel E. Barnes. London: Routledge Classics.

Schein, E. H. 1992. *Organizational Culture and Leadership* (second edition). San Francisco: Jossey-Bass.

Scott, R. 1987. "The Adolescence of Institutional Theory," *Administrative Science Quarterly* 32: 493–511.

Seligman, M. E. 2002. *Authentic Happiness*. New York: The Free Press.
    2003. "The Past and Future of Positive Psychology," in C. Keyes and J. Haidt (eds.), *Flourishing: Positive Psychology and the Life Well-lived*. Washington: American Psychological Association, pp. xi–xx.

Seligman, M. E. and Csikszentmihalyi, M. 2000. "Positive Psychology: An Introduction," *American Psychologist* 55: 5–14.

Staw, B. M. 1986. "Organizational Psychology and the Pursuit of the Happy/Productive Worker," *California Management Review* 18(4): 40–53.

Sutcliffe, K. M. and Vogus, T. J. 2003. "Organizing for Resilience," in K. S. Cameron, J. E. Dutton, and R. E. Quinn (eds.), *Positive Organizational Scholarship: Foundations of a New Discipline*. San Francisco: Berrett-Koeller, pp. 94–110.

Valls, A. 1999. "Self-development and the Liberal State: The Cases of John Stuart Mill and Wilhelm von Humboldt," *Review of Politics* 61(2): 251–74.

Wright, T. A. 2003. "Positive Organizational Behavior: An Idea Whose Time Has Truly Come," *Journal of Organizational Behavior* 24: 437–42.

Wright, T. A. and Staw, B. M. 1999. "Affect and Favorable Work Outcomes: Two Longitudinal Tests of the Happy-productive Worker Thesis," *Journal of Organizational Behavior* 20: 1–23.

Wrzesniewski, A. 2003. "Finding Positive Meaning in Work," in K. S. Cameron, J. E. Dutton, and R. E. Quinn (eds.), *Positive Organizational Scholarship: Foundations of a New Discipline*. San Francisco: Berrett-Koeller, pp. 296–308.

Wrzesniewski, A. and Dutton, J. E. 2001. "Crafting a Job: Revisioning Employees as Active Crafters of Their Work," *Academy of Management Review* 26(2): 179–201.

17 | Corporate sustainability as an indicator for more humanism in business? A view beyond the usual hype in Europe

OLIVER SALZMANN, AILEEN
IONESCU-SOMERS, AND ULRICH STEGER

The terms "corporate social responsibility" and "corporate sustainability" are used (often interchangeably) to describe the situation when companies take on a wider array of social and environmental issues (directly or indirectly) associated with their activities and take actions to mitigate those issues. A so-called business case for sustainability exists if these actions also translate into improved corporate financial performance.

Companies in an ideal humanistic business environment would proactively decide in favor of actions that put society's needs first. In any case, a sound business case for corporate sustainability is an important foundation for the necessary attitudinal change in this regard – and a simple fact of making smart investments. Humanism can be interpreted as a more far-reaching version of corporate sustainability, one that most hard-nosed and myopic managers would most likely disregard as philanthropy.

Sustainability in today's business environment has become increasingly prominent over the years, most recently in the context of climate change: businesses, policy-makers, and NGOs are attempting to surpass each other through – more or less – well-designed initiatives. And the media are happy to feed the heightened societal awareness.

However, how much of this is hype and opportunism? How significant is stakeholder interest in corporate sustainability, as a first step towards achieving humanism in business? To what extent do they reward corporate leaders and penalize laggards?

We hope to provide solid answers on the following pages, and will base them on empirical evidence collected at the International Institute for Management Development. We will primarily report on an empirical study of nine stakeholder groups, namely: NGOs (and consumer organizations), financial institutions, governments, cities and communities, corporate customers and suppliers, media, and unions (cf. Steger 2006). We collected our data between May and November 2005 – most notably at a time when climate change still received significant attention from NGOs and scientists, and focused on five European regions: (1) Great Britain and Ireland, (2) Nordic countries and the Netherlands, (3) Germany, Austria, and Switzerland, (4) France and Belgium, and (5) Spain and Portugal. We conducted 265 semi-structured interviews (including 15 interviews with sustainability experts and managers to benchmark our findings) and complemented those with self-completion questionnaires that we mailed to 16,000 personalized addresses, spread equally across the regions and stakeholders groups. We followed up where possible and appropriate through fax and phone calls, and also used snowball sampling among our interviewees to boost our sample size. The resulting questionnaire sample (307 observations) is sobering in itself and reflects a response rate of roughly 2 percent for the mailed questionnaires.

The importance of corporate sustainability in Europe

Overall, our respondents – with the obvious exceptions of NGOs and consumer organizations – showed little interest in corporate sustainability. We attribute this to three major reasons:

1. Europe's high social and environmental standards, which result from relatively strict legislation and consequent enforcement practices.
2. Europe's struggle for regional competitiveness against emerging economies in Asia in particular. Companies have gained considerable bargaining power over the years, and thus governments were not inclined to tighten social and environmental standards even further. Economic upturns may relieve some of the pressure. Ultimately, however, the parameters within which policy-makers operate do not change.

3. Actual changes in corporate behavior: As most of our respondents confirmed, companies have learned a lesson or two – from being in several rough spots in the 1990s (Shell's Brent Spar, Nike's sweatshops, etc.). They manage issues and stakeholders more systematically.

We noted a clear trend towards cooperation, not only between stakeholders and companies but also among stakeholders themselves, e.g. when politicians – more or less opportunistically – side with unions and publicly criticize major layoffs in companies, right after they had reported windfall profits.

Overall we also see little evidence for the so-called first-mover advantage. The downside potential for laggards is greater than the upside potential for leaders – not only because of the way the majority of stakeholders "tick" but also as a result of media coverage that is dominated by stories of failures, scandals, etc. rather than success stories.

Individual stakeholder – positions and significance

Clearly, the stakeholder groups surveyed differ significantly from each other, in terms of their agendas, their bargaining power, their activities, etc. In the following paragraphs, we will attempt to highlight some of our stakeholder-specific findings – underpinned by a couple of key quotations from our interviewees:

NGOs are clearly by far the most demanding: They are strongly concerned about significant and documented improvements in corporate social and environmental performance, hence their focus on corporate target setting, transparency, and social and environmental impacts in developing countries (i.e. the supply chain). However, they have become more and more frustrated, given (1) the ignorance of other stakeholders, whose buy-in they rely on (e.g. boycotts only really work if consumers participate) and (2) companies' ability to manage their issues and stakeholders more coherently:

The times of the big demonstrations are gone. (Quote from NGO representative)

In the early days, we could not get to the factory gates; today they serve us tea and cookies . . . I was so tired of yet another conference and PowerPoint presentation. Stakeholder dialogues are merely excuses – we are managed. What happens on the ground is not very pretty. (Quote from NGO representative)

In light of this frustration and the willingness to provide an upside for companies, NGOs have also adopted more cooperative strategies to influence companies.

Our supporters are generally happy with us taking money from companies as long as the policy changes companies make are visible. When looking for a corporate partner, we are interested in corporate leadership, in the "willing sinners," preferably in a high-impact sector. (Quote from NGO representative)

However, this trend is still regarded as very controversial – even within the same NGO.

For this reason, it is very important to demonstrate effectiveness of such partnerships:

Prior to engaging with a company, we carry out a due diligence process. We commission a comprehensive assessment of our potential partner – carried out by a third party. Our potential corporate partner pays for this assessment – as a demonstration of goodwill. (Quote from NGO representative)

National and regional governments as well as communities and cities are primarily concerned with regional competitiveness of their region and country. Hence, they see themselves as "enablers" of corporate sustainability and do not seriously consider tighter social and environmental standards.

We try to promote corporate sustainability by setting the right framework, raising awareness, improving knowledge and bringing greater transparency . . . We do not want to burden global companies with an extensive amount of national regulation. Therefore, corporate social responsibility with its voluntary and self-regulating characteristics is the right instrument in the era of globalization. (Quote from city representative)

When it comes to influencing corporate behavior they rely on guidelines, standards, and award schemes and negotiated agreements. Financial institutions and markets are – alongside customers – companies' most important stakeholders. However, our evidence shows that their interests in and influence on corporate sustainability is weak:

Our business model does not allow us to impose additional assessments on our clients. If you want to sell something, it is difficult to address additional [social or environmental] criteria. Currently, our clients could just go to a competitor (Quote from financial investor)

As a public company, you have the obligation to disclose to investors everything that they would consider to be material to their investment decision. An investor will not invest in a company for thirty years. They do not care, for instance, if a company is putting sludge into the ground that is going to be robbed in thirty years' time. If the investors knew, it would be in thirty years from now and nobody else would know it until thirty years from now, they wouldn't give a sugar. That is the reality of the market. They only care about the risk that is going to crystallize tomorrow. (Quote from financial institution)

In the financial sector there are several niche players that have built their business models around corporate sustainability. However, they focus on corporate transparency and accountability rather than actual social and environmental impacts of corporate activities:

We are trying to identify companies that seize opportunities and manage risks deriving from economic, environmental and societal developments better than their peers do . . . Our mission is to be able to measure what companies are doing in terms of management systems and how this leads to specific results. (Quote from Rating Agency)

Companies as stakeholders – i.e. suppliers and customers – have a significant potential to promote corporate sustainability– since they are part of the business system. However in practice, only corporate customers – at least partly – exploit this potential, also becasue they are scrutinized by their own customers and NGOs. They have become increasingly engaged in the environmental and social behavior of their suppliers; they set and enforce standards chiefly in developing countries, in which they often take a quasi-regulatory role.

Our customers expect it from us . . . I have to show them the things that we ask suppliers. If they see hard data – they believe it. When we look at the billions of dollars we spend overall, half is outside our company – therefore our suppliers have to act in a responsible way. (Quote from corporate supplier)

Tackling supply chain issues can be a formidable task: In the food and beverage industry, multinational companies such as Nestlé and Unilever have to liaise with thousands of suppliers, often small farmers:

It is impossible to have 100 percent coverage of the supply chain in terms of environmental and social performance. We have to draw the line and say that at a certain stage we have to stop. (Quote from corporate supplier)

Corporate sustainability is typically not pushed by corporate suppliers; in most cases since they would not dare to bother their customers with it. However, there are exceptions that are characterized by a clear need for risk management and product responsibility (e.g. hazardous chemicals).

There is no room for that – my job is to manage, run and grow the business. From day to day, other than aspects of good management, I do not have space for these issues. (Quote from corporate supplier)

Both corporate suppliers and customers prefer to "cooperate to influence" (rather than to confront). Interestingly, respondents from *both* groups consider the corporate customers' side as clearly more influential than the side of corporate suppliers.

The pressure goes up the supply chain, not down. (Quote from corporate supplier)

Corporate sustainability also holds limited importance for the remaining stakeholders, namely media and unions. Obviously unions are primarily concerned with employment:

We have no declared goal in the field of corporate social responsibility (CSR), but of course, we look out for the rights of our members . . . Employees are primarily concerned about their job security, pay, and safety; CSR is of minor importance. (Quote from union representative)

They are also very sceptical, since they consider companies' activities in the field of corporate sustainability as an attempt to strengthen bargaining positions and forestall regulation:

CSR softens our negotiating position . . . We have a nuanced view on CSR: It is neither inherently bad, nor good. And it is not a substitute for regulation and collective bargaining. (Quote from media representative)

Finally, media exhibit a largely opportunistic approach to corporate sustainability; there simply is no mission or agenda:

Our program is to reflect adequately the topics that are currently most important to society. Unemployment, business relocation, and sustainability are such topics; we try to address the worries and questions of our audience.

Factors influencing the decision for or against a certain story are big names, big numbers, government policy [reason: impact on the whole industry] or shocking findings. (Quote from media representative)

However, they have – in their role as gatekeepers – huge potential. It remains unexploited since only niche players (special interest media such as magazines and websites) act strategically and systematically to create transparency and promote more responsible corporate behavior.

Three stakeholder clusters

A cluster analysis revealed three distinct sets stakeholders, which we refer to as "challengers," "bystanders," and "skeptics":

- Challengers consider corporate sustainability important and are dissatisfied with companies' performance in that area.
- Bystanders also consider corporate sustainability important; they are satisfied with corporate performance.
- Skeptics consider corporate sustainability less important and are dissatisfied.

Some groups are more strongly associated with one cluster than with another. As one would expect, the highest number of challengers can be found among NGOs, the highest number of bystanders among corporate suppliers, unions, and corporate customers; we found the highest number of skeptics among communities and corporate suppliers. It is self-evident that more of our respondents (59 percent) were challengers, followed by skeptics (21 percent) and bystanders (20 percent).

A subsequent analysis of the clusters' perception of individual dimensions of corporate sustainability showed that the challengers primarily focus on issues, regions, and processes, i.e. anything which underpins concrete demands and a solid agenda. They also tend to take adversarial actions against companies (praising and blaming, boycotts, etc.) to push their agenda and primarily target companies' reputations. In contrast, bystanders and skeptics have a narrower and more basic perception of corporate sustainability, e.g. bystanders exhibit a relatively strong concern for employment. Moreover, bystanders prefer cooperative actions to influence companies; hence they also see their influence on corporate innovation (rather than reputation). Skeptics' actions and influence are rather negligible.

Also, based on our response rate to the questionnaire and our interviews, we have to conclude that the stakeholder universe is dominated by both bystanders and skeptics; the dominant share of challengers in our sample is a clear sampling bias. Again this clearly suggests that without a significant environmental or social crisis, stakeholders are unlikely to drive the corporate sustainability agenda.

What the managers think

Our interviews with the fifteen sustainability experts and managers clearly underpinned our findings on the limited significance of stakeholders to the corporate sustainability agenda. The managers clearly regarded confrontational NGOs with skepticism:

I do not think that you can group all NGOs together – there are two basic groups. One group that is trying to solve problems and another group stuck in an "awareness-raising phase." Some are locked into an old product, and the marketplace has moved on.

They also reported improvements in stakeholder relationships (more dialogue, more engagement with NGOs and public agencies) and were confident that future stakeholder pressure – if it was to materialize – could be contained. Our respondents said a lot about NGOs, less about the other stakeholder groups, obviously because of their limited relevance. Among other things, they criticized policy-makers and media for their reactive and opportunistic role:

Politicians are opportunistic, not "sustainable" people – they put sustainability on the agenda just to get votes, that's all.

The media have a bad news–good news working principle. Good news does not have the entertainment value; the public interest is the driver for news picking. Sustainability topics are not set in the media; the rule of the game is that the more exciting and dramatic topics are more important.

Climate change – new momentum for corporate sustainability?

If one looks at the timeline of events related to climate change, it is obvious that events and media coverage culminated in 2007, in particular prior to the G8. In our view, various factors have contributed to this heightened awareness – some more scientific than others: e.g. Hurricane Katrina, the Stern Report, a democratic majority in the US congress, the fourth IPCC assessment report, not forgetting a warm winter and spring in Europe, of course.

However, to what extent can we actually ascertain an increase in stakeholder pressure? Whereas NGO strategies have hardly changed (why should they?), other stakeholders, in particular governments and regulators, have taken a more proactive role. The EU has formulated an ambitious plan to mitigate climate change, which is yet to be fully translated into actual policies. Mayors of some 500 US cities have voluntarily committed to Kyoto. President Bush has finally agreed to emission reductions and a post-Kyoto process – even if with certain caveats. Nevertheless substantial uncertainty remains – e.g. around the next national allocation plans in the EU, a post-Kyoto agreement, the involvement of China and India, etc.

What about business? It is apparent, that most companies are still on the lower end of the learning curve. Some have necessarily become more acquainted with climate-related opportunities and risks as a result of regulation (e.g. the EU emission trading scheme, the Renewable Energy Sources Act in Germany). However, the more significant actions are those that took place early and went beyond compliance. They include for example carbon neutrality (as aspired to by many banks and other less carbon-intensive companies) and a variety of partnerships (some of them already in existence for several years) with different purposes: Some aim to develop managerial and technical capacity to reduce emissions and source from renewable energies. Some even engage in lobbying for legislation (or more precisely a certain kind of legislation, e.g. the US Climate Action Partnership and the Climate Group).

What does this tell us?

Leading companies are ahead of some of their stakeholders and they are most likely aware of significant low-hanging fruits. They expect an increase in the price of carbon and they want to be at the forefront of technological and regulatory developments. The laggards will have no choice but to react to emerging or tightening regulation (giving greenhouse gas emissions a price in their markets).

We are far from corporate sustainability being mainstreamed. With regard to climate change, business models are not yet seriously affected or even questioned (just look at ExxonMobil's "softened but still skeptical" stance on climate change and renewable energies and the windfall profits of the oil and gas majors). However, such a development is not inconceivable and will depend on a variety of factors that would keep up the current momentum. They include extreme weather events, environmental or social crises, geopolitical risks, the depletion of fossil fuels and . . . political and business leadership.

It seems too early to tell where we are heading. Cynics may legitimately call for a severe crisis to increase pressure on policy-makers and business. In light of the evidence presented, they may well be right. Faced with Europe's constant struggle for competitiveness, stakeholders may be even harder pressed to achieve a proliferation of higher social and environmental standards. Coupled with stakeholders' limited willingness to reward leadership (or even punish laggards), it will by no means become easier for proactive managers to build their business case for corporate sustainability, which would ultimately pave the path to increased humanism in business. This situation hints at a future where the failure of the humanistic business agenda is likely (cynics and hard-nosed managers would say "inevitable"). Is it realistic to expect companies to embrace an almost Utopian, holistic humanistic business philosophy, when they fail to fulfill the mere requirements of corporate sustainability?

Using corporate sustainability as a proxy and initial step for humanism in business, empirical evidence provides a view of a sobering reality. However, such a reality check is crucial for future actions. The current situation undoubtedly presents us with an uphill task in instilling humanism in business. A gradual process directed towards bringing about change within the business world is crucial. It requires managerial and technical capacity-building in companies to facilitate smart first moves, but it also requires a humanistic business environment; after all, attitudinal changes have to come from somewhere. Will companies choose to roll out their pilot projects on sustainability without being pressured by external stakeholders; will they give them the benefit of the doubt?

Reference

Steger, Ulrich. (ed.) 2006. *Inside the Mind of the Stakeholder*. Basingstoke: Palgrave Macmillan.

18 | Changing direction: corporations as ambassadors for the environment?

OLIVER RAPF

Hitting hard – corporations and the environment

Nature pays for economic growth

The term *sustainability* was coined over three decades ago, and has since then become a challenge that can no longer be ignored by any major international company. Progress towards a more sustainable society has, however, been slow. During those decades, the economic model on which our global society is based has not become fundamentally more sustainable. Economic development and the creation of wealth still rely on the exploitation of (largely finite) natural resources. Commonly used indicators for progress, such as the measurement of Gross Domestic Product, do not take the depletion of natural resources or the pollution of the natural environment into account. The external costs of resource use and the associated pollution are not being internalized. Rather, society as a whole is carrying the burden, as well as the costs associated with this burden. To make things worse, the burden is shared unequally across the globe: people in poor countries often carry a larger share of the burden than those in richer countries. A good example is the impact of climate change, which, in the form of droughts and extreme weather events, is already affecting developing nations to a much greater extent than developed countries, although much of the problem is being caused by consumption and lifestyle patterns in industrialized nations. Simultaneously, poorer developing nations often lack the means to adapt to climatic changes.

WWF's *Living Planet* report[1] reveals the continuous deterioration of the environmental situation over time. The aggregated indicator,

[1] Hails, Chris (ed.). 2006. *Living Planet Report 2006*. Gland: WWF International. http://panda.org/news_facts/publications/living_planet_report/index.cfm (accessed July 2007).

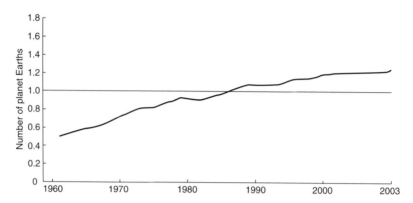

Figure 18.1 Humanity's ecological footprint: estimates of how much of the productive capacity of the biosphere people use

Humanity's Ecological Footprint, demonstrates this graphically. The global population has a current ecological footprint that would require 1.3 times the amount of resources that planet earth has if it were to be sustained over time.

A footprint of one would indicate that humankind is just living on the limit of sustainability. Any truly sustainable society would have an ecological footprint well below one. This would mean that the global society consumes fewer resources than our planet is able to provide in the same time period. Any number higher than one indicates that we are living off the capital of our earth, consuming more than it provides us with.

The outlook is, however, daunting. Even a moderate business-as-usual scenario will lead to a footprint twice the size of the planet by the middle of this century. Figure 18.2 shows how the global footprint will increase if the world continues on the current path.

While this indicator is an aggregated tool consisting of a large number of indicators,[2] it nevertheless reveals the scale of the challenge. Living on a sustainable scale will require significant changes in production and consumption patterns to achieve a global ecological footprint smaller than one. The question remains whether change is in sight.

[2] See the *Living Planet Report 2006* for details.

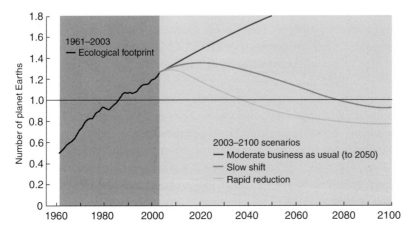

Figure 18.2 Three ecological footprint scenarios: two may lead to sustainability. One path entails a slow shift from our current route, the other a more rapid transition to sustainability.

Who is responsible?

Corporations around the world are following the same economic model as at the beginning of the Industrial Revolution. While industrial centers have shifted geographically and production processes have become more resource-efficient over time, the sheer expansion of industrial activity has overcompensated for the efficiency gains and is leading to an absolute increase in resource consumption, and in waste and pollution.

Who is to blame for this? Governments, industry, consumers? Obviously, there is no single villain. The question under debate is: who should change what and at which speed?

In fact, the model definition of a corporation does not as such allow for other considerations than maximizing profit. It could be argued that corporations only do what they have been founded for: increasing the wealth of their owners and/or shareholders. Corporations – at least the large majority of them – have not been founded to care for social values or the environment. Most people would agree that every corporation has a moral responsibility to care for its employees, the communities in which it works, and from which it draws its resources. Ultimately, however, the existing economic model does not make such a caring stewardship mandatory. In fact, it takes governments and regulating authorities to define rules and guidelines for businesses to protect the interests of employees, citizens, and the environment in general to a certain degree. To which degree is mostly defined by the societal values of the time, and not by scientific rigor, nor necessarily by humanistic values.

Societal values change constantly, influenced by new scientific findings, changing human values, and changing economic realities. In the twenty-first century, companies are more than ever expected to act as caring stewards, and not just rely on government rules and regulations. The issue of climate change is a typical example of a situation where government responses to the problem are considered insufficient compared to scientific findings.[3] As governmental regulation is bound to the nation-state and international regulation develops only slowly, this means political influence alone is too slow to tackle urgent issues of a global extent like climate change. At the same time, much of the problem of climate change is caused by business decisions. Businesses not only decide in which production facilities to invest, thereby defining the energy and carbon intensity of their production processes, but also decide on the products and services to be found in any given market. Currently, there is a growing split between the urgency of addressing climate change, the slowness of the political response, and hesitant business reactions.

Corporate responsibility extends far beyond the factory or office. Companies directly influence their customers' consumption patterns by offering (or not offering) certain services and products. In many multinational companies, marketing budgets are often the largest budget item after investment and labor costs. The marketing budget is used to convince customers to spend money on certain products, directly influencing purchasing decisions. An excellent example of this is the emergence of low-budget airlines. Having taken off in the last decade, tempting offers to fly at a low price are now often regarded as a standard consumer right. Little attention was paid to the environmental effects of this emerging industry when governments liberalized the aviation market, and allowed non-flag carriers to take their share of the market. The question is therefore: who is to blame for the

---

[3] A summary of current climate change science can be found in the *Summary for Policymakers*, published by the Intergovernmental Panel on Climate Change, www.ipcc.int (accessed June 2007).

negative environmental consequences of this industry? An answer to this question would be retrospective, and a blame-and-shame campaign would not solve the problem. Rather, both governments and companies should be proactive in addressing the environmental problems that they cause. Both need encouragement, and sometimes even public pressure, as the current system of rules and regulations alone is insufficient to change things for the better. NGOs are well equipped to push both governments and corporations to "do the right thing."

WWF has chosen to address both target groups, governments and the private sector, to drive change towards a more sustainable future. While many environmental NGOs lobby governments and attack corporations, WWF is one of the few NGOs working strategically and co-operatively with companies on a global level.

NGOs and companies – unlikely partners?

WWF engaging business in partnerships

WWF is one of the largest environmental groups with a global network of offices and projects. The organization is present in almost a hundred countries and its engagement spans a wide range of environmental issues. WWF's mission – to stop the degradation of the planet's natural environment and to build a future in which humans live in harmony with nature – can only be achieved if the current patterns of production and consumption of goods and services undergo significant change that will lead to more sustainable practices on a global level. As a global organization, WWF was and is seeking progressive relationships with the corporate world. This strategy can clearly only succeed if the organization manages to be a trusted partner of companies as well as society and its supporters. This ambiguity means that WWF has to constantly re-evaluate its partnerships with companies, its position in society, and has to take considerable care to maintain the trust of its almost five million supporters around the world. The organization constantly walks a thin line with its business partnerships. Any partnership that cannot be proven to have made a significant change might be called a "greenwash." In fact, the media scrutiny of WWF's business partnerships proves that the public is watching carefully. WWF has therefore introduced an internal system of checks and approvals with the aim of guaranteeing the highest conservation standards.

WWF recognized the need to change business practices early on, and has been the driving force behind the creation and establishment of initiatives to trigger change in corporate practices. Two examples of this work are the founding of the Forest Stewardship Council (FSC) and the Marine Stewardship Council (MSC), both aimed at making the respective sector more sustainable.[4] Both FSC and MSC established an industry standard for business practices and created a labeling process for products that meet sustainability criteria as defined by the group of NGOs supporting both processes.[5] They thus enable corporations to differentiate themselves from others by taking the environment into account and give consumers an indicator of how to "buy responsibly."

The early 1990s saw climate change emerging as a new threat to the global environment. WWF participated in the UN Conference on Sustainable Development in 1992 in Rio de Janeiro, which established the UN Framework Convention on Climate Change. Shortly afterwards, WWF started its first climate change activities in a few of its national offices, particularly in the Netherlands and in Germany. Both countries chose to engage companies in their climate change work early on. In the mid-1990s, WWF started business partnerships with a focus on climate change.

WWF Netherlands (WNF)[6] was the first office to focus on developing best practice case studies with regard to reducing CO_2 emissions, which would serve as an example for entire industry sectors. In cooperation with a construction company, the WWF developed and promoted low-energy houses, which were built in a number of locations in the Netherlands.

WWF Germany had already created a group of corporate supporters for its climate change work in 1995, when negotiations under the UN Framework Convention on Climate Change in Berlin led to

---

[4] See the Forest Stewardship Council's webpage at www.fsc.org and the Marine Stewardship Council's webpage at www.msc.org for more details. Both standards emerged from dialogue with corporations, and the MSC was officially initiated by Unilever and WWF in 1997 – an example of a successful green–business partnership.
[5] FSC is supported by WWF, Greenpeace, Friends of the Earth, and many others.
[6] Wereld Natuur Fonds, the Dutch name of WWF.

the Berlin Mandate to develop a globally binding agreement on the reduction of greenhouse gases. This process led to the Kyoto Protocol in 1997. WWF Germany's "Zirkel 2005" consisted of large German companies, such as Lufthansa, Die Bahn (the national German railway), Springer Verlag (one of the leading publishing companies), and many others. This group focused on supporting the voluntary CO_2 reduction target announced by the German government in 1995,[7] and generated funds to support WWF's climate change work in a number of countries in Europe.

Why do companies partner WWF?

There are many reasons why a company would engage in a partnership with WWF. While reputational benefits for the company may be one of the first reasons from an external perspective, this does not have to be the most important motivation. In fact, many companies do not regard this as the main reason and are often quite reluctant to proactively communicate their WWF partnership. Only later, once conservation results have been achieved through the partnership, do communication activities become more important.

The reasons for a company partnering with WWF are often more strategic in nature. Companies are looking for a partner without a hidden agenda, one that can bring political and scientific expertise on environmental issues to the table. WWF is well equipped for this, as the organization has decades of experience with political lobbying from the national to the global level. At the same time, WWF runs a multitude of field-based projects, gathering and contributing to environmental science in a number of disciplines. Companies are looking for advice on how they can improve their environmental performance in response to and in preparation for changes in the political environment, while ensuring that they are up to date with the latest scientific findings.

For many companies, partnering with WWF is an insurance policy that they "do the right thing" with regard to environmental issues. Being able to claim partnership with one of the leading environmental groups cushions companies against accusations from other pressure

---

[7] In 1995, the German government under Chancellor Helmut Kohl announced a 25 percent CO_2 reduction target compared to 1990 emissions by 2005.

groups. On the other hand, it also pushes companies into the spotlight, as public and media scrutiny can increase. They closely examine whether claims with regard to environmental performance and achievements are actually factual. Companies intending to partner with WWF soon come to the conclusion that they will have to make serious efforts to live up to the expectations of both the public and their partner.

Another important reason for companies seeking to partner with WWF is the need to prepare for upcoming environmental regulations. Rather than wait until regulators force companies to reduce their environmental impact, many want to gain a first-mover advantage by introducing strategies that anticipate later regulation. This is particularly true of the area of climate change policy, with companies preparing early for future carbon constraints.

Companies often hope to avoid government regulation by engaging in voluntary agreements with governments. However, past experiences have demonstrated that these agreements regularly fail to achieve the envisaged environmental targets. A recent example is the automotive industry's failure to meet vehicle CO_2 emissions as agreed with the European Commission. Despite annual monitoring reports, car manufacturers failed to make sufficient progress to reach the target of 120g CO_2 emission per vehicle kilometer, while the European Commission lacked the means to force the vehicle industry to do more. NGOs are in a much better position to put pressure on individual companies, as they do not have to take political issues into consideration. NGOs are inherently expected to create pressure, enabling them to deliver on voluntary partnership goals.

A further reason for companies to address environmental issues proactively is consumer expectations. Today's consumers expect their preferred company and brand to act responsibly and take care of the environment. With increasing consumer awareness about environmental issues, this is not only of concern to all corporate marketing departments, but also increasingly to top management. Past consumer boycotts and the growth of consumer-owned websites on and blogs about products and companies give more weight to consumer opinions and expectations. Companies often find that partnerships with NGOs are helpful in addressing consumer concerns. Partnerships could almost be described as an insurance policy for a company, protecting it against accusations of not fulfilling consumer expectations.

Companies are nevertheless not only concerned with how they are viewed from the outside. A growing number of companies engage with WWF because they want to show to their employees that they are a "good" company. Internal awareness building and training on environmental issues is an important element of many partnerships, and often even the starting-point of a longer engagement. Companies hope to trigger more innovative thinking in employees, which will eventually benefit the company's bottom line.

Finally, economic reasons will also play a role in a company's decision to partner an NGO. Generally, a decrease in pollution saves costs, as fewer resources are used in production. Saving energy, water, or other inputs will help cut production costs. This is often the main reason for bringing the financial department on board in any partnership.

In summary, any company partnering the WWF will benefit from an image transfer, i.e. the positive image WWF enjoys[8] will be associated with the partnering company to a certain degree. It is therefore crucial for WWF to select its partners carefully and rigorously.

Can NGOs help corporations become sustainable?

NGOs' relationship with corporations has changed significantly over the last two decades. Adversary relationships – which dominated the interaction in the 1980s – have evolved into processes through which NGOs guide companies to more sustainable behavior. While few would argue that the occupation of the Brent Spar oil platform by Greenpeace could be described as "guiding" industry, it nevertheless led Shell to choose a more environmentally friendly way of decommissioning the platform than just sinking it. Today, influence is often exerted in a more differentiated way. The increasing wave of corporate responsibility reporting has led to numerous stakeholder consultations that are organized either by individual companies or industry associations. Whether these consultations are just an unavoidable "must" for industry, or whether they are driven by a sincere desire to change corporate practices towards a more sustainable direction, cannot be answered easily. Nevertheless, today hardly

---

[8] See e.g. the *Edelman Trust Barometer 2006*. Source: http://edelman.com/image/insights/content/FullSupplement.pdf (accessed June 2007).

any large multinational company receives its "civil society" license to operate without consulting NGOs.

The balance between transparency and trust

In this respect, WWF also participates in stakeholder dialogues. However, over the years it became clear that corporate practices could not be sufficiently influenced through public stakeholder consultations. WWF realized that driving real change in companies required well-established relationships, mutual trust, and open and critical dialogues – often without the world listening in. The real barriers to change are frequently not discussed in public fora, as they often pertain to confidential corporate information. For competitive reasons, companies are concerned about revealing too much in public debates. WWF's experience shows that it often takes one to two years for a sufficient trust level to be built between partners and the real work towards a more sustainable company can start.

Consequently, transparency about partnerships must be managed carefully. While it is obvious that other stakeholders scrutinize a corporate-NGO relationship carefully, too much transparency can sometimes endanger progress in a partnership. However, results and achievement certainly have to be made public on a regular basis. Public scrutiny helps both sides stay true to their respective roles; therefore, WWF welcomes public interest in its corporate partnerships.

WWF's process of cooperation

Based on its many years of experience with partnership development, WWF has developed a method to define partnerships: the *4 Cs principle*. The four Cs stand for: *challenge, conservation, communication, cash*. Ideal partnerships are those that deliver equally on all four Cs. *Challenge* means that WWF asks the company to abandon its conventional way of thinking, and gives rise to new targets. *Conservation* implies that clear targets have to be set regarding improvement of a company's environmental performance beyond a business-as-usual approach. *Communication* means that WWF wants to communicate the partnership to an external audience. Finally, *cash* means that WWF asks its partner companies to support its work financially.

Obviously, the key question in any partnership is how the four Cs are balanced. WWF International has put a system in place that requires any partnership development to undertake clearly defined steps. A key step is a *due diligence study* that identifies the specific partnership's engagement topics, risks, and opportunities. In the next step, *setting conservation targets*, requires a benchmarking exercise in which the environmental performance of the specific company is compared to that of its peers. This also includes benchmarking the company against the best practices in the relevant industry sector. Based on this analysis, WWF identifies and sets ambitious conservation targets. The publication of these targets creates a *challenge for the whole industry* and defines a *benchmark for the environmental performance* of the relevant companies in the sector.

In any partnership, *both parties reserve the right to disagree*. In fact, WWF and its partners agree to disagree on certain issues. Nevertheless, it is important that the *disagreement does not affect the core issues of a partnership*.

Measuring the success of partnerships

A critical indicator to measure the impact of such partnerships is whether the agreed conservation targets trigger incremental change, or result in fundamental changes in any given company's business decisions. The answer to this question is not straightforward. Incremental steps are often the best way to create awareness at all levels of the corporate decision-making process, and are a necessary foundation to prepare for more fundamental change later on. While incremental changes can be criticized as not being bold enough to address pressing environmental challenges, they nevertheless give a company the opportunity to introduce change management and experiment with solutions. Receiving external recognition for those changes is a welcome side benefit, and increases the motivation of the people in the company. The true challenge lies in making companies change fundamentally and having them question the sustainability of their business model. This is a process that takes time and requires the support of changes within the societal and economic system in which a company operates, as well as of the individuals who drive the company. The level and speed of change in these two systems will certainly influence a company's willingness to ask itself fundamental questions about its sustainability performance.

Cooperation or confrontation?

The environmental NGO community utilizes many different tools to achieve its goals. From an external perspective, it may seem that NGOs can be easily divided into those using confrontational strategies versus those that engage in cooperation. In reality, the situation is far from being that black and white. For NGOs to cooperate effectively and have their voice heard, they need a convincing economic argument, which is often provided by the threat of confrontational tactics like a boycott, etc. While WWF leans more towards cooperation strategies, there are examples where WWF choses to engage in a confrontational strategy with companies – and thus use the *last resort* to motivate them to change. In fact, the strategies complement each other and cannot be regarded as mutually exclusive. Mike Brune, Executive Director of the Rainforest Action Network, remarked with regard to this point:

> The bottom line is that the environmental movement can't save the planet. Big business will either destroy it, or figure out how to be profitable without destroying it.[9]

Thus, the goal must be to help corporations to face this challenge. Some corporations are nevertheless harder to convince than others. This is reflected in their relationship with other NGOs, in which cooperative and confrontational strategies complement and mutually re-enforce each other.

Corporations are starting to change

The growth in the number of corporate (sustainability) reports and the increase in the number of stakeholder dialogues between companies and public pressure groups seem to reflect companies' growing willingness to work on their social and environmental impacts. How

---

[9] From an interview with Mike Brune, Executive Director of the Rainforest Action Network. Source: Doyle, Jim. 2004. "Eco-warriors / Co-founder of Rainforest Action Network and Activist Spouse Take Fight for Environment One Step at a Time," *San Francisco Chronicle* December 17, p. F1.

serious companies are with regard to driving change is very hard to judge from CSR reports, and would warrant significant research.

The question remains, of course, whether any given company is simply engaging in well-dressed public relations activities regarding sustainability or whether it also bases its strategic business decisions on sustainability indicators. WWF's experience shows that *few companies are willing to seek long-term partnerships with a global NGO*, as they are concerned that this group will continuously challenge its partner's business decisions. Many companies invite NGOs to participate in public stakeholder meetings, offering them the opportunity of a ten-minute statement, but do not take the next step of engaging in a recognized relationship that would allow strategic and (often) confidential discussions. However, there are companies that are prepared to make the necessary investment in a long-term relationship with an NGO. WWF has been particularly successful in establishing a range of partnerships with multinational companies. Let us take a closer look at three of those partnerships.

Case studies: WWF's international climate change partnerships

Partnerships with companies to achieve corporate greenhouse gas (GHG) reduction and to promote solutions to climate change are a key element of WWF's strategy to fight climate change. To support the Kyoto Protocol, WWF developed the Climate Savers program[10] in the late 1990s. This program requires companies to set absolute greenhouse gas reduction targets compared to a historical baseline. It mimics the main rule of the Kyoto Protocol, without giving companies the flexibility to buy CO_2 credits to reduce emissions. The program intends to motivate companies to analyze GHG reduction potentials in their own operations, and to develop and implement strategies that deliver reductions. The target is set after an in-depth analysis of the GHG emission situation, which is jointly undertaken by the company, WWF, and an independent third party. Progress towards agreed targets is monitored regularly so that if problems occur, both sides will be aware of this early on.

[10] A summary of all Climate Savers Partnerships can be found at www.panda.org/climatebusiness (accessed June 2007).

Case study 1: Lafarge – setting new standards in the cement industry worldwide

Lafarge, the global cement and construction material company, was one of the first international companies to set strategic conservation targets together with WWF. In 2001, WWF signed a Climate Savers agreement with the company, which committed Lafarge to reduce its energy- and process-related CO_2 emissions by 10 percent below the 1990 emissions in Annex 1 countries.[11] Lafarge was the first cement company to agree to an absolute reduction target. At that time, the general response from the cement industry to this challenge was: "An absolute CO_2 reduction target is not acceptable." By breaking ranks with the mainstream of the industry, Lafarge took the lead and set a new benchmark for the industry's carbon performance. While this involved a certain risk for Lafarge, it created a key benefit as well. By analyzing its CO_2 emission situation carefully and starting to implement a reduction strategy, the company gained valuable experience of how to react to government regulations limiting CO_2 emissions. The company clearly had a head start when the European Emission Trading Scheme came into force in 2005. Having a CO_2 monitoring system in place meant Lafarge had sound economic planning in place that took the price of CO_2 reduction into consideration.

WWF monitors Lafarge's CO_2 emissions annually, with the data verified by an independent third party. Over the years, WWF received proof that Lafarge was in fact reducing its emissions in industrialized countries as had been agreed. However, it also became clear that Lafarge's total global amount of CO_2 emissions was increasing over time because of strong business growth in emerging economies like China. Concerned with this global rise in emissions, WWF challenged Lafarge in 2005 to find strategies to turn around CO_2 emissions from its cement production in emerging economies. This is an ongoing project, but once the results have been published, WWF expects Lafarge to make a strong commitment to leading the sector in reducing CO_2 emissions in their operations in emerging economies.

WWF has also challenged Lafarge with respect to the company's other environmental impacts, such as toxic pollutants, its biodiversity impacts, regeneration of its quarries, and sustainable construction.

---

[11] Annex 1 as defined by the Kyoto Protocol, basically all industrialized countries.

The partnership undergoes constant evaluation by WWF. A team consisting of staff from both parties meets several times a year to monitor progress. The partnership agreements are signed for multi-year periods, requiring an evaluation of achievements and a re-commitment to continue at the end of each period. Public communication through a variety of media is important to inform both WWF and Lafarge stakeholders about conservation achievements, and to keep the relationship's transparency high. Media interest in the partnership has been shown to be rather high, with a number of critical analyses of the partnership appearing in newspapers and magazines. WWF welcomes this public scrutiny, as it increases the transparency of the relationship, and contributes to its credibility. The key parameter for WWF's decision to continue the partnership is whether Lafarge is willing to agree to conservation targets that will demonstrate its leadership of the cement industry worldwide in this regard.

Case study 2: Nike – an ambassador for sustainability

Companies with a globally recognized brand have an enormous influence on their customers. They can be influential ambassadors for sustainability and environmental issues if they have a credible and ambitious change agenda.

One of the global brands that has sustainability high on its agenda is Nike. WWF negotiated and signed a Climate Savers agreement with Nike in 2001 to achieve absolute reductions of CO_2 emissions. On analyzing the carbon footprint of the company, it became clear that a large share of Nike's footprint comes from the shipping of its products from the place of manufacture to its customers. In addition, the supply chain (i.e. the companies manufacturing Nike products) was the source of a large proportion of the company's CO_2 emissions as well. As these entities are not under the direct control of Nike, the initial CO_2 reduction target covered Nike-owned operations only. It was agreed that Nike would develop baselines and indicators to measure emissions by the supply chain.

The initial target year for Nike's CO_2 reduction commitment was 2005. Nike achieved that target, and is now working in cooperation with WWF to set targets for its supply chain. As the suppliers are outside the boundaries normally considered to be a company's responsibility, WWF and Nike are moving onto new ground with this endeavor. WWF believes that it is imperative to continually increase the benchmark for its corporate partnerships to make the mutual investments worthwhile.

In addition to the technical work around quantified reduction targets, WWF also cooperated with Nike to educate the public about climate change. Nike and WWF participated in a number of sports events across the USA, such as the "Race against Global Warming," a running competition held in several US cities. Other activities featured ad campaigns on public transport to raise awareness.

Case study 3: Allianz – driving change in the financial industry

Business decisions are mainly driven by economic considerations; therefore, entities that have a direct influence on costs and return of investments are an important lever to drive change in an industry. Integrated financial services companies that provide services in banking, asset management, and insurance can be drivers for sustainability, provided they integrate tools to analyze the impact of their business decisions according to relevant sustainability criteria.

The carbon footprint of any financial services company is dominated by indirect effects. Whereas emissions caused by offices, business travel, and a company car fleet will be significant, the business decisions leading to investments in a wide range of business sectors (e.g. coal power plants) are likely to cause a much larger amount of greenhouse gases to be emitted along the value chain. Those secondary emissions are outside the direct decision-making of any financial services provider, but can be influenced significantly. If investors were to face a financial penalty when investing in carbon-intensive projects, the economics of any given project would change in favor of carbon-cleaner projects. An example would be if loans and mortgages provided for real estate were to be tied to the energy efficiency of the buildings, making it financially more attractive to invest in those with low energy consumption. Integrating such indicators into daily decision-making remains a big challenge for the finance industry.

In 2005, WWF partnered with Allianz Group to explore the risks and opportunities of climate change and the financial services sector's related policies. The publication of a joint study[12] provided the basis for a multi-year engagement that defines tools to measure and reduce the carbon footprint of Allianz's business decisions with respect to insurance, lending, and investment. Developing carbon screens and introducing these tools into mainstream day-to-day decision-making will be a key element of this industry's climate change strategy. This is the main focus of the partnership between WWF and Allianz, which aims at transforming the financial industry.

Critical evaluation of case studies and partnerships

An environmental NGO's success depends on a small number of factors. Independence, transparency, and scientific rigor are probably the most important assets for any successful NGO. By developing partnerships with actors that follow a very different set of values, an NGO risks trading in its values for the sake of establishing a partnership. It is therefore crucial that partnerships are constantly re-evaluated and checked to see whether they have made sufficient progress towards achieving the set targets.

Partnerships to solve environmental problems are often difficult as there are a multitude of solutions to environmental problems. In the design of any partnership, WWF faces the difficulty of defining targets that the company itself would not achieve alone, but which are nevertheless realistic and can in fact be achieved. The challenge is to be cutting-edge in defining conservation success while staying achievable. Given the sheer size of environmental problems and the urgent need to act, particularly with regard to climate change, the design of any partnership is a long and sometimes tedious process, with WWF always being the party driving the relationship forward.

In order to guarantee constant evaluation of its partnerships, WWF normally does not sign agreements for longer than three to five years. After each period, the partnerships are only renewed if there have been sufficient conservation achievements, and the company agrees to take up new challenges. During such a partnership period, a team of staff from both sides works together to implement and monitor the agreement.

---

[12] See http://assets.panda.org/downloads/wwfallianzclimatechangereportjune 2005.pdf (accessed July 2007).

Often, changes in company practice and environmental successes are not communicated immediately. From an external perspective, it may sometimes seem as if there is hardly any progress, or as if change is too slow. However, for WWF and its partners, it is important to make conservation achievements public at a point when they are solid and will be sustained over time. This requires much trust from WWF's supporters, while the media is often on the lookout for a scandal about a "greenwashing" partnership. WWF nevertheless welcomes public scrutiny of its corporate partnerships; in fact, it helps to maintain the pressure for partnerships to succeed.

Conclusion

The environmental challenges of the early twenty-first century are so large that no actor can successfully address them alone. Partnerships and coalitions between NGOs and companies combine each party's power and influence to turn environmental solutions into mainstream business.

Environmental NGOs engaging in partnerships with the corporate world must be rigorous in defining minimum standards for success. It is crucial that NGOs are transparent about their relationships, even if that means admitting that a partnership has failed.

A key asset of any environmental NGO is its brand and reputation. NGOs must not risk their assets by engaging in partnerships that will not drive real change in the specific industry sector.

WWF is constantly re-evaluating its partnerships and has put a system of checks and balances in place that is designed to avoid partnerships that do not live up to the challenges set. A company engaging with an NGO must be prepared to ask itself uncomfortable questions. Any serious NGO will require the company to undertake a thorough analysis of its environmental footprint and develop strategies to reduce this footprint. Both partners need to understand that the required changes in business practices are not incremental but need to be fundamental. End-of-pipe solutions are not long-term solutions as they treat the symptoms of a problem and not the causes. By shaping consumption patterns and executing investment decisions, companies around the world are co-responsible for the current unsustainable lifestyle and can be an important leverage for change.

Challenging corporations around the world to achieve a truly sustainable global economy will remain a key element of WWF's conservation strategy in the foreseeable future. Where necessary, collaboration will continue to go hand in hand with confrontation. Global corporations are thus well advised to listen and cooperate more with environmental NGOs, which are important players for a company to obtain civil society's "license to operate."

PART 4

The individual as a change agent for a humane business society

19 | *Ethical codes at work*[1]

ADRIAN HENRIQUES

What is related to general human inclinations and needs has a *market price*...but that which constitutes the condition under which alone something can be an end in itself has not merely a relative worth, that is, a price, but an inner worth, that is, a *dignity*.

(Kant 1997)

Kant's remarks, and the idea of the intrinsic worth of people, are central to the meaning of humanism. It suggests that everyone already has an intrinsic worth and that, in this sense, there is nothing that people have to do to gain dignity. However, there may well be actions that they or others might take that could detract from human dignity. In a business context, as elsewhere, those behaviors that detract from human dignity involve a loss of integrity.

This chapter looks at how, at an individual level, the humanity of our work can be preserved in a business context. It first reviews the formal regulation of integrity in terms of "doing the right thing" and then discusses the other meaning of integrity: honesty, interpreted as personal transparency. The chapter concludes with an acknowledgement of the difficulty of maintaining integrity in the workplace.

Encoding integrity

One way of maintaining integrity might seem to work within an agreed code of conduct. Codes of conduct, developed by the companies themselves, are becoming increasingly popular, especially in large companies. These codes ostensibly seek to ensure that employees – and therefore the company as a whole – behave properly. There is, however, some confusion regarding what such codes can achieve. There are

---

[1] This chapter is based on work originally published in Adrian Henriques. 2007. *Corporate Truth: The Limits to Transparency*. London: Earthscan.

also several important areas in which individual ethical behavior can clash with the interests of the company.

There are two key factors giving rise to such conflict:

- whether a particular code applies to the company or to its individual employees;
- who developed the code: this may be the company, one or more individuals within it, or a third party.

In general, a code will lack legitimacy unless those who develop it are those to whom it applies. In order for a code to not only have legitimacy but also *humanity*, it is necessary for individuals (rather than the interests of organizations of one sort or another) to be dominant in the code development process as well.

Taking a broad view of the term "code of conduct," the entire system of law may be regarded as a "code of conduct" applying both to society as a whole and, in different ways, to the various components of society including individuals and companies. Under democratic conditions, the law as a code will be legitimate and may also be humanistic in the sense defined above. However, this legal corpus is not readily available to either companies or ordinary people trying to make daily decisions. Nevertheless, the law does cover many of the situations also covered by codes of conduct, and, as we shall see, codes of conduct usually refer directly to the law.

Outside the field of "hard law," there have been calls for codes to regulate the conduct of multinational companies since the 1960s, although again the practical usefulness of such codes (even when they do exist) can be extremely limited. These codes have varying status and are often described as "soft law." Examples include the OECD Guidelines™ (OECD 2000), which covers issues such as bribery and corruption and bears quite directly on the behavior of employees. However, the OECD Guidelines does not resemble a code that prescribes the behavior of employees directly. Codes such as the OECD Guidelines try to ensure that a company's management also ensures that its employees do not resort to or accept bribery.

Another example of a code that applies to companies, but has been developed through a process that includes them, is the Fair Labor Association (FLA), whose code of conduct prescribes acceptable behavior in relation to the following issues (FLA 2005):

- forced labor
- child labor
- harassment or abuse
- nondiscrimination
- health and safety
- freedom of association and collective bargaining
- wages and benefits
- hours of work
- overtime compensation.

It is noteworthy that this code explicitly covers the behavior of the *company* towards its employees. This is a crucial factor in enabling individuals to maintain their dignity.

Much more widespread and perhaps more relevant to individuals' decisions (rather than the conditions in which they work) are the various codes of conduct that professional institutions have developed over time. Almost all professional associations – from doctors and lawyers to engineers, estate agents, and even politicians – now have codes of ethics. These describe, with practical examples, what is considered ethical conduct, unethical conduct, and (usually) how to deal with doubtful cases. The principal reason why such codes are common is that the alternative to such self-regulation is regulation by the law and control of the profession being taken from its practitioners.

Professional codes occupy an intermediate position in several respects. "Professions" are not organizations; professionals are individuals who practice a certain profession. Their codes of conduct typically not only describe ethical rectitude, but also technical competence. This is appropriate, as technical incompetence is likely to damage clients and practitioners alike. But how far are such codes appropriate to the conduct of employees in general or to the behavior of professionals within employment but outside their professional practice?

Codes of conduct applicable to individuals but developed by third parties are quite common. The field of religion abounds in such codes and these may well have relevance to the individual's behavior at work. There are also codes of conduct developed by individuals for themselves. These may be described as "humanist" codes of conduct.

How, then, do the corporate codes of conduct found in many companies work in relation to individual integrity? The position is surprisingly unclear, both as to whether these codes applies to companies or to individuals and as to who has or should develop the code. At first glance, the content of many corporate codes seems directly concerned with the behavior of its individual employees. Yet, the avowed reason for the code is usually to ensure that the corporation as a whole behaves with integrity. The existence of such "higher"-level codes, or at least corporate integrity, is of course important. As Jamison and Steare have observed: "personal integrity cannot flourish outside a context of corporate integrity" (Jamison and Steare 2003). However, can a corporate code substitute a personal code or personal integrity?

The confusion over to whom the code belongs is evident in the following quotation from BP's website:

Our code of conduct is the cornerstone of our commitment to integrity. As Lord Browne, the group chief executive, affirms: "Our reputation, and therefore our future as a business, depends on each of us, everywhere, every day, taking personal responsibility for the conduct of BP's business." The new BP code of conduct is an essential tool to help our people meet this aspiration. The code summarizes our standards for the way we behave. All our employees must follow the code of conduct. It clearly defines what we expect of our business and our people, regardless of location and background. Ultimately it is about helping BP people to do the right thing. (BP 2006)

It is brave to dictate what is expected of people "regardless of location and background." This is not just because individual morality varies in important respects with culture, but also because an individual's "code of conduct" is rarely as explicitly articulated as required of a corporate code. An exception may be those individuals who acknowledge an articulated religious code. One of the strengths (as well, perhaps, as one of the weaknesses) of the way individuals express their moral views is that moral judgments are highly context-specific and appropriate to a given situation. The essence of personal moral judgment is not to be found as a compilation of predefined answers to questions such as "would you ever lie to your boss?"

This is perhaps one of the reasons why corporate codes of conduct are usually greeted with such cynicism by employees. No one really believes in them; the financial interests of the company are thought to come first. Most employees suspect that only the most egregious cases could ever really justify pushing sales targets, for example, into second place. There is thus a paradoxical effect whereby the active management of morality may be counter-productive. This may partly explain the findings of a survey of the impact of "ethics officers" some years ago. The survey found that while ethical commitment affected financial performance positively, a formal commitment to ethics management systems was not important (Verschoor 1999).

Therefore, while it may be useful for both companies and their employees to have moral codes, it is not possible for one to fill in for the other. However, it may be possible for personal and corporate codes to interact. When they do, both may benefit. One way to think about this is to consider how corporate codes come into existence. There are many possible ways: some may be developed by a group of interested mid-level or senior managers; alternatively, a third party may be consulted to develop something suitable; a further possibility is that the code is developed as a result of discovering what staff think is important. It is fairly predictable that codes that are developed without staff involvement are not recognized by the staff as their own. It follows that such codes are far less likely to be adhered to.

Conversely, those codes developed in conjunction with staff are more likely to be taken seriously. This has another implication: given that the turnover of staff is increasing in many organizations, it follows that codes of conduct need to be constantly redeveloped if they are to continue to remain relevant. The nature of a "corporate" code is thus a proper subject for stakeholder dialogue.

What do corporate codes of conduct cover? BP's code of conduct covers a number of different stakeholder concerns: health and safety, security, the environment, employees, business partners (including suppliers), governments, communities, company assets, and financial integrity. It makes clear, for example, that employees should not resort to or accept bribes and should use personal information about other employees only as intended.

Yet, from another perspective, BP's code deals only with issues regarding temptation and confusion, or more precisely, what should be avoided and what to do when it is not clear what to do. The list of matters to be avoided is of course closely connected to the list of stakeholder concerns set out above. What should be done about those matters that are not clear is much more limited, but essentially involves asking for advice. The code concludes with the following: "Ask if you are ever unsure what is the right thing to do. Keep asking until you get an answer with which you are comfortable" (BP 2006).

This is an optimistic note on which to end the code, as it presupposes that it is possible for a troubled employee to find someone who can supply a satisfactory answer. Nonetheless, even, or perhaps especially, in a large company, it cannot be presumed that an employee's values and interests will necessarily coincide with those of the company as a whole.

Thus, while corporate codes appear to be quite paternalistic in the way in which they try to regulate individual behavior, they also assume that individuals have a high level of personal moral development.

Personal revelation

At one level, honesty, or personal transparency, is a good example of an area that codes of conduct are intended to regulate. Transparency is, moreover, also important as it facilitates the ethical behavior that codes attempt to achieve through articulation, external imposition, and compliance. When transparency is a personal commitment, it can promote ethical behavior.

At a personal level, transparency is challenging. The transparency of our personal behavior opens us to the scrutiny and potential judgment of others. Too strong a fear of judgment may inhibit any transparency at all – but when it is less overwhelming, it can serve as an ethical catalyst. What, then, is the proper role and extent of personal transparency in a work context? Or put another way: how far should we expect ourselves, and others, to be open with one another when working for a company?

The culture of a company will have a profound effect on whether personal transparency can flourish. In a very supportive culture, in which staff in general and management in particular are genuinely concerned for employees, it will naturally be easier for individuals to be open with one another.

On the other hand, in a combative culture, transparency will be inhibited. For example, in one company, the sales force competed fiercely to demonstrate commitment. The salesmen's hour of arrival in the morning was viewed as a key sign of commitment, the evidence for which was the presence of their car in the car park. The sales manager came in extremely early in the morning, therefore some of the sales staff took to leaving their cars in the car park overnight and traveling by other means to demonstrate commitment (without actually making it). The sales manager subsequently became suspicious and started checking the temperature of the car bonnets on his way into the car park. This is obviously a pathological situation in which fear inhibits transparency. The consequences of this behavior extend well beyond the apparently trivial area described here. Knowing this situation would create a lack of trust in any sales figures produced by this sales team. The adverse business consequences of a lack of transparency are never far away.

The appropriate level of individual transparency varies according to the context. There are three main contexts, involving:

- employee–employee relationships;
- employee–third party relationships;
- employee–company relationships.

It may seem obvious that what two people say to each other is nobody else's business: privacy is a basic right and should be respected. The level of transparency within that relationship is a matter for the individuals concerned. However, if another party is adversely affected, the situation becomes more complex, and those affected may claim that they are entitled to know what has been said and may even wish to control the level of transparency.

This is certainly the case with regard to companies. The BP code states that:

Consistent with its respect for employee privacy, BP does not normally take an interest in personal conduct outside of work – unless such conduct impairs the employee's work performance or affects the reputation or legitimate business interests of BP. (BP 2006: 24)

BP appears to believe that it has a right to know – and perhaps interfere in – its employees' private lives if it is in its interest to do so. This is at best insidious, and, while it may accurately capture BP practice, it is difficult to conceive how such a statement could be part of any *ethical* code.

While it is not acceptable for a third party to demand transparency of private relationships, some companies seek to foster communications between staff in the hope that benefits may emerge. Many companies seek to harness the energy of personal relationships (at least within management) in order to tap into the intellectual capital of their staff; they encourage an informal "water-cooler culture" in which ideas are freely exchanged and shared. The benefits of this approach are considered to greatly outweigh any commercially "unproductive" exchange of gossip that may occur.

What a member of staff may say to third parties pertains to very different issues. In general, companies do not actively encourage transparency in such cases. This may sometimes be justified on the grounds of commercial confidentiality, but is usually rather thinly veiled fears for a loss of company reputation. The BP code of conduct says, in relation to external speaking engagements:

> Even where the venue is informal, such as a trade association event, if possible, seek review of your presentation by your line manager **and in all cases take care not to cause any harm to the reputation of the BP group.** (BP 2006: 52, emphasis added)

There are many subtleties here: it would seem entirely reasonable for a member of staff to be completely open about issues at work to their families, if they so wish. This would apply regardless of the nature of the issue. It would not, for example, be claimed that an employee who divulged fraud to her husband had done wrong. By extension, it would be hard to claim that a similar disclosure to a friend would be wrong.

If, however, the individual to whom an employee speaks is not a family member or friend, but a reporter, then the policy of most companies is even stricter. A fairly common maxim is to advise staff to disclose nothing to reporters that they would not like to see publicized in the media.

Finally, what sort of transparency should one expect between individuals and companies? Companies need to know information about their employees to a certain degree, but they must respect an individual's privacy. Furthermore, it should be borne in mind that if the company knows something about an individual, in almost every case so will another individual within the company (such as a personnel officer).

Consequently, there is a need to underline the privacy of the individual–company relationship and protect that information from inappropriate disclosure. For BP, this means:

> Those with access to personal employee data must only use it for the purpose for which it was collected and adhere to the highest standards of confidentiality in using it. Never provide personal employee data to anyone inside or outside of BP without proper authorization. Personal data must

not be held longer than necessary to meet the legal or business reason for which authorization was given. (BP 2006: 24)

Keeping a sense of proportion

Transparency is not an unconditional good. Ibsen's play *The Wild Duck* reminds us that transparency can be a destructive, if not simply embarrassing, force when pursued without any thought of the consequences. Most of the time, however, the problem is not too much transparency, but too little. At any rate, the exercise of transparency requires judgment.

Besides meaning honesty, integrity also means "whole" and has the same root as the word "integer." This suggests that it is not possible to separate one aspect of integrity from another. If you expect integrity in maintaining the company's records, then you must expect it when an employee speaks to the outside world – whether or not that is in the company's direct interests. Some companies recognize this, in that they have a "whistleblower" policy, whereby staff who report unethical behavior are protected, particularly while their claim is investigated. However, such policies rarely extend to support for staff who seek the help of the press in combating unethical behavior.

One important reason for companies to have codes of behavior and ethics is that they cannot rely on all their employees to have a well-developed moral sense. As we have seen, codes are, however, both general in application and inflexible in nature. Conversely, the nature of the moral sense that individuals develop is both flexible and highly context-specific. "Whistleblowing" policies are a partial response to this situation: when a moral breach is sufficiently serious, they permit an individual's moral sense to be exercised appropriately.

Corporate ethical codes are a management response to a problem. The essence of most management solutions is a system that can "run itself." While this may seem rational, this approach is simply not possible – or advisable – for moral codes. In practice, codes require interpretation, and the nature of and approach to interpretation are crucial. Interpretation is important in two senses:

- it preserves the moral capacity of those who undertake the interpretation, acknowledging their contribution to the resolution of the issue in question;

- it allows the specific circumstances of the issue to be more fully taken into account in a way in which the rigid or unthinking application of a rule would not do.

Perhaps all of us at times feel that we know what we want to do at work and that we know what is expected of us. We may be clear about the goals of the organization for which we work and even enjoy achieving them, and do not doubt that we can call on the support of sympathetic ears when the path is not so clear. These times are the sunlit uplands of working life.

For the rest of the time we need integrity and/or honesty. This is hard work. It would be much easier simply to follow (someone else's) rules without question. To acknowledge the inherently "unfinished" nature of ethical codes may not seem rational in the usual sense of that word. However, it is true to the original meaning of the term, which has the same root as the word "proportion." If we are to keep our sense of proportion, we can go a long way to preserving the dignity of people in the workplace. As William Blake put it:

He who would do good to another must do it in Minute Particulars: General Good is the plea of the scoundrel, hypocrite and flatterer, For Art and Science cannot exist but in minutely organized Particulars And not in generalizing Demonstrations of the Rational Power. (Blake 1972: 687)

References

Blake, William. 1972. *Complete Writings*. Oxford: Oxford Paperbacks.
BP. 2006. *Code of Conduct*. Available at www.bp.com/ sectiongenericarticle. do?categoryId=9003494&contentId=7006600 (accessed May 2006).
Fair Labor Association (FLA). 2006. *Workplace Code of Conduct*. Available at www.fairlabor.org/all/code/index.html (accessed May 2006).
Jamison, Christopher and Steare, Roger. 2003. *Integrity in Practice*. Crawley: The Soul Gym.
Kant, Immanuel. 1997. *The Groundwork of the Metaphysics of Morals* (original edition 1785). Cambridge: Cambridge University Press.
OECD. 2000. *The OECD Guidelines for Multinational Enterprises*. Paris: Organisation for Economic Cooperation and Development.
Verschoor, Curtis 1999. "Corporate Performance is Closely Linked to a Strong Ethical Commitment," *Business and Society Review* 104(4): 407–15.

20 | The daunting challenges of globalization and the power of individuals in cross-stakeholder networks for a humanistic face of globalization

JEAN-PIERRE LEHMANN

The new world order and disorder

Towards the end the first decade of the twenty-first century, it is quite clear that things have not turned out quite as had been expected in those early euphoric years that followed the collapse of the Berlin Wall and what the American scholar Francis Fukuyama termed "the end of history."[1] Fukuyama did not, of course, mean that the world was coming to an end, but rather that the ideological confrontation between collectivism and individualism – translated in economic terms into the battle between the central command and control economy and the liberal market economy – had been irrevocably won by the individualist-oriented market economy, with all the social and political freedoms that it represents. For over two centuries the ideological battle had raged, resulting in millions of publications and, in real-life terms, the establishment of collectivist regimes under both fascist and communist rule throughout most of the twentieth century and all the harm they inflicted. With the deaths in the mid-70s of the Iberian fascist dictators, Franco of Spain and Salazar of Portugal, fascism as a system of state in Europe was finished. The fall of the Berlin Wall on 9 November 1989 presaged the collapse of communism. What the scholar Fukuyama called the end of history, the American president, George H Bush, termed "the new world order."

---

[1] Fukuyama, Francis. 1989. "The End of History?" *The National Interest* 16: 3–18, subsequently published as Fukuyama 1992.

At the time President Bush (*père*) proclaimed the new world order, Thierry de Montbrial, director of the French Institute for International Relations (IFRI), commented: "it is not a new world order, but a chaotic transition to uncertainty."[2] Indeed, a recapitulation of the events, forces, and developments that have occurred in the course of the almost two decades since the fall of the Berlin Wall reveals how chaotic these times have been, how the most unexpected has actually occurred, and how uncertain prospects remain. To cite only one of a myriad examples: in June 1989 Beijing witnessed the Tienanmen massacre; in August 2008 held the Olympic Games, with Tienanmen Square as the site for beach volley. China has emerged as the world's banker and especially the chief lender to the US. Money talks in any language, at any time. But who would be so unwise as to disclaim the great uncertainty that continues to hover over China's future trajectory? The chaotic transition to uncertainty is still with us.

While undoubtedly chaotic, on balance in 2007 the planet is a better place than it was in 1987. Of that there can be little doubt. To cite only two of, again, a possible myriad examples: in 1990 the proportion of the world's population living under $1 a day was 32 percent, it has now fallen to less than 20 percent. On July 14, 2007, at the military parade in Paris to mark the French national "Bastille" day, army contingents from all twenty-seven EU countries, including Poland, Hungary, Estonia, etc., marched down the Champs-Elysées, whereas these same armies in 1987 were poised to kill each other. The world is a more prosperous and peaceful place than it was, and, if things are done right, it should be even more prosperous and peaceful in 2027.

That perspective, however, cannot be taken for granted. Indeed, it would be extremely dangerous to do so. As Jean-François Rischard has so compellingly and trenchantly argued in his excellent book *High Noon* (Rischard 2002), the planet faces a series of highly daunting challenges and it is running out of time. The chaotic transition to uncertainty contains many powder kegs with multiple fuses, many of which are short and rapidly getting shorter.

The cause of all this ambient turbulence, the high-speed bulldozer driving across the planet, is the process and phenomenon of

---

[2] To my knowledge Thierry de Montbrial never actually wrote that phrase. It came out at a meeting convened at his institute in Paris in 1991 and I made careful note of it: clearly an excellent example of *le mot juste*.

globalization. Globalization, as many authors have reminded us, is not a twenty-first-century "invention." What is occurring at present is a twenty-first-century variation on a theme that stretches back almost to the origins of mankind. In one of the latest publications on the subject, the author Nayan Chanda, editor and director of Yale Global Online, argues that there is a recurring pattern of four primary actors in the globalization script: "The same human desire for a better life that prompted traders to brave the waves, the same political ambition of warriors to occupy foreign lands, the same urge for preachers to set out to convert others to their ideas of the good, and the same drive of adventurers to seek new lands and opportunities are still working to shrink the world" (Chanda 2007: xv).

These four actors, traders, warriors, preachers, and adventurers, are conspicuous by their presence in both the great expansion of the Arab-Islamic empires of the seventh to the fourteenth century, as they were in the European-Christian empires of the fifteenth to twentieth century. Indeed it was in the course of the latter half-millennium that the ascendancy of the West, beginning with the emergence of the Portuguese seaborne empire in the Age of Discovery, became inexorable and overwhelming. Western traders, warriors, preachers – whether religious or secular – and adventurers called the global shots. The power of Europe and its colonial settlement offshoots, mainly the US, came to be greatly re-enforced in the course of what historian Robert R. Palmer referred to as the dual political and industrial revolutions of the late eighteenth and early nineteenth century (Palmer 1969). The successive waves of globalization in these five centuries were dominated by the West and it was propelled to full ascendancy – especially the British empire, over which the sun never set – with both the establishment of democratic-capitalist institutions and the advantages gained in transport and communication technologies by the inventions and engineering applications of the Industrial Revolution.

Twenty-first-century globalization is also being driven by dual revolutions, both of which are extremely profound, and in combination are bringing about the biggest transformation the planet has seen since Ferdinand Magellan first circumnavigated the globe in 1519. Conveniently, the landmark date for both revolutions can be traced to the same year: in 1989 the Berlin Wall fell, precipitating the global market revolution, while in the same year the world wide web (www) was launched, precipitating the information and communication technology (ICT) revolution. In the course of the first heady five years or so of the global market revolution, country after country after country abandoned their hitherto command and control import substitution protectionist industrialization policies in favor of market liberalization and a more open economic agenda.[3] With the high growth that these reforms entailed in many countries and the opportunities for trade, investment, outsourcing, etc., that arose, the term "emerging markets" entered the global business lexicon.

More astute observers, however, noted that in some cases, and notably those of the two Asian giants, India and China, which together account for 40 percent of world population, it was not so much a case of "emergence" as a case of "re-emergence." The inexorable rise of the West since the early sixteenth century notwithstanding, still at the dawn of the nineteenth century India and China together accounted for about 50 percent of global GDP and both economies dominated world manufacturing. By the mid-twentieth century, as India gained independence (1947) after 190 years of the British raj and as China achieved its liberation (1949) after 150 years of civil and foreign wars and untold humiliations, the combined share of global GDP of these two "giants" accounted for less than 8 percent (Maddison 2005). The reforms carried out in both countries (China more so) have unleashed highly powerful forces for economic growth. Though we remain in uncharted and choppy waters, one can reasonably assume that the growth of these two economies will be sustained in the next several decades.

The global market revolution has led and will increasingly lead not only to high growth and rising competitiveness among both emerging and re-emerging economies, but also to a considerable paradigm shift in global business (see Lehmann 2006). Intriguingly, whereas sub-Saharan Africa became the proxy battleground between the two superpowers during the Cold War, the same continent is increasingly being seen as the battlefield where the rivalry between Chinese and Western global economic reach may be determined.[4]

---

[3] For a detailed description of how this process evolved across the world, see Yergin and Stanislaw (1998).

[4] There have been numerous publications and studies on this subject; see for example: De Lorenzo (2007), two anonymous 2006 articles in the *Economist* and *Financial Times*, and the special issue of *Inside AISA* 2006.

Thus, while the global market revolution has given rise to unprecedented and indeed until recently unimaginable opportunities, it has also, inevitably, led to a considerable amount of turbulence. Turbulence per se can be good. The issue is how this turbulence is managed. In the work cited earlier, Jean-François Rischard makes the point that while markets and technology have experienced exponential change, institutions and mindsets have, at best, achieved linear change. There is between the two what he calls a yawning governance gap. The inability of the members of the WTO, and especially the new *quattuor* of leading trade policy powers, the US, EU, Brazil, and India, to reach a satisfactory conclusion to the Doha Development Round bears evidence to the reality of this chasm.[5]

Thus, while the global market revolution has exerted powerful centripetal forces, it has also resulted in equally powerful centrifugal forces. To cite perhaps the most glaring and most daunting current example, while the Chinese and American economies have never been so intertwined, also never has there been so much potential acrimony in the relationship, at least since 1949. A trade war between China and the US could be the devastating blow that could knock twenty-first-century globalization off track, comparable to the earlier conflict that arose between the established power of Britain and the rising power of Germany, culminating in the First World War, which reversed the process of globalization that had developed in the late nineteenth and early twentieth century, resulting in a global fracture that lasted through most of the twentieth century.

The global market revolution has been both enhanced and rendered more turbulent by the ICT revolution. It has certainly opened vistas in transacting business that are mind-boggling, and this may be only a beginning. For the financial trader, ICT is simply a tool that can result in constant innovations and new products and in moving vast amounts of capital. As with any technology, ICT is morally neutral; however, also as with any technology it can be used to different moral ends. ICT can bring the international community closer together, we can learn much more about any society or culture (e.g. through Wikipedia) so phenomenally more quickly than in the past, but it can also serve as a means of spreading suspicion and hate. Winston Churchill's famous

---

[5] Lehmann, Jean-Pierre. 2007. "Death of the Doha Dialogue of the Deaf," *The Evian Group Communiqué*, www.eviangroup.org/p/1566.pdf.

aphorism that "a lie gets halfway around the world before the truth has a chance to get its pants on," has taken on exponentially greater meaning since the arrival of the internet. As is well known, the forces that would seek to destroy globalization are among the most adept in using the technological tools of globalization.

While globalization has resulted in forces of animosity and disintegration between communities and cultures at the global level, it is also witnessing considerable rising forces of suspicion and animosity within national or regional boundaries. No doubt the most acute example in this decade has been the fissures that have occurred in the Islamic world. Millions of Muslims are hit, as they see it, by a double globalization whammy. On the one hand, with only a few exceptions (such as Malaysia and Turkey) most Muslim economies have not been particularly successful either among the "emerging" or the "re-emerging" economies. In the winners versus losers twenty-first-century globalization league, most Islamic societies have so far been more in the ranks of the losers, or at least have perceived themselves as such. This global phenomenon has been compounded by the intense divisions within many Islamic societies, not just, or indeed particularly, between the rich and the poor – though that chasm is deep in many Islamic societies – but also between those who are seen as globalizers – supping, so to speak, or, indeed, even worse, wining with the infidels – and the purists (fundamentalists) who see absolute cultural resistance as the only means to safeguard their identity.

Contrary to what is often asserted and to the numerous publications purporting to show the Islamic roots of terrorism, this phenomenon of militant – indeed suicidal – rejection of the dominating force of globalization is quite universal. There are many examples of such movements throughout history, notably in China, Japan, and Korea in the face of rising Western dominance in the nineteenth and twentieth centuries; the Chinese Boxer Rebellion of 1900 is a quite vivid illustration (see Cohen 1997), as the militant peasant nationalist Chinese, imbued with a sense of invulnerability, rose up with fanatical zeal to combat the "Western" forces of trade, technology, and religion (Christianity). Though the Chinese today are seen mainly as the emerging winners of globalization, there were between the Boxers in 1900 and the global Chinese capitalists of 2000 a number of intermediary phases, including not all that long ago (1966–76) the fanaticism and xenophobia of the Cultural Revolution.

However, before writing the "end of Chinese history" – i.e. its alleged irreversible conversion to economic liberalism – the point needs to be stressed that globalization in China, as elsewhere, has witnessed phenomenally rising inequality. It is very probable, as has been argued, that it is not globalization that causes inequality, but technological change, which displaces skills and hence the value of labor, both by rising unemployment and depression of wages in areas requiring no more than basic skills. What is important here, however, is not so much reality, but the perception of reality. Thus while, as noted earlier, the planet is a more prosperous place, and overall poverty has indeed been greatly reduced, nevertheless it is also a much more unequal place. To be more precise: while the inequality between some of the hitherto poor developing countries and the rich indus-trialized countries on a GDP *per capita* basis has decreased, the often astronomically rising inequality is *within* economies. This applies as much to developing economies as it does to mature economies. And what makes it all the more unbearable is that "thanks" to the ICT revolution, the inequality has become far more visible. Whatever the reality may be, the culprit for all this is widely seen as globalization. And globalization in turn, whether in China, India, South Africa, Brazil, France, or the United States, is widely seen as the profitable monopoly of a small global elite.

This perception is in fact quite accurate on two counts. First, it is the case that in the early twenty-first century, some 20 percent of the world's population consumes 85 percent of the world's goods and services. Second, it is also the case that globalization has spawned a global elite who tend to be totally on the same page whether in Shanghai, Mumbai, Cape Town, São Paulo, Paris, or Chicago, but are seen as distant and aloof by their own more local compatriots. Goldman Sachs may be the epitome of what authors John Micklethwait and Adrian Woolridge in their excellent book *A Future Perfect: The Challenge and Hidden Promise of Globalization* have referred to as the emerging "cosmocracy": Goldman Sachs Man and Goldman Sachs Woman are a universal species who speak the same language, dine in the same restaurants, drink the same wines, read the same papers, and are totally on the same cultural page, irrespective of their ethnic origins (Micklethwait and Woolridge 2000). Even among the well-to-do, therefore, there is a growing cleavage between those who see the great potential gains of globalization (the Goldman Sachs tribe) and those who see their privileges and positions eroding or who live in despair of ever improving their lot.

The *big* risk that globalization faces on the basis of current trends is a vast and intense series of backlashes that will occur at national level, but that governments may deem politically expedient to transfer as policy at the global level. On the basis of current trends, this seems inexorably the direction the world is going in. It is always critically important, however, to remember that trends can – and arguably in light of the world we are living in now, must – be reversed.

How can we do that?

The power of humanist social leadership

In the course of the successive waves of globalization – the main propelling forces of which, as we have seen, are economic, techno-logical, military, and ideological (or religious) power – there have also been movements that, whatever their origins may have been, have resulted in a global impact. This has of course especially been true of the great religions. Little could the inhabitants of Nazareth in the early first century CE have imagined that their local boy-wonder Jesus would become such a global icon and influence. More recent times have seen the emergence of very powerful social move-ments aimed at righting wrongs and improving the moral fabric of society.

A striking example from the last century is the emergence of the "suffragette" movement in the years before the First World War in the UK, which laid the political and ideological foundations for the eventual worldwide force of feminism. The goal of the suffragettes was to obtain the vote for women. Women's enfranchisement, with the exception of some remaining male chauvinist redoubts, has become pretty universally accepted. Indeed in more and more coun-tries, including Islamic states, women not only vote, but also are political leaders. Yet, it is extraordinary today, in the early twenty-first century, to reflect on how "radical" the cause appeared, and the trials and tribulations that the suffragettes (and other feminist leaders) had to undergo. They were imprisoned, went on hunger strike, resulting in their being force-fed, and indeed one of the early activists, Emily Davison, who had earned the highest academic results from

Oxford,[6] killed herself in 1913 by throwing herself under George V's horse at the Epsom Derby. In the opposition to women being granted the vote and gaining their civic rights, there were, of course, what today would be described as die-hard male chauvinists. For many people, however, "passive opposition" simply came from the fact that it seemed "natural" that men should vote and women should not. That was the situation that had prevailed; change tends always to be viewed with suspicion.

Living in the US as a student in the early 1960s, I was actively engaged in the civil rights movement and the freedom marches, and highly privileged to have been at the Lincoln Memorial on the occasion when Martin Luther King delivered his famous "I have a dream" speech. Combating the desire of African Americans to gain emancipation and dignity, there were of course the out-and-out racists like the then-infamous governor of Alabama, George Wallace. But arguably the biggest obstacle, as with the suffragettes, was the general apathy and inertia of the broader public. These people were not necessarily racists, at least not consciously so, but the fact that Negroes (as Blacks were referred to at the time) should ride in the back of the bus, eat at different restaurants, not sit on public benches reserved for whites, let alone use "whites-only" toilets, all seemed to be in the natural order of things and should not be changed. The Negroes who sought to change things, like Martin Luther King, were referred to in "polite society" as "uppity."

Those who sought to abolish slavery in the nineteenth century encountered very much the same syndrome. In his remarkable book *Bury the Chains*, Adam Hochschild recounts how in the early nineteenth century roughly 20 percent of humanity was held in one way or another in bondage. The abolitionists came across the familiar barrier to change. Obviously, those who profited from slavery and the slave trade – which included the Church of England, which possessed profitable plantations in the Caribbean worked by slaves – would oppose the abolitionists. But for many other persons, the abolitionists appeared bizarre, Utopians, dreamers, who had difficulty coming to terms with reality. Having a slave seemed a very natural thing. Slavery had always existed; which in fact it had (Hochschild 2005).

[6] Women were not at that time admitted to degrees at Oxford University but were allowed to take exams.

The biggest challenge for the abolitionists, the suffragettes and feminists, and the civil rights activists was to raise awareness, to get society to understand that what was being taken as natural, was in fact not natural; indeed it was evil.

Although women today are far from having gained full emancipation, not only in conservative Islamic societies, but also, albeit to very different degrees, in the "advanced" West; although racism remains, alas, a blight in much of the world; and although slavery has not been totally abolished, nevertheless it can be said that at least so far as "awareness" is concerned, it is generally recognized in civilized societies that women should be seen as equals, racism is wrong, and slavery abominable. Although this may sound obvious in the early twenty-first century, under no circumstances should it undermine the Herculean efforts that were required on the part of those who fought so valiantly for these major human causes.

These three humanist social movements had three key features in common, that tend to prevail in most of history's great social movements for change and betterment: (1) they all had very strong, dedicated, persistent leadership, usually beginning with one dominant figure – Emmeline Pankhurst for the suffragettes, Martin Luther King for the civil rights movement, and William Wilberforce[7] for the abolitionists – who in turn spawned other leaders; (2) they had to combat not only fierce opposition, but also, at times even more so, indifference, apathy, and inertia; (3) no doubt in good part for that reason, all three movements took a generation or more to achieve their short-term objectives, while atavistic legacies lingered on. In the case of slavery, while Britain banned the trade and abolished slavery in the United Kingdom in 1807, it persisted in the US into the 1860s and in Brazil into the 1880s. Martin Luther King's "dream" remained quite a nightmare during a good number of years after his assassination (1968), and perhaps only towards the end of the last century did blacks in the US really begin to gain solid political and social legitimacy. In the West, women mainly got the vote in the years after the Second World War, a process which spread out to most of the world where elections are held, though with strong resistance still in a

---

[7] The two hundredth anniversary of the abolition of slavery in Britain has seen the publication of several books on the subject, including one by the former Tory leader, William Hague, 2007.

number of Middle Eastern and Central Asian countries, in which, however, women's movements are active as catalysts of change and led by courageous personalities.[8]

Perhaps the most striking contemporary example of a strong social movement is that of environmentalism. The World Wildlife Fund for Nature (WWF) was founded in Morges, Switzerland, in 1961, Friends of the Earth in San Francisco, California, in 1969, and Greenpeace in Vancouver, British Columbia, in 1971. As with most other social movements, the environmentalists also were initially marginalized and seen as dreamers. The one-generation rule of thumb also seems to apply. Forty to thirty years since these movements arose, today we have, for example, Al Gore's adoption of the cause of environmentalism, the setting of environmentalism as a key priority in the G8 agenda and the most important minister, immediately after the prime minister, in the cabinet of the new French President Nicholas Sarkozy responsible for the environment; clearly environmentalism has entered the mainstream. As with the other movements, the agenda is by no means finished; there will remain very daunting challenges ahead and much opposition from vested interests and social inertia, but as with the other social movements cited above, the persistence of the early leaders is beginning to pay off. Again, as with the other movements, one of the earliest key challenges for the environmentalists was to raise the level of awareness. Even if imperfectly, that has now been done.

In the pantheon of persons in the twentieth century who raised consciousness and left a huge mark, among by far the greatest are Mahatma Gandhi and Nelson Mandela. Although Gandhi's main struggle was national, aimed at achieving India's independence from Britain, his impact was and remains universal. Two strands of Gandhi's philosophy stand out: his advocacy of non-violence, which in turn had considerable influence on both Martin Luther King and Nelson Mandela, and his social inclusiveness, seeking both to destroy barriers between castes and include the outcastes, and to join together in one common political and social space Hindus and Muslims.

---

[8] See Smith (2006), Khalaf (2007), and also see as an eminent example of a women's social movement for change, the Arab International Women's Forum, www.aiwfonline.co.uk/.

Nelson Mandela's attributes as one of the twentieth century's greatest leaders lies not only in his courageous and persistent struggle for the abolition of apartheid, but perhaps even more so in bringing about reconciliation after apartheid had been ended.

The point to make is this: during a good deal of the history of globalization, slavery was a feature and indeed a force. Cotton and coffee, to name only two of the earliest most globalized products, were intimately connected with the slave trade and the use of slave labor. As business was roaring along, driven by the emerging full throttle of the Industrial Revolution and the exponentially increasing trans-Atlantic trade, for contemporaries it was very difficult to imagine a world without slavery, or indeed how business would function without slavery. This "consensus" as noted was shared not just by traders and financiers, but also by the established Christian Churches of the Western world. Opposing slavery required all the attributes we have mentioned, along with the need to educate the public and to make policy-makers aware that globalization based on slavery would become unsustainable. It was unsustainable not so much from an economic viewpoint, arguably more from a social and political one, as slaves began to revolt, as they did for example in the bloody uprisings in Haiti under Toussaint Louverture in 1803 (Dubois 2005), but especially from a moral viewpoint. It was gradually recognized that slavery was wrong, full stop. An immoral state will ultimately sow the seeds of its own destruction.

Thus as there may be compelling economic reasons to engage in certain practices because of their business returns, there may be strong moral reasons to resist and indeed oppose these forces. This is not opposing globalization or indeed business, but realizing that globalization and global business will not be sustainable if these practices persist. Just as slavery "made sense" from a business perspective in the nineteenth century, bribery "made sense" in the twentieth century and continues to do so in the twenty-first. This no doubt is the reason that the government of Tony Blair sanctioned, even if indirectly, the huge bribery engaged in by British Aerospace (BAe) in order to secure contracts in Saudi Arabia, which, the government insisted, was good for British business and for British jobs (Anonymous 2007). Corruption as a means of conducting business is, in the long run, unsustainable. At present this seems not only not evident to governments that appear at the bottom of the Transparency International index,[9] but indeed to the UK government, which should know better. But it can be confidently predicted that if global business retains this cancer of corruption, global business will perish.

One globe, two planets

In 1845, three years before the publication of *The Communist Manifesto* by Karl Marx and Friedrich Engels, the British Tory politician Benjamin Disraeli published a novel entitled *Sybil*. In this book, Disraeli wrote of: "Two nations between whom there is no intercourse and no sympathy; who are as ignorant of each other's habits, thoughts, and feelings, as if they were dwellers in different zones, or inhabitants of different planets. The rich and the poor" (for a reprint, see Disraeli 1998). This was in reference to the UK at the time, as it was clear to Disraeli that the chasm had to be narrowed, lest Britain experience the same bloody revolutions that were spreading across the Continent.

There is today much talk and much wringing of hands on how the world continues to experience dire poverty, especially among the 2.4 billion people, 40 percent of humanity, who live on less than $2 a day. Monetizing poverty, however, misses the point. It is not just the division of income that divides the world, but access to resources and to public goods. If twentieth-century history could in large part be written in terms of oil (Yergin 1991), the twenty-first century may be written about in terms of water (Nilekani 2007). It is the greatest divide between the two planets that inhabit the same globe.

Imagine an eight-year-old girl we will call Karen who lives in Beverly Hills, California, and, across the globe, a fraction of a nano internet second away, another eight-year-old girl we will call Gudiya, who lives in a village in the Indian province of Bihar. Karen and Gudiya are not just separated by the multiple-figure difference in income of their respective parents, the two-car garage of the former's house and the bullock as main means of transport for the latter's family, the ample availability of electricity for Karen, allowing simultaneous multiple use of TVs, computers, electronic pianos, kitchen appliances, lawn

---

[9] In the 2006 Transparency International Corruption Perception Index, the UK features in eleventh place and Saudi Arabia in seventieth, out of 163, with Haiti in the last place (www.transparency.org/policy_research/surveys_indices/cpi/2006).

mowers, etc., and the absence of electricity for Gudiya, but especially by the fact that while Karen's home includes a swimming pool, a Jacuzzi, ample water supply to keep the garden's flower beds fresh and beautiful, and toilets flushing with fresh water, Gudiya has no access to potable water at all. Thus, when Karen is driven off to school on weekday mornings, Gudiya, seven days a week, must get up before dawn and walk several hours to a well to collect water for the family (Luce 2004). After walking to the well, queuing at the well, and walking back to the village with the water jug on her head, even if there is a school in the village, Gudiya may be too late and in any case will be too exhausted. Because of water, Gudiya is condemned to a life of illiteracy, which will also almost certainly condemn her to a life of poverty. Gudiya's plight is especially poignant in comparison with that of Karen, but needless to say it is also a very far cry from the life of the eight-year-old girls whose parents are part of the Indian IT success story in Mumbai, Bangalore, or Hyderabad.

On this globe with just over 6 billion people, some 1.1 billion have no access to potable water, 2 billion have no electricity, 2.4 billion live without proper sanitation, and as many as 4 billion live without sound wastewater disposal systems.

For Gudiya to rise in the world, as things currently stand probably only a miracle would help. Gudiya, condemned at childhood, has no or only very, very little hope. Hers will most likely be a life of hardship and suffering. As the population's planet is expected to grow substantially in the course of the next couple of decades, and with about 98 percent of growth occurring in developing countries, often the poorest ones, the "hope index" will become increasingly pertinent. Thus, while the suffering and hardship of many youth who are and will be populating this planet in the first quarter of the twenty-first century may not be as dire as Gudiya's fate, nevertheless their sense of appurtenance and worth will be acutely tested. If one takes the Middle East, which will experience the biggest population increase during this period, where over half the population is under 20, and where youth unemployment already hovers at the 25–40 percent mark, where rapid urbanization is resulting in the erosion of family and village ties, clearly it does not require a Nobel Prize to discern that all this constitutes quite explosive chemistry.[10]

[10] "Middle East: Population Growth Poses Huge Challenge", *Oxford Analytica*, 18 January 2007.

If slavery was the great cause of the nineteenth century, and discrimination on the basis of race, religion, and gender the great cause of the twentieth century, the great cause of the twenty-first century must be acute, intrinsic poverty and the kind of gross inequality that separates Karen and Gudiya. Just as it came to be widely accepted that it was morally reprehensible that people should be enslaved, and as it came to be widely accepted that it was morally reprehensible that they should be discriminated against on the basis of race or gender, so will it become urgently necessary for it to be widely recognized that it is morally reprehensible for global society to allow Gudiya to live in the conditions that she does and in the hopelessness that envelops her.

Gandhi's favorite aphorism that "there is enough in this world for everyman's need, but not for everyman's greed" holds even truer today, partly because the world has shrunk so much and even Gudiya will become aware of the chasm that separates her from those who have. At this dawn of the twenty-first century, when the amount of accumulated wealth and the remarkable advances in technology can result in so much enhancement of prosperity, it is clear that unless this prosperity is reasonably distributed, but much more important is used to eradicate hopelessness and instead provide hope, globalization will almost certainly be brutally derailed.

This challenge will not be met by conventional sources of authority and especially not by political leaders. As with the movements to abolish slavery and the movements to end racial and gender discrimination, it is necessary to constitute multi-stakeholder networks committed to raising awareness, to educating the public, to engaging in dialogue, to generating understanding and action, and to being prepared to recognize that it will take time.

Recognizing that it will take time must also be understood in a context, however, where time is of the essence. In the book cited above, Jean-Louis Rischard argues that we have roughly twenty years. We are on top of an environmental and social waking volcano. The means of course exist for raising global awareness much faster than in the past, thanks to the ICT revolution. Yet, as also noted, while technology has made prodigious advances, mentalities lag.

Twenty-first-century globalization, as was noted in the beginning of this chapter, has seen a twin revolution: the global market revolution and the ICT revolution. For globalization to be sustained into the twenty-first century and to avoid another human disaster comparable to those experienced last century, there must be a third major revolution: a humanist revolution.

References

Anonymous. 2006a. "China in Africa: Never Too Late to Scramble," *The Economist* 26 October: 53–6.

2006b. "China Winning Resources and Loyalties of Africa," *Financial Times* 22 February. http://us.ft.com/ftgateway/superpage.ft?news_id= fto022220061535118320..

2007. "An Arms Deal That Stinks of Hypocrisy," *Financial Times* 7 June. http://us.ft.com/ftgateway/superpage.ft?news_id=fto060720071 746509311.

Chanda, Nayan. 2007. *Bound Together: How Traders, Preachers, Adventurers and Warriors Shape Globalization.* New Haven and London: Yale University Press.

Cohen, Paul. 1997. *History in Three Keys: The Boxers as Event, Experience and Myth.* New York: Columbia University Press.

De Lorenzo, Mauro. 2007. "China and Africa: A New Scramble?" *Jamestown Foundation China Brief* 7: 2–5.

Disraeli, Benjamin. 1998. *Sybil: Or the Two Nations,* Oxford: Oxford Paperbacks.

Dubois, Laurent. 2005. *Avengers of the New World: The Story of the Haitian Revolution.* Cambridge, MA: Belknap Press of Harvard University.

Fukuyama, Francis. 1992. *The End of History and the Last Man.* London: Penguin Books.

Hague, William. 2007. *William Wilberforce: The Life of the Great Anti-Slave Trade Campaigner.* London: HarperCollins.

Hochschild, Adam. 2005. *Bury the Chain: The British Struggle to Abolish Slavery.* London: Macmillan.

Inside AISA. 2006. *Special Issue: China in Africa,* Oct–Dec. Pretoria: Africa Institute of South Africa (AISA).

Khalaf, Roula. 2007. "Women Challenge Age-old Prejudices," *Financial Times* 14 June. http://us.ft.com/ftgateway/superpage.ft?news_id=fto 061420070549280120.

Lehmann, Jean-Pierre. 2006. *The Times They Are a'Changin': Tomorrow's Challenges.* Lausanne: IMD.

Luce, Edward. 2004. "A Thirst for Change," *Financial Times* 22 July: 16.

Maddison, Angus. 2005. *The World Economy: A Millennial Perspective.* Vancouver: University of British Columbia Press.

Micklethwait, John and Woolridge, Adrian. 2000. *A Future Perfect: The Challenge and Hidden Promise of Globalization*. London: Crown Business.

Nilekani, Rohini. 2007. "Is Water the Next Oil?" *YaleGlobal Online* 31 May.

Palmer, Robert R. 1969. *The Age of the Democratic Revolution: A Political History of Europe and America 1760–1800*. Princeton: Princeton University Press.

Rischard, Jean-François. 2002. *High Noon: 20 Global Problems, 20 Years to Solve Them*. New York: Basic Books.

Smith, Helena. 2006. "From Iraq to Oman, the Future is Female," *Observer* 23 April: 5.

Yergin, Daniel. 1991. *The Prize: Epic Quest for Oil, Money and Power*. New York: Simon & Schuster.

Yergin, Daniel and Stanislaw, Joseph. 1998. *The Commanding Heights: The New Reality of Economic Power*. New York: Simon & Schuster.

21 | The leader as responsible change agent: promoting humanism in and beyond business

THOMAS MAAK AND NICOLA PLESS

The findings of a global survey carried out for the World Economic Forum 2007 show a growing lack of confidence in leaders, both in politics and in business, to improve the lives of people on this planet (Gallup 2007). Respondents all over the world, but especially in Europe and the Americas, worry about safety and they don't trust current business leaders to ensure a prosperous world for the next generation. Obviously, even a few years after the corporate scandals in the United States and elsewhere, business leaders still face a significant lack of trust in the wider public.

Not surprisingly, then, we find an exponential increase in corporate social responsibility (CSR) activities and reporting over the past years through which businesses want to show that they act responsibly, are good corporate citizens, and contribute to the well-being of societies in which they operate. "Re-building public trust" is arguably a priority for business leaders at home and abroad, and corporate responsibility among their core challenges. In fact, there is widespread agreement that it takes *responsible leadership* to build and sustain a business *in* society. The UN Global Compact and the European Foundation for Management Development (EFMD) call for "Globally Responsible Leadership" as a "global exercise of ethical, values-based leadership in the pursuit of economic and societal progress and sustainable development" (EFMD 2005: 2) And in business schools around the world, but especially in the US, we see "a frenzy of activities," as the late Sumantra Ghoshal (2005) notes in his pledge to rethink business education.

These actions, programs, and initiatives in responsible leadership obviously reflect a real demand, whether we look at business school education, leadership development, or business practice. The real challenge, however, is whether, and how, the call for responsible leadership can be answered. If "business schools have lost their way," as Bennis and O'Toole (2005) contend, and if "bad theories are destroying good practices," as Ghoshal (2005) argues, then we face some fundamental challenges to develop and sustain responsible leadership in business. How can they be met? What needs to be done to infuse responsible leadership in theory – and in practice? In other words, what needs to be done to educate current and future leaders to develop a humanist perspective that guides them to act as agents of social change and betterment, rather than for individual glory and enrichment?

In what follows we want to shed some light on these questions by highlighting the challenges of leading a responsible business *in* society, by looking at selected profiles of responsible leaders and by arguing that business leaders should consider themselves as *responsible change agents*. Mahatma Gandhi once said "You must be the change you wish to see in the world." If business leaders want people to trust them (again) they need to be seen as active contributors to solving world's problems, and cannot afford to be considered a part of these problems. In other words, they need to inspire and spearhead a humanist business culture that seeks to serve human needs, solve social and environmental problems, and generates well-being and prosperity for everyone.

Leadership in times of complexity, connectivity, and concern about the state of the world

The past decade has seen a seminal shift in the business environment: global interdependence and interconnectedness are a reality. Leading a business in an interconnected, global business environment means navigating in a world of complexity, diversity and uncertainty, requiring from leaders an appropriate cross-cultural perspective (Bartlett and Ghoshal 1998; Black *et al.* 1999) and the ability to deal with a high level of complexity (Dalton 1998). Since values are everywhere (Diermeier 2006), it also requires a *values radar*, that is, the ability to scan moral, social, ecological, and cultural developments, and to assess and weigh the impact of organizational behavior on all relevant stakeholders (Pless and Maak 2005). This places new demands on leaders, namely to balance multiple interests, reconcile potential dilemmas (Trompenaars and Hampden-Turner 1998), and navigate a business successfully and responsibly in a fast moving environment, while building sustainable relationships and trust with stakeholders.

There is widespread agreement that the stakeholder framework has proved useful to analyze the strategic and normative challenges organizations face, and that good stakeholder relationships are key to organizational viability and business success (Donaldson and Preston 1995; Freeman 1984, 1994; Post *et al.* 2002; Svendsen 1998; Wheeler and Silanpää 1997). Still, there are both theoretical and practical challenges with respect to identifying, evaluating and balancing stakeholders' claims. More often than not the claims made by employees, clients, shareholder, suppliers, NGOs, communities, government, nature, and on behalf of future generations collide and need to be reconciled. This calls for proactive engagement (Burke 2005) and requires leaders to address stakeholder salience and determine whose claims are legitimate (Jones *et al.* 2007; Mitchell *et al.* 1997). The leadership challenge here is to enable *inclusive* stakeholder engagement and dialogue, to facilitate a legitimating discourse (Apel 1988; Habermas 1991) and to help balance diverse claims to enable ethically sound decision-making.

Ethically sound decision-making too is among the key challenges leaders face. If we look at the many scandals and examples of "bad leadership" (Kellerman 2004) and ethical failures *in* leadership (Price 2005), we see leaders struggling with questions that make up the very core of leadership. On the one hand there is the ethical challenge of leadership as such: responsible leadership needs *leadership ethics*. This might seem like stating the obvious. So far, however, with few exceptions (e.g. Ciulla 1998; Maak and Pless 2006), the persisting "industrial paradigm" (Rost 1993) in leadership research has hindered a truly humanist paradigm from emerging. While ethics is at "the heart of leadership" (Ciulla 1998) a theory of responsible leadership has yet to be developed. On the other hand, moral dilemmas in an interconnected and multicultural world are almost inevitable. How can one adhere to fundamental moral principles while still respecting cultural differences and taking into consideration different developmental standards (Donaldson 1996)? What needs to be done to secure "uncompromising integrity" (Moorthy *et al.* 1998) in the global marketplace?

Moreover, balancing different stakeholder claims, including those of the natural environment, future generations and less privileged groups "at the bottom of the pyramid" (Prahalad 2005) creates social, ecological, and humanitarian challenges. Against this backdrop leaders are confronted with the challenge to create and lead a sustainable business in society. While many corporations have adopted a "triple-bottom-line" approach (Elkington 1998) and integrated social and environmental considerations into their values creation, only few so far have taken on the *humanitarian* challenges – poverty, hunger, diseases and injustice – which prevent large parts of the human community from participating in the global economy in the first place; let alone benefiting from it. The actual challenge at hand is twofold – on the one hand to exercise active global corporate citizenship, fighting problems such as HIV/AIDS or human rights violations, and thus live up to the responsibility that comes with the increased power that multinational corporations have acquired; on the other hand to create a "more inclusive brand of capitalism, one that incorporates previously excluded voices, concerns, and interests" (Hart 2005: xli). There is agreement in both business and society that multinational corporations and their leaders have an enormous potential for contributing to the betterment of the world (WBCSD 2006).

Thus, as the world is changing, businesses need to adapt to a seamless environment, in which hunger and diseases in Africa, the speed of knowledge work in India, environmental degradation in China, consumer behavior in developed countries, and an increasing skepticism as to what the future state of the world will look like are all interconnected. The problem is that not all leaders are aware of it and most are not yet equipped to deal with the above challenges because a dominant mechanist fiction blocks the way.

The "theatre of illusions" of leadership as we know it

The prevailing research approach towards leadership assumes the existence of an uncontestable reality that is to be discovered by applying empirical methods just as in the natural sciences, to capture this reality in scientific language, and to explain social phenomena as causal relationships (Gergen and Thatchenkery 2004; Pless 1998). Rost (1993) calls this the "industrial paradigm" of leadership research. It assumes that only positivist knowledge generated by empirical methods counts as true knowledge. Calas and Smircich show that this approach ultimately resulted in the search for the "Rosetta Stone" of leadership (1988: 224), which one hoped to discover and decode by breaking the subject-matter of leadership into smaller and smaller units of inquiry; thereby, however, losing the main code of leadership. Furthermore, the industrial paradigm builds on possessive individualism (Macpherson 1962) and dyadic relationships, creating a subject–object understanding of leadership, with the leader as subject and possessor of superior qualities. These qualities separate leaders from followers, who as subordinates become objects of a "strictly top-down, command and control" (Ghoshal 2005) leadership style. It views the leader as a rational agent and "bureaucratic expert" whose expertise is "morally neutral" (MacIntyre 1984).

Yet MacIntyre (1984) has argued compellingly that this master of effectiveness and "central character of modern society" is not much more than "contemporary moral fiction" (107). It is neither value-neutral, as the positivist paradigm wants us to believe; nor is the notion of leadership effectiveness anywhere close to being realistic, let alone desirable. In fact, it is a "peculiarly managerial fiction embodied in the claim to possess systematic effectiveness in controlling certain aspects of social reality." MacIntyre stresses that this claim of effectiveness cannot be morally neutral, because it is "inseparable from a mode of human existence in which the contrivance of means is in central part of the manipulation of human beings into compliant patterns of behavior" (74). And the "permanent unpredictability of human life" contradicts the notion of control and effectiveness (106). As it turns out, then, leadership and managerial effectiveness function as "a fictitious, but believed-in reality, appeal to which disguises certain other realities" (76), thereby lacking appropriate justification. The mechanist view that these leadership facts have to be value-free and that leadership expertise leads to effectiveness is a mere prophecy that was translated into social performance which disguises itself as "factualization." Thus, the positivist leadership paradigm is a "moral fiction," a "folk-concept." Leadership, as we know it, is a *theatre of illusions* (MacIntyre 1984: 77).

In other words, what we perceive as leadership is not "effective" social control but a more or less skillful *dramatic imitation* of such control (107), based on misguided beliefs and misunderstanding. Still, it is this "malaise of modernity" (Taylor 1991), which hinders responsible leadership from emerging and instead causes a "coercive inauthenticity" (Trilling 1972) in much of what falls under the umbrella term "leadership." Thus, in addition to the aforementioned contextual challenges we face an additional conceptual one: the reconstruction of the *moral ontology of leadership*.

Reconstructing the moral ontology of leadership

Since this task exceeds by far the limits of this chapter we can only highlight some of the key aspects. First, leaders and leadership researchers need to understand that ethics is at the heart of leadership (Ciulla 1998, 2006). The task of being effective in moving others to do something is a moral one because its very nature is based on *normative decisions* as to "*how* leaders get people to do things (impress, organize, persuade, influence and inspire) and *how* what is to be done is decided (forced obedience, voluntary consent, dictated by the leader or a reflection of mutual purposes)" (Ciulla 2006: 21). In other words, the very way leadership is defined contains in it normative assumptions about the role of the leader, the purpose of leadership and about the relationship between leader and followers.

Second, as for the relationship between leader and followers, we find an odd discrepancy between the image of the leader as decoupled expert and pursuer of managerial effectiveness on the one hand, and the reality of leading a business in society on the other. Leading a responsible and sustainable business in today's and tomorrow's world requires orienting knowledge that reflects the complexity and diversity of leadership relationships. As a consequence, instead of focusing on the dyadic leader–subordinate relationship alone, a wider range of multiple relationships needs to be considered. If we broaden the view from leader–subordinate relationships to leader–stakeholder relationships, that is if we start to think of followers as stakeholders and stakeholders as followers, then the leadership project actually consists of a web of relationships, some of which may still be hierarchical, most of which, however, will have a different configuration. The leader engages with different stakeholders who are ultimately of equal status and do not necessarily depend on him. In fact, in some cases the leader might be the follower, e.g. when he follows the advice of scientists or NGOs on matters such as sustainability. Against this background we suggested elsewhere (Maak and Pless 2006a) that responsible leadership should be understood as a relational phenomenon which occurs in social interactions with those who affect or are affected by leadership and have a stake in the purpose and vision of the leadership relationship (Freeman *et al.* 2006). Moreover, "the purpose of leadership can be understood as to build and cultivate sustainable and trustful relationships to different stakeholders inside and outside the organization . . . to help to realize a good (i.e. ethically sound) and shared business vision" (Maak and Pless 2006b: 103).

Third, and connected to the idea of having a commonly shared purpose and vision, we want leaders to do the right thing and do things right. Leaders who listen, who care for others and not only themselves or their organization and who are able to align different, sometimes conflicting values into a common vision to serve a purpose that is higher than one self or one organization. At the core, then, the leader is *trusted to serve a valuable common purpose*. In other words, leadership is essentially not about the person of a leader, or about being a "great man," but about the purpose and the people he or she serves. It was Robert Greenleaf (1977), after reading Hermann Hesse's *Journey to the East*, who first elaborated on the idea of leadership being about leaders serving followers rather than the opposite. He asked "Do those served grow as persons?" If the answer is yes and if "followers" are likely to become servants themselves, then the leader did a good job, i.e. he was effective. Clearly, this notion of effectiveness is inseparable from the notion of *good leadership* and rests on moral principles. The "is" and the "ought" of leadership are therefore inextricably connected to each other. We can only judge what good leadership is, or if someone's a good leader, if we consider the "what" and the "why": *what* leaders and followers do (effectiveness/action) and if their acting is desirable and legitimate, that is, *why* they do it (ethics/purpose). In this sense, too, leadership research needs to overcome the prevailing "moral fiction" (MacIntyre 1984) and rediscover the proper role and true calling of leadership in promoting humanism in business, not egoism, and in weaving sustainable relationships to serve the common good. The idea of *servant leadership* might prove to be helpful in this endeavor; being *authentic* in this endeavor is indispensable.

Therefore, a fourth aspect in reconstructing the moral ontology of leadership is the *recovery of moral authenticity* in leadership. It means in Charles Taylor's terms (1991) overcoming "the primacy of instrumental reason" and to reconnect to what Rousseau called *le sentiment de l'éxistence*. Authenticity is essentially a social virtue. It can best be described as "being true to who you are in what you do" and involves the ability to be a reflective actor who discerns what is genuinely worth pursuing within a given social context (Guignon 2004: 147–55). *Moral* authenticity in leadership, however, implies more; it requires leaders to align principles, purpose, and process of leadership in ways that all stakeholders (as followers) consider genuine and worth pursuing. Being authentic in this sense means doing the right thing because it is the right thing to do, not because it is beneficial. It means being aware of moral challenges, being able to reconcile moral dilemmas, and having a moral vision as to what role business should play in contributing to the common good. It means having values, living values, and showing "attitudinal respect" (Taylor 1989: 15) to issues that demand dignity. These values, "the values of the authentic leader," writes Bill George (2003: 20), "are shaped by personal beliefs, developed through study and introspection, and consultation with others – and a lifetime of experience. These values define the holder's moral compass." In this sense, George notes, good and authentic leadership is like a continuing journey for a leader to find the true self and the purpose of life's work.

Fifth, given the challenges in both business and societies, we need business leaders who not only take part in, but also trigger positive transformation, who use their means and ideas to contribute to a sustainable future. In other words, we need business leaders who act as responsible change agents in and beyond their businesses. In what follows, we look at three profiles of responsible leaders who incorporate this idea, discuss some of their key character traits and sketch in more detail what we mean by "responsible change agent."

The leader as responsible change agent

When Ray Anderson, CEO of Interface, the world's largest manufacturer of commercial floor covering, with headquarters in Atlanta, Georgia, picked up a book in the early nineties entitled *The Ecology of Commerce* and began to read it, it dawned on him: he was a plunderer of the earth. "Some day," he now likes to say at one of his frequent speaking engagements, "they will put people like me in jail." Anderson realized that he was exploiting the earth's natural resources without thinking about the ecological footprint his company would leave for coming generations. He was leading a business *as if* there was no tomorrow; no children or grandchildren to consider. For him, reading Paul Hawken's book was an epiphany. In the years since, he set out to lead one of the biggest and most fundamental transformations in today's business world, inspiring innovations that impacted many other organizations and industries, to create the cleanest, most creative, most innovative, biggest, and most profitable industrial carpet manufacturer in the world. This is by no means a small achievement. The business of producing commercial carpet and floor tiles is a toxic one; it uses nylon and adhesives that are primarily created from oil and chemicals. In 1994, Interface was using more than 500 million pounds of raw material each year, producing more than 900 million tons of emissions and over 2 billion liters of wastewater (Rothman and Scott 2003). Under Anderson's leadership, however, what once was a polluting business with a huge environmental footprint aims at being a zero-emission business by 2020. In fact, what began as a "mid-course correction" (Anderson 1998) is now spearheading what the company calls a "new industrial revolution" to create the ultimate sustainable enterprise, not only reconciling economic, environmental, and social bottom lines, but enhancing all of them at the same time. In other words, "doing very well by doing good" (Rothman and Scott 2003: 42).

While Anderson is both passionate and modest about his achievements he incorporates in many ways the prototype of the leader thinking and acting as *responsible change agent*. And while he initially acted on the grounds of a personal epiphany, the transformation of Interface's business to become a sustainable enterprise is a common achievement by Anderson, his managers, engineers and employees, Interface suppliers, scientists, and shareholders. Acting as responsible change agent Anderson had the vision of what he wanted the organization to become; he inspired and motivated his people to think about uncommon solutions and help build the sustainable enterprise; he convinced suppliers to follow him in this endeavor; his engineers tapped into the right scientific resources to make the radical changes in production happen; and he earned the trust from shareholders to continue on the path taken even in times of financial crisis. Thus, stakeholders followed a responsible leader in his way of transforming a business to create a sustainable, i.e. better future.

A well-known example of a responsible business leader is Anita Roddick, founder of The Body Shop, the UK-based cosmetics producer and retailer. While social and environmental values were a company staple from the very beginning it was not until a defining moment when The Body Shop went public that Anita Roddick decided that the company needed to transform its heritage into market power; that as a publicly traded company it should use its power to set an example. In one of her books she remarks on this moment.

A lot of people – those who did not know us very well – thought that after going public we would perhaps sell up and retire to a life of indolent luxury. Gordon and I never remotely considered doing such a thing . . . When we got home that night we sat in front of the fire and Gordon said, "OK, what do we do now?' . . . We now had wealth and status in the business community. Wealth plus status equalled power. How were we going to use that power? And what were the social responsibilities of business? Should not a business that relied on the community for its success be prepared to give something back to the community? Should there not be a trade in goodwill as well as in commerce? All this, and much more, we talked about long into the night, and it began to dawn on us – no matter how trite it may now sound – that The Body Shop had both the potential, and the means at its disposal, to do good. (Roddick 1991: 109)

After that night the Roddicks made a principled decision to be a force for common good which led to the formulation of the company's mission: "To dedicate our business to the pursuit of social and environmental change." Anita Roddick became an active proponent of fair trade, engaging many communities in developing countries to become suppliers to The Body Shop while helping them to build sustainable businesses and communities. And it became a hallmark of her leadership to take a stand, to speak up, and lead, and live, an activist approach to raise awareness for issues such as animal testing, climate change, active self-esteem, domestic violence, and human rights. Under her leadership The Body Shop conducted more than thirty campaigns to promote social and environmental change; and an important task for her as a leader was to set an example for campaigning, to provide a campaigning platform to create a culture of citizenship, to communicate that citizenship is an integral part of doing principled business, and to use her influence as a leader to mobilize different stakeholders to take coordinated action for the common good (Pless 2007).

Thus, Anita Roddick acted in many ways as a responsible change agent, transforming not only her own business but also the cosmetics industry. Moreover, she symbolizes a shining example that even one business leader can be a powerful, transformative force for the good and that with the power embedded in this role comes social and environmental responsibility. Inherent in being a responsible business leader, we argue, is the calling to improve the human condition and make this world a better place.

This idea of a striving human community at home and in the workplace is also at the heart of a business leader who acts as a responsible change agent in the very mainstream of the consumer production business. Tex Gunning is president of Unilever Bestfoods Asia, the Asian operation of the Dutch–British consumer product giant Unilever. When Gunning joined Unilever in the mid-90s markets were saturated; there were no real innovations in the pipeline; the giant was going through troubling times. Brought in as an expert in restructuring, which at that time was just an open code word for laying off workers, he decided to seek new, uncommon ways to grow the business without laying off people. He decided to build a human community where human individuals work together, enjoy what they are doing, care for each other, and – based on values such as trust, honesty and authenticity – take the business in creative and innovative directions (*What Is Enlightenment?* 2005). As a result, the business turned around in an almost dramatic way. A key to this success were multiple "breakouts," demanding experiential learning retreats in places like Jordan, India, China, or Malaysia. And as president of Unilever Bestfoods Asia Gunning not only started the food business in fifteen countries, but also set as his goal to significantly improve the nutrition and well-being of children in Asia (*What Is Enlightenment?* 2005). After all, the number of malnourished children in India exceeds that of Africa. The vision for improving the livelihood of people (rather than selling products), the impact of living a social mission intrinsic to the business on a daily basis; the caring spirit unleashed by "breakouts" to the real world with real problems, all this is highlighted by the Tsunami relief efforts of Unilever Best Foods in Sri Lanka, which are documented in a book called *Sri Lanka* (Unilever 2005). Here, Gunning reflects back on the journey of more than a hundred employees and asserts:

In fact we realized again that if we inculcate a meaningful spirit, if we develop the right values of service, care and belonging and we help our people to grow as human and business beings that the rest will follow much more easily. As leaders, we need a whole new level of consciousness about the functioning of organizations. Recognize that it is a living and therefore continuously changing organism, adjusting itself to its new circumstances and adjusting to the human players that make up the organization.

As a responsible change agent Tex Gunning incorporates the future of business leadership: emphasizing that even when times get rough business does not have be mean, but in fact should have a *meaning*, a social purpose and vision to improve the lives of all stakeholders; a leader who is at the same time caring, concerned, and committed to improving the state of the world in which he operates. When asked what makes a leader outstanding, he answered: "Average leaders take care of themselves and their families. Good leaders take care of themselves, their families and some of the community. Great leaders – and great companies – not only take care of these stakeholders but also want to change the world. They want to leave the world better than they found it" (*What Is Enlightenment?* 2005: 96).

Responsible leaders like Tex Gunning, Anita Roddick, and Ray Anderson know that their calling is not to enrich the few (shareholders, managers, themselves) but to enrich the lives of the many and to make this world a better place. They consider the power vested in them as a powerful trust to initiate change and social transformation through business. They engage in relationships with all stakeholders, have a vision of a better future, and act based on this vision as responsible change agents. In other words, they care for others and for our common future as human beings and want to tackle the challenges facing humanity. And if we paraphrase Gandhi again, we can very well say that they live the change they want to see in the world. They are *transforming leaders*.

The concept of transforming leadership was developed by the historian James MacGregor Burns (1978), drawing on research on needs, values development, and moral development. Burns argues that transforming leadership aims at having a profound impact: "a radical change in outward form or inner character" (Burns 2003: 24). The transforming leader takes the initiative "in mobilizing people for participation in the process of change, encouraging a sense of collective identity and collective efficacy, which in turn brings stronger feelings of self-worth and self-efficacy." It creates a sense of meaningfulness in the work and lives of followers and is a source of inspiration (Burns 2003: 25–6). The transforming leader empowers, energizes, and enables; and ultimately leader and follower raise one another to higher levels of moral awareness. Transforming leaders inspire responsible behavior and are engaged in a dialogue about values. A good transforming leader makes followers into leaders (Ciulla 2006: 29). Ray Anderson, Anita Roddick, and Tex Gunning as responsible change agents are living examples of transforming leaders in much the same sense that Burns imagines leaders should be.

Conclusion: business leaders as agents of world benefit

Responsible leadership, in this sense and in view of the challenges we outlined at the beginning, is to a large extent transforming leadership. It is about responsible business leaders who take on human challenges as challenges for their businesses, who ignite strength and inspiration, who say what they do and do what they say, who make followers leaders in their own right, and who strive to reconcile their organization's bottom lines – economic, social, and environmental – in principled ways. This sort of change is by no means an easy task. It might imply having to "build the bridge as you walk on it" (Quinn 2004). Responsible leaders, however, grow with the challenges they encounter. In fact, it is part of their moral quality and strength: "It comes from and may expand to all the world; it is rooted deeply in the past and faces toward the endless future . . . the quality of leadership, the persistence of its influence, the power of coordination it incites, all express the height of moral aspirations, the breadth of moral foundations" (Barnard 1938: 484). Ultimately, business leadership is *moral* leadership, too, or should be, as it takes moral ambitions to make this world a better place. This world is the "real" world with "real" problems and not a "theatre of illusions." Some business leaders have embarked on a journey to change this world for the better, to improve the human condition. They act as agents of world benefit and promote humanism in and beyond business. Hopefully many others will follow.

References

Anderson, R. C. 1998. *Mid-course Correction, Towards a Sustainable Enterprise: The Interface Model.* Atlanta, GA: Peregrinzilla Press.

Apel, K.-O. 1988. *Diskurs und Verantwortung*. Frankfurt am Main: Suhrkamp.

Barnard, C. I. 1938. *The Functions of the Executive*. Cambridge, MA and London: Harvard University Press.

Bartlett, C. A. and Ghoshal, S. 1998. *Managing across Borders: The Transnational Solution*. Boston, MA: Harvard Business School Press.

Bennis, W. and O'Toole, 2005. "How Business Schools Lost Their Way," *Harvard Business Review* 83(5): 96–104.

Black, J. S., Morrison, A. J., and Gregersen, H. B. 1999. *Global Explorers: The Next Generation of Leaders*. New York, London: Routledge.

Burke, E. M. 2005. *Managing a Company in an Activist World: The Leadership Challenge of Corporate Citizenship*. Westport, CT and London: Praeger.

Burns, J. M. 1978. *Leadership*. New York: Perennial.
2003. *Transforming Leadership*. New York: Atlantic Monthly Press.

Calas, M. B. and Smircich, L. 1988. "Reading Leadership as a Form of Cultural Analysis," in J. G. Hunt, B. R. Baliga, H. P. Dachler, and C. A. Schriesheim (eds.), *Emerging Leadership Vistas*. Lexington, MA: Lexington Books.

Ciulla, J. 1998. *Ethics: The Heart of Leadership*. Westport, CT: Quorum.
2006. "Ethics: The Heart of Leadership," in T. Maak and N. M. Pless (eds.), *Responsible Leadership*. London and New York: Routledge.

Dalton, M. A. 1998. "Developing Leaders for Global Roles," in C. D. McCauley, R. S. Moxley, and E. Van Velsor (eds.), *The Center for Creative Leadership Handbook of Leadership Development*. San Francisco: Jossey-Bass.

Diermeier, D. 2006. "Leading in a World of Competing Values: A Strategic Perspective on Corporate SRcial responsibility," in T. Maak and N. M. Pless (eds.), *Responsible Leadership*. London and New York: Routledge.

Donaldson, T. 1996. "Values in Tension: Ethics away from Home", *Harvard Business Review* September–October: 48–62.

Donaldson, T. and Preston, L. E. 1995. "The Stakeholder Theory of the Corporation: Concepts, Evidence, and Implications," *Academy of Management Review* 20(1): 65–91.

EFMD 2005. "Globally Responsible Leadership: A Call for Engagement." Online. Available HTTP: www.efmd.org/html/Responsibility/cont_detail.asp?id=041207trlv&aid=051012qnis&tid=1&ref=ind (accessed October 18, 2005).

Elkington, J. 1998. *Cannibals with Forks: The Triple Bottom Line of 21st Century Business*. Gabriola Island, Stony Creek, BC: New Society Publishers.

Freeman, R.E. 1984. *Strategic Management: A Stakeholder Approach.* Boston: Pitman.

1994. "The politics of Stakeholder Theory: Some Future Directions," *Business Ethics Quarterly* 4(4): 409–22.

Freeman, R. E., Martin, K., Parmar, B., Cording, M. P., and Werhane, P. H. 2006. "Leading through Values and Ethical Principles", in R. J. Burke and C. L. Cooper (eds.) *Inspiring Leaders*. London and New York: Routledge, vol. I, pp. 149–74.

Gallup International Asscociation 2007. Gallup International Voice of the People. http://weforum.org/en/media/Latest%20Press%20Releases/voiceofthepeoplesurvey (accessed January 26, 2007).

George, B. 2003. *Authentic Leadership*. San Francisco: Jossey-Bass.

Gergen, K. J. and Thatchenkery, T. J. 2004. "Organization Science as Social Construction: Postmodern Potentials," *Journal of Applied Behavioral Science* 40: 228–49.

Ghoshal, S. 2005. "Bad Management Theories Are Destroying Good Management Practices," *Academy of Management Learning & Education* 4(1): 75–91.

Greenleaf, R. K. 1977/2002 *Servant Leadership. A Journey into the Nature of Legitimate Power and Greatness* (twenty-fifth anniversary edition). Mahwah, NY: Paulist Press.

Guignon, C. 2004. *On Being Authentic*. London and New York: Routledge.

Habermas, J. 1991. *Erläuterungen zur Diskursethik*. Frankfurt am Main: Suhrkamp.

Hart, S. L. 2005. *Capitalism at the Crossroads*. Upper Saddle River, NJ: Wharton School Publishing.

Jones, T. M., Felps, W., and Gigley, G. A. 2007. "Ethical Theory and Stakeholder-related Decisions: The Role of Stakeholder Cultures," *Academy of Management Review* 32(1): 137–55.

Kellerman, B. 2004. *Bad Leadership*. Boston, MA: Harvard Business School Press.

Maak, T. and Pless, N. M. 2006a. "Responsible Leadership: A Relational Approach," in T. Maak and N. M. Pless (eds.), *Responsible Leadership*. London, New York: Routledge.

2006b. "Responsible Leadership in a Stakeholder Society. A Relational Perspective," *Journal of Business Ethics* 66(1): 99–115.

MacIntyre, A. 1984. *After Virtue* (second edition). Notre Dame, IN: Notre Dame University Press.

Macpherson, C. B. 1962. *The Political Theory of Possessive Individualism: From Hobbes to Locke*. London: Oxford University Press.

Mitchell, R. K., Agle, B. R., and Wood, D. J. 1997. "Toward a Theory of Stakeholder Identification and Salience: Defining the Principle of Who and What Really Counts," *Academy of Management Review* 22(4): 853–86.

Moorthy, R. S., DeGeorge, R. T., Donaldson, T., Ellos, W. J., Solomon, R. C., and Textor, R. B. 1998. *Uncompromising Integrity: Motorola's Global Challenge.* Schaumburg, IL: Motorola University Press.

Pless, N. M. 1998. *Corporate Caretaking: Neue Wege in der Gestaltung organisationaler Mitweltbeziehungen.* Marburg: Metropolis.

2007. "Understanding Responsible Leadership: Roles, Identity and Motivational Drivers. The Case of Dame Anita Roddick, Founder of The Body Shop," *Journal of Business Ethics* 74(4): 437–56.

Pless, N. M. and Maak, T. 2004. "Building an Inclusive Diversity Culture: Principles, Processes and Practice," *Journal of Business Ethics* 54(2): 129–47.

2005. "Relational Intelligence for Leading Responsibly in a Connected World," in K. M. Weaver (ed.), *Proceedings of the Sixty-fifth Annual Meeting of the Academy of Management,* Honolulu, HI.

Post, J. E., Preston, L. E., and Sachs, S. 2002. *Redefining the Corporation: Stakeholder Management and Organizational Wealth.* Stanford, CA: Stanford University Press.

Prahalad, C. K. 2005. *The Fortune at the Bottom of the Pyramid: Eradicating Poverty through Profits.* Upper Saddle River, NJ: Wharton School Publishing.

Price, T. L. 2005. *Understanding Ethical Failures in Leadership.* New York: Cambridge University Press.

Quinn, R. E. 2004. *Building the Bridge as You Walk on It. A Guide for Leading Change.* San Francisco, CA: Jossey-Bass.

Roddick, A. 1991. *Body and Soul: Profits with Principles.* New York: Crown Publishers.

Rothman, H. and Scott, M. 2003. *Companies with a Conscience.* Denver, CO: The Publishing Cooperative.

Rost, J.C. 1993. *Leadership for the 21st Century.* Westport, CT and London: Praeger.

Svendsen, A. 1998. *The Stakeholder Strategy.* San Francisco: Berrett-Koehler.

Taylor, C. 1989. *Sources of the Self.* Cambridge, MA and London: Harvard University Press.

1991. *The Ethics of Authenticity.* Cambridge, MA and London: Harvard University Press.

Trilling, L. 1972. *Sincerity and Authenticity.* Cambridge, MA and London: Harvard University Press.

Trompenaars, F. and Hampden-Turner, C. 1998 *Riding the Waves of Culture: Understanding Diversity in Global Business* (second edition). New York: McGraw-Hill.

Unilever. 2005. *Sri Lanka. Journey to Greatness.* Unilever Bestfoods Asia.
WBCSD. 2006. *From Challenge to Opportunity. The Role of Business in Tomorrow's Society.* Geneva: World Business Council for Sustainable Development.
Wheeler, S. and Sillanpää, M. 1997. *The Stakeholder Corporation.* London: Pitman.
What Is Enlightenment?. 2005. "I Have No Choice: An Interview with Tex Gunning," *What Is Enlightenment?* 28 (March–May): 95–8.

22 | Quiet leadership: a way to sustainable positive change[1]

JOE BADARACCO

Every profession and walk of life has its great figures, leaders, and heroes. Think of the men and women who create or transform major companies, the political leaders who reshape society, the firefighters who risk their lives to save others. We exalt these individuals as role models and celebrate their achievements. They represent, we feel, the true model of leadership.

But do they really? I ask this because, over the course of a career spent studying management and leadership, I have observed that the most effective leaders are rarely public heroes. These men and women aren't high-profile champions of causes, and don't want to be. They don't spearhead ethical crusades. They move patiently, carefully, and incrementally. They do what is right – for their organizations, for the people around them, and for themselves – inconspicuously and without casualties.

I have come to call these people *quiet leaders* because their modesty and restraint are in large measure responsible for their impressive achievements. And since many big problems can only be resolved by a long series of small efforts, quiet leadership, despite its seemingly slow pace, often turns out to be the quickest way to make an organization – and the world – a better place.

Stories of heroic effort do teach us indispensable lessons in courage and dedication. They also show us the highest human ideals and help parents and teachers pass on important values. And these are not merely stories: Without the efforts of great individuals, our world would be an emptier and meaner place. We owe these men and women our admiration and gratitude.

[1] Excerpted with permission from: Joseph L. Badaracco. 2002. *Leading Quietly.* Boston: Harvard Business School Press.

The problem is that the heroic view of leadership looks at people in terms of a pyramid. At the top are the great figures. They have clear, strong values and know right from wrong. They act boldly, sacrifice themselves for noble causes, set compelling examples for others, and ultimately change the world. At the bottom of the pyramid are life's bystanders, shirkers, and cowards. These are T. S. Eliot's "hollow men," afraid to act and preoccupied with self-interest. They inspire no one and change nothing.

But where does this view leave everyone else? Most people, most of the time, are neither saving the world nor exploiting it. They are living their lives, doing their jobs, and trying to take care of the people around them. The pyramid approach, by saying little about everyday life and ordinary people, seems to consign much of humanity to a murky, moral limbo. This is a serious mistake.

Consider the view of Albert Schweitzer, a man who, by any standard, was a truly heroic leader and a humanist. In his late twenties, Schweitzer abandoned two promising career paths – one as a musician, the other as a theologian – that would have led to a comfortable, settled, and secure life. Instead, he became a medical missionary and spent most of his life serving lepers and victims of sleeping sickness in Central Africa. His decades of hard, lonely, and sometimes dangerous work were rewarded with the Nobel Peace Prize in 1952, and Schweitzer used the funds from the prize to expand his hospital. He worked there until his death at the age of ninety.

Schweitzer changed many lives and inspired countless others. Yet, in his autobiography, he wrote these words about the role of great individuals shaping the world:

Of all the will toward the ideal in mankind only a small part can manifest itself in public action. All the rest of this force must be content with small and obscure deeds. The sum of these, however, is a thousand times stronger than the acts of those who receive wide public recognition. The latter, compared to the former, are like the foam on the waves of a deep ocean.

This is a remarkable, almost radical statement. Here is Albert Schweitzer, a great man, telling us to rethink and even devalue the role of great figures in human affairs. He compares their efforts to "foam" and instead praises "small and obscure deeds."

Schweitzer's view represents a profoundly different way of thinking about leadership. Consider, for example, the Tylenol episode of the early 1980s – probably the most famous tale of responsible business leadership in the last twenty years.

In 1982, someone put cyanide into a number of Tylenol capsules, resulting in the deaths of seven people. The national media seized the story and wouldn't let go. Millions of Americans panicked, fearing their medicine cabinets contained deadly poison. Instead of hunkering down, Johnson & Johnson's chairman, James Burke, took immediate and bold steps to lead the company through the ensuing crisis. He cooperated swiftly and fully with public authorities and the media, defining the crisis as an issue of public health, not corporate profits. He immediately withdrew all Tylenol from the market, costing the company millions of dollars. Johnson & Johnson then quickly introduced triple-seal packing for Tylenol, and the industry soon followed its example. Burke received enormous credit for his efforts and surely earned it.

This story is dramatic and inspiring and has been told and retold countless times. Yet, from Schweitzer's perspective, this chronicle of leadership can easily mislead us. Is the Tylenol episode the real story of responsible leadership at Johnson & Johnson during the 1980s? What was everyone else in the company doing during this period? Were there thousands of managers, supervisors, and other employees just cranking out Tylenol capsules, Band-Aids, and the other products – all the while enjoying a nice moral holiday?

The answer to this question is clearly no. Like people in organizations everywhere, they were dealing with the difficult everyday challenges of life and work: making sure the products they sold were safe, helping coworkers with personal problems, developing new drugs and medical devices, and making sure their employees were treated with fairness and respect. The "non-heroes" at Johnson & Johnson did all this without the resources and support available to the company's executives, and they did these things day after day and year after year. In the grand scheme of things, their cumulative effort made the world a much better place. In fact, from Schweitzer's perspective, their efforts *were* the grand scheme of things.

To understand and learn from what these men and women did, we have to take Schweitzer's perspective to heart. This means looking away from the great figures, extreme situations, and moments of historical drama and paying closer attention to people around us. If we look at leadership with a wide-angle lens, we can see men and women who are far from heroes and yet are successfully solving important problems and contributing to a better world.

Messy, everyday challenges

This broader perspective reveals that the vast majority of problems calling for leadership are everyday situations. These situations don't come labelled as strategic or critical, and they aren't reserved for people at the top of organizations. Anyone can face these challenges at almost any time. Hard choices don't involve "time out" from everyday life, but are embedded in its very fabric.

Imagine, for example, that you could hover over a town, lift the roofs off houses, offices, and other buildings, and watch what is going on inside. In one home, a couple is arguing about moving the man's father into a nursing home. In an office, two government officials are talking quietly about investigating a long-serving employee rumored to be pilfering funds. The head of a hospital emergency room stares at a spreadsheet, wondering if she can avoid imminent reductions in the number of indigent patients her unit treats. A loan officer at a bank has just discovered a serious accounting error: Should he report it and create an organizational mess or just leave things alone?

These are everyday practical problems, routine and unremarkable – or at least, that is how they look at first. But a closer inspection reveals something else. Ostensibly ordinary problems can be incredibly messy, complicated, ambiguous – and important. As such, they are real leadership challenges.

Take the case of the loan officer. What could be more mundane, even tedious, than an accounting problem? But once the loan officer stopped and looked carefully at the issue, he found there was nothing simple about it. Why, for example, has such a large problem been overlooked for so long? One dismaying possibility was that senior management had buried the error and wanted it to stay that way. Bringing the problem to light could cost a colleague his job and cause one of the bank's clients to go bankrupt. But concealing the problem would be a violation of the law and the loan officer's sense of professionalism and integrity. In this case and many others, the "everydayness" of problems disguises their real complexity.

The loan officer, like men and women in organizations everywhere, was dealing with just one of a multitude of difficult, commonplace challenges. What do you do, for example, when you don't have time or the resources to do what you really believe you should do? What if doing the right thing involves bending or breaking the rules? What if a situation is so murky and uncertain you don't even know what the right thing is? What if someone with a lot of power is pressuring you to do something wrong? Questions like these define the complex territory of responsible, everyday leadership.

The loan officer did the right thing – but in ways that don't fit the heroic model. He found a way to disclose the problem, got the loan restructured, protected his colleague's job, and avoided risking his own. He accomplished this without doing anything dramatic or heroic. Instead, he followed many of the guidelines presented here. His efforts were cautious and well planned, he moved shrewdly and kept his political antennae fully extended, and he bent some of the bank's rules in the process of doing what was right. In short, he resolved his problem through a distinctive, unorthodox, and extremely useful way of thinking and acting.

Surprising approaches

My understanding of this approach to leadership emerged after I carefully examined scores of situations in which someone, typically a manager in an organization, faced a difficult ethical challenge and resolved it in a practical, responsible way. I found that in these situations, individuals rarely took bold, courageous steps. They did not articulate values and inspire a large number of other people to follow them. They had little interest in self-sacrifice. Often, they weren't even sure how to get a handle on the problem in front of them.

As individuals, these men and women were modest and unassuming, skeptical or shrewdly realistic, and had a healthy sense of their own self-interest. They weren't charismatic, had little power, and didn't see themselves as leaders in the conventional sense. Their idea of taking action was working behind the scenes – patiently, carefully, and prudently.

In the end, they did the right thing or at least got it done. They handled difficult choices and tough situations in ways that made the world a better place. The basic guidelines they employed can be summarized briefly. The first principle advises people facing difficult problems not to kid themselves about how well they understand the situation or how much they can control. A second principle recommends trusting mixed motives, as in difficult situations people should expect their motives to be mixed and even confused.

The other guidelines follow very pragmatic aspects. Count your political capital and spend it carefully. If your situation is uncertain or hazardous, find a way to buy time before you do anything. Use the time not to moralize or preach, but to drill down into the technical and political aspects of your situation. Search hard for imaginative ways to bend the rules. Instead of moving aggressively to solve a problem, try to nudge, test, and escalate gradually. Finally, don't dismiss compromise solutions – quiet leaders see the crafting of creative compromises as an invaluable practical art and the essence of responsible leadership.

Although the guidelines can be stated simply, using them well is a tricky business. For one thing, they can be misinterpreted and misused. Bending the rules can shade into breaking them. Some compromises are nothing more than unimaginative exercises in splitting the difference, while others are sell-outs of basic principles. Each of the guidelines for quiet leadership is a two-edged sword, and all of them can become excuses for doing nothing or taking sleazy shortcuts. Hence, each guideline has to be understood fully and examined carefully.

The guidelines can be misleading if they are viewed as the right way to deal with *all* really hard organizational problems. There are times when the right course of action is clear, when compromises betray important values, and when leadership means taking a stand and paying a price. Quiet leaders understand that some situations require direct, forceful, courageous action, and a few even call for heroism. Hence, it is critical to have a sense of when and how these tools should be used and to understand their limits and risks.

In general, however, quiet leaders see their approach as the most useful way to deal with the difficult problems that come their way. They view strong measures and heroism as a last resort, not the first choice or the standard model. This is why Navy fliers, the brave men and women who land streaking jets on aircraft carriers, are told in training that "there are no old, bold pilots." In other words, preparation, caution, care, and attention to detail are usually the best approach to everyday challenges.

There are no little things

But what do these patient, unglamorous, everyday efforts add up to? The answer is they are almost everything. The vast majority of difficult, important human problems – both inside and outside organizations – are not solved by a swift, decisive stroke from someone at the top. What usually matters are careful, thoughtful, small practical efforts by people working far from the limelight. In short, quiet leadership is what moves and changes the world.

This conclusion is both important and easy to dismiss. From the time we are very young, we learn to admire great leaders, the men and women whose vision, courage, and sacrifice have made our world a much better place. But thinking only about great figures and bold, historic acts can make it hard to understand why quiet, everyday leadership matters as much as it does.

Sometimes small efforts are snowballs that roll down hills and accumulate force. Sometimes, in situations poised on the knife's edge, they tip things in the right direction. Sometimes ostensibly small acts influence other people months or even years later by taking root in their experience, gestating, and shaping their development. And, even when larger consequences do not flow from small acts, these acts matter simply because they are right. Bruce Barton, a remarkable business executive who founded a major ad agency, served in Congress, and wrote widely about religion, observed,

Sometimes, when I consider what tremendous consequences come from little things – a chance word, a tap on the shoulder, or a penny dropped on a newsstand – I am tempted to think there are no little things.

Don't kid yourself

Quiet leaders are realists. They try hard to see the world as it is. This means recognizing, almost as a sixth sense, that all sorts of things can happen and often do. And they happen because people act for all sorts of reasons, virtuous and vicious, clear and muddle-headed, sensible and nutty. Realism, in other words, isn't pessimism or cynicism. It is making ample room for the many ways in which people and events can surprise, dismay, and astonish.

Sometimes things turn out worse than expected and simple-looking problems turn out to be treacherous and complicated. This is why quiet leaders move carefully, put together contingency plans, and watch their backs. Sometimes things turn out much better than expected, so they are ready to seize opportunities. And, quite often, things simply turn out very differently from what anyone expects. Then they are ready to scramble and maneuver.

Quiet leaders see the world as a kaleidoscope rather than a fixed target or a well-mapped terrain. In most organizations, most of the time, self-interest, shortsightedness, and chicanery are tumbling together with shards of loyalty, commitment, perseverance, and integrity. The churning is continuous – propelled by the dynamism of the modern economy, the restlessness and vibrancy of contemporary life, and the age-old drivers of human nature.

Hence, quiet leaders value trust, but they don't forget how fragile it can be. While they aren't cynics, they don't overestimate the idealism of other people – or their own. They are acutely aware of the limits and subtleties of power, even for people with impressive job titles. And quiet leaders don't forget that the world is divided between powerful insiders, vigilantly guarding their interests, and ambitious outsiders, vying to reach the inner circle. These are among the many reasons why they move step by step to deal with serious problems.

Trust mixed motives

Why do some men and women take action when the safe and sensible thing is to get out of the line of fire? The answer is that sometimes people find they can't walk away from a person or a situation. Something engages them. And then they go to work, resolutely and creatively, and they persevere, despite inconveniences, uncertainties, long hours, and professional hazards.

Altruism is a natural but potentially misleading way to explain these efforts. A common view is that leaders are people who willingly sacrifice their comfort and convenience for the benefit of others. In the New Testament, for example, St. John sets out a heroic ideal of self-sacrifice: "Greater love hath no man than this, that a man lay down his life for his friends."

Stories of heroic self-sacrifice are deeply inspiring. They show us the heights the human spirit can sometimes reach and work as antidote to self-pity, selfishness, and the natural tendency to inflate one's efforts and contributions. In reality, however, very few people are willing to become martyrs or risk everything for a cause – which is precisely why we praise and revere the handful of people who do so, calling them saints or heroes. The rest of us have basic instincts that are less noble and more complex. Many people care, sometimes very strongly, what happens to other people and to their organizations, but many care also about themselves. Self-interest and altruism run together in their veins. Hillel the Elder, the great Jewish scholar and teacher, suggested the complexity of their motives when he asked, "If I am not for myself, who will be for me? If I am only for myself, what am I?"

Conventional stories of leadership stress the purity of leaders' motives, their unfaltering dedication to high aims and noble causes, and their willingness to challenge the system. At best, these stories provide inspiration and guidance. At worst, they offer greeting-card sentimentality in place of realism about why people do what they do. They also tell people with mixed and complicated motives that they may be too selfish, divided, or confused to be "real" leaders.

The philosophy of quiet leadership offers a very different perspective. It starts by acknowledging that leaders' motives are almost always, in Nietzsche's phrase, "human, all too human." It also holds that, when quiet leaders succeed, it is usually *because* of their mixed and complicated motives, not despite them. In other words, people who embrace complexity, in the world around them and inside themselves, are more likely to succeed at difficult everyday challenges than individuals who try to airbrush away these stubborn realities.

Buy a little time

When faced with a challenge, effective leaders rarely rush forward with "The Answer." Instead, they do something quite at odds with the conventional view of leadership. Instead of charging the hill, they often look for ways to beg, borrow, and steal a little time. This tactic can make the difference between success and failure. Time lets turbulent waters settle and clarify. It lets people discuss their situations with each other and think things through on their own. Time gives people a chance to assess their real obligations, and gives sound instincts a chance to emerge. It lets them observe and learn, understand some of the subtle ways in which individuals and events interact, and look for patterns and opportunities in the flow of events.

There are of course situations in which time just isn't available. Also sometimes stalling only delays the inevitable. Sometimes it reveals weakness in a leader, rather than prudence and responsibility. If bosses play these games, others may do the same, making the organizations more bureaucratic and political, and, while these games are quite common, some of them involve deception and subterfuge. Because quiet leaders are realists, they understand all this. But, as realists, they also know that they sometimes don't have a choice. In other words, they have to get their hands dirty.

This is why quiet leaders use the time they have and buy more time when they need it. In a world that sometimes moves in nanoseconds, there often isn't much time available, but that makes scarce moments even more valuable. And once quiet leaders have secured a little breathing room, they go to work – with restraint, modesty, and patience.

Invest wisely

In fact, quiet leaders are exceedingly careful how they invest their time, energy, and effort. They think more like investment bankers than would-be heroes. Before they charge a hill, they measure it carefully. Before they get involved in risky, uncertain efforts, leaders do something surprising: they check to see just how much "capital" they have. What they are checking up on, however, isn't cash, but something more complicated and important – political capital.

This elusive entity consists mainly of a person's reputation and relationships at work. As such, it is invisible and intangible. In other words, political capital consists mostly of perceptions in the minds of other people. While no one can actually count it or put it in a vault, political capital is the hard currency of organizational life. And, when quiet leaders take action on a difficult problem, they pay close attention to how much of it they are risking and the likely returns on their investment.

Drill down

Something important is missing from most stories of heroic leadership. Its absence simplifies these accounts and makes them more vivid and powerful, but it does so at the cost of realism and relevance.

The missing factor is the technological and bureaucratic complexity that pervades life and work today.

All around us, life and work today are rapidly subdividing, like amoeba, into ever more specialized spheres of complexity. Even dogs are now specialists: some sniff out drugs, others help the blind or deaf, others provide seizure alert or detect accelerants in arson investigations. Because of these developments, people working in organizations of all kinds often face problems enmeshed in technological, legal, and bureaucratic complexities. Sometimes they can turn to an expert for help, but often the problem is theirs. They have to figure out what to do. When this happens, stories of heroic endeavor are of little use. The basic need isn't to summon courage, moral vision, or the corporate credo, it is to understand what is *really* going on.

Quiet leaders know that moral commitment and high principles are no substitute for immersion in the complexities of a particular situation. When quiet leaders face a problem entwined with complexities, they work patiently and persistently to get a grasp of what they know, what they need to learn, and whose help they require. These efforts to learn are not a prelude to responsible leadership – they are its essence. The alternative approach – some well-intentioned combination of moral fervor and amateurism – usually leads nowhere.

Bend the rules

Bending the rules isn't something we associate with responsible leadership. If anything, it's what politicians do, or devious lawyers, or kids trying to get around a curfew. Real leaders, according to the conventional view, obey the law and play by the rules – because they see it as their duty and it sets the right example. They know when leaders fiddle with the rules, others do the same.

Yet things are often more complicated. Consider, for example, telling the truth. This is something we are all supposed to do, but we also recognize exceptions to this rule. Some are trivial: You may decide not to tell a friend what you *really* think of her new scarf. Other exceptions are profound: During the Second World War, some families in Europe hid Jews from the Nazis and lied about it. Between the trivial and the profound cases are countless everyday situations in which strict adherence to the rules may do more harm than good. The basic problem is that no one is smart enough to throw a net of rules over all the possibilities – the world is simply too varied and fluid, too ambiguous and uncertain. Quiet leaders respond to these ambiguous situations in a particular way. They are reluctant, for a variety of good reasons, to break the rules, but they don't want to obey them mechanically and cause harm. So they look, imaginatively and creatively, for ways to bend the rules, they seize the opportunity and use it to uphold their values and commitments.

But bending the rules is a tricky business that involves walking some very fine lines. Quiet leaders do not bend the rules casually, nor do they view cleverness and maneuvering as ideal ways to deal with problems. But sometimes the complexities of situations give them no choice. Drilling down doesn't produce an answer, and they can't buy more time. So they look for ways to bend the rules without breaking them. Their aim is not to avoid responsibilities, but to find a practical, workable way to meet all of their responsibilities.

Nudge, test, and escalate gradually

Despite careful efforts – such as drilling down or checking how much political capital they have – their strong commitment to do something rather than walk away leads them into situations where the path ahead is far from clear. They can't plan or look the answers up in a book. They have no choice but to improvise. This means finding ways to nudge, test, and carefully escalate their efforts. Their aim is not to solve problems with a brilliant insight, inspiring words, or a decisive act. Instead of trying to crack the case, they look for ways to work the problem. In fluid situations with many contingencies, the challenge often isn't hitting the target but locating it. In these circumstances, successful leadership depends on learning, and learning involves taking the right small steps. By testing, probing, and experimenting, quiet leaders gradually get a sense of the flow of events, hazards to be avoided, and opportunities they can exploit. Instead of a problem–solution paradigm, they rely on an act–learn–act–learn approach.

Craft a compromise

When principles are at stake, compromise is morally suspect. It smacks of mutual back scratching and the transactions of politicians and lobbyists in smoked-filled rooms. The ethical problem with compromise is that it seems to be basically a matter of splitting the difference. This may be fine for many activities but not for basic values. Quiet leaders accept this of fundamental moral principles, but they don't find it particularly useful in most situations. They view compromises in a different light. They regard them as challenges and look for opportunities in the flow of events. They buy time and invest their political capital wisely. In short, they follow a mix of practical and theoretical guidelines in order to craft compromises that express and defend the values they hold dear. When they succeed, they are practicing leadership in its best form.

Three quiet virtues

Quiet leadership is, in part, a set of tools, a collection of useful tactics. But this creates a serious risk. What if these tools end up in the wrong hands? There is an additional crucial element to quiet leadership which goes beyond mere "tactics." It is a matter of character. Quiet leaders are men and women who rely heavily on three unglamorous virtues: restraint, modesty, and tenacity. Each of these is a habit of mind and action, and each helps men and women use the tools and tactics of quiet leadership in responsible, effective ways. Notice that these are quiet, everyday virtues. None is readily associated with heroic leadership. There is no mention of undaunted courage, charismatic personality, willingness to sacrifice everything, noble passions, or unwavering commitment to a cause. If anything the virtues of restraint, modesty, and tenacity seem all too ordinary. But this is, in fact, the source of their value. They are accessible virtues. They are familiar, natural, sensible ways of thinking and acting. As a result, almost anyone can practice and cultivate the simple virtues of quiet leadership. They aren't reserved for special people or extraordinary events.

23 | *Everyone a changemaker: social entrepreneurship's ultimate goal*

WILLIAM DRAYTON[1]

Rodrigo Baggio grew up in Rio de Janeiro loving computers. As he matured into an extraordinarily tall, thin man with a hugely wide smile, he became a computer consultant. However, from early on, he was one of the few in his generation who noticed – with concern – that the young people growing up in the favelas on the hills overlooking his middle-class neighborhood had no access to this digital world.

Because he has the great entrepreneur's tenacity of observation and thought as well as action, he decided he had to take on the digital divide – well before the phrase came into currency – and he has been pursuing this vision relentlessly ever since. While beginning to work toward this dream as a teenager, he learned just how motivated and capable of learning the young people in the favelas were. And also how competent the favela community was in organizing. This respect underlies the central insight that has allowed Rodrigo to have a growing multi-continental impact.

Rodrigo provides only what the community cannot: typically computers, software, and training. The community does the organizing, finding space, recruiting the students and faculty, and providing ongoing administration. The result is a uniquely economical model, and also one where, because the investment strengthens the broader community, it is self-sustaining and a foundation for other initiatives long into the future. Rodrigo's chain of hundreds of community-based computer training schools now serves hundreds of slums across Latin America and Asia. These schools now have 700,000 graduates.

I got a sense of Rodrigo's power when he came to Washington shortly after being elected an Ashoka Fellow. Somehow he convinced

---

[1] Excerpted with permission from: William Drayton. 2006. "Everyone a Changemaker: Social Entrepreneurship's Ultimate Goal," *Innovations* 1(1): 80–96.

the Inter-American Development Bank to give him its used (but highly valuable) computers. Somehow he convinced the Brazilian Air Force first to warehouse and then to fly these computers home. And then he somehow managed to persuade the Brazilian customs authority to allow all these computers in at a time when Brazil was trying to block computer imports. That is how entrepreneurs work. Having decided that the world must change in some important way, they simply find and build highways that lead inexorably to that result. Where others see barriers, they delight in finding solutions and in turning them into society's new and concrete patterns.

That much is easy to observe. However, there is more to it. Somehow, an unknown, young, lanky Rodrigo, the head of a new and unknown citizen organization, persuaded the managers of one after another of society's big institutions to do things they never would have imagined. He knew they were the right and logical things to do. Somehow they sensed that inner confidence and found it surprisingly persuasive. What were they sensing? Rodrigo's words and arguments no doubt helped, but few people are willing to step out beyond the safely conventional merely on the basis of good arguments. Rodrigo was persuasive because his listeners sensed something deeper. What Rodrigo was proposing was not just an idea, but the central logic of his life – as it is for every great entrepreneur. He mastered and came to love the new digital world from the time he was a young boy. More important, his values from early on drove him to care about the poverty and inequality he could see on the hillsides rising behind the middle-class Rio in which he was growing up. His values and his temperament had him taking on the digital divide before the term was invented.

As a result, when Rodrigo sat across the table from the much older, powerful officials he needed to move, they were confronting not just a good idea, but deeply rooted and life-defining values: non-egoistic, kindly determination and commitment. This values-based faith is the ultimate power of the first-class entrepreneur. It is a quality others sense and trust, whether or not they really fully grasp the idea intellectually. Even though they would not normally want to step out in front of the crowd, a quiet voice tells them to trust Rodrigo and go with his vision.

Any assessment of Rodrigo's impact that stopped with his idea, let alone his business plan, would not have penetrated to the core of his power. Our field has been impoverished by too many assessments that never get to the essence. Nor is Rodrigo's most important impact his schools or the life-changing independence and mastery he provides his students. Consider the impact Rodrigo has on a community when he introduces his program. It is not a school created by the government or outsiders. It is a school created by, funded by, managed by, and staffed by people in the community. The students are responsible for learning and then making their way. Think how many patterns and stereotypes are crumpled by these simple and very obvious facts. The psychological impact is a bit like India emerging from fifty years of falling behind to suddenly be recognized as the new challenger at the cutting edge of the most advanced part of the world's economy.

Accompanying this disruption of old patterns of action and perception is another contribution, and I believe it is Rodrigo's and every entrepreneur's greatest one: the idea of catalyzing new local changemakers into being. Unless the entrepreneur can get someone in one community after another to step forward and seize his or her idea, the entrepreneur will never achieve the spread that is essential to his or her life success. Consequently, the entrepreneur presents his or her idea to the local community in the most enticing, safe, understandable, and user-friendly ways possible.

Of course, the entrepreneur's own life story is in itself a beacon encouraging hundreds of others to care and to take initiative. This also increases the number of local changemakers. Moreover, when these local champions then build the teams they need to launch the idea they have adopted, they are providing not only encouragement but also training to potential next-generation local changemakers.

As the field of social entrepreneurship has grown and multiplied and wired itself together across the globe over the last twenty-five years, the rate of this plowing and seeding at the local level has accelerated dramatically. Ten years ago, the probability of an idea from Bangladesh affecting a community in Brazil, Poland, or the US was very limited. Now it is common (the best-known example being Muhammad Yunus' impact on the global spread of micro-credit) and becoming more common every year.

As the number of leading pattern-changing social entrepreneurs has been increasing everywhere, and as the geographic reach of their ideas has been expanding ever more rapidly, the rate of plowing and seeding therefore has multiplied. As have the number of local changemakers.

This whole process is enormously contagious. As the number of large-scale entrepreneurs and local changemakers multiplies, so does the number of support institutions, all of them making the next generation of entrepreneuring and changemaking easier. Not only do people not resist, but in fact, they respond readily to this change. Who wants to be an object when they could be changemakers, when they could live lives far more creative and contributory and therefore respected and valued? As important as Rodrigo's impact is on the digital divide and on the lives and communities he serves, I believe this second dimension of his impact is far more important – especially at this transitional moment in history.

The most important contribution any of us can make now is not to solve any particular problem, no matter how urgent energy or environment or financial regulation is. What we must do now is increase the proportion of humans who know that they can cause change. And who, like smart white blood cells coursing through society, will stop with pleasure whenever they see that something is stuck or that an opportunity is ripe to be seized. Multiplying society's capacity to adapt and change intelligently and constructively, and building the necessary underlying collaborative architecture, is the world's most critical opportunity now. Pattern-changing leading social entrepreneurs are the most critical single factor in catalyzing and engineering this transformation.[2]

Everyone a changemaker

The agricultural revolution produced only a small surplus, so only a small elite could move into the towns to create culture and conscious history. This pattern has persisted ever since: only a few have held the monopoly on initiative because they alone have had the social tools. That is one reason that per capita income in the West remained flat from the fall of the Roman empire until about 1700. By 1700, however, a new, more open architecture was beginning to develop in

[2] As Ashoka has come to understand this more clearly, it has clarified its ultimate goal. Challenged several years ago by eBay's Pierre Omidyar, Ashoka came to understand, given its understanding of these historical forces it came into being to serve, that its ultimate goal is an "everyone a changemaker" world. Before that, it had talked chiefly in terms of the intermediate goal of building an entrepreneurial/competitive citizen sector.

northern Europe: entrepreneurial/competitive business facilitated by more tolerant, open politics. The new business model rewarded people who would step up with better ideas and implement them, igniting a relentlessly expanding cycle of entrepreneurial innovation leading to productivity gains, leading to ever more entrepreneurs, successful innovation, and productivity gains. One result: the West broke out from 1,200 years of stagnation and soon soared past anything the world had seen before. Average per capita income rose 20 percent in the 1700s, 200 percent in the 1800s, and 740 percent in the last century.[3] The press reported the wars and other follies, but for the last 300 years this profound innovation in how humans organize themselves has been the defining, decisive historical force at work.

However, until 1980, this transformation bypassed the social half of the world's operations.[4] Society taxed the new wealth created by business to pay for its roads and canals, schools and welfare systems. There was no need to change. Moreover, no monopoly, public or private, welcomes competition, because it is very likely to lose. Thus, the social sector had little felt need to change and a paymaster that actively discouraged it. Hence, the squalor of the social sector. Relative performance declining at an accelerating rate. And consequent low repute, dismal pay, and poor self-esteem and élan.

By the nineteenth century, a few modern social entrepreneurs began to appear. The antislavery leagues and Florence Nightingale are outstanding examples. But they remained islands. It was only around

---

[3] Interview with economist Will Baumol in his office. See also, Baumol, William J. 2002. *The Free-Market Innovation Machine*. Princeton University Press.
[4] The "social" or "citizen" half of the world's operations includes education (students, faculty, organizations), health, environment, emergency relief, rural and slum development, human rights of all sorts, and all the other areas of human and environmental needs – except when these needs are served by the business other half. Eventually the distinction will fade as the accidental division created over the last three centuries of rapid business productivity growth and social-sector stasis erodes. Ashoka and a growing number of other citizen-sector organizations ask that everyone stop defining us as not government (NGO) and not business ("nonprofit"), respectively, the European and American initial reactions to our newly emerging sector. It does not make sense to define half of society by what it is not. We suggest the use of "citizen sector" and "citizen organization" instead. One or more citizens caring and organizing to provide a service or spark a change are the active ingredients. And, as this chapter articulates, our most important impact is our "everyone a changemaker" – aka citizen – role.

1980 that the ice began to crack and the social arena as a whole made the structural leap to this new entrepreneurial competitive architecture.[5] However, once the ice broke, catch-up change came in a rush. And it did so pretty much all across the world, the chief exceptions being areas where governments were afraid.

Because it has the advantage of not having to be the pioneer, but rather of following business, this second great transformation has been able steadily to compound productivity growth at a very fast rate. In this it resembles successful developing countries like Thailand. Ashoka's best estimate is that the citizen sector is halving the gap between its productivity level and that of business every ten to twelve years.

This rapidly rising productivity means that the cost of the goods and services produced by the citizen sector is falling relative to those produced by business – reversing the pricing pattern of the last centuries that led to the much-criticized "consumer" culture. As a result, as resources flow into the citizen sector, it is growing explosively. It is generating jobs two and a half to three times as fast as business. There are now millions of modern, competing citizen groups, including big, sophisticated second-generation organizations, in each of the four main areas where the field has emerged most vigorously: Brazil-focused South America, Mexico/the US/Canada, Europe, and South and Southeast Asia. (The field is also growing vigorously in Africa, the Middle East, East Asia, and Australia/New Zealand, but these are much smaller clusters.) All this, of course, has dramatically altered the field's élan and attractiveness. This is where the job growth is, not to mention the most challenging, value-rooted, and increasingly even well-paid jobs. Just listen to today's "business" school students.

Given the results-based power of this transformation of the citizen sector, more and more local changemakers are emerging. Some of these learn and later expand the pool of leading social entrepreneurs. To the degree they succeed locally, they give wings to the entrepreneur whose idea they have taken up, they encourage neighbors also to become changemakers, and they cumulatively build the institutions and attitudes that make local changemaking progressively easier and more respected. All of which eases the tasks facing the next generation

---

[5] Ashoka was conceived in the 1960s to serve this historic transformation, but it only began work in 1980, when it perceived that the time was ripe.

of primary pattern-change entrepreneurs. This virtuous cycle cata-
lyzed by leading social entrepreneurs and local changemakers is the
chief engine now moving the world toward an "everyone a
changemaker" future.

No matter how powerful this dynamic is, however, several other
changes are necessary if society is to navigate this transition successfully:

- Most important, society cannot significantly increase the proportion of adults who are, and know they are, changemakers and who
  have mastered the necessary and complex underlying social skills
  until it changes the way all young people live.
- Although it is normal for support areas like finance to lag behind
  change in the operating areas they serve, the emergent citizen sector
  is now at significant risk unless it can quickly engineer major
  structural changes in both its institutional finance sector and the
  broad grassroots sources of support in its post-breakeven zone.

Transforming the youth years

There are well over 500 Ashoka leading social entrepreneurs (roughly
a quarter of the total), whose primary goal is getting society to do a far
better job of helping all children and young people to learn and grow
up successfully. Each has a powerful, proven, society-wide approach.
(Between 49 percent and 60 percent of those elected by Ashoka have
changed national policy within five years of their startup-stage
election.)

However, each of these approaches is a partial answer. It is built
around one insight or principle, works through one delivery system,
and addresses one or two client groups. Ashoka's "mosaic" process
brings all these powerful elements together, draws out the few universal principles that open major new strategic opportunities for the
key decision-makers in a field (e.g. in this case, those who run schools
and youth programs), and then markets these principles. In effect,
these mosaic collaborations promise our community the ability to be
entrepreneurs together, an advance that produces a far bigger impact
than anything the sum of our solo ventures could achieve.

Roughly two-thirds of these 500-plus youth-focused Ashoka entrepreneurs have learned the same three powerful principles. Because they

need human resources to implement their vision and cannot realistically get more teachers, they turn to young people. That young people are a huge, and in fact usually the only significant available human resource is the first insight. The other two follow logically: first, the unconventional assumption that young people are or can be competent; and second, the idea that one must transform youth communities (e.g. in schools) so that they become competent at initiating and organizing, and then train and reward their young people in these skills. Applying these three principles in hundreds of different ways and across the globe produces strikingly similar and powerful results: motivated students, better academic results, and young people who are experiencing being in charge. And a very different feel to those schools and programs from the moment one walks in.

Whether these social entrepreneurs discovered and developed these principles to solve their staffing problems and/or with broader educational purpose, collectively they have created a most powerful set of tools to transform the youth years. Moreover, the repeated success they have had in large-scale and highly diverse applications of these principles leaves one with enormous confidence in the power and practicability of these principles.

Ashoka's young people's mosaic also identified another principle that fits closely with this first cluster: anyone (or any group) who does not master the complex social skill of guiding his or her behavior through applied empathy will be marginalized. Since this is the enormously cruel, destructive state of perhaps 30 percent of the world's people, helping young people master empathy is proportionately important.[6] One of the best ways of doing so is by encouraging them to build teams to contribute important changes and/or services. If their team is to succeed, they must master teamwork, which in turn rests on applied empathy.

If young people do not grow up being powerful, causing change, and practicing these three interlocked underlying skills, they will reach adulthood with a self-definition that does not include changemaking and a social skill set that largely precludes it. Just as one must develop

---

[6] Canadian Ashoka Fellow, Mary Gordon and her Roots of Empathy program is one example of the innovation building in this area. See Gordon, Mary. 2005. *Roots of Empathy: Changing the World Child by Child*. Markham, Ontario: Thomas Allen Publishers.

strong emotional foundations in the first three years of life or suffer for a lifetime, young people must master and practice these social skills and the high art of being powerful in and through society while they are young.

The children of elite families grow up at home and usually in school being expected to take initiative and being rewarded for doing so. This confident ability to master new situations and initiate whatever changes or actions are needed is in essence what defines the elite. Entering adult life with confidence and mastery of empathy/teamwork/ leadership skills is what has ultimately given this small group control of the initiative and therefore of power and resources for millennia.

However, the other 97 percent grow up getting very little such experience with taking initiative. Adults control the classroom, work setting, and even sports and extra-curricular activities. And this situation, coupled with society's attitudes, drums home the message to this majority: "You're not competent or perhaps even responsible. Please don't try to start things; we can do it far better." Teachers, social workers, and others are comfortably in control; and, in fact, most school and other youth cultures are not competent and do not train, support and respect initiative-taking. Instead, the peer group culture, not surprisingly, is resentful and in the worst cultures, quite negative.

Do these inarticulate, frustrated youth cultures bring analogous prior situations to mind? Over the last century, many other groups – including women, African Americans, those with disabilities, even colonial peoples – had to make their way from debilitating stereotypes and little prior practice in taking the initiative to becoming fully accepted, capable contributors. These groups, although very different from one another, had to travel strongly similar human and community transformation paths.

Young people are the last big group to set out on this journey. They are also different; but, in the underlying psychological and organizational transitions ahead, they can learn a great deal from the experience of these other groups.

The Ashoka community is now well into the launch of a global "civil rights" or "women's" movement for young people. Its four levels of leverage reinforce one another powerfully. Every young person it helps to transform his or her idea – be it a tutoring service or a virtual radio station, into a team and then an ongoing reality – knows they are powerful. They will be changemakers and role models for life. Each such team typically has roughly twenty-five other young people doing the tutoring or coaching – and they are all practicing empathy and teamwork and also getting the idea they can lead.

Once a school gets four or six such powerful peer groups, the overall youth culture can readily switch from resentful/passive and not competent to energized/initiatory. All this leads to engaging society in seeing the need to change the youth years worldwide.

Needed: new social financial services

Citizen organizations of all types and sizes urgently need a new social financial services system. Where can two fifteen-year-old African American girls go when they need $900 seed funding to launch a teen-to-teen late-afternoon confidential telephone hotline? Or a fourteen-year-old who needs $800 startup and working capital to buy T-shirts to imprint and sell in order to fund an Ecuadorian support group of young people with diabetes? Or a group of boys who need funds to seed what eventually will become a successful effort to build a municipal skateboard park?[7]

They cannot go to a foundation or a government agency. They typically cannot even open their own bank account. What if their parents cannot or will not pay? Or if it is important to the young people to do it on their own (so they can do it their way)?

As we have just seen, society's core interests are in making it easy, not impossible, for young people to take initiative and build ongoing services. But our existing financial services institutions fail us. This is only one of many such failures of today's social financial institutions. Social entrepreneurs need social investors who will value new ideas. The most important innovations cut across the disciplinary and organizational boundaries created to solve old problems. Governments are bound by narrow, rigidly and impermeably bounded "stovepipes" defined by legislation and refined ever more narrowly by the organizations and regulations that follow. Foundations are captive to internally formulated "strategies," their institutional stovepipes, and staffs who typically follow specialist lateral career paths. Moreover, a program officer confronting a crosscutting idea will have to learn

---

[7] These are typical of the sort of venture Youth Venture has found among teens in the US.

more, think harder, and consult and share decision-making much more than when facing a familiar idea that neatly fits his or her program. (Can you imagine what would have happened to the digital revolution if its entrepreneurs had to fit similar strategy/stovepipe straitjackets created by Deutsche Bank or Bank of America?)

Social entrepreneurs need and deserve loyalty. Their work is not a job; it is their life. And they are, day by day and year after year, central to the iterative process of creation that is the essence of the value being built. But making and sustaining the commitments that would constitute loyal partnering requires judgment, very-long-term perspective, and true understanding of entrepreneurship – all of which are difficult for large institutions to muster. Social entrepreneurs need medium- to long-term and often substantial investments. They must test and refine an idea (an inherently unpredictable process), learn how to market it and cause many other institutions to change (also resistant to tight scheduling), and then build an institution and movement. Almost all governments and foundations, guided by their own internal one-year budgeting imperatives, provide one-year funding. Social entrepreneurs need support in building strong, major institutions; governments and foundations avoid the "overhead" this would entail.

There are further systemic reasons why governments and foundations fail the citizen sector. Their structure keeps them from seeing and often from serving whole classes of potential clients well. Moreover, because they are not subject to competitive discipline, they do a poor job of rewarding high performing citizen groups and closing or merging poorly run ones. Society's resources are, consequently, allocated poorly. Worse, the citizen sector cannot become as productive as business as long as this undisciplined condition continues. If the incumbent institutions seem unlikely to transform themselves to provide the types of services a rapidly evolving and increasingly diverse citizen sector now needs so urgently, where can the sector look? To the enormous, highly competitive, client-focused for-profit financial industry it provides business a kaleidoscopic diversity of services that are minutely fitted to client needs and that change, if anything, faster than the clients.

The first for-profit financial firms that recognize that there is a huge, highly attractive new business waiting to be born here and that open it up will profit handsomely – and make a profound contribution. There are many factors coming together now that make such a move timely.

The citizen sector is now both very large and the fastest growing sector of society. It also has many large, solid institutions. At the same time, there is huge existing, and more latent, demand for quality social investments, with varying mixes of social and economic return and in different subject-matter and geographic areas. There also is huge actual and latent demand for engagement in the social sector. People want access to quality personal opportunities ranging from volunteering and internships to full careers for themselves and their families and friends. They also want to spot and land the new business/social opportunities that are now developing. A smart bank will develop a web of products and services that will allow its bankers to serve every investor client's individual needs with a tailored package of varying mixes of financial, social, and engagement values.

The transaction costs of government and foundation grant-making, taking into account only the direct (not opportunity) costs to donor and donee, now run at 20 to 45 percent, roughly ten times what is normal for business finance.[8] This difference offers huge scope for financial firms to find efficiencies and capture some of the savings through fees.

The now huge socially responsible investment industry achieved this scale chiefly by investing in subsets of existing financial stocks and bonds that exclude objectionable (e.g. tobacco, arms) securities. The new commercial microcredit funds that have been introduced over the

---

[8] William F. Meehan III, Derek Kilmer, and Maisie O'Flanagan explain the reasons for this, in "Investing in Society," *Stanford Social Innovation Review* (Spring 2004): "For starters, [government and foundations do] not have cost-efficient transaction processes, when compared to for-profit benchmarks. In the for-profit capital market, companies spend between $2 and $4 raising capital (e.g., legal, marketing, and administrative expenses) – for every $100 they raise. In the social capital market, however, nonprofits spend between $10 and $24 for every $100 they earn through fundraising (e.g., obtaining donor lists, sending direct mail, or making phone calls). Nonprofit chief executives, meanwhile, spent between 30 and 60 percent of their time pursuing donations with such 'soft costs' unevenly accounted for in fundraising costs. Foundations and government grantors, meanwhile, spend about $12 to $19 on administration (including general overhead and reviewing grant applications) for every $100 they allocate. Federated givers, those intermediary organizations such as the United Way and Jewish Community Federation that collect individual donations and then allocate dollars to charities, spend approximately $13 million for every 100 to cover their expenses. That means that in the social capital market, the cost of raising capital consumes roughly 22 to 43 percent of the funds raised, a dreadfully inefficient process."

last few years are the first major example of the next step: the for-profit finance industry profitably providing direct investments in citizen-sector work to the broad public. They are able to do so because there are 120 to 150 large, safe, well-established microcredit lenders, with clear, stable track records, in whose securities these funds can invest large sums safely without incurring significant expense (relative to investment) in case-by-case due diligence reviews.

Although this success is enormously encouraging, it is far, far from enough. It illustrates the principle, but it cannot provide either the volume or the choice the huge latent demand needs, let alone what is required to build a substantial business for the industry overall. Therefore, a critical part of the Ashoka strategy to encourage for-profit finance firms to enter the social financial services business is to catalyze the development of many, very large, reasonably uniform and safe, and therefore securitizable, new classes of social investment. The single most important source of these new investment opportunities flows from our gracefully named "business/social hybrid value-added chain" (HVAC) work.

Sketching the story of one HVAC on which Ashoka is working will help make this change more concrete. Over most of the planet small farmers do not have access to drip irrigation equipment. It is not profitable for the piping and irrigation firms to serve them. The companies' costs are too high for the poor rural economy, and the companies do not understand or trust the small farmers or their environment. In Mexico, a partnership between Amanco (the leading piping company in Latin America), Ashoka, and local citizen groups is now beginning to demonstrate how to close this gap. Over the last decade, large, competent citizen groups have developed to serve small farmers. Their cost structure is that of the "other Mexico," that of the poor and of the rural areas. They understand and have the trust of their clients. Moreover, the sector has increasingly mastered relevant skills, ranging from large-scale/low-cost organizing to knowing how to help poor people save reliably. These now large, skilled economic citizen groups can provide the missing bridge between the company and a huge untapped new market, between the farmers and access to a technology that will provide them with more income, more stable income, water conservation, and environmental benefits.

Everyone benefits enormously. The farmers earn much more, more securely. The environment benefits, and the country produces more,

more reliably. The first citizen groups to join are the only source, at least for a while, that can provide these benefits to their farmer clients. This gives them a huge competitive advantage vis-à-vis both government and other citizen groups. Moreover, they get the same markup that businesses playing similar roles receive – a huge (especially relative to their cost structure) and growing revenue flow that promises them independence from governments and foundations. Amanco will be the first into this market and should settle in long-term with a significant share, even recognizing that competitors will follow. The company has established key relationships and is quickly coming up the learning curve to mastering this new market, which is making it harder and harder for others to catch up quickly.

After demonstrating this hybrid value chain principle in a half dozen very different industries, Ashoka's focus will shift to encouraging business and social competitors to enter. Already several management consulting firms are introducing hybrid value chains to their clients as a major new practice opportunity.

Where are we going?

The daily news is chronically dispiriting, a reportage of follies that seem to be taking place in a world without a compass. That is probably so in part because this is a time when deep historical tides are moving with unprecedented speed and force. The millennium when only a tiny elite could cause change is coming to an end. A generation hence, probably 20 to 30 percent of the world's people, and later 50 to 70 percent, not just today's few percent, will be changemakers and entrepreneurs. That world will be fundamentally different and far safer, happier, more equal, and more successful place. To get there, we must end the infantalization of young people. They and the rest of us must enable all young people to be fully creative, initiatory, and powerful changemakers. We must also build the wisest possible financial and other institutions so that, as these young people become adults, the new citizen sector will draw them fully into an "everyone a changemaker" world.

24 | *Social business entrepreneurs are the solution*[1]

MUHAMMAD YUNUS

Capitalism is interpreted too narrowly

Many of the problems in the world remain unresolved because we continue to interpret capitalism too narrowly. In this narrow interpretation, we then create a one-dimensional human being to play the role of entrepreneur. We insulate him from other dimensions of life, such as the religious, the emotional, the political, and the social. He is dedicated to one mission in his business life: maximizing profit. Masses of one-dimensional human beings support him by backing him with their investment money to achieve the same mission. The free-market game, we are told, works out beautifully with one-dimensional investors and entrepreneurs. Have we been so mesmerized by the success of the free market that we don't dare to question it? Have we worked so hard at transforming ourselves absolutely into one-dimensional human beings – as conceptualized in economic theory – to facilitate the smooth functioning of the free-market mechanism?

Economic theory postulates that you contribute to society and the world in the best possible manner when you concentrate on squeezing out the maximum for yourself. Once you get your maximum, everybody else will get theirs too. As we follow this policy, we sometimes begin to doubt whether we are doing the right thing by imitating the entrepreneur created by theory. After all, things don't look too good around us. We nevertheless quickly brush off such doubts by maintaining that bad things happen as a result of "market failures" – properly functioning markets do not produce unpleasant results, do they?

I do not think things are going wrong because of "market failure." The causes lie much deeper. Let us be brave and admit that they are

---

[1] Based on a contribution to Nicholls, A. (ed.) 2006. *Social Entrepreneurship – New Models of Sustainable Change.* Oxford: Oxford University Press.

the result of "conceptualization failure." More specifically, it is the failure of economic theory to capture the essence of human beings. Everyday human beings are not one-dimensional entities; they are excitingly multi-dimensional and indeed very colorful. Their emotions, beliefs, priorities, and behavior patterns vary so greatly that they can be more aptly described by drawing an analogy with the millions of colors and shades that are produced by mixing just three basic colors in varying proportions.

Social business entrepreneurs can play a key role in the market

Let us postulate a world with two kinds of people, both one-dimensional but with different objectives: the profit-maximizing kind and the non-profit-maximization kind. The second type is totally committed to making a difference in the world; they are driven by social objectives. They want to give other people a better chance in life. They want to achieve their objectives by creating and supporting a special kind of enterprise. Such businesses may or may not earn profit, but like any other business, they must not incur losses. We could describe this new class of businesses as "non-loss" businesses.

Do we find this second type of person in the real world? Yes, we do. We are all familiar with "do-gooders." They are the people referred to as "social entrepreneurs" in formal parlance. Social entrepreneurship is in fact an integral part of human history. Most people take pleasure in helping others and all religions encourage this quality in human beings. Governments reward social entrepreneurs with tax breaks, and special legal facilities are created so that they can create legal entities to pursue their objectives.

Some social entrepreneurs use money to achieve their objectives; some just give away their time, labor, talent, and skill or make other useful contributions. Those who use money may or may not try to recover part or all of the money they invest in their work by charging a fee or a price.

Social entrepreneurs who use money can be classified into four categories:

- no cost recovery
- some cost recovery

- full cost recovery
- more than full cost recovery.

Once a social entrepreneur operates at 100 percent or beyond the cost recovery point, he has actually graduated into another world, the business world with its limitless expansion possibilities. This is a moment worth celebrating. He has overcome the gravitational force of financial dependence and is now ready for space travel! This is the critical moment of significant institutional transformation. The social entrepreneur has migrated from the world of philanthropy to the world of business. To distinguish him from the first two types of entrepreneur listed earlier, we will call him a "social business entrepreneur."

Social business entrepreneurs make the marketplace more interesting and competitive: interesting because two different kinds of objectives are now at play, creating two different sets of frameworks for price determination; competitive because there are now more players than before. These new players can be as aggressive and enterprising at achieving their goals as traditional entrepreneurs.

Social business entrepreneurs can become very powerful players in national and international economies. If we were to add the assets of all the social business entrepreneurs in the world today, the total would represent the merest fraction of the global economy. This is not because these assets lack growth potential, but because conceptually we neither recognize their existence, nor make room for them in the market. They are considered freaks and kept outside the mainstream economy. We do not pay attention to them because we are blinded by prevailing theories.

If social business entrepreneurs exist in the real world – as it seems they do – it makes no sense that they are not accommodated within current conceptual frameworks. Once we have recognized social entrepreneurs, the supportive institutions, policies, regulations, norms, and rules can be developed to help them enter the mainstream.

The neoliberal free market is often considered ill equipped to address social problems. Indeed, the market is often identified as a significant contributor to social problems such as environmental hazards, inequality, polarization of political power, health problems, unemployment, ghettoes, crime, etc. Since the market is perceived as having no capacity to solve social problems, this responsibility is handed over to the public sector. This arrangement was widely considered the only solution until command economies – such as in the former Soviet Union – were created in which the state took over everything, abolishing the free market.

But this did not last long. With command economies gone, we have returned to the artificial division of work between market and state. In this arrangement, the market is the exclusive playground of the personal gain seekers, overwhelmingly ignoring the common interest of the people and the planet. In recent years, initiatives that make profit seekers aware of social responsibilities while maintaining their profit-maximizing objective have gained momentum. These sometimes take the form of self-imposed restrictions on activities and/or of the creation of a philanthropic window with profit.

With the global economy continuing to expand year on year, personal wealth in many developed countries reaching unimaginable heights, technological innovations accelerating this trend, globalization threatening to wipe weak economies and the poor off the map economically, it is time to consider the case for social business entrepreneurs more seriously than before. Not only is it unnecessary to leave the market solely to personal gain seekers, it is extremely harmful to mankind as a whole. It is time to move away from a narrow interpretation of capitalism and broaden the concept of the market by giving full recognition to social business entrepreneurs. Once this has been done, they can make the market work as efficiently for social goals as it does for financial goals.

A social stock market

So, how do we encourage the creation of social business entrepreneurs? What are the steps that we need to take to facilitate social business entrepreneurs playing an increasingly larger role in the marketplace?

First, we must recognize social business entrepreneurs in our theory. Students must learn that there are two kinds of businesses:

- business to make money
- business to do good.

Young people must learn that they have choices to make about which kind of entrepreneur they would like to be. If we broaden the interpretation of capitalism, they will have a wider choice to mix these two basic types in proportions that suit their personal objectives.

Second, we must make social business entrepreneurs and social business investors visible in the marketplace. As long as social business entrepreneurs operate within the cultural environment of the present stock markets, they will be restricted by the existing trading norms and conditions. Social business entrepreneurs must develop their own norms, standards, measurements, evaluation criteria, and terminology. This can only be achieved if we create a separate stock market for social business enterprises and investors – a "social capital market." Investors could invest money in the causes in which they believe and in the companies that they think are achieving particular missions best. Some companies listed on this social capital market may be excellent at achieving their missions, while simultaneously making very attractive profits. Obviously, these companies will attract both social, goal-oriented investors and personal, gain-oriented investors.

Making a profit does not disqualify an enterprise from being a social business enterprise. The basic deciding factor is whether a social goal is the enterprise's overarching goal and is clearly reflected in its decision-making. There will be well-defined, stringent entry and exit criteria for a company to qualify for listing on the social capital market and, if applicable, to lose that status. Soon companies will emerge that will succeed in mixing social and personal goals. Investors must remain convinced that companies listed on the social capital market are truly social business enterprises.

To this end, I suggest several rules and guidelines. These include:

- Profit making by social business enterprises is legitimate, on condition that investors do not receive any dividends or receive only token dividends. A social business enterprise is designed and operated as a business enterprise to pass on all the benefits to its customers. It reverses the profit-maximization principle by means of the benefit-maximization principle.
- Social business enterprises should generate enough surpluses to repay the invested capital to the investors as early as possible. It is up to the investors to decide how quickly they want their money back. They may get their money back to reinvest in other social business enterprises or in traditional profit-maximizing enterprises. They may even decide to reinvest the surplus in the same social business enterprise that generated the profit.

- Social business enterprises should generate surpluses for their expansion, the improvement of quality, increased efficiency, introduction of new technology, and innovative marketing to reach the deeper low-income layers, particularly women, children, and disadvantaged communities.
- Investors will need to be clear that they are investing in a social business enterprise for a return that is much broader than an immediate gain in dollars and cents. They invest in a social business enterprise because they feel an urge to make a difference and share their lives with other people. They invest because they feel that they can contribute their creativity, innovativeness, and entrepreneurial abilities to solve complex social and economic problems and, consequently, improve the quality of people's lives – including their own. If an investor wishes to withdraw his investment from a social enterprise, he may do so by selling his shares to the existing shareholders or to a new shareholder who accepts the philosophy, practice, and conventions.

Until social stock exchanges are created, existing stock exchanges could open a window to facilitate the trading of social business enterprise stocks. All companies categorized as social business enterprises could be listed under a separate category of companies. For easy recognition of social business enterprises, each company could identify itself by adding the suffix "SBE" to its name, as in Grameen Danone Foods SBE.

My feeling is that there are many people around the world who are ready to make investments in social business enterprises if only they could reach out to them. Foundations and philanthropists may find it very attractive to invest part of their charity money in social business enterprises.

Together with the creation of a social stock market, we'll need to create rating agencies, appropriate impact assessment tools, indices to understand which social business enterprise is doing more and/or better than others, so that social investors are correctly guided. This industry will need its *Social Wall Street Journal* and *Social Financial Times* to make all the exciting stories, as well as the negative ones, and analyses known to keep social entrepreneurs and investors properly informed and forewarned.

Within business schools, we can start producing social MBAs to meet the demand of social business entrepreneurs and to prepare young people to become social business entrepreneurs themselves. I think young people will respond very enthusiastically to the challenge of making serious contributions to the world by becoming social business entrepreneurs.

We will need to arrange financing for social business entrepreneurs. New banking models need to be developed. New angel investors will have to emerge. Social venture capitalists will have to join hands with social business entrepreneurs.

The potential for social business enterprises

I believe there are many potential developments that – once understood – may fuel the growth of social business enterprises. These include:

- Existing companies of all shapes and sizes may launch their own social business entrepreneurs to test the water. A part of their annual profit may be devoted to the creation of social business entrepreneurs as a part of their corporate social responsibility activities. They may create social business enterprises themselves or they may partner known or potential social business entrepreneurs. Specialized companies may be created to provide matchmaking services between traditional entrepreneurs and social business entrepreneurs in respect of possible partnerships.
- Many companies with their own foundations may create "Social Business Enterprise Investment Funds" in addition to their philanthropic activities. The advantage of such a social business enterprise fund would be that money would keep on growing, giving the companies more financial power to create more social business enterprises.
- Individual entrepreneurs who have achieved success and/or suffered failures in conventional businesses may feel an urge to try their creativity, talent, and management skills in establishing and running their own social business enterprises. If they succeed at their first social business enterprise, they may be so inspired that it may even become a habit. They may discover just what an exciting business social business can be.
- International and bi-lateral donors could start creating "Social Business Enterprise Funds" in recipient countries to support social business enterprise initiatives.
- Children of successful business families could decide to devote themselves to social business enterprise because their traditional businesses are already successful and there is little challenge for them. They may be attracted by new challenges and the rewards of social business enterprises.

- Young entrepreneurs without inherited businesses may decide to start out their careers with social business enterprises rather than traditional businesses because they seem so "cool."

How to make a start

One good way to get started would be to launch a design competition for social business enterprises. There could be local, regional, and global competitions. Prizes for successful designs could come in the form of equity financing for social enterprises and/or partnerships to implement social projects. All the submitted social business proposals could be published so that these could become the "open source" starting-points for social business entrepreneurs in the next cycle.

A social business entrepreneur could even start the social capital market as a social business enterprise. A business school or several business schools could join hands to launch this as a project and trigger serious business transactions.

We should not expect a social business enterprise to provide all the answers to a social problem right from its founding. It will most likely proceed one step at a time. Each step may lead to the next level of achievement. Grameen Bank is a good example in this regard. I never had a blueprint to follow when creating Grameen Bank. I took one step at a time, always thinking that this step would be my last. But this was not to be. That one step led me to another step – a step that was so interesting that is was difficult to walk away. I faced this situation at every turn.

I started my work by giving small amounts of money to a few poor people without any collateral. Then I realized how good these people felt about these loans. I needed more money to expand the program. To access bank money, I offered myself as a guarantor. To get the support of another bank, I converted my project into the bank's project. Later, I turned it into a central bank project. Over time, I saw that the best strategy would be to create an independent bank to do the work. So we did. We converted the project into a formal bank, borrowing money from the central bank to lend money to the borrowers. Donors became interested in our work and wanted to support us. We received loans and grants from international donors. At one stage, we decided to stop taking money from donors. This led us to focus on generating money internally by mobilizing deposits. We soon arrived at a stage when Grameen Bank had more money in deposits than it lent to borrowers. Today it lends out half a billion US dollars a year in loans (an average of $130 per loan) to 6 million borrowers without collateral and maintains a 99 percent repayment record.

We introduced many programs in the bank: housing loans, student loans, pension funds, loans to purchase mobile phones to become the village telephone ladies, loans to beggars to become door-to-door salespeople. One led to another.

Besides Grameen Bank, we have also created many other companies: a renewable energy company (Grameen Shakti), Grameen Healthcare Services, Grameen Phone, Grameen Telecom, Grameen Agriculture, Grameen Fisheries & Livestock, Grameen Communications, etc. The latest company that we launched is of particular interest to this chapter: a 50:50 joint venture between Grameen and Danone called "Grameen Danone Foods, a Social Business Enterprise." (I include some relevant sections of the joint venture agreement in the Appendix.) I invite all companies to think of creating social business entrepreneurs as part of their business. They'll find it an exhilarating experience.

Social business entrepreneurs are the solution

We started out by assuming a world with two kinds of people: one kind wants to make money; the other kind wants to do good. But in the real world there are only people of one type with two types of interests in varying proportions. It is important that we recognize these two types of interests in our business world, because it is important for mankind and the planet. As people become increasingly worried about the current state of capitalism, the potential for social business entrepreneurs is growing. If we create the right environment, social business entrepreneurs can use market mechanisms significantly and make business an exciting place for fighting social battles in ever more innovative and effective ways. Let us now get serious about social business entrepreneurs. They can create hope for the future of human society and brighten this gloomy world for us all.

Appendix: Extracts from "Grameen Danone Foods – A Social Business Enterprise," Joint Venture Agreements

Purpose:	Mission: ***Reduce poverty by a unique proximity business model which brings daily healthy nutrition to the poor.*** The JV (company) will be designed and operated as a social business enterprise and will aim at sharing the benefits with its community of stakeholders.

Specific objectives:

Daily healthy nutrition to the poor:
Allow lower income consumers of Bangladesh, to have access (in terms of affordability and availability) to a range of tasty and nutritious foods and beverages on a daily basis, in order to improve their nutritional status.

More specifically, help children of Bangladesh grow strong, thanks to tasty, nutritious food and beverage products they can consume every day, so that they can have a better future.

A unique proximity business model:
Design a manufacturing and distribution model that involves local communities.

Reduce poverty:
Improve the economic conditions of the local low income population by:

- Upstream: involving local suppliers (farmers) and helping them to improve their practices;
- Production: involve local population via a low cost/ labor intensive manufacturing model;
- Downstream: contributing to the creation of jobs thanks to the distribution model.

Operating profit/ Distributions:	In terms of P&L, the JV (company) should be a no-loss operation company. This means that no shareholder should lose money in their participation in the business model; the business model should be profitable for each Party and any profits (beyond cost of capital) generated by the JV (company) will be reinvested in the development of its business in a manner to be mutually agreed upon by the Parties.

The JV (company) will be designed and operated as a social business enterprise and will aim at sharing benefits with the community of its stakeholders.

Bottom line for the JV (company) will be to operate without incurring losses while serving the people, particularly disadvantaged people, in the best possible manner.

The JV (company) will generate enough surpluses to pay back the invested capital to the parties as early as possible. It is up to the parties to decide how quickly they want their money back. Parties may decide to reinvest the surplus in the JV (company) for expansion, improvement of quality, increasing efficiency, introducing new technology, innovative marketing to reach the deeper layers of low-income people, particularly women, children, and disadvantaged communities, undertake research and experimentation, to improve and diversify products and services.

The JV (company) will try to pay back the Parties' capital out of the profit within a time period agreed upon by the Parties.

Even after the capital amount is paid back, GDF (company) will pay a 1 percent dividend annually to the shareholders.

25 Concluding observations

ERNST VON KIMAKOWITZ, MICHAEL
PIRSON, HEIKO SPITZECK, WOLFGANG
AMANN, AND SHIBAN KHAN

Be bold – allow yourself to envision a life-conducive economy

Throughout this book, authors from diverse personal and academic backgrounds have argued that the purpose of economic activity should be to serve mankind. This may look somewhat idealistic or even naïve at first sight. However, we believe the arguments presented in this book build a strong case for working towards a more life-conducive economy. We have learned that there have been humanistic principles throughout history, within different religious and cultural traditions across the globe, as well as in the development of economic thought. In practice, we also increasingly find examples of humanists using entrepreneurial means to foster genuine life-serving developments, while topics such as business ethics, social entrepreneurship, and corporate social responsibility continuously deepen their footprint in management education and research.

Clearly, building a more life-conducive economy and redefining the role of business in society accordingly means aiming high. Simultaneously, we should realize that our economic activities are not governed by laws of nature, but follow man-made rules. We chose to adopt these rules and, consequently, we can also choose to change them or at least allow them to evolve in the light of new knowledge – free of (sometimes dogmatic) status quo conserving defense mechanisms.

If one is asked to decide whether changes in any context are positive or not, one depends on a vision of a desired outcome. How else would one know if progress is being made, if not by aiming at a regulative idea and assessing changes against it? We can only work towards what we can envision. Our economic development will therefore, in part, depend on having such a vision. In a global economy, this vision will have to be based on ideas and ideals that are appealing to mankind as a whole, regardless of cultural, religious, or regional backgrounds. Perhaps it is idealistic to argue that the purpose of economic activity is to serve mankind, but it is certainly not naïve.

In this book, we have discovered that humanism has the potential to guide the development of this common vision, as it is founded on humanity itself. It is through its universal appeal that humanism allows for any number of cultural, religious, and regional identities while working towards the development and fulfillment of common ideals.

As editors of this book, we believe that a global economy in which man is the measure of all things is an ideal worth striving for.

Be prepared – allow yourself to challenge mainstream thinking

In the following section, we extract some of the key findings and arguments in this book to help us retrace a few of the ideas presented and to gain a perspective on how the various contributions form a bigger picture.

Part one – philosophical grounds and implications

As the title of this book suggests, humanism as a philosophy is our point of departure. To obtain a better understanding of what humanism could mean in the business context, we have invited philosophical scholars to shed some light on the philosophical grounds of humanism, its relation to culture and religion, the rich history from which it derives, and its implications for economics and business studies.

Granting us an entry-point to the philosophical roots of humanism, Julian Nida-Rümelin presented four mutually dependent key elements. These four key elements of humanism are:

- human nature is not given – it can be refined; education and learning are adequate means with which to refine human nature;
- reasoning and reason – that which is called *logos* in Greek;

- universalism – humanism addresses everybody. There are no essential differences in ethnicity, nation, race, social status, or culture as far as humanism is concerned;
- opposition to collective identities – humanistic values address the individual, not the collective.

Humanism is often associated with European Renaissance thinking, but while the term "humanism" stems from that period, its underlying beliefs can be traced back several thousand years. In ancient India, China, Greece, and Rome, great thinkers had developed ideas that we would today call truly humanist thinking. In the Muslim world too, humanist thought had a strong presence in the works of religious leaders and cultural figures. It was, however, only in the early nineteenth century that European thinkers called this tradition "humanism." The term was based on the fifteenth-century Italian term *umanista*, which was used to designate a teacher or student of classic literature. These nineteenth-century thinkers were often inspired by Muslim sources that were themselves based on the findings of Greek and Roman works.

As Matt Cherry argued in his chapter on the history of humanism: "These rich humanist traditions reveal that common principles can arise in the most diverse environments, and suggest that the humanist goal of living an ethical and fulfilling life guided by reason is an aspiration with universal appeal." This universal appeal that Julian Nida-Rümelin identified as one of the four key elements of humanism was also emphasized by Greg Epstein when he pointed out that: "Clashes occur when we take pride in our own culture but fail to see how others could take pride in theirs; or when we apply the laws of rationality – and cynicism – to discussing another's inherited religious beliefs or customs, but fail to understand that we too have beloved traditions that seem bizarre in the eyes of others." He then concluded that: "As our world grows smaller and more interconnected, we are in ever greater need of a universal ethic for all humanity. A truly transnational Humanism for the modern world is one that allows us to actively celebrate our distinct cultural and other kinds of identity, while still affirming universal Humanist principles."

As such, humanism can provide an inclusive platform for people from any cultural, religious, or regional background, and can therefore help establish the common ground required for a globalizing economy.

From Claus Dierksmeier, we learned that globalization poses ethical challenges, especially when businesses operate in what seems to be ever-growing uncertainty. In his chapter on the requisite journey from business ethics to economic philosophy, he argued that: "Since discussion in business ethics is often influenced and framed by the theoretical foundations of academic economics, the demand for a new business ethics translates into the need for a critique of the economic paradigms underlying traditional business ethics."

Drawing on that view, Stephen B. Young critically analyzed the global economy from a moral and cultural perspective. He reflected on the difficulties when determining a moral point of view from which one can offer a credible critique of the global economy and came to the conclusion that one aspect of humanism, stewardship, offers assistance. Stewardship is understood as an action orientation of human decision-making that is partly utilitarian but simultaneously integrates notions of duty, obligation, and responsibility to a larger whole – a community of interest and purpose.

Following this economic analysis, Omar Aktouf and W. David Holford took a look at the implications of humanism for businesses. They suggested that at first sight, various streams in management and business studies seem to be increasing their focus on the human being. They nevertheless continued: "Yet let us not fool ourselves into thinking that these various streams reflect any significant attempt at creating business frameworks or management practices that embrace man's emancipation as a finality onto itself, or 'man as the measure of all things'." They argued that the current socio-economic process is caught in the endless pursuit of maximization of profits that leads to a truncated understanding of the human being, and called for a humanistic approach within business activities. They embraced a participatory vision of the employee in businesses where workers are not viewed as a cost to reduce but as an ally to convince. They concluded that human beings should no longer be viewed as instrumental servants of profitability.

Next, Domènec Melé critically addressed the lack of a life-conducive business character. His findings suggested two mainstream tendencies that he described as a humanistic and an "economistic" one. In the first, humans come first; in the latter, economic results receive priority over human dignity, human rights, and human growth. After discussing these two tendencies, he concluded his chapter by sharing some encouraging trends with the reader. These are that job designs and organizational structures have become more person-focused; that organizations have increased their employees' degree of involvement, commitment, and participation; that firms are no longer viewed as a set of contracts but as a community of people; and that management focused on maximizing shareholder value is increasingly turning to management by values.

The contributions of the first part gave us a basic understanding of humanism and allowed us to philosophically substantiate the challenges addressed to mainstream economic thinking in the subsequent parts of this book. Humanism is a useful catalyst for framing these challenges, as it is, in principle, globally applicable and compatible with free markets and liberal ideals, although its view of the purpose of economic activities differs profoundly.

Part two – the systemic level

Peter Ulrich opened the second part of this book by remarking: "It's *not* the economy, stupid – it's society!" With this thought-provoking recollection of Bill Clinton's well-known 1992 presidential campaign slogan ("It's the economy – stupid!"), he suggested that we need to "learn again to make a clear difference between economy and society to bring them into a sensible relationship, instead of confounding both levels as it is common practice in neoliberal thinking with its standard recipe for nearly all socio-economic problems: more market and more competition." Given that many of our societal problems are the outcome of the success story of liberalized and rationalized economies, simply increasing the dosage will not resolve the problems, he maintained in a clear-cut argument. He continued by envisaging a republican-liberal political order that focuses on the general and real freedom of citizens in which individuals are "in principle willing to bind themselves to the ethical principles of a fair and decent living together in a free society." He suggested that civilizing the market economy by establishing this republican-liberal political order could be a solution for the "inconvenient awareness and handling of the societal consequences of a highly productive market economy."

In line with these ideas, Amartya Sen shared his particular approach to development as "a process of expanding substantive freedoms that people have." He first elaborated on the interdependence between freedom and responsibilities, since only the person who has freedom can be held responsible, while having substantive freedoms also imposes responsibilities. In an argument based on four points, he first argued for the primacy of substantive freedoms in evaluating social achievements and failures. Second, he maintained that the perspective of substantive freedoms can accommodate considerable variation, which is necessary, as freedoms "are inescapably of different kinds." Third, we learned that a shared recognition (within society) of what may not be part of an acceptable society could depend on an open discussion of issues and feasibilities. And fourth, "an approach to justice and development that concentrates on substantive freedoms inescapably focuses on the agency and judgment of individuals; they cannot be seen merely as patients to whom benefits will be dispensed by the process of development. Responsible adults must be in charge of their own well-being; it is for them to decide how to use their capabilities." Sen, thus, suggested an alternative, non-utilitarian perspective on development, which would help to assess true "humanistic" progress within national economies as well as globally.

In the following chapter, Klaus Leisinger examined the possibilities for business organizations to contribute to the promotion and pre-servation of human rights. His work distinguished three levels of corporate conduct with respect to human rights. The first level refers to the essentials ("must have"), which are based on obeying the law and adhering to regulation, as companies that "are in breach of the most important consensus of the international community place themselves outside the corridor of legitimate activities." The second level refers to what the author called enlightened self-interest ("ought to have") and is based on wise strategic decisions leading to corporate citizenship that goes beyond legal duties: "where national laws are not in harmony with what is defined by enlightened consensus of the international community, moral obligations come into play." Cor-porate philanthropy ("can have") constitutes the third level, with a "nice to have" character, while the borderline between good man-agement practices and corporate responsibility excellence is not fixed but lies somewhere within a strategy of enlightened self-interest. He concluded by building a business case for corporate human rights engagement, confirming his belief that good companies are part of the solution by promoting the freedom, well-being, and dignity of individuals in all societies.

Next, Lynn Sharp Paine argued that the public has undergone a value shift. In most societies, the amoral character of the corporation is no longer accepted and businesses have to react by merging social and financial imperatives to remain successful. While the paths to value-driven management that have merged these imperatives are varied, "more and more companies are rejecting traditional ideas of management as a 'value-free' science and business as an 'ethics free-zone'." She concluded that it is unlikely that these changes can be reversed under the pressure of external forces and that we are "thus likely to see continuing calls for companies to be more efficient and more profitable, and at the same time more responsive to their constituencies, more accountable for the impact of their activities, and more respectful of law and generally accepted ethical standards."

Ulrich Steger outlined the various deficiencies of our current system and called for concerted action to reverse the trend. He sees the financial industry as a leverage for change and holds that "life is more than consumption". Addressing the future academic community, he poses some challenging questions to be answered, pointing to a more humane future.

Following the philosophical grounding in the first part, the second part focused on the system-level implications of creating a more life-conducive economy. The starting-point was a depiction of a humane society and businesses' role within such a society, as well as an introduction to development theory beyond utilitarian calculus. These chapters were then complemented by an examination of three domains relevant for business: human rights, shifting public values, and the harsh reality with which humanistic thought is often faced under current globalization practices.

Part three – the organizational level

The third part presents management support for enlightened business leaders and organizations at the forefront of humanistic thinking in business practice. In his chapter, Allen White analyzed current governance failures and corporate governance initiatives, arguing that a democratization of the corporation is needed. He believes that democratized, stakeholder-governed corporations will be able to deal with the current challenges much better than those with shareholder-centric governance structures.

"Democratizing the corporation . . .," he concluded, "promises a different future. Whether through the voluntary actions of corporations themselves or mandatory actions imposed by governments, transitioning to stakeholder governance will help end the 'disharmony' that stands in the way of corporations reaching their full potential as agents of sustainable development."

Michael Pirson outlined the newly emerging phenomenon of social entrepreneurship and indicated how current organization managers could learn from it. Social entrepreneurs are people motivated to effectively contribute to social change. They employ business methods to achieve social objectives, and therefore represent a blueprint for humanistic business. The description of different models of social enterprise presented guidelines for strategically reorganizing a traditional corporation to serve authentic human needs.

Claudia Peus and Dieter Frey stressed the importance of positive leadership and organizational culture. They presented their center for excellence model that describes organizational cultures that have a strong philosophical grounding and have, simultaneously, been found to be characteristic of exceptionally successful organizations. Such cultures emphasize constructive criticism, creativity, employee participation, and development, thereby following humanistic principles. Thereafter they conversely argued that: "Where organizational cultures and leadership styles do not reward employees' performance, or where human dignity is even violated, employees' ability to work under pressure and their overall performance is substantially limited." They thus challenge the often implicitly expressed management practitioner view that there is an inherent conflict between upholding business performance and following humanistic principles.

Supporting humanistic management, Miguel Pereira Lopes, Miguel Pina e Cunha, Stephan Kaiser, and Gordon Müller-Seitz introduced the concept of positive organizational scholarship (POS). POS was presented as the academic backbone of humanistic management, focusing on the study of positive outcomes, processes, and attributes of both organizations and their members. Consequently, POS embraces studying the pursuit of human growth and self-development. As pragmatic humanists, the authors' message for organizational leadership is twofold: "First, adopt a multi-stakeholder viewpoint on what is considered humanistic management, instead of centering humanistic claims on working and living conditions only. Management action should not be seen as inhumane or self-interested without a deep examination of their reasons. Second, search for evidence that shows that only genuinely true concerns about treating people grounded in the fundamental human values can lead to business success and development. This will ultimately discourage everyone from adopting opportunistic behaviors, and engage people in productive and genuinely virtuous relationships at work."

Oliver Salzmann, Ulrich Steger, and Aileen Ionescu-Somers cautioned against an overly optimistic view, and presented research results gained from interviews with more than 250 executives. Their general finding is that corporations have learned to deal with and fend off outside pressures, but do not feel compelled to promote a more human-centered approach to business. They have learned how to "manage" stakeholders, but there is little evidence that a true transformation has resulted. The authors therefore called for a more concerted scrutiny of actual business behavior and increased pressure on corporations. The good news is that there are willing change agents within corporations that could be partners for positive change.

These potential partnerships were elaborated on in Oliver Rapf's description of WWF and its corporate allies. He concluded by arguing that: "The environmental challenges of the early twenty-first century are so large that no actor can successfully address them alone. Partnerships and coalitions between NGOs and companies will help to combine power and influence to turn environmental solutions into business mainstream."

The third part thus created a platform for rethinking mainstream management approaches and provided practitioners with more grounded propositions on how to manage humanistically. Many questions are still unanswered and much remains to be done, but a first practical outlook for a discourse has been provided.

Part four – the individual level

The fourth and final part consisted of action-oriented approaches that highlighted the role of the individual in a humanistic transformation of business. Adrian Henriques started out by reminding us of the threat to individual dignity in economic environments by citing Immanuel Kant: "What is related to general human inclinations and needs has a market price . . . but that which constitutes the condition under which alone something can be an end in itself has not merely a relative worth, that is, a price, but an inner worth, that is, a dignity." His chapter focused on the question of how humanity on an individual level can be preserved in a business context by regulating integrity through ethical codes and by facilitating behavior of integrity interpreted as honesty or personal transparency. In both cases, the culture of the organization is crucial for the preservation of dignity, as the development and subsequent adherence to ethical codes, as well as the personal risks that an employee faces when being personally transparent, are both closely linked to the supportiveness of corporate cultures.

Jean-Pierre Lehmann manifested his belief in the power of the individual and the flexibility of our system in integrating human needs to the fullest. A special role for that transformation is ascribed to leaders. Individuals like Martin Luther King, Mahatma Gandhi, Emily Davison, and others had a tremendous impact on the world around them. He observed: "The biggest challenge for the abolitionists, the suffragettes and feminists, and the civil rights activists was to raise awareness, to get society to understand that what was being taken as natural, was in fact not natural; indeed it was evil."

Thomas Maak and Nicola Pless also ascribed a crucial role to leadership in positive transformation processes. Their understanding of leadership is, however, unorthodox, presenting leaders as responsible servants of their followers. Responsible leaders are committed to a purpose higher than making profit, ignite strength and inspiration, say what they do, and do what they say. They make leaders of followers, and strive to reconcile their organization's bottom lines – economic, social and environmental – in principled ways.

Joe Badaracco then introduced us to people whom he calls *quiet leaders* and to the way they work. His argument is built on his own research and observations that "the most effective leaders are rarely public heroes. These men and women [quiet leaders] aren't high-profile champions of causes, and don't want to be. They don't spearhead ethical crusades. They move patiently, carefully, and incrementally. They do what is right – for their organizations, for the people around them, and for themselves – inconspicuously and without casualties."

He outlined the virtues and mechanics of quiet leadership and described a set of tools and useful tactics that quiet leaders need to possess. These are, however, not sufficient, as the quiet leaders about whom he writes have to have a character based on restraint, modesty, and tenacity. He closed his argument by saying that because these virtues are familiar, natural, and sensible ways of thinking, they are very valuable, as "almost anyone can practice and cultivate the simple virtues of quiet leadership. They aren't reserved for special people or extraordinary events."

William Drayton shared these ideas – aligned to the view that almost anyone can cultivate the virtues of quiet leaders – on how everyone can become a changemaker. He told the story of Rodrigo Baggio, a Brazilian who overcame multiple obstacles to import donated computers to his home country. While this story provides strong evidence of Rodrigo's entrepreneurial spirit, it caught the author's attention because Rodrigo is driven by a social objective – the computers were used to help bridge the digital divide in Brazilian favelas even before the term was invented.

Drayton highlighted this example as a role model for individuals that strive to make a difference by using entrepreneurial means to follow social objectives. He suggested several changes for the transition to an economy in which social entrepreneurs are no longer an "exotic species" but become part of the very fabric of our economies. His vision is a world in which a large proportion of the population will be changemakers, creating a world that will be a "fundamentally different and far safer, happier, more equal, and more successful place."

In the final chapter, Muhammad Yunus argued that capitalism is mostly interpreted too narrowly, and explained that: "In this narrow interpretation, we create a one-dimensional human being to play the role of entrepreneur. We insulate him from other dimensions of life, such as the religious, the emotional, the political, and the social." He then described a new breed of entrepreneur, the social-objective-driven entrepreneur, who wants to give others a better chance in life. These entrepreneurs run businesses that may or may not earn profits but, like any other business, they must not incur losses. What sets them apart is that they do not subordinate social objectives to maximize profit. He argued that we need to create organizations that support these entrepreneurs. These businesses also need access to funds; he therefore conceptualized a social stock exchange in which social enterprises are able to attract the funds required for their operations.

Fundamentally, Muhammad Yunus argued that we need to reinterpret capitalism, but remains hopeful, as people "become increasingly worried about the current state of capitalism, the potential for social business entrepreneurs is growing." We require the right environment to allow this new breed of entrepreneurs to use market mechanisms in innovative and effective ways to promote social objectives.

Be realistically optimistic – allow yourself to make an impact

Crucial for the understanding of this book is its interdisciplinary approach. The editors have deliberately chosen to integrate voices from philosophical, economic, business studies, and entrepreneurial backgrounds in the hope of two outcomes.

First, to ascertain if there is common ground for a discussion of the role of business in society that challenges some of the beliefs on which our current economies are built. We further hope that such a discourse will also find reverberation amongst policy makers and practitioners alike. We can only expect more real-world changes if those people who either shape the economic framework or operate within it are engaged in an open and uncoerced discussion. This is no easy task. On the one hand we hope that those who experience the described challenges in their daily actions will find it encouraging to read about the numerous examples of life-conducive business conduct presented in this book. On the other hand, we hope that they will realize that they can draw on the findings of researchers in multiple disciplines to provide the intellectual ammunition required for a discourse with those upholding the status quo. Everyone can be a changemaker.

Second, our aim is to establish whether the elements in such an open discourse form a common research agenda to further our knowledge and generate new insights.

As stated at the beginning of these closing remarks, redefining the role of business in society is a challenging and complex endeavor. The editors therefore believe that there is much to learn from integrating the voices of different disciplines in this discourse. We will benefit from a better understanding of our philosophical heritage just as much as we will benefit from knowing how management by values can impact performance-related success factors in businesses. We need to understand the kind of environment that allows a small social enterprise to thrive as much as we need to understand what makes a large transnational corporation a good corporate citizen. If we are to expand our view of the human being to something broader than a business-focused, economistic individual, we need to seek input from outside the economics and business literature. Simultaneously, one needs to study the business drivers that generate competitive advantages in the marketplace if one is to promote social objectives through market mechanisms, so that these drivers can be put to innovative use. In short: the more we are willing to give up (rather) insular thinking in various research disciplines, the more we will be able to provide actionable input to nourish the diverse and multifaceted discussion of a more life-serving economy.

We therefore hope that the diversity that lies in the various chapters of this book will also be a stimulus for further research in this field.

A brief reflection

As the title of this book suggests, humanism as a philosophy is our point of departure, and this book's ultimate target is humanism as a guiding framework to help redefine the role of businesses in society.

Let us therefore look back and reflect on some of the thoughts presented. Reviewing the role of the market and businesses in society could lead to more life-conducive economies; nevertheless a widespread prescription for addressing societal problems is still a strong focus on GDP growth. Are highly developed economies truly in need of just a little extra growth to obtain the resources required to address the problems they face? Putting people first in business organizations would allow companies to benefit strongly from increased employee commitment and motivation. However, many studies reveal widespread mistrust and alarming inner withdrawal rates amongst employees – particularly those of large corporations. Responsible leadership is in great demand – but the reality is top managers who often cultivate a "pop star" image and have little interest in the inclusion of social objectives in their decision-making. Correcting our (economistic) view of the human being and interpreting capitalism more broadly could have a great positive impact on how and why we use market mechanisms – but social entrepreneurs only make rare appearances and, although admired, are generally presented as a rather exotic species.

Three reasons for being realistically optimistic

How can we then be optimistic? There are three reasons for this. First, we find philosophical arguments that are supportive of the optimistic mind. We as humans have the ability to enter into a discourse. We have the gift to identify the reasonable, and we have the capacity to develop universally accepted norms through a process of giving and criticizing reasons for holding or rejecting particular claims (Habermas 1985; Kant 1991).

Second, some of the assumptions in economics and business sciences that may have played a part in creating the challenges that we face are currently under scrutiny. In particular the utility-calculating and maximizing *homo oeconomicus* is increasingly facing opposition from behavioral economics (Hammond 1998). Furthermore, the assumption that the endless pursuit of economic growth per se provides live-serving solutions is being questioned by human development theory (Sen 2000), as well as from an ecological perspective (Meadows *et al.* 2004). The belief that businesses can, for the most part, operate free of ethical concerns as long as they adhere to the law has shielded them well from responding to stakeholder claims more proactively. Currently, however, an increasing number academics are no longer supportive of this view and endorse the need for companies to seek societal legitimacy beyond the boundaries of legal and regulative compliance (Ulrich 2008).

The third reason for being cautiously optimistic is that we can find a multitude of examples of market mechanisms and entrepreneurial tools used successfully to achieve social objectives. It is currently possible to identify flourishing niches of life-conducive economic activities almost everywhere. In fact, this book demonstrates just that. We identified the philosophical implications of humanism for economic activities and businesses in the first part. In the second part, we demonstrated what an economic system that puts people first could look like and how private sector actors could, and in some cases already do, play a role in getting us there. In the third part of the book, we learned that more and more companies of all sizes and in all corners of the world are rethinking their role in society. These companies are beginning to turn themselves into values-based organizations that embrace their responsibilities towards their stakeholders. In the fourth part, we have seen that people from all walks of life can become changemakers in their own right.

Consequently, even though the status quo does not always seem favorable, a more life-serving economy is not out of reach as individuals, businesses, policy makers, and researchers lead by example, working towards an economy where people come first. While status quo maintaining actors increasingly face new challenges, the number of positive cases increases by the day. We believe that these are very encouraging signs.

We may just be at the beginning of an economic revolution, one that is happening quietly, gradually, and from the bottom up; one that is constantly gaining momentum, despite (or perhaps because of) its lack of revolutionary fanfare, making it more thoughtful and balanced, and thus more likely to succeed.

References

Habermas, J. 1985. *The Theory of Communicative Action.* Boston: Beacon Press.

Hammond, J., Keeney, R., and Raiffa, H. 1998. "The Hidden Trap in Decision Making," *Harvard Business Review* 9–10: 47–58.

Kant, I. 1991. *Kant: Political Writings* (second edition), ed. H. S. Reiss, trans. H. B. Nisbet. Cambridge Texts in the History of Political Thought. Cambridge: Cambridge University Press.

Meadows, D., Randers, J., and Meadows, D. 2004. *Limits to Growth – The 30 Year Update.* Vermont: Chelsea Green Publishing.

Sen, A. 2000. "A Decade in Human Development," *Journal of Human Development* 1(1): 17–23 (also available online at http://hdr.undp.org/docs/training/oxford/readings/Sen_HD.pdf).

Ulrich, P. 2008. *Integrative Economic Ethics. Foundations of a Civilized Market Economy.* Cambridge: Cambridge University Press.

Index